The publisher gratefully acknowledges the generous contribution to this book provided by the Ahmanson Foundation Humanities Endowment Fund of the University of California Press Foundation.

Scenes of Instruction

Academia meets Hollywood: Professor Karl Waugh, dean of arts and sciences at the University of Southern California, tests the emotionometer on the Great Stone Face, Buster Keaton, while Gwen Lee looks on, ca. 1920. (From the USC Moving Image Archive.)

Scenes of Instruction
The Beginnings of the U.S. Study of Film

DANA POLAN

University of California Press
BERKELEY   LOS ANGELES   LONDON

University of California Press, one of the most distinguished university presses in the United States, enriches lives around the world by advancing scholarship in the humanities, social sciences, and natural sciences. Its activities are supported by the UC Press Foundation and by philanthropic contributions from individuals and institutions. For more information, visit www.ucpress.edu.

University of California Press
Berkeley and Los Angeles, California

University of California Press, Ltd.
London, England

© 2007 by The Regents of the University of California

Library of Congress Cataloging-in-Publication Data

Polan, Dana B., 1953–.
   Scenes of instruction : the beginnings of the U.S. study of film / Dana Polan.
      p.   cm.
   Includes bibliographical references and index.
   ISBN 978-0-520-24962-2 (cloth : alk. paper)
   ISBN 978-0-520-24963-9 (pbk. : alk. paper)
   1. Motion pictures—Study and teaching—United States.   I. Title.

PN1993.8.U5P58   2007
791.43071'073—dc22   2006025495

Manufactured in the United States of America

16 15 14 13 12 11 10 09 08 07
10 9 8 7 6 5 4 3 2 1

This book is printed on New Leaf EcoBook 50, a 100% recycled fiber of which 50% is de-inked post-consumer waste, processed chlorine-free. EcoBook 50 is acid-free and meets the minimum requirements of ANSI/ASTM D5634–01 (*Permanence of Paper*).

For Marie and Bob Sturken, Ken and Elaine Langsam

Contents

	Buster Keaton, Professor Karl Waugh, and Gwen Lee	*frontispiece*
	Acknowledgments	ix
	Introduction: Toward a Disciplinary History of Film Studies	1
1.	First Forays in Film Education: The Pedagogy of Photoplay Composition at Columbia University	33
2.	A Brief Interlude as the Movies March On: Terry Ramsaye and the New School for Social Research	90
3.	"Younger Art, Old College, Happy Union": Harvard Goes into the Business and Art of the Movies	113
4.	Between Academia and the Academy of Motion Picture Arts and Sciences: The University of Southern California Ventures into the Cinema	175
5.	Politics as Pedagogy, Pedagogy as Politics: The Rather Brief Moment in Time of Harry Alan Potamkin	236
6.	Appreciations of Cinema: Syracuse Discovers Film Art	263
7.	Cinematic Diversions in Sociology: Frederic Thrasher in the World of Film Appreciation	299
8.	Middlebrow Translations of Highbrow Philosophy: The Film Fandom of the 1930s Great Books Intellectuals	344
	Notes	377
	Index	401

Contents

	Buster Keaton, Professor Karl Waugh, and Gwen Lee	*frontispiece*
	Acknowledgments	ix
	Introduction: Toward a Disciplinary History of Film Studies	1
1.	First Forays in Film Education: The Pedagogy of Photoplay Composition at Columbia University	33
2.	A Brief Interlude as the Movies March On: Terry Ramsaye and the New School for Social Research	90
3.	"Younger Art, Old College, Happy Union": Harvard Goes into the Business and Art of the Movies	113
4.	Between Academia and the Academy of Motion Picture Arts and Sciences: The University of Southern California Ventures into the Cinema	175
5.	Politics as Pedagogy, Pedagogy as Politics: The Rather Brief Moment in Time of Harry Alan Potamkin	236
6.	Appreciations of Cinema: Syracuse Discovers Film Art	263
7.	Cinematic Diversions in Sociology: Frederic Thrasher in the World of Film Appreciation	299
8.	Middlebrow Translations of Highbrow Philosophy: The Film Fandom of the 1930s Great Books Intellectuals	344
	Notes	377
	Index	401

Acknowledgments

Of necessity, the historian of a discipline has to rely on the graciousness of colleagues, friends, and associates. For my study, I was blessed with a network of scholars and "native informants" who gave invaluable advice and provided necessary pieces of the historical puzzle in the form of documents, productive leads, personal testimony, and so on.

Haidee Wasson, Peter Decherney, and Anne Morey investigated areas of film history that overlapped somewhat with mine and thankfully were willing to share the results of their groundbreaking, rigorous research with me.

A number of scholars helped with documentation and essential background information: Mark Langer, Ian Jarvie, David James, Janice Radway, Donald Crafton, Jonathan Auerbach, Cari Beauchamp, John Belton, and especially Kathy Fuller-Seeley, who used her unparalleled eBay prowess to track down fascinating incunabula from early film history and its early study. I also learned much from scholarly conversation with Scott Bukatman, Jon Lewis, Eric Smoodin, William Buxton, Kaveh Askari, and Henry Breitrose. A special thanks to Herb Farmer, Eleanor Hickey, Frances Feldman, and Richard Bare for firsthand accounts of the early days of film pedagogy at the University of Southern California, and to George Comenetz for his anecdotes on the beginnings of St. John's College. Children or colleagues of some of the figures in this study provided fascinating biographical material: Oren Jacoby (for his father, Irving), Mark Morkovin (for his father, Boris), and Victor Garwood (a colleague of Boris).

I presented versions of some of the chapters of this book in academic venues—Art History at Stanford University, the Steinhardt School of Education at New York University, Film Studies at King's College (London), American Studies at Doshisha University (Kyoto), Film Studies at the Université de Montréal, the Columbia University Film Seminar, Cinema Studies at the University of Pennsylvania, and the Wolfe Institute for the Humanities at Brooklyn College—and I deeply thank both the organizers of these events and the audience members who engaged in productive dialogue around my topics.

I could not have conducted my historical research without the immeasurable aid of librarians and archivists at a number of institutions: the archives of New York University, the New School for Social Research, St. John's College, and Columbia University (Columbiana); the American Jewish Archives; Special Collections at the Joseph Regenstein Library at the University of Chicago; the Hoover Institute at Stanford University; the Moving Image Archive of the University of Southern California; Special Collections at Syracuse University; the clippings files division of the Lincoln Center Performing Arts Library; the British Library; the Manuscript Division, Special Collections, of the New York Public Library; the John F. Kennedy Presidential Library (Joseph P. Kennedy Papers); the Baker Library of the Harvard Business School; and the Margaret Herrick Library of the Academy of Motion Picture Arts and Sciences (a special thanks to Barbara Hall!).

Thanks to my intrepid graduate assistant researchers: John Frankfurt, Mina Shin, and Nam Lee, all at USC, and Lisa K. Broad, at NYU.

Mary Francis is, quite simply, the dream editor and was wonderfully supportive of a big project with lots of archival detail behind it. The commitment of the University of California Press to publishing ambitious work in film studies is so heartening, as is their particular devotion to research that carefully sets out to document the history of cinema as an important cultural form of our modernity.

This project was supported by a Scholar's Award from the Academy Foundation of the Academy of Motion Picture Arts and Sciences. I can sincerely admit that I have waited all my life to say, "I wish to thank the Academy for this award"!

My deepest thanks go to my family. My uncle Ken and aunt Elaine have always been there for me. I gain the riches of life from my parents-in-law, Marie and Bob Sturken, and from my brothers- and sisters-in-law and their spouses: Cheryl-Anne and Carl Sturken, Bill and Barbara Peterson. My nieces—Kelly, Leigh, Kyra, and Moira—are a constant source of vitality and inspiration.

Marita, I trust, knows all she has brought to this project—and, more important, to me.

Introduction
Toward a Disciplinary History of Film Studies

In 1929, a glossy movie magazine, *Motion Picture Classic*, ran a series of short reflections by editors of college newspapers on Hollywood films' image of campus life. After a number of months on "What College Men Think of the Movies," the magazine turned over its October issue to editors at women's colleges. In one article, Eugenie M. Fribourg, writing for the *Barnard Bulletin*, found the movies wanting in accuracy of depiction of college life, although their flaws of representation did not seem to repel students, who flocked to the cinema in droves. In fact, as Fribourg noted, "[T]he movie industry, at the moment, has much in common with the present college student. Both have lived about the same amount of time, both are not quite mature, and both are now interested in a happy future." Jokingly, Fribourg depicted the rush of college kids to local movies as so much an element of daily routine that filmgoing could seem a part of their curriculum:

> One course that the college catalogue neglects to print is the four years' Survey of American and Foreign Movies. The course is a popular one and is attended regularly by over half the college. As courses go, it is a comparatively new one, and therefore not always recognized as a part of the regular curriculum. To the student, however, it occupies a definite position in college activities. . . . Few go because they are really thrilled with what they see, or because they enjoy the movies as an art. They go to kill time.[1]

Fribourg perhaps could use the fictional idea of a movie curriculum in ironic fashion because the very notion of movie study seemed so fanciful. If the movies were in fact of the same age as the college student, no doubt such unproven youthfulness might make them seem *not* a propitious object for scholarly attention.

And yet from early on in the life of the movies—as early as the mid-

1910s, when they began to grow into the complex form of the narrative feature film—some institutions of higher learning *had* studied movies and studied them, moreover, as an important element—whether in moral force or aesthetic value—of modern society. In the following pages, I set out to tell the story of these early ventures in film education.

My primary goal is to give film scholars and film students some of the prehistory of their discipline in a manner comparable to the burgeoning industry of disciplinary histories in other fields of the humanities. Beginning in the 1980s, a number of such fields witnessed the publication of studies that focused attention inward to the disciplines themselves, setting out to examine their fundamental premises and their habitual practices. Here I am thinking of investigations such as Gerald Graff's *Professing Literature* (1989) and Robert Scholes's *The Rise and Fall of English* (1998) for the field of English; Richard Rorty's *Philosophy and the Mirror of Nature* (1981) for philosophy; Peter Novick's *That Noble Dream: The "Objectivity Question" and the American Historical Profession* (1988) for history; David Shumway's *Creating American Civilization: A Genealogy of American Literature as an Academic Discipline* (1994) for American literary study; and Donald Preziosi's *Rethinking Art History: Meditations on a Coy Science* (1989). Some of these works were situated primarily on a theoretical level, outlining and, at times, debating the foundational assumptions of the fields in question. Others aimed at a more everyday material level by looking at concrete institutional operations by which and through which the fields functioned. Still others took an avowedly historical approach by chronicling how the fields had come into being and how their practitioners had extended—and sometimes fought over—basic premises, methods, and objects.

Recently, we have even seen the emergence of a new academic field concerned with the study of fields. Here there is analysis not just of individual disciplines but of what has been labeled "disciplinarity" per se. A key signpost of this attempt to examine what disciplines share, no matter their differences, was the anthology *Knowledges: Historical and Critical Studies in Disciplinarity* (1993), intended to initiate a book series of analysis of individual disciplines and of reflection on disciplinarity overall.[2] In their first pages, the editors define their goal as the examination of "what makes for disciplinary knowledge *as such*" (my emphasis), and their volume's essays catalog common and standard practices of various disciplines. Thus, sections of the book cover such topics as the work of boundary policing wherein disciplines legislate proper research conduct for their members (i.e., a discipline is involved not only in deciding what is "proper" knowledge but also in deciding what is "improper"—not solid, hard, rigorous, or objective, or whatever terms the field uses to draw lines between legitimate and illegitimate forms of knowledge); the basic operations of disciplines (the rhetorics they employ, the rituals they perform, the characteristic spaces in which they operate); and their "socializing practices" (how they choose, train, and credential their practitioners). Disciplines, the editors of *Knowledges* explain, work to constitute a field of study (what objects to attend to, what methods will be legitimated in that attending); to produce practitioners (i.e., they train and then credential those deemed to have properly demonstrated effective mastery of disciplinary skills); to produce value (e.g., they create jobs, they bring in funding, they build up marketable prestige); and to construct, as the editors say, "the idea of progress" (i.e., they outline which kinds of knowledge are allowed to become objects of study for the discipline, and how the discipline's survey of knowledge grows and gains in ever-greater effectiveness).

While numerous disciplines have turned to an analysis and even an anthropology of their own practices, there has not yet been an extended *historical* investigation of the institutions and concrete activities of film studies. To be sure, the emphasis on *theory* as a central activity of that field has encouraged reflexivity and self-interrogation. It becomes inevitable to ask such disciplinary questions as What does it mean to do film theory? Which theory? Should one do something other than theory? Here we might cite David Bordwell's *Making Meaning: Inference and Rhetoric in the Interpretation of Cinema* as a key text in its attention to the operative premises of the field.[3] As the reference to "rhetoric" in his subtitle suggests, Bordwell is concerned centrally with the shared languages of film studies and with the critical activities that the discourse most encourages. But it is interesting to note how Bordwell, to a large degree, dis-embodies the practices of the field's participants and disconnects them from concrete institutional operations. For example, Bordwell offers extensive quotations from theorists, but these remain unnamed in the body of the text, with attribution only in footnotes. This is in keeping with Bordwell's evident intent to see film theory as governed by rules and codes of investigative conduct that transcend individual personalities. But it does mean that material bodies, institutions, and individual identities become of secondary importance. Bordwell is not interested here in the personalities that are doing theoretical work but in the common discursive field in which that work is expressed, no matter the individual theorist.

No doubt, the long-range history of film studies has not been written because, ironically, an alternate, abbreviated history has taken its place and tenaciously become the standard narrative for the field. Specifically, it is customary to imagine a history of film studies as gaining momentum only as late as the end of the 1950s, then crystallizing in the foundation of the field's professional society (then called the Society of Cinematologists) in 1959, and flourishing in the media-explosive and express-yourself-through-new-arts context of the 1960s. For example, in the retrospective reflection "Ruminations of an Ex-Cinematologist," film historian Jack Ellis—a key participant in the formation of film studies at the time—isolates a number of factors in the 1960s that were propitious for the field's development:

> To oversimplify, three things had happened by the mid-1960s. The first was auteurism. The films of Federico Fellini and Ingmar Bergman had increased the amount and intensity of interest in film more than those of us teaching it had previously managed to do. . . . The second thing that had changed the teaching of film was television. These new cinema students had . . . learned the language of the moving image accompanied by sound before they could speak intelligible sentences. Third, in the late sixties, the years of civil rights demonstrations and antiwar protests, students' attraction to film was combined with anger directed toward the traditional institutions and values of their society, including those of education. The movies had a youthful, democratic aura; they became part of the rebellion.[4]

The reasons for the endurance of this substitute history are several. First, the story it offers is quite seductive in that it allows film studies practitioners to imagine the beginnings of their discipline in heroic terms. Specifically, the narrative that has film studies emerging into the 1960s is the story also of its emergence *out of* the 1950s, that period in which so much intellectual reflection on culture was dominated by a disdain for what one fairly denunciatory volume termed "mass culture: the popular arts in America."[5] But for a few exceptions, which film studies will then treat as heroic figures who separated themselves from the crowd of complainants against popular culture, intellectuals of the 1950s tended to see the mass arts as a homogeneous bloc of superficiality, formulaic triteness, soulless pandering, degradation of higher reason, and so on.[6] Film studies in the 1960s, then, frequently had to do with redemptive tales in which various figures fought to stand out from the morass of mass conformity. Sixties auteurism, for example, pictured the object of its study, the Hollywood directors, as heroes themselves who managed to find personal voice within the constraints of the studio system—"the film director as superstar," as one book title at the end of the period put it.[7]

The narrative of film studies' inspiration in 1960s culture is attractive also because it makes argumentative sense. It assumes a series of causes—

for example, experimentation in cinema by avant-gardists and new wavists that distinguished itself from mainstream formulaicness and thereby called out for recognition and analysis—that might well have had as one effect the academic institutionalization of film appreciation that took as its mission to understand just what was going on with cinema in the period.

In this respect, for all its exalting the moment in heroic garb, the discourse of film studies' disciplinary emergence in the 1960s is not inaccurate. To the extent that we can define the concretization of a discipline by such signs as the rise of professional societies, the legitimation of some critical practices (and a concomitant delegitimation of others, deemed to be less scholarly, rigorous, or scientific), the regularization of practices of credentialization (the granting of degrees and diplomas, for instance), the garnering of academic respect through the publication of books that become standard points of reference, the crystallization of networks of dialogue and interchange among credentialed practitioners through such venues as conferences, the perfection of channels for the dissemination of disciplinary research in the form of scholarly journals, and so on, then the 1960s are indeed the period when film studies as an academic field did begin to take on disciplinary solidity and regularity.

But the very extent to which the discipline's solidification has traditionally been rendered in heroic terms means that earlier efforts in the teaching of film have been downplayed. Starting in the 1960s and 1970s, academic writing on the study of film tended, as if by necessity of self-justification, to view the decisive contributions of the past as deriving either from figures outside academia or from within the university world *but outside* anything so field specific as film studies. The assumption appeared to be that there may have been people examining film in earlier periods but they did not do so in any memorable fashion within a specifically academic context. For *modern* film studies to be imagined heroically as an achieved professional discipline, the figures who came before had concomitantly to be imagined as nonprofessionals in the area.

Take, for instance, modern film studies' fascination with an early, quirky figure like Hugo Münsterberg, who in the mid-1910s wrote one of the first aesthetics of cinema. Although Münsterberg was a Harvard professor, his film writing had only indirect connection to his academic specialization in philosophy and psychology, and this perhaps was part of his appeal to the burgeoning professional film studies of the 1970s. Thus, one story about Münsterberg had him discovering the joys of cinema in a nonprofessional context: waiting to make a train connection, Münsterberg happened into a movie theater, where he discovered the films of Annette Kellerman and became enthralled by cinema's capacities to appeal to the emotions and imagination. It was as an amateur—literally, a lover—that Münsterberg came to the movies, not as a rule-bound academic. Münsterberg may have used some of his scholarly rigor to reflect on film, but he never directly became a professional film scholar, and this aided his heroic or romantic appeal for a future film studies discipline.

In the following pages, I want to offer a revision of film studies' typical story by bringing to light the pedagogical efforts of teachers who set out to provide film instruction in institutions of higher learning between 1915 and 1935. During this period, a number of such institutions came to be venues either for individual courses on film or even for ambitious initiatives to develop broad curricula in cinema study. Many of the questions this early pedagogy confronted would recur in the discipline, and film studies scholars still wrestle with them today: for example, what might the connections be between the critical study of film (whether as an art or as a social practice) and practical instruction in *filmmaking*? To what extent does the teaching of movie *criticism* as engagement with individual films encourage the elaboration of a broader aesthetics of cinema overall as art form? Is the examination of film as expressive art or form of culture compatible with the study of business practices and the political economy of the cinema industry? Is such cultural or aesthetic examination compatible with the analysis of film's psychosocial effects on behavior and morality? Is there a particularity of film among the arts, and to what extent should film's independence—or derivation—from other arts (such as literature) be emphasized in the elaboration of a cinema aesthetics? To what degree should the study of film culture center on its historically dominant form (i.e., Hollywood-inflected narrative fiction)? To a large degree such questions still drive the field, and it is useful to look back on the ways the very first film pedagogues came to grips with them.

Despite the length of my study, I want to emphasize a certain modesty to the enterprise. Although the academic contributions of many of the figures I examine were unsung—both at the time they taught their courses and in subsequent accounts that offer a history of critical reflection on cinema—it is perhaps best not to imagine these early film instructors as heroes. Their efforts were frequently of an unassuming nature, and their impact was limited. We do not find here an alternate history of *an academic discipline,* for these random ventures in film instruction did not coalesce into a coherent field solidified around fixed questions and sets of practices. For instance, the early efforts in film pedagogy cannot be thought of as constituting a pre-paradigmatic moment in the ways that Thomas Kuhn outlined the processes of disciplinary consolidation in the sciences. For Kuhn, the preparadigmatic phase in a science's history involves conflicts between various scientific groups, each claiming that its methods have the greatest scope for addressing the important questions of the field. The pre-paradigmatic moment has also to do with the realization that there are some questions that the methods, instruments, and guiding principles of only some of the contenders within the internecine groups can answer.

In these respects, the period of the early study of film cannot really be termed pre-paradigmatic. There was little conflict, not because questions had been answered but because there was little common space in which practitioners could come together even to pose questions and debate answers. For the most part, the early instructors of film operated without taking much account of each other. At best they would cite each other as bibliographic items in reading list, but almost as if the very fact of citation meant that they did not need to engage with each other's ideas in extended fashion. Significantly, in the one situation where there was some direct contact among film instructors—the case of several teachers in the 1930s who tried to examine film's potential for aesthetic and moral betterment—the sites in which they would meet to exchange insights about film were not themselves academic venues. Where scholarly conferences offer a means for academic professionals to assemble, exchange thoughts, and thereby solidify the discipline, the 1930s proponents of betterment through film did not yet have access to academic conferences as a venue for dialogue. They met, rather, in the context of nonacademic civic institutions—in particular, public conventions of reform agencies such as the National Board of Review, which expected research to lead to policy and action rather than further academic study.

Although the efforts of these early figures failed to coalesce into a disciplinary tradition of film studies, I find their stories worth telling. At the very least, if these figures were not heroes, they were often distinctive, even fascinatingly eccentric, and their tales have an intriguing quality. They speak of a time before academic specialization and before the institution of a sharp divide between amateur and professional. Consequently, the very blending in their work of art and science, enjoyment and rigor, helps us reflect on the ways academic inquiry both demarcates itself from, and yet frequently mixes with, nonscholarly modes of popular knowledge. Looking at the early history of the study of film can perhaps provide salutary distance from our ensconced positions within the field and enable us to look at our practices anew.

Moreover, beyond the history of a discipline, the story of film studies is intimately linked to, and is a constitutive part of, the history of film itself. And it is also a part of the history of higher education as it enters the twentieth century. While we should not ask too much of several random courses in film, it is illuminating to see how these few cinema classes played out the pressing pedagogical issues of the day: the necessity or not of higher education for the masses rather than a privileged elite; the extent to which modern education should devote itself to vocationalism or professionalization, or both, rather than to the inculcation of general values (perhaps to be found in a canon of great works of Western culture); the degree to which humanistic inquiry still could offer valuable lessons in an age geared to an increasingly instrumental reason that might seem better addressed by social sciences than by the looser culturalist interpretations of the humanities.

Chapter 1 of this study chronicles the very first university instruction in film, the course Photoplay Composition at Columbia University, which began in 1915 and was taught for a few years by Victor Freeburg before being taken over for decades by Frances Taylor Patterson. Freeburg and Patterson assumed, on the one hand, that the cinema in its current context was not being encouraged to become an art—it was presently little more than a morass of (negative) social effects—but they also believed, on the other hand, that the cinema could become a force of artistic uplift, and they viewed their own pedagogy as a means of training students to help bring about this desired state of affairs. The chapter examines how Photoplay Composition's role in the university's extension program was inflected with a Progressivist desire to offer meaningful instruction—both practical and cultural—to new social constituencies in the urban context. Revealingly, Frances Patterson imagined that not all her students actually expected to become professional photoplay writers, and she intended her version of the course to serve as much as a lesson in consumption as in production: that is, she assumed that proper understanding of the techniques and higher aesthetic function of the well-made photoplay would help *all* citizens to become better viewers of film and push them to demand better stories. There would thus be an ameliorative feedback loop between consumption and production. This chapter not only examines course syllabi and related documents but also looks at the extensive critical writing by Freeburg and Patterson in order to pinpoint their aesthetic presuppositions about a possible art of cinema.

The photoplay course discussed in the first chapter was administered by Frances Patterson for almost four decades; chapter 2, in contrast, deals with a fleeting example of pedagogy. In 1926, the renowned film historian Terry Ramsaye offered a lecture course on cinema at the New School for Social Research timed to coincide with the publication of his massive history of film, *A Million and One Nights*. Ramsaye was not an academic, and the New School distinguished itself from other institutions of higher learning both by not offering degrees and by trying to reach an older constituency than the average college student. These distinctions themselves constitute some of the interest of Ramsaye's instruction. Ramsaye wrote his large-scale history in populist terms: film was the cultural form that through direct visual impact most achieved the age-old wish for artistic communication that would be imaginative and affective, as well as easy and accessible. But Ramsaye was also deeply Americanist: his version of film history argued its ultimate incarnation in Hollywood narrative film, which he viewed as the veritable destiny of the art form as it evolved to realize an ancient dream of popular artistic expression. In this respect, Ramsaye's course version of his book both responded to one aspect of the New School's philosophy of adult education, centered as it was on a populist dream of a pedagogy for nontraditional school populations, *and* ultimately differed from the New School's overall mission, which was devoted to opening those populations to the newest efforts of a culturally challenging European experimentation.

Although Columbia's Photoplay Composition course did take as one of its constituencies the profession-minded adult who wanted to break into the film business by becoming a photoplay writer, both Photoplay Composition and Terry Ramsaye's lecture series in film history were targeted as much at the urban denizen desiring little more than a quick cultural fix from contact with a glamorous new art form. The audience for such courses might range from the movie fan wanting more material about the art, to the socialite looking to spend a few hours in cultural uplift, to the consumer of films hoping to refine his or her critical discernment and demand the best in cinematic art.

If these first courses addressed, then, the cinematic amateur, chapter 3 initiates a look, extending over several chapters, at the ways in which the increasing rationalization of the motion picture industry through the 1920s led to classes that set out to produce trained workers who could take up professional positions in film. Thus, chapter 3 chronicles the attempt at Harvard University in 1927 to use a Business School course on the film industry to mold managers who would assume administrative jobs in the world of film production. Sponsored by Harvard alumnus Joseph Kennedy, who hoped to use the course to lend prestige to his recent incursion into the movie business, the Harvard course brought luminaries of the industry—such as Will Hays, Marcus Loew, Louis B. Mayer, and others—to lecture on their efforts as cinema entrepreneurs. But for all its difference from a more culturally concerned course like Photoplay Composition at Columbia University, the

Harvard Business School course did not ignore aesthetic issues and questions of value. There was, for instance, a constant emphasis in the industry leaders' speeches on film as a moral, social, and aesthetic good, and on the assumption that an ever more rationalized industry could only become an ever more ethical industry. The Harvard course was a public relations effort by the film industry to present itself in the best moral light, and this led the entrepreneurs to argue that even though they produced a commodity seemingly comparable to others, theirs was in fact a product of a superior nature, one that added artistry to the world. The Harvard course is valuable in the ways it shows yet another attempt to mediate art and commerce in the early days of both the film business and the business of film teaching.

This story of industrial rationalization, and of the encouragement of a pedagogy professional enough to deal with it, continues in chapter 4, which outlines the attempt by the Academy of Motion Picture Arts and Sciences (AMPAS) to create a curriculum—first at the University of Southern California (USC) and then at Stanford University—of professional training in filmmaking in order to meet the new needs of motion picture production in the sound era. Significantly, however, for all the interest in practical training, the AMPAS-sponsored courses also emphasized—like the Harvard Business School course—aesthetic value and the need for effective film production to be directed toward moral and cultural amelioration. Thus, the USC curriculum came to be directed by a professor of comparative literature, Boris Morkovin, who matched his classroom pedagogy with strong efforts in moral reform through cinema (in the 1930s, for example, he published a reform journal, *Cinema Progress,* and founded a league for ethical and aesthetic betterment through high-class film). In complementary fashion, the Stanford course was taught by an expert in the psychology of aesthetic response and dealt with issues of art's specificity. But in both cases, instead of the tension between the practical and the cultural leading to an effective mediation of art and industry (as perhaps occurred with Victor Freeburg's and Frances Patterson's notion of a feedback loop between production and appreciative reception), there was conflict: at USC, production students felt that the emphasis placed on film's cultural and social meanings just was not practical enough, and they alienated Morkovin from the program, leading to a long-enduring marginalization of critical studies approaches to film. At Stanford, by contrast, the production aspects of the curriculum never really got support (even from its own instructor, who seemed to have no particular love of film), and film pedagogy moved from the discipline of psychology to the more humanistic field of fine arts, where it remained for several decades.

The next three chapters deal with several ventures in film studies in New York State in the early to mid-1930s. Here, there emerged a more specifically humanities-oriented understanding of film that treated it as a cultural and artistic form as much as a social force. Significantly, although the three figures I deal with worked in relative isolation—literally so in the case of Sawyer Falk, off in western New York at Syracuse University, where he shaped one of the first film courses to recognize the aesthetic potential of a cinematic avant-garde—they all were active members of the same organization for cinematic uplift, the National Board of Review, and seemed inspired by that reform institution's desire not only to promote proper cinematic content but also to foster an appreciation of cinematic form.

These three chapters coalesce somewhat around shared intellectual projects in a common geographic space. Chapter 5, the first of these chapters, outlines efforts by the Marxist critic Harry Potamkin to teach a film course at the New School for Social Research just before his untimely death early in 1933. Before his demise, Potamkin had also elaborated plans for a broad university curriculum in film studies. That project has received some attention in the critical literature of film, whereas his New School course has passed unnoticed. Significantly, if Terry Ramsaye's earlier venture at the New School perhaps overemphasized an Americanist tradition of cinematic populism, Potamkin's pedagogy promised to be more in keeping with the New School philosophy. On the one hand, he matched the school's general commitment to liberal if not radical causes. On the other hand, he focused much of his interest in cinema on an appreciation of European experimental traditions in ways that would have been in line with the New School's reputed role as American disseminator of cutting-edge traditions in European arts. In fact, Potamkin never saw his Marxism as incompatible with a philosophy of aesthetic appreciation—for him, a politically healthy society was reflected in vibrant and formally adventurous cultural production—and his pedagogy revolved around the attempt to mediate film's social responsibilities with its aesthetic potential.

The second New York pedagogy, outlined in chapter 6, came from beyond the metropolitan arena of New York City: from 1934 until his death in 1961, theater professor Sawyer Falk taught a cinema appreciation course at Syracuse University. His concern was to establish film as an art independent of other cultural forms such as literature or drama, independent even of narrativity. Falk, a strong proponent of abstract or pure cinema, filled his classes with analyses of medium-specific techniques of film such as montage and dynamic composition. Falk seems to me to be rare among the early film professors in elaborating so complex an analysis of film as an art in its own right, and I carefully outline the lineaments of his aesthetic position and the ways this was translated into classroom pedagogy. (In fact, Falk kept extensive notes from his class, and it is possible to reconstruct his teaching in sharp detail.)

In chapter 7, I look at New York University, where education sociologist Frederic Thrasher taught film in the School of Education starting in the early 1930s. Significantly, Thrasher initiated his course as a study in what today's communication scholars term "media effects." That is, he was concerned initially with examining the social impact of movies. He had even been enlisted as one of the researchers in the Payne Fund Studies on the movies, the famous (or infamous) attempt by moral custodians to use the social sciences to pinpoint film's supposed contribution to social problems such as juvenile delinquency. The author of a 1927 book on youth gangs and on the mass culture in which they were immersed, Thrasher would have seemed a likely proponent of a denunciatory approach to film, but in the 1930s, he shifted from a purely sociological understanding of film to a more aestheticized one in which it was assumed that good films could counter the effects of bad ones and be a source of cultural uplift. Thrasher's course, originally entitled The Motion Picture and Education, mutated into one called The Motion Picture: Its Artistic, Educational, and Social Aspects, and to this course he brought critics, filmmakers, and cultural commentators, all in an attempt to praise the cultural worthiness of film.

The last chapter of the book chronicles a curious and yet striking attempt in academia to deal affirmatively with the popular art of film and to claim for cinema a respectable place as object of humanistic inquiry. In 1937, the philosopher Scott Buchanan became the first dean of the newly restructured St. John's College, which was famously about to devote its curriculum to regularized study of the reading program known as the Great Books of the Western World. Buchanan drafted a detailed philosophical justification for such study but ended his proposal by arguing that the Great Books curriculum should culminate in examination *of film aesthetics and film production,* since, he argued, film was *the* dialectical art of the modern age and summed up and synthesized all the learning of the Western tradition. Where the culture wars of the 1980s and 1990s often involved neoconservatives lamenting the study of popular culture and calling for a return to high literature, Buchanan had defended the high culture of the Great Books *while* arguing also for the necessary mediation of popular and high traditions through the work of cinema. Buchanan's inspiration came from the earlier enthusiasm for the movies expressed by two of his fellow defenders of Great Books: the philosopher Mortimer Adler, who had written a seven-hundred-page aesthetics of cinema, *Art and Prudence,* and the poet and critic Mark Van Doren, who served in the mid-1930s as film critic for the *Nation*. I find the willingness of this Great Books cohort (they had all been graduate students of Columbia's John Erskine, who had launched the idea of Great Books study at the university) to see film as quite compatible with an Arnoldian valorization of "the best that has been thought and said" a fascinating revision of the historical record, which in its neoconservative version necessarily assumes conflict between Great Books and popular culture. It seems a fitting way to conclude a study that deals with the variable and often welcoming means by which intellectuals approached film in the early decades of its history. As a convert to Thomist Catholicism, Mortimer Adler had argued that the arts offered an imaginative transcendence of worldly responsibilities, and he had pointedly written *Art and Prudence* to claim for philosophy the understanding of the arts—both popular and high—and to remove them from the clutches of social science. With Adler, the arts and humanities literally moved toward theology.

While this study will be at pains to eschew any narrative logic which assumes that the isolated film courses appearing between 1915 and 1935 developed in necessary stages and established a teleology, it is intriguing to note how the history I recount bears a resemblance to the broader argument that some historians have made about the concerns that occupied higher education in the first decades of the century. For example, in an influential study, *The Making of the Modern University: Intellectual Transformation and the Marginalization of Morality,* education historian Julie Reuben outlines how the twentieth-century university reacted against the spiritual and even theological vocation of earlier institutions of higher education in at least three successive ways.[8] First, there was an attempt to eschew theology in favor of activist social sciences as modes of knowledge that could elaborate practices for social betterment: where theology relied on dogma, intuition, rhetorical suasion, and mere faith in its hope of improving the lot of humanity, the social sciences promised objective analysis, predictable conjunctions of problem and solution, and moral commitment buttressed by reliable experimentation. The social sciences became a new "theology." Second, however, there was a backlash in these same social sciences against the very attempt to push knowledge toward action: a number of social scientists vociferously railed against what they saw as the enslavement of free inquiry to pragmatic ends, even if morally justifiable ones, and they argued for the social sciences as a space of value-free, nonutilitarian research and reflection for its own sake. Many proponents of the social sciences withdrew from a concern with morality, and this coincided with, if not contributed to, an increasing specialization in social science disciplines that no longer offered a total theory of the social but looked at isolated empirical phenomena. In a third moment, then, the humanities and the arts gained strength as the new site in which questions of value and totality, of morality and life's deeper meanings, could still be addressed. The humanities were now the newest "theology."

In this respect, it is revealing to note how frequently the study of film in its first decades revolved around questions of social reform versus cultural appreciation, as if hesitating between a social science–based and a humanities-based understanding of this new artistic form. In the story I am telling, we see clear moves increasingly to claim film as an object for humanistic inquiry and to suggest that it possessed aesthetic qualities that would enable it to transcend the positivism of social science. For instance, Frederic Thrasher at New York University's School of Education came to the study of film *from sociology* and had expected initially to treat cinema in terms of its no doubt deleterious social impact, only to discover that increasingly he *admired* cinema as a complex art form to be appreciated for the beauties it added to the world. Thrasher's trajectory was a veritable conversion from social scientific analysis to humanistic advocacy of the art of movies. Similarly, several humanists in the 1930s used an appreciation of movie art precisely to attack social science as a pretender that was out of its specialized depths when it tried to deal with aesthetic and cultural realms of value, beauty, and higher meaning. Thus, the cohort of humanists allied behind the pedagogy of Great Books took perhaps somewhat surprisingly to the cinema, which they appreciated as a humanistic venture comparable in its own fashion to the deeper promise of canonic, high-culture liberal education.

At the same time, however, I want to avoid making it appear as if the stories I am telling had necessarily to culminate in this aesthetic, humanistic appreciation of film. Actually, chapter 8 ends somewhat pessimistically by arguing that the valorization of film that we find in the Great Books cohort represented an ill-fated moment in the history of the study of cinema. Scott Buchanan's plan for film study at St. John's never reached fruition, Mortimer Adler never addressed film again in as public or positive a fashion, and in fact it seems that the Great Books proponents came to harden their faith in high culture in ways that increasingly left little room for an appreciation of the more popular art of cinema. By the end of the 1930s there appeared the first glimpses of a mass-culture critique that took the popular arts to be the enemy of cultural uplift and that retarded the serious academic study of film for quite some time. The late 1930s are as much the end of a vision of ambitious film studies as its beginnings.

If I have structured my study as a chronology, then, it is not from a desire to imply a teleology, especially a triumphalist one in which the early study of film *had* to culminate in an aesthetic appreciation so strong that it swept up even the high humanists and made them unflagging enthusiasts of cinema. On the contrary, chronology serves here because it offers a "zero degree" of narrativity, one in which history is rendered in its episodic nature, vulnerable to accident (who would ever have expected a Great Books venue like St. John's College to be a site for cinema appreciation?), and subject to unexpected influences and sudden reversals of fortune. Quite modestly, again, I have set out to chronicle all the cases, whether consequential or not, whether punctual or persistent, in which institutions of higher learning opened their doors to film classes. I have not attended to film pedagogy in elementary or secondary schools except where this became a topic in university courses. (For example, in his NYU School of Education course on film, Frederic Thrasher presented his ideas on film uplift to K–12 teachers in hopes that they would introduce film-betterment classes to their schools.)[9] Additionally, I try to concentrate on those cases in which film was treated as a cultural or social form in its own right rather than as a transparent vehicle for the pedagogical transmission of concepts from other fields. Hence, my concern here is not with the use of film as a medium of visual education, although not all courses of the time made such a clear distinction.[10]

The bulk of my narrative of the early days of the study of film stops in 1935—although this heuristic punctuation of the history is exceeded somewhat in my attention to Scott Buchanan's venture at St. John's in 1937. It was in 1935 that the Film Library of the Museum of Modern Art (MoMA) began its operations and definitively established new possibilities for the academic study of cinema. In particular, MoMA's rentable series of historic films offered universities a set of supposedly canonical works around which courses could be organized. Although the Film Library engaged in myriad activities—collecting and archiving films; establishing a study center with films, books, journals, stills, and related documents that scholars could consult in their research; putting on exhibitions of film-related materials; running a New York–based film series—its greatest contribution to the growing awareness of film and its history was its circulating series of films. There now could be historical traditions of film, legitimated by the prestige of a museum and maintained and transmitted through the generations by a well-grounded pedagogy. Virtually overnight there was a proliferation of scattered courses in film appreciation or film history that were based on the MoMA collection and that regularized the study of film in standard patterns that would still be in place when universities came more systematically to introduce film curricula in the 1960s. For example, chapter 4 describes how in the case of Stanford University, a course in the aesthetics of the photoplay that had been stumbling along since its beginnings in the 1930s in the psychology division was reborn and reinvigorated in the middle of the decade when the availability of the MoMA collection enabled the university to justify a move of film to the fine arts department. As D. M. Mendelowitz, the fine arts instructor for the course's new manifestation, wrote in a letter that was proudly quoted in MoMA Film Library material, "I have just completed a year's use of your film programs in conjunction with my course, Graphic Art 66, 'Lectures on the Motion Picture' and I wish to acknowledge the assistance your services have been to me. I planned my course before the Film Library Series became available but found it impossible to assemble a sufficiently adequate body of illustrative material to justify giving the course. Your programs have fitted into my needs admirably and I am showing them as laboratory assignments in conjunction with my lectures."[11]

The momentous impact of the Film Library on film culture has been well documented and analyzed in *Museum Movies: The Museum of Modern Art and the Birth of Art Cinema* by film scholar Haidee Wasson.[12] As Wasson's book shows, the Film Library both was in continuity with earlier efforts to treat film as a worthy form of cultural attention *and* constituted a rupture from those efforts insofar as it set out to make itself a—if not the—key player in the legitimation of film art. Wasson clarifies the extent to which Film Library personnel saw themselves quite directly as "custodians" of film who had to militate against improper forms of film viewing and for what they considered aesthetically correct ones. They themselves became "pedagogues" of a sort. Films were often accompanied by print material—either program notes or explanatory titles added to the beginning of the films—as if to imply that the film object did not bear its meanings in the direct encounter of spectator and film. Rather, meaning came *from study*, from the surrounding of film in a literally discursive context of facts, explanations, and descriptions.

By the end of 1936, the Film Library could report that its series had been shown in such academic venues as Bryn Mawr, Colgate, Cornell, Dartmouth, Mount Holyoke, NYU, Princeton, Smith, Stevens Institute of Technology, the University of Chicago, Indiana, the University of Pittsburgh,

Vassar, and on and on. To be sure, most of these showings occurred at film society screenings and other extracurricular events rather than in courses, but they were clearly taking place as educational activities rather than as mere amusement. By attending the MoMA series, for instance, a student would gain culturally accredited exposure to what was being presented as *the* canon of a contemporary art form. The screenings offered a form of pedagogy, sometimes in concert with, sometimes as a substitution for, classroom activities.

For example, at Dartmouth College the initiation in the mid-1930s of a so-called course in the development of film was directly keyed to the MoMA series. As an article in a local newspaper explained, the "course," to be sponsored by the Department of English and the Department of Art and Archaeology, would be closely based on the MoMA series. From this article—which mentioned no professors and no lectures, and instead simply listed classic titles to be shown from the MoMA circulating collection—it is easy to take away the impression that the course would essentially be self-taught through nothing more than the viewing of the films. That is, what was being referred to as a course was really just a set of coherent screenings. Perhaps the very fact that the series from MoMA were offered precisely as series—that is, organized either historically or thematically rather than presented as a mere assemblage of individual works—enabled Dartmouth to imagine that the screenings themselves were a credible form of pedagogy.

Not only did the MoMA Film Library's series promise to render coherent previously disorganized approaches to film history and to lend scholarly study an air of systematicity, but MoMA would set out to establish what film history was and should be. To take just one example, when in the latter part of the 1930s the Film Library began to work with Columbia University on a film curriculum to be taught with MoMA staff and resources, MoMA assistant curator Richard Griffith wrote to his boss, Iris Barry, to indicate far-reaching ambitions for college film teaching that went beyond collaboration with Columbia alone:

> I think our job is to put together a complete (year or half year?) course on "The History of Motion Pictures"—lectures accompanied by films, an exhaustive job covering history, aesthetics, and commercial development. The lectures should be, must be, I think, so final and authoritative as to deserve publication in book form—*the* course on motion pictures, in other words. If the Columbia project goes through, this will of course be done in connection with it and the work thus much simplified. But, I do not think the initiation of this project should be made conditional on the fruition of the Columbia plans. Even if Columbia should fall through,

> I think our destiny forces us to put the results of the Film Library work into teaching form and make it available. That's the next, the obligatory next, step forward for us. This lecture course can find its way into one college after another, in one form or another, if we really make it better than any now available and put all our steam behind it.[13]

Whatever Barry thought of this particular proposal, it is interesting to note that she herself got caught up in imagining the MoMA Film Library as the veritable initiator of serious film studies. Thus, in a retrospective look at the first decade of its accomplishments, Barry herself pictured the Film Library as a break in habitual ways of doing things:

> Until 1935 much had been written and said about the cultural and social influence of the film and about its inherent artistic qualities, but little had been done to treat the motion picture as though it actually did possess aesthetic qualities, and nothing whatever had been done to make possible a consistent study of its content, style, development or aesthetics. The Museum of Modern Art was the first independent institution to acclaim and accept the motion picture as a contemporary art form on a footing of equality with the other arts.[14]

Barry went on to assert that the course she helped organize at the end of the 1930s at Columbia had no predecessors: "The first credit-course on motion pictures to be given in an Eastern university was held for Columbia University by the Film Library during the three years 1937–39. The students attending this course later furnished personnel to the film industry as well as teachers on film history to other colleges."[15]

In claiming this, Barry effectively wiped away a large sweep of the history of film pedagogy—the history I will be recounting in the following pages. Film had indeed been taught in American universities before 1937. Ironically, Barry herself had even been a guest lecturer in at least one of the courses: specifically, from the mid-1930s on, she regularly came to speak on "The Art of the Motion Picture" in Frederic Thrasher's for-credit course on film appreciation at NYU. And she certainly would have been aware of other early initiatives in film pedagogy. Even before the MoMA Film Library began to circulate its film series, it had been in touch, for instance, with Sawyer Falk, who had been teaching cinema appreciation at Syracuse University since 1934—that is, one year before the beginning of operations for the library. Falk would even be invited to collaborate in pedagogical projects in film at MoMA. By reconstructing the facts of film studies' history to elide such early ventures, Barry no doubt enabled the construction of a heroic narrative in which MoMA initiated film studies, but she also engaged in an activity of deliberate historical "forgetting." (Ironically, Sawyer Falk too would participate retrospectively in such forgetting: whereas in the 1930s he had initially presented his new course as one among several such initiatives, by the 1950s he was describing the course as "one of the first of its kind, if not the very first.")

MoMA's circulating library of films certainly did constitute a break in the history of film studies, but it was not the inventor of the field that Iris Barry claimed it to be. What was new was the possibility MoMA provided for a solidified canon that could offer the regularity and systematicity that had been lacking in haphazard earlier ventures. In this respect, I find it useful to go back to the earlier moment precisely because it allows us to witness a field of study in the moment of self-invention, as its first practitioners worked to devise the very terms of discussion and the very questions they would pose to their object of study. I have sometimes described the present project to friends and colleagues as a history of early U.S. "film studies," but it is more accurate to refer to it as a history of the early U.S. "study of film." The difference has to do with the ways in which "film studies" appears to signal the formation and concretization *of a discipline.* Film was studied before 1935, but largely without disciplinary solidification into an academic tradition. The notion of "the beginnings of the U.S. study of film" emphasizes *episodes* that transpired *before* the coalescence of film study into an established field with lineages, legacies, commonly shared assumptions, and regularized procedures. I am setting out, then, to tell the story of the ways in which a number of academic instructors began to imagine film as an object worthy of serious study, and how to that end they designed the first courses in which film was the center of attention.

Although I will be concentrating in the following pages on those specific cases in which figures *within institutions of higher learning* took film to be a specific, definable, and teachable object of academic attention, it is often individuals who never specifically taught film that today's cinema studies scholars refer to when they outline the history of the discipline and seek a lineage for their own current work. For example, virtually any official historical account by today's practitioners will predictably cite as a disciplinary antecedent the poetic and often wacky ramblings of the folk poet Vachel Lindsay in his book *The Art of the Photoplay* (1916). Lindsay never actually was a film professor, but his text became formative for the discipline. In contrast, one can search with difficulty for more than cursory references in the critical literature of film studies to pedagogues like Victor Freeburg or Frances Patterson, who were the first teachers of a university course *specifically on film* and who each wrote two volumes on film.

There are a number of reasons for this skewing of the history, not all of them wrongheaded. Lindsay did write a full-fledged aesthetics of film, whereas Freeburg and Patterson—who were teaching courses with a large practical component (specifically, how to succeed as a photoplay writer)—tended often to use their own writing to less philosophical ends. Their practical textbooks do not raise foundational questions in as systematic or explicit a fashion. Indeed, as Freeburg and Patterson themselves admitted, much of the more aesthetically reflective aspects of their own volumes derived directly from Lindsay and Hugo Münsterberg.

We should not, then, overemphasize the theoretical contributions of figures like Patterson or Freeburg. But their early efforts in film instruction help to pinpoint the irony of a situation in which those who taught a field of popular culture were not regarded in the same manner as those who made the reputed and recorded contributions to the elaboration of the field's critical literature. Even as late as the 1960s, film studies found its useful literature not in the efforts of film *scholars* (one of the rare published books on film by a university instructor of the art was *Motion Pictures: The Development of an Art from Silent Films to the Age of Television* [1960], by Purdue professor Albert Fulton) but in works of criticism (e.g., the writings of Pauline Kael or Andrew Sarris [who later would go on to have an academic career]) or in scholarly writings by people in other fields (e.g., Erwin Panofsky, who gave one of the first keynote talks for the newly founded Society of Cinematologists at the end of the 1950s). No doubt cinema's assumed status as an object of popular taste about which everyone has opinions has meant that much of the available writing on film has been nonscholarly, but it is still striking to encounter an important field of critical attention where for so much of its history, the respected discourse on the object of study has been offered by figures other than those who actually approach the object as scholars.

I must confess that part of my interest in chronicling the efforts of these early figures who have been lesser known in the history of film studies has to do with my ongoing concern for the ways in which the practical efforts of day-to-day pedagogy generally are downplayed in the historiography of disciplines. Academic *rhetoric* frequently invokes a necessary interconnection between research and teaching, but historiographical practices proceed often as if only the former contributed in any substantial ways to defining the contours of disciplines and their practices.

Disciplines, their historians seem to say, are formed through professional activities and institutions such as scholarly journals, professional societies and their meetings, the reading and writing of specialized research, the credentialing of graduate acolytes, and so on, but rarely through what happens in the average classroom session. It is as if the everyday work of imparting instruction to a student population is taken to be a secondary activity with no direct impact on the field's constitution and continuance. Symptomatic in this respect is the explicit decision by David Shumway in his genealogy of the discipline of American literary studies to pay less attention to pedagogy and curriculum, and to concentrate instead on research and the scholarly discourse of professors among themselves. In Shumway's words, "My focus is on research practices as revealed in publications of scholarly articles and books. I have also been concerned with pedagogy and curricular practices, but I have not treated these in as much detail, because a discipline, as I understand it, is dedicated to the production of knowledge, so that under the disciplinary model, transmission of knowledge becomes a mere means to further production."[16] What Shumway appears to be saying is that to the extent that disciplines revolve around "the production of knowledge," this occurs in the form of writings destined for other professors: the knowledge that students take away from the classroom is not really a part of what characterizes a discipline. The classroom, Shumway seems to contend, merely transmits a produced knowledge but adds nothing—and leads to nothing of consequence for the discipline.

Shumway follows this sentence with a footnote in which he adduces an additional reason for not attending to pedagogy: the sheer practical difficulty of finding traces of classroom activity. Here, at least, one can concur. Indeed, in the following pages, we will often encounter the challenges of reconstructing everyday classroom practice when so much data and detail have disappeared. But these material problems are largely unrelated to the larger resistance to the classroom that Shumway demonstrates. His broader attitude has theoretical implications for how we understand the production of knowledge: in his view, that students absorb a body of knowledge is not consequential for the meaning of a field and its development.

In the effort, then, to draw attention to the everyday activities of teaching, my study sets out to reconstruct as much as it seems possible to discover of early film pedagogy. The accounts that follow derive from extensive archival research: the goal is to establish the identity of those who taught film, how they went about it, what presuppositions they started from, how their courses originated, and what they intended to accomplish. Since much of this history is uncharted, I will offer a fair amount of quoting from documents, and there will be a fair amount of narrative recounting. I want first of all to establish the historical record.

In the following pages, then, there will often be a great deal of detail about specific courses, curricula, and their content. Given how little of this history has been available to film scholars and students, I deliberately err on the side of providing more rather than less. At the same time, I do not want my attention to the irreducible particularity of individual pedagogies to lead us to lose sight of larger implications of this early history of what would later become a solid discipline of academic endeavor. In fact, I intend this study as not only an archival history but also an *intellectual history*. At the very least it asks: What did it take for academia to treat film as an acceptable object of study? What were the possible forms of that study at the time? What were the larger contextual forces in higher education, and in American society more generally, that enabled academic institutions to begin to deal with the popular culture of the movies?

As they moved deeper into the twentieth century, institutions of higher education found themselves forced to come to grips with new demographic conditions in the United States—in particular the shift to city living, the influx of immigrant cultures, and the growing need attendant upon industrialization for a trained, disciplined, and, some might say, trained-to-be-subservient labor force. On the one hand, academia became a site for reflection on the conditions of modernity, with the social sciences in particular promoting themselves as the modes of knowledge most propitious for this reflection. On the other hand, the universities and colleges also became venues in which new citizen-subjects could gain skills to make their way through that modernity. As David O. Levine shows in his book *The American College and the Culture of Aspiration, 1915–1940*, this was a period of great faith in college as a place in which ordinary citizens (and not just a privileged elite) could learn strategies for contemporary living and material success. In Levine's words, "After World War I, institutions of higher learning were no longer content to educate; they now set out to train, accredit, and impart social status to their students. The curriculum became inextricably tied to the nation's economic structure, particularly its burgeoning white-collar, middle-class sector."[17]

There was, however, no obvious, inevitable form and content to such a curriculum. To the extent that, as Levine puts it later in his book, the new academic world was "poised between its traditional function of transmitting past culture and its modern function of occupational and social training" (210), it was as possible to argue that a college education adequate to the demands of a new modernity might be one that stressed the higher cultivation of the whole human being as much as one that emphasized trades and professions. For example, World War I certainly brought awareness of the need for engineers and scientists, but it also led many old-style humanists to argue that their classic curriculum, too, was essential insofar as it taught the deeper values that governed war and peace.

In like fashion, the modern academic system had no definitive attitude about the place of everyday or popular culture in the curricula of institutions of higher education. Popular culture might be one of the threats to a new humanity, but it also might be the site of new career options. And in the hands of a Mortimer Adler, as we see in chapter 8, popular culture might even itself be claimed to foster a sense of higher humanity.

In the first decades of the century, the question was being raised as to what to do about new forms of popular culture and their impact. For example, in their classic study, *Middletown* (1929), Robert and Helen Lynd had found that mass-media forms such as cinema were becoming the social glue for urban experience, replacing previous modes of socialization such as church, school, and family. While many academics ignored the new mass culture or disdained it as deleterious, a few set out to understand its impact. There was a need in the beginning of the twentieth century, with its overload of experience and its increasing commodification of everyday life, for people to know what they should read and see *and* to learn how to pass themselves off as skilled in the interpretation of the everyday culture around them. There was a need also, as people moved into the new consumerist age, for what Joan Rubin in *The Making of Middlebrow Culture* and Janice Radway in *A Feeling for Books: The Book-of-the-Month-Club, Literary Taste and Middle-Class Desire* refer to as the middlebrow "cultural mediators" so prevalent in the first part of the twentieth century: that is, intellectuals who could bring culture to the masses and offer them salient lessons in dealing effectively with that culture.[18] Radway, for instance, examines how the judges for the Book-of-Month-Club literary selection served as popular pedagogues who could select for ordinary citizens those narratives that would help them make their way through the modern moment. The books chosen were often narrative works of emotional and sometimes intellectual uplift, and they offered the image of a world that was still narratable, that still made coherent sense. In like fashion, we will encounter in the following pages a select number of pedagogues who set out to present film as something that could be used to improve the present age and offer narrative cues for making one's path through it. Cinema became for these professors a force that could help new citizens wend their way through the complicated terrain of contemporary life. Film was imagined either as a force for *moral* uplift (this, for example, was the approach of NYU's Frederic Thrasher, whose cinema course in the 1930s treated film as itself a form of popular education) or as a source for the production of *aesthetic* value (thus, for instance, Sawyer Falk's cinema appreciation course at Syracuse University tried to introduce students to the best works in European cinematic modernism).

In the moment of Progressivism, educational institutions joined with various initiatives in government, religious organizations, reform institutions, Chautauqua institutes, and so on, to deal with the new qualities of American life by trying to find points of integration for diverse social constituencies within civics and corresponding cultural and social realms. In this Progressivist context, reformers sought out and promoted the potentially beneficent aspects of everyday culture, which helps explain the increasingly positive acceptance of film as an object of academic study. Film was a profession but also potentially an art, and pedagogues worked with the assumption that proper training in spectatorship would help ordinary citizens improve their cultural lot. And by promoting an education in film, the educators also promoted themselves: in teaching that to view the new visual art of film properly one could not just absorb it distractedly but had to reflect on its techniques, the pedagogues of cinema were saying that their instruction was necessary, something that citizens required.

It is important to understand Progressivism not so much as a single movement but as a series of initiatives and debates conducted by individuals, organizations, and institutions that did not necessarily have a direct relation to each other and could, indeed, display conflicting notions and methods of social-cultural reform. In one early guise, a moralistic discourse dominated Progressive reform and posited that the new conditions of everyday life in America offered its citizens dangerous temptations, and therefore that there should be moral instruction as defense against noxious influence. But where many of the moralists militated as impassioned amateurs (e.g., reformers such as Jane Addams), the rising academic professionalization of American social sciences meant that its practitioners were increasingly able to take on the mission of Progressivism without enclosing amelioration within a moralistic or religious framework and could claim instead for themselves a scientific objectivity. Everyday life and its popular culture turned from being the target of well-meaning reformers in the world at large to offering an object of study for professionals within academia.

The moral guardians in the first decade of the twentieth century had tended to regard film with suspicion as one of the seductions into salacious misbehavior that faced ordinary people in the public sphere. The closing of New York's moving picture exhibition venues at the end of 1908 is the most famous example of the moral disciplining of cinema in this first moment. But this moralistic disapprobation received quick riposte. First, pragmatically astute reform groups such as the People's Institute (a key player behind the foundation of the National Board of Censorship) set out not to condemn the movies but to find paths toward their betterment. Second, and more to our purposes, a number of educators worked to turn film into the object of a positive analysis and approbation in which it was imagined that, with the right instruction, exposure to the art of cinema and the working of its techniques could have an uplifting effect. This concern with ameliorative forms of instruction in the popular culture of the age was institutionalized in the curricula of outreach programs at Columbia, the New School, and New York University, which increasingly tried to target new constituencies and find an acceptable, even beneficial, popular culture for them.

There were no guarantees that the early pedagogues would succeed in this attempt to justify cinema as a respectable object of study. In his book on the history of cultural studies, John Hartley argues that the dominant, high-culture aesthetic tradition can constitute something as art only if it is seen as abstracted from worldly cares.[19] In this respect, the problem of cinema for so many cultural custodians at the beginning of the twentieth century was that it seemed too rooted in a worldly context: for example, the majority of films came from an industry that appeared to treasure financial benefits over either moral or aesthetic goodness.

However, a series of tactics were available to intellectuals hoping to construct film as worthy object. First, they could study that very worldliness, try to master it and pull positive benefit—both moral and financial—from it. Thus, for instance, when in 1927 the Harvard School of Business initiated what it hoped would be an ongoing course on the *business* of film (with strong backing from the Hays Office, the Hollywood public relations and industry trade bureau most known for its attempt to legislate a moral code for film content), it intended that course as a means of making the industry appear as efficient and as moral as possible, and as thereby possessing the greatest chance of creating publicly responsive and uplifting popular art. In other words, the pedagogy was designed to mediate art and industry and to suggest that each grew beneficially from the other.

Second, to present film as worthy of attention, intellectuals could make the argument that the cinema was potentially a form of art no less transcendent of worldly cares than any other. In this view, the business of film had only incidental effect on the essential aesthetic vocation of the art. This was a position taken by Sawyer Falk at Syracuse and by the group of figures (Scott Buchanan, Mortimer Adler, and Mark Van Doren) who tried to argue for a pedagogy of film as the culmination of the Great Books tradition. This was also the position of Columbia's Frances Taylor Patterson, who asserted a distinction between the personal industriousness of the creative artist and the film industry, which she pictured as a set of external pressures that the artist could and should fight against.

A third possibility was to argue that the very premise—that art had to transcend the worldly—was inadequate. Instead, some intellectuals claimed, art's value could come precisely from the practical aid, the very worldliness, it offered citizens to make their way through the everyday world. For example, while Frances Patterson's invocation of *industriousness* did have to do with the ways in which citizens could learn to make art, it also seemed more simply to valorize a personally meaningful work activity. By the studious application of rules, citizens would learn aesthetic techniques, but they would also learn to appreciate the very act of making. To find a meaningfulness of personal endeavor within the complexities of modernity, people needed *craftsmanship*, a word that figured in the title of one of Patterson's cinema books and in fact showed up endlessly throughout the period of the 1910s and 1920s, along with the complementary term *workmanship*, to suggest the social value of industrious personal enterprise. Uplift here came not from the rush of emotion in the face of great art but from pride in learning a skill and participating in a job well done.

Craftsmanship indeed is a key aspect of the American tradition. It involves valorization of the maker, the doer, the hobbyist, the tinkerer: the assumption is that you make yourself by making things. The lauding of human skill and dexterity—which no doubt also fuels an American interest in hobbies, science fairs, basement tinkering, gadgetry and invention, and everyday arts and crafts—became in the historical moment of craftsmanship and workmanship a celebration of the American dream less as the pioneer adventure it had been in the nineteenth century than as an adventure-in-place, the discovery of the ingenuity by which one coped industriously with the objects in one's immediate purview. And such crafting did not necessarily have to lead to a career. Hence, Frances Patterson taught photoplay writing to noncredit extension students and adult-education students who seemed to follow the instruction as much for the sheer enjoyment of the enterprise as for any hopes of industry employment. The point was not to give students careers but to teach them the valuable act of workmanship in itself. Such a crafts pedagogy was an example of that growing concern with the therapeutic and with the bolstering up of the self against the ravages of the contemporary world that American studies scholars such as Warren Susman and T. J. Jackson Lears have seen as central to the intellectual history of this period.[20]

From the start, then, film study welcomed the conjunction of aesthetic appreciation and practical instruction in film. Both made people better. But for this conjunction actually to work, industry had to be seen as a source of quality, a mark of individual moral worth; even Harvard's course claimed that the men it was training for the film business would engage in their work with inspired respect for cinema's artistic and cultural possibilities. From the opposite direction, Mortimer Adler would argue in the 1930s that appreciation of cinema's accomplishments increased all the more when one took into account the practical efforts and active skills that had to be employed in moviemaking. As he put it in *Art and Prudence*, his massive aesthetics of film, "It may be objected, as it has been in certain quarters, that the movies are not an art but an industry and that, therefore, they do not deserve the same kind of consideration which is given to music and poetry. . . . [T]his objection reveals a failure to understand the status of the cinema as fine art. . . . The moral and political criticism of an art is usually distorted by a lack of sensitivity to its problems of workmanship and production, its artistic aims and its technical means."[21]

Many early film courses were concerned with issues equally of filmmaking and of film appreciation. Indeed, it is important to note how educationally productive was this confusion of two pedagogies—a confusion useful to Progressivist ideology, in which all forms of self-improvement from the moral-aesthetic to the practical were promoted. The activities both of photoplay making and of photoplay appreciation were integral components of an overall process that envisioned film's function as moral, aesthetic, and practical self-amelioration alike.

Film studies arose within this context of reform and self-improvement. It seems not coincidental that the very first course—Columbia's Photoplay Composition—developed at virtually the same moment as the publication of aesthetics of film by such luminaries as Münsterberg and Lindsay. For film to stand as a positive object for university study, it had to achieve a certain level of respectability and aesthetic ambition, and this happened in the teens with the shift to the feature film. Certainly, there had been some attention by intellectuals to cinema before this moment. For example, as Richard deCordova notes in his *Picture Personalities*, the emergence of cinema had been accompanied by a scientific discourse on the technology of film and its ability to bring reproduced pictures to life.[22] But it is unlikely that academic study of film would have arisen from the mere need to dissect cinema's technical wizardry. Indeed, as deCordova points out, the savants who set out to explain the gadgetry of early cinema found easy venues for their explanations of new technology in the columns of widely disseminated popular science journals: they did not need to bring film into the classroom in order to study how its images were produced technologically.

To be sure, the emergence in the teens of a powerful and artistically ambitious, narratively complex cinema did not *necessitate* the concomitant emergence of an academic study that set out to explain its powers. In fact, the very extent to which film worked as a visually immediate art of affect and emotion easily available to all might have suggested that it did not need explanatory discourses, academic or not, to make sense of it: cinema, in the directness of its impact, might seem to wear its meanings on its sleeves. What could one say about an art whose workings were so visible and which itself seemed so vocal? What could one teach?

Among the practices of everyday culture, cinema posed a problem for pedagogy: there was the widespread assumption that film's power—both positive and negative—was that it was a popular art that spoke accessibly to everyone. If such was indeed the case, what could academic discourse add to cinema's evident, easy functioning as democratic culture? Throughout the 1910s, and especially in the 1920s, writings about film repeatedly invoked its potential to serve as a universal language, a "visual esperanto" (as Edward S. Van Zile called it in his 1923 volume *That Marvel, the Movie*).[23] There was even an emphasis on cinema as a veritable pedagogy in itself insofar as film's photographic nature enabled it to transmit images of the world and thereby offer instruction about it. In its explicit presentation of everyday knowledge, film could substitute for other forms of learning. Cinema supposedly transmitted the facts of existence with greater immediacy and greater impact than the more mediated, distanced efforts of the traditional verbal discourse of classroom pedagogy. In Edward Van Zile's case, for instance, we even find the author proposing an end to universities and their replacement by a universal archive of film images that could recount all of human knowledge. (It is worth noting that this assumed the necessity of re-creating past events through staged performances. Even as it intended to valorize film as documentary transmission of the world, the invocation of film as universal language had a necessary place for fiction and imaginative reconstruction.)

If this were the case, if film was already a fully effective form of visual pedagogy, what role would there be for the film instructor? What could he or she say about film that film itself did not say already?

To grant themselves a necessary role in the understanding of film, the early pedagogues could resort to a number of strategies. At the very least, they could displace attention from the films themselves to their context. They could, that is, offer instruction in the ways to best create this powerful universal language and make it available to the greatest number of citizens: hence, courses in film production and in film business (especially the distribution and selling of film to its audience). Conversely, they could study the context of reception: if film was indeed a universal language of direct impact, was this good or bad for society? How might viewers be better trained to receive the fullness of film's messages? Hence, courses in cinema appreciation.

But the pedagogue could also find ways to focus on the films themselves, even when these seemed quite vocal about their own effects and affects. For example, the pedagogue might argue that film was indeed a universal language but only at an affective and nonrational level; the professor of film could set out, then, to make manifest the meanings that remain emotive in the art itself. Or the pedagogues could agree that, yes, film was a universal language but only for some people some of the time: spectators needed training in a visual literacy that would render them properly receptive to the art. This, as we will see, was an argument that NYU's Frederic Thrasher made when he contended that juveniles were assailed by too many influences in the modern world and were not learning how to be properly receptive to the right influences embodied in the highest-quality films.

Yet another strategy involved the assertion that even if cinema was an art of power and emotional richness, different films in different contexts achieved their potential in their own ways. There needed, then, to be a history of cinema—what it had achieved as cultural form, what it might still achieve—as well as a typology of genres and even, from early on, a cataloging of the expressive talents of individual directors as veritable auteurs. Even before they had the MoMA canon to guide them in categorizing films along historical, generic, and authorial lines, some film teachers engaged in the systematization that comes from classifying an art according to its creative achievements.

But if the early pedagogues displayed a variety of ways of talking affirmatively about film, it is not necessarily the case that their words had institutional impact—that anyone of consequence in the hierarchy of higher education was listening to their lessons. If film was able to enter the academy so early on in the century, it was not only for the important intellectual historical reasons that I have outlined here. There is also a much more banal and benign explanation. As we will see throughout the following pages, film also slipped quietly and easily into academic settings as much because no one was really paying attention. Here, we might reference historian Laurence Veysey's classic account of the emergence of the modern university, which argues that it took on the shape of a vast bureaucracy in which there could no longer be centralized oversight of each and every intellectual enterprise. In Veysey's oft-cited words, "The university throve, as it were, on ignorance." Or as he elaborates, "The university throve on the patterned isolation of its component parts, and this isolation required that people continually talk past each other, failing to listen to what others were actually saying."[24] Film studies, then, may have benefited from the sheer complexity of modern academia as a new twentieth-century bureaucracy: this was a period in which increasing specialization, creation of new academic units, multiplication of courses, and so on became the norm. In this moment of what the historian of academia John Higham terms the "departmentalization of universities," curricular initiatives proliferated, and rather than seeking ways to pull the strands back to a common core, many colleges and universities found it advantageous to use proliferation to reach out to diverse new populations of students and thereby to appear pluralistic and democratic.[25]

Again, then, modesty is called for in our history of these early days. The first teachers of film were not revolutionaries or trailblazers but merely professionals trying to do a job. In some cases their commitment to film was fickle and lasted for no more than a course or so. In others, they engaged unflaggingly with the art of film over decades but in a patient, even plodding, way, quietly continuing a pedagogy that in many ways had become habitual. It might be comforting for film scholars to imagine that their predecessors created their pedagogy in acts of intellectual heroism. But in the larger scheme of things, these early efforts were absorbed into university business as usual.

In a remembrance of his student days at Cambridge University, the cultural critic Raymond Williams wrote of the dangers of exaggerating in historical memory the intensity of intellectual life on a college campus:

> [M]emories are selective. This is clear even in those cases in which people profess to be remembering a group (it is usually brilliant; it is always unique). . . . The successful, obviously, are more easily remembered; the others, equally important at the time, can be made to fade. People talk of the Cambridge of Moore and Russell, or of Wittgenstein and Richards, and so on. Yet at any time such figures are a tiny minority in the whole intellectual life of the university. It is falsifying, in a particular way, to project the place through these few figures, who are as often as not relatively isolated, or quite uncharacteristic.[26]

Perhaps, then, it is enough to tell the story of film studies as it was, without romanticizing. Perhaps it is useful to counter the impression that the only important things that happen to a discipline happen outside the classroom and apart from the daily clockwork of pedagogy's ordinary and routine functioning. The early film pedagogues are a part of the history of the discipline even if no one sings their praises.

1 First Forays in Film Education

The Pedagogy of Photoplay Composition at Columbia University

> Where is the quiet and study essential to the study of art to be had? In the dark silence of motion-picture theaters.
> FRANCES TAYLOR PATTERSON, instructor for Photoplay Composition, Columbia University, *Scenario and Screen* (1928)

Among the handful of letters between Will Hays, head of the Motion Picture Producers and Distributors Association (MPPDA), and Columbia University president Nicholas Murray Butler in the university's archives, the very last one, from 1945, is particularly amusing.[1] Hays and Butler maintained over the years a correspondence that was simultaneously professional and somewhat personal: for example, in 1920, Butler asked if he might receive tickets for himself and his family to the Republican National Convention (of which Hays was chairman), and Hays wrote back with his willingness to oblige. The correspondence also offers an ongoing glimpse of the busy life of the university president in a period when institutions of higher learning increasingly were being run as veritable big-business bureaucracies (and lamented as such by such cultural commentators as Thorstein Veblen). The modern university had evolved into a massive operation in which responsibilities for individual programs and projects were ever more frequently delegated to subunits, such as individual departments, in the institutional hierarchy. Presidents did not have time to keep track of everything: they were just too busy fund-raising and serving as symbolic beacons for the university. Throughout the years, Butler would take an interest, both academic and personal, in the movies, but he did not always have time to commit himself to film culture in extended fashion.

The November 10, 1945, letter is revealing in its image of a busy college president for whom running the university has become an all-consuming responsibility. The letter came from R. B. Parker, Butler's personal secretary, and was written to Will Hays to thank him for sending the president a copy of Raymond Moley's official history of the Hays Office. President Butler, Parker recounted, was very grateful to have the volume. He would, Parker promised, "have it read *to him* at the very first opportunity" (my empha-

33

sis). The image here is of the university president as overly occupied and preoccupied administrator—not so unlike our typical image of the classic Hollywood producer on several phones at once—who can get by only through what we now term *multitasking*. Butler might from time to time take an interest in the movies and the business behind them, but he too had a business to run, and the movies could demand only so much attention from him.

Delegation of responsibility and benign indifference to local decision making at the departmental level became necessary to the workings of the modern university as it entered the twentieth century. With the increasing fragmentation of divisions and the increasing diversity of functions any one campus performed, there was no way the administration could keep track of every component, and there was a concomitant need to let individual units proceed in relative autonomy from direct supervision. Units could generally do as they wished as long as they did not stray too far from basic assumptions about what the university mission was or open themselves up to scandal. At the same time, university administrators in the twentieth century increasingly began to ignore the academic projects on campus in large part because their administrative energy had turned elsewhere—to public relations, to fund-raising, to the cultural image of the university in the world at large.

University presidents, for instance, ceased to be academic figures primarily—the titular leaders of their faculty—and instead turned into figureheads who lobbied for the university with nonacademic publics (e.g., trustees, donors, parents, journalists, and legislators). Tellingly, one of historian Laurence Veysey's own descriptions of this new outward-oriented activity of college leaders uses a metaphor from film: "For their part, university administrators (whose deeper sympathies more frequently lay with the marching feet [i.e., the publicly attractive activities of campus athletics and parades]) took pride in the accomplishments of their faculties, even if they did so in the manner of the neighborhood theater owner who never watches the films he books but keenly knows the drawing power of the actors."[2] In like fashion, in 1932, the secretary of Columbia, Frank D. Fackenthal, used a film metaphor when he wrote on President Butler's behalf to turn down an invitation to a screening from Adolph Zukor (for Paramount's movie *The Man I Killed*): as Fackenthal explained, "He [President Butler] is sort of a motion picture himself these days and does not seem certain that he can stop long enough to drop into the Criterion."

It is no doubt risky to read too much into a few letters in a (perhaps incomplete) archival file. However, the anecdote of President Butler engaged in other activities while one of his minions reads him a film book can serve as a fitting allegory for one destiny of early cinema pedagogy in the Ivy League context. Early in the twentieth century Columbia flirted with film, but it was not central to the university's overall mission—such that there might still be one singular mission in an age of increasing academic compartmentalization—and the specific activity of film pedagogy seems to have found its way into the curriculum less because it mattered to anyone high up than because, quite the contrary, it did not make a splash and passed quietly under the radar. Starting in the fall of 1915, Columbia would begin offering a pedagogy in Photoplay Composition in its adult-education extension program and then in its home-study (i.e., correspondence school) program, and this course would continue to be offered for several decades. From a single item in the curriculum, the course would expand into multiple sections and multiple levels (from beginners to advanced). It would come close to spawning a spin-off production course at the beginning of the 1920s, and would almost be absorbed at the end of the 1920s into a broader, more ambitious attempt at Columbia to create a full degree-granting program in cinema. Through all this, however, film teaching just moved along—not much fanfare, but also not much outcry. One searches in vain for administrative notice—positive *or* negative—of this first pedagogy of film. From our vantage point within the established discipline of today's film studies, we would like perhaps to look back and imagine that things were more exciting and more heroic, and that the "birth" of the field was an event of high drama. When writing the history of a discipline, it is easy to get so caught up in the local efforts that marked the trajectory of the field that one imagines that everyone in the university setting (and even perhaps persons beyond the ivy walls) must have felt a sense of momentousness and followed the story with close attention. But the modern university had become such a massive and fragmented space that it would be hard for any new pedagogy to do more than quietly find its own little corner.

Offered in the nether region of extension programs, noncredit lecture series, and professional divisions removed from the mainstream humanistic mission of institutions of higher learning, the first film courses slipped stealthily into the academic context and, in some cases, endured most likely by exploiting the benign neglect that frequently resulted from bureaucratic ignorance.

That the researcher does not find documents concerning the history of a discipline does not always mean they have disappeared; it can also mean they never existed to begin with. That is, what we might take to be an interesting or even exciting history that everyone must have been commenting on at the time can turn out to be part of an initiative so local or minor it was absorbed into the running of university affairs "as usual," and thereby merited no special attention or extended commentary. Silence and a lack of documents represent the other face of benign ignorance.

Take, for instance, a series of letters in the Wills Hays folder at Columbia that went back and forth in late 1926 between President Butler and several figures in the film industry (not just Hays alone): Butler wrote to Hays admitting that he (Butler) did "not know anything about the motion picture industry" but had been wondering if his book *Building the American Nation* might form the potential basis for a motion picture; Carl Laemmle at Universal wrote to invite Butler to a screening of an adaptation of Jules Verne's *Michael Strogoff* (Butler declined); and in yet another letter Laemmle asked him to be one of the judges for a high school photoplay contest in honor of Victor Hugo (Butler accepted). The correspondence is sparse, but nonetheless it has several intriguing aspects. First, we might wonder why letters to or from Carl Laemmle ended up in a file supposedly devoted to Will Hays. Of course, it could be an after-the-fact accident of filing: someone in Butler's office may have simply put all letters relating to the film business together. At the same time, it is worth noting that Hays, as we will see in more detail, seems to have been an important behind-the-scenes figure in a number of enterprises around film in higher education, and it might well be the case that Hays actually instigated the various attempts by Laemmle to forge contacts with Butler and his university.

There is yet another intriguing aspect to the letters from 1926. One learns from other documents at Columbia and from Will Hays's own papers that *concurrent with* the bits of tentative contact evident in these letters between Hays, Laemmle, and Butler, there had already been fairly advanced discussions between industry officials *and* Columbia administrators and faculty regarding the development *of a degree program in film study* at the university. Butler did not directly take part in the discussions about the program, but he knew of them and gave them his imprimatur and close attention. Later I will discuss details of this project, which was given its greatest elaboration in 1927. For now I only want to register the fact that none of Butler's correspondence with industry figures like Laemmle alluded to the curricular project in film in any way. Hays and Butler talked about the idea of a Hollywood adaptation of the college president's book without any mention of the initiative (in which they were both involved) to bring film study to Columbia. Likewise, Hays made no mention of the project in his letters to Laemmle. Perhaps some of the discussion of the program occurred outside of letters (e.g., there may have been unrecorded telephone conversations). Perhaps the film activities that Butler was being asked to involve himself in, such as the Victor Hugo contest, were ways of establishing social contacts and opening channels of communication so that the curricular idea could then be examined. But it is again interesting to see the extent to which these bureaucrats could so compartmentalize their concerns that their letters on one topic seem to engage in a sort of deliberate ignoring of their own activities in other, complementary areas.

In this respect, it is additionally striking to note that the 1926 discussions between film industry officials and the Columbia administration regarding the creation of a degree program in film gave minimal recognition to the fact that for about ten years Columbia had already been offering film courses—namely, the series of classes starting in 1915 on photoplay composition that had been offered through the university's active extension program. The instructor who taught the photoplay course, Frances Taylor Patterson, was not mentioned in any documents about the new film curriculum proposed in 1927; neither was the man who had taught it before her, Victor Freeburg. Patterson served on no committees geared toward implementation of that curriculum, and she appears not to have been consulted for her views on a film major. As we will see later, Freeburg's and Patterson's courses were vaguely alluded to by planners of the new program but merely as existing offerings that could easily be absorbed into the proposed curriculum. There was little sense that Patterson's own views on the topic of course development in film mattered in any way. Her photoplay composition pedagogy, at best, was something taken for granted and, at worst, something ignored.

Nonetheless, the photoplay composition courses that began at Columbia in the mid-1910s represent, as far as we can tell, the first academic offerings on film in the United States, and for that reason they matter to the historian. One reason for their marginalization in the university's consciousness is that they were offered through various branches of Columbia's extension program, and to a degree, the lack of attention paid them reflects the low intellectual status granted by higher education to extension study overall. To be sure, universities saw advantages to be gained from their extension programs, but these were not always imagined by administrators and regular faculty as *intellectual* benefits. From the late nineteenth century on, a number of elite institutions of higher learning had begun programs in adult or extension education, and their reasons were not always scholarly: adult education made for good public relations, it fit in with the ameliorative spirit of the Progressive age, and with efficient organization, it could be a new source of revenue for the institutions. Indeed, Columbia seems to have been driven by a number of these factors, especially as its "rival to the south," New York University, seemed to be getting all the glory of extension education. Additionally, as we will see later, extension programs also functioned in some cases as laboratories where courses could be tried out in a low-risk environment before being proposed as for-credit offerings to the regular body of matriculating students.

Few extension programs offered their courses for credit. At Columbia specifically, *no* extension courses were allowed to fulfill regular curricular requirements. (However, one newspaper story reported that a student in the photoplay course, who was a regular matriculating Columbia undergraduate, was able to petition successfully to have the course count toward his major.) Even though some of the extension courses were taught by regular Columbia teaching staff who simply offered noncredit adult-education versions of the same courses that matriculating Columbia students took from them for credit, the administration insisted that extension courses not be considered a regular part of the university's curriculum. Fundamentally, early American adult education instituted a division between the regular university curriculum, considered to represent the real core of the university's educational offering, and another track of courses imagined as serving very different needs. To the various constituencies involved in both kinds of curriculum—not only students but also teachers, administrators, and the general public—the courses on either side of the divide were imagined to entail a range of pedagogical advantages and disadvantages. On the one hand, President Butler seems to have wanted to assign extension courses a lesser status, not really a part of genuine university education and not really for the elite college student. As he put it bluntly in 1926, "It is almost as important to keep certain young men and young women from going to college as to induce others to do so."[3] On the other hand, in a 1923 report, James Egbert, the head of Columbia's extension program, boldly pictured his division as so fully meeting the requirements of a rigorous commitment that it often surpassed many degree-granting programs in terms of seriousness of education. These, he argued, rested on their laurels and were often little more than socializing clubs for degree-seeking students more interested in useful contacts and the prestige of a diploma than in real learning. In Egbert's words, "The opinion exists in the minds of many that colleges throughout the country are being regarded by students and by people in general as athletic and social clubs primarily and not as educational institutions. The students in University Extension attend for the purpose of obtaining an education, and are not drawn aside from this goal by the allurement of athletic sports or social engagements."[4]

Was extension learning an entertainment that sold out the real educational mission of the university? Conversely, did it offer the seriousness that the university system was all too often lacking in its social-club undergraduate programs? Did its seriousness tip too often into an overly pragmatic emphasis on a teaching of vocational and practical skills that itself betrayed the university mission of liberal education? Such questions about university initiatives in adult education were replayed in specific ways with regard to the photoplay composition courses at Columbia. These courses, as we will see, hovered between several identities: for example, they alternately (or simultaneously) were a light pastime for New York culture mavens, a form of vocational training, and (at least in the rhetoric of the instructors in charge) sites for deeper liberal uplift through aesthetic education in a new modern cultural form—the art of cinema.

Columbia began its extension program early in the twentieth century with courses offered on the university campus itself and at various sites throughout the metropolitan New York area. In 1913, the Institute of Arts and Sciences was added as a subsidiary part of the extension program. Where the extension program overall offered courses that generally would run for the whole semester and might involve homework and class assignments (since students could get certification for successfully completing the courses even though they could not use such courses to matriculate at the university), the Institute of Arts and Sciences was conceived as a place for more punctual public events such as lectures, concerts, recitals, and performances of various sorts. Many of the events at the institute were artistic. For example, there was a series of very successful choir performances, which evidently helped in legitimating an eventual for-credit track in choir at the university. But the institute also involved lectures or demonstrations with a more practical orientation: for example, "how-to" sessions on this or that topic of practical training. And there were also lectures with a broader mission of civic uplift: for instance, at the same moment that Photoplay Composition began to be taught through the extension program, the institute's bulletin announced lectures on such topics as "The New Prison System," "Food Preparation," and a series of three talks on "Women Who Helped Mould England." Whereas the extension division director, James Egbert, came from the regular faculty at Columbia, the first appointed head of the Institute of Arts and Sciences, Milton J. Davies, had been educational director of the Central Branch of the Young Men's Christian Association, had previously been involved with the Chautauqua Institution, and had also served as supervisor of the Brooklyn Institute of Arts and Sciences. In this background, we see very clearly the concern with the transmission of cultural uplift through public outreach.

The general educational efforts of the extension program, and its more specifically artistic offerings through the institute, were complemented in 1919 by the creation of a home-study program in which students could take courses, often similar to those offered on-site in extension, by mail. Importantly for our concerns, all three programs—general extension, the Institute of Arts and Sciences, and home study—offered instruction about film.

A 1916 budget breakdown for the extension division offers an immediate sense of the place of Photoplay Composition in the overall scheme of things. In that year (the second in which Photoplay Composition was given), the total budget for the extension division was $130,516, with $10,850 allotted to English, a very successful track in terms of enrollment, while a mere $350 was designated for what was termed the film "department." Other documents from the time, such as an interview with the first photoplay instructor, Victor Freeburg, in the *New York Times* in 1917, also referred to a "department" but it cannot have been imagined with any great ambition, given its meager allotment within the extension division.

Through the first years of the 1920s, the photoplay course had a steadily increasing enrollment, although it was never overwhelming in number. By the middle of the decade, it seems to have stabilized at around fifty students.[5] We can make some tentative guesses about the place that Photoplay Composition may have occupied within the extension curriculum by extrapolating from a statistical study of Columbia's home-study program conducted in the mid-1930s by a philosophy student, George Baxter Smith, for his Ph.D. thesis, published as *Purposes and Conditions Affecting the Nature and Extent of Participation of Adults in Courses in the Home Study Department of Columbia University, 1925–1932*.[6] By analyzing enrollment patterns and student interest as indicated on registration cards they filled out, Smith set out to examine the areas of greatest popularity in the home study courses and the needs they were expected to fill. Smith's study looked at 5,700 registration cards (one-tenth of the total) from the Columbia home-study program between 1925 and 1932 and performed a number of statistical analyses on them.

From his 10 percent sampling, Smith examined those home study courses that had more than fifty persons enrolled in sessions during his sample period. Of all the areas of study, courses in English—which is where Photoplay Composition was located in the home-study catalogs—ranked highest overall in enrollment numbers, with classes in commercial subjects (i.e., accountancy, secretarial training, business methods) coming in second. Utilitarian motives seem to have governed the majority of enrollments in English: the top-ranked English courses were not in literary appreciation or literary history but in such areas as grammar, composition, and business English. For these preferred courses, students tended to cite cultural motives, such as a desire for general education, much less frequently than purely vocational concerns as their reason for enrollment.

Given the high ranking for these other forms of professional writing, then, it is perhaps worth wondering why Photoplay Composition did not fare better in enrollments. Of course, there may have been contingent factors we are not aware of: for example, it may have had a word-of-mouth reputation as not being particularly helpful for those seeking a writing career, and there may have been specific campaigns to build enrollments for rival courses (just as today some professors advertise their courses through glossy flyers). Additionally, it is clear from her interviews and writings that Frances Taylor Patterson, who taught the home-study course on the photoplay, imagined the course to concern broad questions of aesthetic appreciation and critical discernment as much as practical technique, and this may have discouraged students who wanted directly beneficial training in screenwriting. In other words, her very attempt to establish film as an art rather than as just a professional path may have dissuaded students who wanted career training from their English division courses.

One possible explanation for the relatively lower ranking of the photoplay course compared with vocational writing courses is suggested by another of George Smith's statistics: he found that 80 percent of the sampled enrollees either already had some background in their chosen course of study or indicated they had some prior sense of the practical issues and applications of the vocation they wanted to study. Thus, students taking a class in short-story writing might feel they already had some sense of what it was like to write a story. Insofar as students would not have had a previous background in photoplay writing, the writing of photoplays might have appeared as an imposing new activity where students had no existing skills to build on. The short story or magazine article, to name two forms of writing that *did* lead to high-enrollment classes, did not seem to undergo a substantial change from the written page in one's home to printed words in publication, whereas the words of the photoplay underwent a mysterious transformation as they were taken over by the machinery of film production. It may have been less apparent to students that they could have success in this field. Additionally, the increasing length or complexity of feature films from the mid-1910s on may have given students the impression that photoplay writing, in contrast to, say, short story production, was not a minor vocation to be conducted during breaks from full-time employment in another arena. Short stories or magazine articles might easily be knocked off in one's spare time, but not perhaps a feature-length scenario. (Revealingly, in her courses, Patterson actually tried to teach students not to assume that a sample full-length original screenplay was the necessary ticket into the film industry: better to work on synopses that would have more chance at getting read. In other words, she tried to lower the ambitions and expectations of her students in order to make their effort more effective.) For those students who imagined that entrance into the world of writing for the film industry should be easy, perhaps the many privately run schools and correspondence programs that promised quick paths to success might have seemed more inviting and less imposing than a somewhat formalized course of study from a major university. To the extent that we can extrapolate from Smith, we can conclude simply that the writing courses that students most desired were ones that had vocational intent, often as training in a secondary profession to be pursued in one's spare time. For whatever reason, the home-study writing courses that had highest enrollments did not include Photoplay Composition. To the attitude of benign neglect the university administration displayed toward its film offering (which was then overdetermined by the low intellectual status that administration granted to extension study overall), we must add neglect by an adult student population that did not flock to the course and may have felt that it was not sufficiently utilitarian.

With such caveats in mind, we can proceed to an examination of the course itself. A short piece by Arthur Leads in *Writer's Monthly* offered a useful early notice of the class:

> Columbia University has a course in photoplay writing. . . . The course is in charge of Professor Victor O. Freeburg, who has for years been interested in the drama and who has a book on the Elizabethan drama just off the press. Feature films will be run in the classroom and in discussing the picture twelve questions will be put to students, among which are: "Is it novel, and why?" "If it isn't novel, what does it remind you of?" and "Why was this scenario bought by the producer?" . . . [I]n offering this new course Columbia University shows that recognition is being given to one of the most popular literary forms in the history of authorship, and I hope that Professor Freeburg's pupils may eventually be able to turn out some scripts that will make jaded scenario editors sit up and take notice.[7]

As this article indicated, the first instructor in Photoplay Composition was Victor Oscar Freeburg (1877–1953). Freeburg had recently received a

Ph.D. in English for his study "Disguise Plots in Elizabethan Drama" (i.e., that dramatic genre whose narratives revolve around characters who disguise and then unveil themselves at dramatically consequential moments). A 1917 *New York Times* discussion of connections between Freeburg's general aesthetic position and his photoplay course pedagogy offered a colorful biography of the pedagogue: "His own career has been somewhat of a movie. Raised on a Western ranch, has served a year at the United States Naval Academy, spent two summers in Europe and captured three degrees from Yale and Columbia. He has also written a standard book on the Elizabethan drama. He has been actor, playwright, dramatic coach, stage director, and college professor."[8]

It is hard to know just how Freeburg came to teach the course. It is risky to accept a newspaper account at face value, but it is worth noting that the *New York Times* profile on Freeburg implied that he was *selected* for the course rather than initiating it himself, hinting that the decision to offer a photoplay class derived from curricular interests at a higher level of the university hierarchy. (Perhaps the impulse came from extension division director James Egbert, who seemed over the years to have ambitions for a film pedagogy.) As the article puts it, "When Columbia decided to open her academic gates to the movies, Dr. Freeburg, still in his thirties, *was called upon to take up the work*" (my emphasis).

Indeed, based on research for his New York University dissertation on early film archives and collections, film scholar Peter Decherney argues that Columbia may have had very practical and pecuniary reasons for founding a film course.[9] Decherney found evidence of shared ventures involving film industry representatives and Columbia University around the time that the photoplay course started, and it may well be, as Decherney posits, that the university undertook the course itself as a means of solidifying relations and taking advantage of financial offerings from the industry. As we will see in the following pages, the development of cinema studies tracked the geographic situation of the film industry. In the 1920s, for instance, production was centered in Los Angeles while administrators stayed in New York, and the bifurcated placement of film study in universities on both coasts reflected this division. In the prior decade, while the split was still under way, the industry had found its home in New York; it was perhaps inevitable that an academic institution there should seek some sort of alliance with an important film company.

In particular, as Decherney shows, the Lasky studio was looking for a place to archive its films, and Columbia seemed a likely prospect. The university would offer not only facilities but also intellectual and cultural prestige if it housed the collection. Decherney shows that Lasky and Columbia University explored additional joint ventures that would accompany the foundation of the archive, and he believes that the photoplay course itself was one of these studio-sponsored activities. In fact, within a month of the beginning of the first photoplay course, the Lasky Company announced a scholarship for the best story idea to emerge from Freeburg's course. In virtually identical language (obviously from a press release), *Moving Picture World* and *Motion Picture News* described the scholarship:

> To further encourage the study of the art of photo-dramatics among the students of Columbia University, which announces that it has just opened a special course of lectureship on motion pictures and their making, the Lasky Feature Play Company, through its executive head, Samuel Goldfish [i.e., Goldwyn], has offered a scholarship to the university. It has been accepted by Victor O. Freeburg, professor in charge of the new department, and the student who, in the opinion of William C. de Mille, chief of the Lasky scenario staff, writes the best original photoplay during the college term, will receive, all expenses paid, a trip from New York to the Lasky studios at Hollywood, Cal., and return. If suitable for commercial production the play will be produced by Lasky with a star in the leading role and released through Paramount Pictures Corporation. Equitable compensation will be made to the author. The decision of Columbia University to start a photo-dramatic department under the direction of Dr. Freeburg is of great interest to the industry. Through the efforts of Professor George Pierce Baker of Harvard, many talented young dramatists, including Edward Sheldon, Percy Mackaye, Frederick Ballard and others, have trained to write for the legitimate field. Mr. Goldfish in his letter says that the photoplay producers of the future will look to the colleges [for material].[10]

In the event, the winner of the competition was Robert Ralston Reed, a New Jersey physician. After a reworking by Margaret Turnbull, a professional screenwriter, his story was adapted into the Paramount release *Witchcraft* (1916).

It may well be, then, that Lasky was a sponsor for Freeburg's course and that Egbert or others saw it as one way of procuring money from an industry (or at least one studio) that seemed to be seeking the prestige of academia. We can only guess at why, if indeed the course originated not with Freeburg himself but with higher-ups, it was in fact Freeburg who was picked to teach it. Certainly, seemingly pliable junior faculty often are requested to undertake new projects desired by the university administration, and Freeburg had just begun as an instructor in English at Columbia. He had taken up his post in June 1915 and immediately taught a literature course in the extension division's summer session. The very next teaching he did was the photoplay course. That Freeburg started his instructorship by teaching in the extension program may suggest that he was "on the radar" of the extension administration and represented an easy or obvious choice for the photoplay class. Perhaps his interest in drama was viewed as parallel to the concerns of photoplay study.

It is hard to know the extent to which Freeburg had any special or deep knowledge of film, or whether he regularly had followed the critical literature on the subject. In another short piece about Freeburg in *Writer's Monthly*, Arthur Leads lauded Freeburg's knowledge of film practice, but that may have just been hype. Freeburg, Leads said, "is a very sincere, earnest worker with a real faith in the future of the photoplay. Moreover, in his teachings at the college, he is at all times essentially practical.... He knows the inside workings of the studios, and understands very completely the technique of writing for the camera. He will shortly bring out a book on the photoplay which, I know, will be a distinct and valuable addition to the worthwhile volumes that have already been written."[11]

For what it is worth, the book version of Freeburg's doctoral thesis, *Disguise Plots in Elizabethan Drama*, which came out just as he started teaching Photoplay Composition, made no reference to films even in contexts where they might have seemed the perfect example to adduce as the modern embodiment of the dramatic and theatrical strategies Freeburg was examining.[12] For example, at one point Freeburg noted that the new theatrical realism of the early twentieth century had made it harder for the legitimate stage tradition to convey the somewhat excessive and often implausible narrative upheavals of the disguise plot, but he suggested that such sensationalist entertainment as the disguise story might still find contemporary life in more low and popular theatrical forms such as melodrama, detective stories, or farce and light comedy. A reference to film melodramas and farces of the time, which often involved disguises and unveiling of concealed identities, would have seemed obvious here, but Freeburg made no mention of the movies. Perhaps the exigencies of writing a dissertation in what was still, after all, a fairly traditional field, devoted to literary canons, required Freeburg to eschew any reference to modern mass cultural forms. Or perhaps he was not yet a fan or scholar of the movies.

In any case, Freeburg appears to have taken his new pedagogical task to heart. During his time at Columbia, for instance, Freeburg helped found the Cinema Composers Club, which continued after he left the university. The club obviously built on his photoplay course but appears to have had a separate existence as a venue in which students could meet to talk about film and even have contact with film production activity. (A short piece in the *New York Times* for April 2, 1922, reports that twenty-four members of the club had had bit parts in the Fox production *A Stage Romance*.) Even after he completely gave up teaching at Columbia in 1919, Freeburg continued to take an interest in film and in 1923 published a second volume on film, *Pictorial Beauty on the Screen*, to follow his first, *The Art of Photoplay Making*, which he had written under the immediate influence of his photoplay pedagogy.

Freeburg taught Photoplay Composition until 1917, when he enlisted in the navy, where he served as a lieutenant during the war. From his employment record on file at Columbia, it appears that he returned one last time in 1919 to teach Photoplay Composition and then left academia to edit the *Swedish-American Trade Journal* (later named the *American-Swedish Monthly*). Given his interests in understanding film as an art of—in large part—pictorial beauty, it is perhaps amusing to note that upon his retirement to Rockport, Massachusetts, he became a regular participant in local art associations as an amateur painter (evidently of landscapes primarily).

During the Freeburg years of the course, there were two levels of photoplay instruction—elementary and advanced—with classes meeting weekly and individual sessions varying from one hour to an hour and a quarter in length. Eventually, the elementary class was divided into two sections. (Perhaps this was in response to increasing enrollments: the *New York Times* reported that registration numbers went from sixteen students the first time the course was offered in the fall of 1915 to sixty by spring 1917, although the latter figure seems inflated.)

The description for the elementary course reads as follows:

> This course is concerned with the methods of preparing dramatic plots, old and new, for the motion pictures. The photoplay is studied as an independent art of dramatic expression, in some respects inferior, in others superior, to the stage play. Special attention is paid to the art of arousing and maintaining interest, the proper dramatic arrangement of incidents and situations, the various methods of delineating character, the effective use of mechanical devices, and the pantomimic and pictorial qualities of a good photoplay. Films will be exhibited and analyzed before the class, and visits will be made to the studios of first-class motion picture companies. Each student is required to write finished, technically correct scenarios of at least one adaptation and one original photoplay.

The following is the description of the advanced course:

> This course is open regularly to those who have completed successfully the work in the elementary course, and to any others who can present evidence of equal training. It is designed to give a limited number of

scenario writers an opportunity for development of individual genius and for a general study of the finer problems and possibilities of the photoplay. There will be discussion of such topics as the psychology of dramatic characters, symbolism, allegory, the spectator's imagination and the dramatic use of settings. Each student is expected to write one complete feature photoplay or several shorter works of equivalent total length during the Session. Students must consult the instructor before registering for this course. [This last sentence does not appear in all listings for the advanced course across the years.]

In the foreword to *The Art of Photoplay Making* (1918), Freeburg specifically declared this first film book of his to be a distillation of concepts he had presented in the photoplay classes (as well as in other venues), and in this respect it is useful to look at the volume for what it might tell us about the content of Freeburg's pedagogy. Above all, the book clarifies the extent to which Freeburg intended the notion of "composition," which remained in the title of the course over the decades, to refer to more than just the mechanical activity of screenplay construction. For Freeburg, the potential photoplay creator was a veritable composer, weaving together both narrative elements of story and visual elements of mise-en-scène to create a unified work of pictorial and dramatic impact alike. (*The Art of Photoplay Making* concentrated most on the structure of effective narrative, whereas his follow-up book, *Pictorial Beauty on the Screen* [1923], tended to look more carefully at issues of visual design. Ultimately, however, Freeburg argued that the dramatic and visual levels of film were necessarily linked, and any critical emphasis on one or the other was merely heuristic.)[13]

Even as he argued for film's uniqueness among the fine arts and its concomitant right to its own pride of place alongside them, Freeburg found cinema's nature to lie in a hybridity of artistic influences: cinema was an art both of plot and of pictorial arrangement, an art both of image and of story, as well as rhythm (Freeburg frequently analogized cinema to the flows of music). A full appreciation of—and training in—the art of cinema had to respect all its aesthetic dimensions, as well as understand how they might work together in the fully composed cinematic work. In this context, the photoplay writer could not act as if his or her stories were not going to take on visual form but had to make their visual embodiment part of the very planning of the photoplay. That is, the writer would have to include precise indications of the look of the film—both the design of its sets and the composition of its images—in the original photoplay.

Already in *Disguise Plots in Elizabethan Drama*, Freeburg had given glimpses of a aesthetic position based on a notion of the unification of visual style and narrative content. In that volume, Freeburg assumed that the strongest writers for a performed visual art, such as theater, were those whose scripts detailed not only the narrative structure but also its best means of being enacted in a concrete form that would be as much visual as verbal. Freeburg reacted against those critics who separated the words of the Elizabethan dramatists from their embodiment in an art of staging. Such critics, he said, "imply that the dramatist, soaring loftily in the heights, condescended reluctantly to mere devices of stage representation." For Freeburg, what happens corporeally on the stage was in large part something that the playwright could—and, more important, should—determine by integrating staging suggestions organically into the script. As he went on to assert,

> But the voice, mimicry, pantomime, and external physical auxiliaries, or technically speaking, the tricks of reading and impersonation, costuming, stage business, setting and stage properties, all of which perished with the performance, were by no means scorned by the poets, for they were playwrights, too. The evidences that the Elizabethans did everything in their power and knowledge to make stage representations realistic to eyes and ears, are palpable to the scholar, and should not be ignored when discoursing on the poetic drama of Shakespeare and his contemporaries.[14]

Likewise, the successful playwright needed to imagine how his or her film would look on the screen and, to that end, write a photoplay that would provide as much guidance toward that visualization as possible.

Anticipating the auteur theory of later film studies, but also turning it on its head, Freeburg argued that one person—and one person alone—should ideally be in charge of the total expressive design of a film both in the story it told and in the look of the images it offered, and he asserted that the photoplay writer most deserved this creative responsibility. This did not mean simply that directors had to respect the stories offered them by writers, but that writers had the responsibility to learn enough about cinema as *visual* art that their photoplays systematically would incorporate instructions regarding the film's pictorial look. The important point here is that Freeburg was doing more than granting the screenwriter status as the primary creator of a film's narrative. Importantly, he was expanding the province in which he claimed the screenwriter should make essential contributions. Freeburg contended that the photoplay writer, or cinema composer, should be the primary figure in the design, both visual and narrative, of the film work. The writer should be responsible for more than a well-constructed plot. As Freeburg put it in *The Art of Photoplay Making*:

> [S]ome scenario writer might say, "Why should I worry about all this? It is the business of the photographer and the director to produce pictures. I only produce plot." To him we must reply, If you are a cinema composer at all, if you are endeavoring to compose a play in pictures instead of in words, then you must conceive, see clearly, and enable the director, actors, and photographer to actualize adequately the pictures, that is, the materials, which constitute your play.... If the cinema composer hopes to achieve art he must become the master of his medium. Furthermore, he must become the master of his servants, his workmen. He must command, advise, and supervise the director, the actor, the photographer, the joiner, these workmen who are endeavoring to put into physical form the picture-play which he, the cinema composer, has conceived and developed in his imagination.... [I]f we all strive together we will some day bring about the state of affairs where the author is master of all the forces which he mobilizes in expressing himself to an audience.[15]

This meant that the budding photoplay writer had to be instructed not only in techniques of dramatic construction but also in visual aesthetics and the psychology of perception. Even though Freeburg's book militated for recognition of the irreducible specificity of film among the arts, he imported concepts from fields like painting to explain how the writer needed to understand tonality, balance, effective composition, and so on. Freeburg's pedagogy, then, would set out to train students not only in the nuts and bolts of photoplay writing but also in the creative refinement of an art.

We might suggest at least a double meaning to the title of Freeburg's *Art of Photoplay Making*. On the one hand, in keeping with an emphasis on art as human-made artifact with teachable compositional techniques, "art" could refer to the talents necessary to the elaboration of successful film compositions. In this respect, it spoke of a quality to be possessed by the makers—in this case, the photoplay writers as total cinema composers—of potential aesthetic objects. Art, then, was a sort of special human skill in creativity. On the other hand, there was also a reference to the "art" that such photoplay writing made, the Art of cinema that was its object and its result. Writers learned an artful skill and learned how to make Art from it.

Central to this argument, of course, was the assumption that the cinema indeed was, or could become, an art. Writing on film at an early point in its history, Freeburg took the aesthetic potential of the movies as a given—not so much in the sense that cinema was by nature an art but in his belief that, with proper training of producers and consumers, it could well turn into one.

Admitting that film was rooted in photographic reproduction, Freeburg asserted nonetheless that cinematic art came into being when the mere givens of such reproduction were transcended. Trick effects, visual symbolism, allegorical narratives, and so on all gave cinema the ability to imply meanings and mysteries beyond the everyday world reproduced on the screen. To take just one example, in a central chapter of *The Art of Photoplay Making*, aptly titled "The Appeal to the Imagination," Freeburg examined how objects distant from the camera and filmed with less sharpness than close-up objects exuded hints of a "beyondness" that exceeded mere worldliness. In his words, "[T]he magic of distance throws the spectator into a momentary reverie, when his imagination weaves beauties which would depreciate or disappear if brought close to the searching lens of the camera" (95).

Significantly, Freeburg posited that plot too was a form of imaginativeness that transcended the merely photographic image. If pictorial beauty was one form of transcendence (analyzed in detail as such in the later *Pictorial Beauty on the Screen*), *The Art of Photoplay Making* attended to the ways in which the forward movement of story—and the suspense-driven guesses made by audiences regarding where that story might be going—also went beyond the photographic image. The forward movement of the narrative, for Freeburg, projected a film beyond the present in ways that were not merely emotive, since spectators had to employ higher reason in their guesses about plot outcome. Narrative spoke to the spectator's imagination but also went beyond it in appealing to processes of intellection.

But for all his emphasis on visual and narrative form as aesthetic transcendence of photographic reproduction, Freeburg's formalism was in no way a modernist valorization of stylistic free play or of avant-garde experimentation. For him, the formal transcendence that art offered had to do with classical virtues of balance, harmony, grace, ease, and so on.

In *The Art of the Photoplay Composition*, Freeburg spoke, for instance, of the proper work of art as encouraging "contemplative repose." We might contrast this with Walter Benjamin's valorization of cinema as an art of modernity that encouraged reflection through a series of shocks that move the spectator away from calm contemplation. Thus, if Benjamin expressed some admiration for the surrealists and their actively disruptive yanking of images out of the easy continuum of everyday life and into vibrant juxtapositions, Freeburg eschewed all pictorial juxtapositions that might not find a harmonious interweaving of elements. None of Lautréamont's chance encounters of the umbrella and the sewing machine on an operating table for him:

> [W]hatever the setting be, whether palace or hovel, shop or club house, church or saloon, pathway or street, brook or waterfall, field or forest, mountain or sea, it, too, must satisfy the demands of beauty.... Thus

for any one photoplay the materials multiply until the problem of arranging them into a pictorial composition is by no means easy of solution. It cannot be solved at all unless the subjects chosen are suitable for the composition desired. For example, let us conceive an extreme case; a Roman centurion, a skating rink, and a lady's fan may be separately pleasant or picturesque to the eye, but they do not lend themselves to composition, because the moment we think of them as parts of the same picture they become mutually repellent. (35–36)

Within the modernity of the early twentieth century, Freeburg would seem to belong, then, to that countertradition that the American studies scholar T. J. Jackson Lears has analyzed as modern "anti-modernism," the attempt by a number of cultural critics and artists in the period to use the new arts of modernity to attempt to return to experiences that had seemingly not yet known the ravages of technology, industry, and urbanism.[16] Freeburg took one of the most industrially and scientifically developed technologies of modernity—the cinematic apparatus—and looked for ways it could restore an ease of living not (yet) alienated by the age of the machine.

It is noteworthy that when Freeburg did talk about those subjects within the image that could encourage repose, many of these tended to be images drawn from nature, from the rural—in other words, from realms ostensibly untouched by technology. His primary example of an appealing image was that of the gently rippling rings created when one throws a stone into the water. A list of other instances in which the viewer might take enjoyment from the graceful contemplation of visual form included "the pouring rush of a waterfall, the rhythmic undulations of the sea, the fan-like spreading of a sky rocket, the slow curling of smoke from a factory funnel, the varying balance of a bird in flight, the steady forward thrust of a yacht under full sail" (12). (It might seem as if the mention of a factory would put us squarely back in the context of modernity, but it is important to note that what Freeburg enacted here was a sort of "aestheticization" of the factory: it would be appreciated for the formal beauty of the smoke that wafted out of it. Its own role in industrial life was elided.)[17]

The assumption that cinema became art when it offered images and stories of a harmoniousness that transcended the givens of worldly experience would guide Freeburg's pedagogy. Photoplay writing would be taught not just as one craft among the many that humans are capable of but as a special and privileged skill capable of producing those supreme objects of human achievement that are Works of Art. While *The Art of Photoplay Making* included practical advice—especially in its last chapter, titled "Commercial Needs"—that film industry executives might pressure photoplay writers to observe, the bulk of Freeburg's conceptualization in his book had to do with the elaboration of an aesthetic and, in large part, with the ways in which the responsible and well-trained photoplay writer could contribute to the elaboration of that aesthetic. Art mattered too much for pedagogy about it to be reduced to mere pragmatic concerns. Against utilitarians who argued that the intrinsic nature of movies was to make money, and not to offer the uplift of Art, Freeburg answered that it was necessary to militate for the art of cinema precisely because it was too important an art to be ignored or debased and made subservient to mere pecuniary consideration. If the public did not demand better films, Freeburg contended, it would continue to be deluged with substandard works by a callous, money-driven business.

Importantly, Freeburg argued the value of photoplay study not just for prospective writers planning careers in the industry but for all citizens, who should care about the role of art in democratic society. If the properly trained photoplay writer could have an impact on aesthetic potential at the point of production, the properly instructed everyday spectator might have an indirect, yet no less powerful, effect at the point of consumption. The box office was a sort of ballot box in which spectators voted for quality by supporting films they preferred and eschewing the rest. Like other reformers from that time who advocated cinematic uplift through education, Freeburg assumed a sort of feedback loop in which production and consumption were linked and in which pedagogy was the mediating force.

One bit of advice about moviegoing that Freeburg offered in his *Pictorial Beauty on the Screen* can stand as a pithy example of his sense that consumption could be made to influence business practices (in this case, those of distribution, exhibition, and, indirectly, production):

> Go to the movies. Whenever you find that you enjoy the films thoroughly do not stop to analyze or criticize. If you enjoy any particular film so much that you are sure you would like to see it two or three times every year for the rest of your life, you may be happy, for you have discovered one of the classics of the screen. Do not analyze that film either, unless you are in the business of making pictures. But if a film makes you uncomfortable, if it is so bad that you are quite disgusted with it, then, though you must become a martyr to it, please stay and see it again. Compare the good parts of the film, if there are any, with the bad parts; study it in detail until you see where the trouble lies. And when you have discovered the real causes of ugliness in that film, wouldn't it be a public service to express your opinion in such a way that the manager of your theater might hear it?[18]

It is worth noting Freeburg's argument here that not all acts of moviegoing necessarily served as an occasion for pedagogy. In particular, the spectator who already had reached a higher level of aesthetic refinement could rely on that acquired taste to enjoy great films without the need always to analyze them. Pedagogy was as much a negative activity—teaching audiences what to dislike and to formulate that in aesthetic principles—as a positive one, confirming them in their higher sensibility. There was even the risk that too much pedagogy in the case of "classics" and good works might interfere with spontaneous enjoyment.

To a large degree, then, Freeburg's pedagogy involved liberating spectators from unrefined modes of spectatorship. Effectively trained spectators could achieve a "spontaneity" of honest response in which the classics would clearly separate themselves off from the bad works that currently dominated the cinematic scene. Conversely, the untrained spectators' seeming spontaneity of response really was inadequate, unrefined, and too easily accepting of the junk that the industry foisted upon them.

But in formulating a conception of uplift in this way, Freeburg's pedagogy opened itself up to two tensions. First, it was not always clear if audiences had an innate, albeit submerged, capacity to sense and seek the valuable work of art or if their innate inclination rather was toward a wallowing in the bad from which they had to be forcefully weaned. In the former case, the film industry would be guilty of misleading audiences and diverting them from the true course of art. In the latter, there could be a veritable blaming of the audience for its own bad taste.

In fact, Freeburg was not free of an elitist fear of the mass's inherent lack of refinement. In "The Psychology of the Cinema Audience," the second chapter of *The Art of Photoplay Making,* he contrasted his notion of the proper reception of film, which most likely would come only through an activity of training and education, with the inadequate consumption he felt most films received from the mass audience. He posited the spectator's reception of art as taking place at several levels or stages. Each stage would be more refined than the previous one, and the goal of education would be to help spectators attain the highest of levels. The role of instruction in spectatorship was to aid the audience in a salutary transition from "primitive" forms (his term) to advanced ones. Freeburg contended, for instance, that "three classes of appeal exist in every film that tells a story. They are: first, the sense appeal to the eye; second, the emotional appeal; and, third, the intellectual appeal" (11). It was the first that Freeburg characterized as "primitive," the basic delight taken in pleasurable sensations and immediately striking forms, a "delight experienced by every spectator whether he be an infant or a mature man of culture . . . a delight in the subject itself" (11). For Freeburg, spectatorship of this sort was at best superficial and at worst dangerous, since it denied the human capacity for imagination and intellectual progress. As he put it, the response to sensation alone was one that would be experienced by the sort of spectator "who might be too stupid to understand the story and yet might thoroughly enjoy the picture" (11).

And if each individual had inside him- or herself some degree of primitive response, that response was all the more likely when individuals assembled as a crowd and let themselves be swayed by mass psychology. As Freeburg put it,

> It must never be forgotten that the theatre audience is a crowd. A crowd is a compact mass of people held together by a single purpose during any period of time whether long or short. . . . The close contact gives the crowd a peculiar psychology. The individual in the crowd is not the same as when alone. He is subconsciously influenced by his companions or neighbours until his emotions are heightened and his desire or ability to think is lowered. . . . In the crowd, he is more responsive, more demonstrative, more kind, more cruel, more sentimental, more religious, more patriotic, more unreasoning, more gullible than when alone. A crowd, therefore, is more emotional and less intellectual than its members were before they came together. (7–8)

Freeburg's description of crowd psychology is a familiar one. From the nineteenth century—with such key works as Gustave Le Bon's book *The Crowd*—and on into the twentieth, the mass psychology of crowd behavior had provided a common theme for cultural analysis, often with a fear of the moral consequences that would arise when individuals formed into an aggregate. The crowd was imbued with a life and energy of its own, one that removed individual differences and brought everyone, no matter their individual knowledge, down to a common level governed more by passion than by intellect, rendering people malleable and less able to make decisions based on individual discernment. Predictably, the flip side of this suspicion of the crowd was often the valorization of an *educated* public that supposedly rose above the mind of the mob. In Freeburg's words:

> While the crowd is single-minded the public is many-minded. The public may be looked upon as a vast web-like association of unified groups, families, cliques, coteries, leagues, clubs, and crowds. A crowd can never exist as such for more than three or four hours at a time, or while the close contact is maintained and the single interest is held. But a public may have space between its units and time between its sessions. Furthermore, the public is permanent in its existence. Its groups come in contact, though not simultaneously; views are exchanged, discussions

are carried on, letters are written, until as a result of all this reflection a deliberate expression is arrived at. This deliberate expression is called public opinion. (8)

Freeburg did not assume the spectator came to art automatically equipped with all the tools for refined understanding. Even in cases where the spectator did possess those tools, crowd psychology could be so overwhelming that the individually discerning spectator might be induced to regress to ever more primitive, or even stupid, responses. It was here that the educator could step in to provide spectators with mechanisms of aesthetic reception strong enough both to resist base emotional appeal and to enable them to appreciate deeper, more intellectual qualities of art. Freeburg's aesthetic posited the existence of gaps between the work of art and its correct consumption, and it granted education the power to surmount such gaps. In this respect, it is noteworthy that a number of the qualities Freeburg attributed to effective "public opinion" in the preceding quotation approximate an ideal of what is supposed to happen *in the classroom:* exchange of views, the conducting of discussion, a recourse to writing as a means of articulating an argument—all these activities encouraging "reflection" and culminating in "deliberate expression."

The beneficial feedback loop between educated spectators and properly motivated producers that Freeburg hoped for required as an initial step the transformation of naive consumers (the crowd of spectators) into a discerning public. One key agent of this transformation was the pedagogue, that cultural mediator I referred to in my introduction and whose role Freeburg was positing for himself by teaching his course and by writing his film aesthetics. As Freeburg put it at the end of the first chapter of *The Art of Photoplay Making*:

[T]here can be no fair appraisement [of the potentials of an art form like the new art of film] without knowledge. There can be no helpful criticism of a new art without sympathetic insight into its special scope and its unique possibilities. What the photoplay world needs at present is more definite canons of criticism. It needs critics of taste and training expressing themselves in the periodicals and newspapers; it needs careful studies in book form; it needs photoplay leagues; it needs to be protected against the inartistic no less than against the immoral; it needs most of all something which will in time result from the constructive criticism of specialists, a general knowledge and understanding on the part of the public of just what it is they would rather see on the screen than the inanity and hodgepodge that now so often claim their attention. (5–6)

But here a second tension in Freeburg's philosophy of uplift could arise, since it fails to necessitate that only through *formal* pedagogy does amelioration of taste occur. In other words, if the classroom pedagogue was a likely source of beneficial instruction, it was also possible for such education to occur by means other than that of the cultural mediator who offers lessons in a classroom to students. One did not need to be in a classroom with a teacher at the front in order to learn about movies. The very fact, for example, that Freeburg indicated that spectators could learn what was wrong with a bad film simply by repeated viewings implies that the literal presence of an official educator was not always essential to the pedagogical process.

Freeburg even imagined the widespread distribution of home movie projectors that could allow spectators to see films again and again, and he clearly viewed this domestic and analytic possession of the film as a veritable form of study. Pedagogy would enter the home. As Freeburg put it in an interview with the *New York Times:* "When a motion picture that can be exhibited repeatedly at will and *studied* at leisure is possible, the photoplay writer will have a tremendous incentive for careful creation. It will be profitable and necessary for the cinema composer, as I like to call him, to exert his utmost efforts to achieve artistic and lasting excellence."[19]

This perhaps was the paradox of extension education (and of educational outreach more generally) in the Progressivist age of reform: if the pedagogue succeeded in his or her instruction, the lessons would become so democratized and so internalized by ordinary citizen-students that they would no longer need the official help of the mediator. They would be able to parse their culture by themselves: Freeburg, for instance, trusted the newly refined spectator not to need to analyze the classics but simply sit back and watch them work their ameliorative effect. By internalizing the lessons of Photoplay Composition, students transformed some part of their own faculty of judgment into a personal "cultural mediator" that allowed them to judge which works were good for them and which were bad, and eventually dispense with the need for a teacher in a classroom setting. It appears almost a logical consequence of the promise of ordinary spectators' internalization of rules that Photoplay Composition should soon become part of the newly established extension program's home-study branch where students were assumed to be able to master a subject by mail.

When Freeburg left Columbia and the Photoplay Composition course to go into military service in 1917, he was replaced by Frances Taylor Patterson, a young woman who in 1914 had received a bachelor's degree in English from Trinity College, Connecticut. In several extension program catalogs, Patterson's husband, Rowland Patterson, who worked in the public schools in areas of health education and athletics, was also listed as teaching some sections of Photoplay Composition, but it is clear that Frances was the primary figure in the development of the course. University records and journalistic notices indicate that Frances Patterson regularly taught the Photoplay Composition course until at least the late 1930s. In the 1920s, she also taught versions of the photoplay course through the home-study program as well as in the classroom. For this correspondence version of the course, Patterson followed standard practice in the home-study program, preparing extensive week-by-week breakdowns of topics and assignments (many of which were keyed to her first book on film, *Cinema Craftsmanship* [1920]) and evaluating material that students sent in from afar.

Vassilios Koronakes, a former Rutgers student who tried a few years ago to track down information about Patterson, suggests (in an unpublished seminar paper) that Frances Patterson was a student of Freeburg's, but I have not found confirmation of this.[20] In the foreword to her *Cinema Craftsmanship*, she did, however, acknowledge the influence of the famous drama professor Brander Matthews, who was also Freeburg's dissertation adviser. Thus it may be that there was a circle of influence around Matthews that included both Freeburg and Patterson.[21] It is perhaps revealing that the last part of Patterson's book reproduced the scenario for *Witchcraft* as a model of efficient photoplay writing and proper manuscript formatting. We should remember that the original story for *Witchcraft* had been written in Freeburg's first photoplay class five years earlier and had won the Lasky studio writing prize. It is almost as if by including *Witchcraft* in her own pedagogical material Patterson was confirming the continued importance of Freeburg's original teaching to her own ongoing effort to promote the art of photoplay writing in the course she had inherited.

Certainly, in taking over Freeburg's course, Patterson offered a pedagogy in keeping with some of Freeburg's aesthetic impulses. For example, a section of *Cinema Craftsmanship* on the need for pictorial beauty in film (61–63) reads as if inspired by Freeburg's investigations of the requirement for the well-composed photoplay to establish unity between visual style and narrative construction. Likewise, a quick discussion of disguise plots in drama and film (27–28) might be indebted to Freeburg's own book on the disguise plot in Elizabethan drama (although in that book, as I noted earlier, Freeburg himself never extended discussion of the genre with film examples). But Patterson also appears to have made the course her own and, as we will see in more detail later, let her own aesthetic inspire it. Although the differences should not be overemphasized, Patterson's aesthetic of film appears (at least on paper) to have diverged in several ways from Freeburg's.

She emphasized plot construction and character over pictorial beauty, and she clearly saw her role as instructing writing students to craft effective narrative more than to create visual pleasure (not that she ruled out the latter; she simply gave it much less priority than Freeburg). She was in no way a mere acolyte of Freeburg. In this respect, although there is not enough in her writings to make us imagine her as a trailblazing feminist who stood up for her own rights, it is worth noting that in her second book, *Scenario and Screen*, Patterson made an assertion of women's independent spirit: "Such nonsense is the idea that there is sex in character.... In the past women may have shown certain similar group reactions, but these may be traced to training and tradition more than to any inherent characteristics or instincts.... Women are throwing off their man-given character cloak.... The new freedom allows them to break the yardstick of tradition and take their own measure."[22]

Similarly, Patterson clearly set out to develop her own approach to film study in her pedagogy for Photoplay Composition. For example, she was quite active in bringing guest lecturers to the class: thus, the 1924 sessions included talks by writers Rupert Hughes, Clara Beranger, and Paul Bern and directors Rex Ingram and William de Mille, among others. Likewise, her 1920 book, *Cinema Craftsmanship*, referred to a class visit by Thomas Ince, the important producer and director (58), and included the transcript of a 1919 lecture by a Lasky studio continuity writer, Eve Unsell. Patterson also worked to incorporate new pedagogical technique into the course. In 1924, for instance, she seems to have been instrumental in getting the university to equip an auditorium with analytical projectors so films could be studied in detail. Even more ambitiously, her desire to get her students to appreciate the details of filmic construction and the cinematic employment of specific formal devices appears to have led in the early 1920s to the production of a film that she apparently commissioned for training purposes. In the words of the *New York Times*:

> Scenes from photoplays which show the various uses of the iris, the fade-in and fade-out, double exposure, the dissolve, the close-up, the semiclose-up, the long shot, the panorama and other cinematographic devices have been incorporated in a film to be used for purposes of instruction in Mrs. Frances Taylor Patterson's classes in cinema composition at Columbia University. Pictures of studio interiors, directors at work and laboratory methods are also included, as well as identical strips of positive and negative film.... To compose a photoplay that has any character of its own, a person must think in terms of moving pic-

tures, and to think in terms of moving pictures, a person must have an easy command of these pictorial idioms. So it is encouraging to learn that the students at Columbia are studying cinema composition with the aid of this graphic film, which, incidentally, the Famous Players-Lasky Corporation has prepared for them.[23]

Patterson clearly had much ambition for Photoplay Composition. Another piece in the *New York Times* provides a sense of the broader activities of the course:

> Mrs. Frances Patterson's course in Photoplay Composition at Columbia will begin its sixth year. . . . The field work of the course, it is announced, will be considerably extended, arrangements having been made for the students to study lighting, the construction of sets, developing, tinting, cutting, titling, etc., in the studios and laboratories in and near New York. In addition, scenario editors and directors will address the class and Mrs. Patterson will exhibit for purposes of analysis, "Nanook of the North," "Sir Arne's Treasure," "The Cabinet of Dr. Caligari," and "The Four Horsemen of the Apocalypse."[24]

Over the years, Patterson put a great deal of effort into her photoplay class. She appears to have used various trips to Hollywood to collate information about the industry to convey to her students. She built up documentation on the film business—especially on manuscript submission procedures at the studios—and worked to keep her students abreast of developments in film industry protocol. Evidently, the materials she accumulated were made available to the students through a mini-library that she referred to over the years as a "Photoplay Museum." In addition to listings of studios to which students could submit photoplays, the "Museum" included magazines, books, stills, actual photoplays, and "famous paintings" so that students could see classic examples of visual composition (thereby suggesting a connection to Victor Freeburg's concern with pictorial beauty in cinema).

To the extent that we can trust journalistic reports, several newspaper accounts of Patterson's efforts for her photoplay course suggest that she diligently put more than a fair amount of time into course research and preparation. For example, a 1930 *New York Times* article on the photoplay class quoted Patterson to the effect that she assembled a great deal of data as background for the course. In her words, she had "for many years been conducting what might be termed an independent research bureau of the screen. I have been watching the trend of motion pictures from year to year and drawing my own conclusion. I have been comparing productions, visiting studios, consulting with authors."[25] Likewise, a short piece in *Variety* in 1938 reported, "A survey of the conditions facing writers who desire to turn their attention to photoplay writing has been completed by Frances Taylor Patterson, who has just returned from Hollywood, where she interviewed producers and writers on the lots of the major companies. Mrs. Patterson is in charge of motion picture work at Columbia University and the survey is intended for the use of students in the course which is to be held on Monday evenings during the academic year beginning Oct. 2."[26]

Patterson herself offered commentary on her course in an article she wrote for *Photoplay* in January 1920. Undoubtedly, much of what she asserted about the class must be taken with more than a grain of salt as promotional plug for the course, but it is still worth quoting some of her description.[27] Here, for instance, is what she said about the makeup of the class sections:

> The students range from the veriest amateur who has rosy hopes of writing a photoplay in three lessons . . . to the blue-stocking who is going in for a Ph.D. degree and plans to use the science of aesthetics as applied to a comparative study of the photoplay and the drama for her thesis. . . . There are young women who feel they ought to be able to form bright and new opinions upon the latest photoplay as well as the latest books or the latest plays or the latest turns in the political situation. A dramatist came in to adapt his play to cinematic form. . . . Short story writers have come for the same reason. . . . Teachers of English come that they may find out which plays can be used as objective illustration in teaching the classics. . . . One man high up in the world of advertising was sent by his firm to learn more about photoplays the better to advertise them. There have been actors and actresses in the class who were ambitious to write stories as well as to act them. One young director, who had a "movie star" for a wife, was eager to prepare himself to write the vehicles in which she was to be starred. . . . Then there are college students who want the course as a necessary part of a liberal education in this day and age when there is scarcely anyone, "highbrow" or "lowbrow," whose pleasure and recreation does not embrace at least a "movie" or two a week. There is the young reporter who has learned that a part of the course is devoted to the development of cinematic criticism which will be more analytical and more adequate than much of the so-called criticism that is being offered at the present time.

Perhaps more significant than this undoubtedly hyped-up description of her course was the hint she offered in the same article that the original impetus for the course came from the university's broader desire to institute film instruction and that she was simply responding to administrative directive when she took over the course:

> Columbia has the distinction of being the first college or university to recognize the tremendous possibilities of the gentle art of story telling by means of *pictures,* to realize that the photoplay in its highest form is essentially artistic, and that wielded by trained and skillful writers its power is illimitable. Columbia felt that a day would come when there would be a demand for scenario writers of culture and undisputed ability, and in addition there was the immediate need to teach people the appreciation of the finer things in the photoplay, which appreciation will eventually result in a demand for better plays on the part of the public.

Just as the *New York Times* profile of Victor Freeburg from 1917 had implied that he was picked to teach the course rather than having come up with the idea himself, there is the suggestion here that Patterson assumed a task that the university administration itself had devised. But like Freeburg, Patterson appears to have taken her assignment to heart.

In fact, even more than Freeburg, Patterson became actively involved, once she started teaching film, in the general cinema culture of the time, and she used that larger effort as a source of insights for her course. She also used her activities in the field of film at large as an occasion to open up her instruction to a broader public. For example, she initiated a series of screenings of art films, open both to her students and to the general public, along the lines of the Little Theatre movement of the time, with its concern to present less commercial works of aesthetically experimental ambition. As a brief notice in the *New York Times* announced, "Under this arrangement there will be shown certain films of outstanding merit, including exceptional foreign productions which may not have been released in this country. There will be lectures by well-known directors, scenario writers and producers."[28] At Columbia, Patterson actively organized events at the Institute of Arts and Sciences. For example, one syllabus for her courses mentions an institute lecture, open to the general public, by film theorist (and poet of the people) Vachel Lindsay, which she had organized under the auspices of the Cinema Composers student club. Likewise, a series of postcards she sent out in 1928–29 shows that she organized several symposia on film through the university's Writers Club, and that these meetings included figures from the film business such as story editors Bertram Bloch and Albert Howson, de Mille Productions general manager John C. Flinn, and Roxy Theatre impresario S. L. Rothafel, as well as such experts on cinema aesthetics as theorist Alexander Bakshy.[29]

From the beginning of the 1920s, Patterson served as a member of various committees of the National Board of Review (NBR), the film-betterment and reform organization, and also was a regular writer for the NBR's monthly magazine. Throughout her career, she was quite concerned with encouraging higher quality in photoplay scenarios. (Thus, as noted by Richard Koszarski, she put together what can be considered the first university press book on film, *Motion Picture Continuities,* which reproduced several scenarios as models for the well-constructed film.)[30]

Patterson is even credited with a produced script for the Yiddish film *Broken Hearts,* an adaptation of a famous play. Jim Hoberman describes the film's production history in his classic history of Yiddish cinema, *Bridge of Light,* and it would seem that the film's somewhat domineering director, Maurice Schwartz, had as much creative input as the scriptwriter, if not more. In this case, it is ironic that the one film written by Patterson, who always militated for the screenwriter as the fundamental auteur of a movie, was an adaptation directed by someone who clearly saw himself as in control.[31]

Patterson wrote regularly on film for specialty film journals but also for more general culture-related publications such as the *New Republic,* the *North American Review,* and the *New York Times.* Here, she called for recognition of the independent art of cinema (especially in relation to the live stage), railed against incomprehension of this independence on the part of Hollywood producers (whom, she felt, overestimated the contributions theater could make to film), and promoted those films that she felt best signaled cinema's artistic potentials. Significantly, the films that the *New York Times* indicated that she assigned her class to analyze in depth—namely, *Sir Arne's Treasure, The Cabinet of Dr. Caligari, The Four Horsemen of the Apocalypse,* and *Nanook of the North*—were all works that she specifically lauded in her published writings. Clearly, her efforts as a writer brought her into contact with works of cinematic art that she then considered important to introduce to her students.

Through her occasional writings, Patterson gained some influence beyond the classroom. For example, on at least one occasion the *New York Times,* which regularly reported on her course, turned to her for commentary when its own reviewer could not cover an important art film. In a column from December 25, 1921, the *Times* film reviewer, after offering praise to a recent Hollywood production (William de Mille's *Miss Lulu Betts*), admitted to not being able to see all new releases and deferred to Patterson, who had sent in a long missive, which the newspaper cited in toto, in praise of the Swedish film *Sir Arne's Treasure,* directed by Mauritz Stiller.[32] Patterson's comments did not merely reveal much about her overall value system for film—for example, she thought the film offered a unity of pictorial form and dramatic function—but also showed her to be an active champion of film art, particularly of those works (European ones, for example) that might not get attention in a culture dominated by Hollywood product.

Nonetheless, it does seem less productive to set out to extrapolate a general aesthetics of film from Patterson's writings, similar to that found in Freeburg's volumes on the art of cinema. First of all, if our goal is to imagine the content of Patterson's pedagogy, we do not need such an extrapolation. More than with Freeburg—who left behind little that explicitly touched upon his course other than brief catalog descriptions, several notices in professional writing journals, and a few comments in one *New York Times* interview—there exists a great deal of very specific material describing what Patterson did in her course, even on a session-by-session basis. Not only do we have Patterson's books and numerous articles, but the Columbia University archives include two fairly detailed syllabi for her courses from early on in her teaching. One—for a home-study version of the course in 1920—is quite specific, as would be expected for a document to be mailed to students who would have little or no contact with the instructor and little to go on other than what was sent them. Called a syllabus, it is in fact twenty-nine pages long and stands as a veritable mini-manual on the art of photoplay writing. The other syllabus appears to be from around the same time and seems an in-class (rather than at-home) version of Photoplay Composition. Although it is also termed a syllabus, presumably for a single course, it actually includes detailed lists of topics for *three* levels of instruction—elementary, intermediate, and advanced. Both of these syllabi offer a wealth of information about Patterson's course itself and render hypothetical extrapolations from her broader writings less essential.

At the same time, it seems that Patterson's general writings are much less geared to the elaboration of a general philosophy of film than was the case with Freeburg. Although there was some practical detail in Freeburg's books, his greater interest appears to have been in aesthetic rumination. While he did acknowledge prior aesthetic ventures such as Vachel Lindsay's and Hugo Münsterberg's books on film published just a few years before his own explorations, Freeburg had little else to go on in militating for an independent art of cinema. Presenting her own books and essays just a few years later than Freeburg's contributions, Patterson, in contrast, could both rely on a larger sweep of prior writings—thus, *Cinema Craftsmanship* provided three pages of bibliography on the literature of film—and take a much less militant, much less explicitly conceptualizing approach to the art of film.

Indeed, there is a greater sense in Patterson's writings that even if the local battles to enable specific films to be deemed art have yet to be fought, the larger struggle to even consider cinema as a potential art form has been brought to positive fruition. The sheer possibility of cinematic art is now assured even if individual works do not always achieve that ideal. Thus, Patterson's writings could go in more practical directions than Freeburg's— more critical engagement with specific films, more advice on immediate issues of narrative form, more discussion of concrete aids in the achievement of film art, and so on—and bracket out broader questions of film aesthetics. Patterson's books on film were practical guides rather than broad philosophical manifestos, and significantly, they paid much more attention to the everyday workings of the film industry than Freeburg's ever did. It is as if Patterson was admitting that the extent to which individual films might not achieve the status of art had to be explained concretely in terms of direct institutional impediments that could be pinpointed and that practical advice could lead one to avoid in the future. On one side lay the higher realm of cinema as art, on the other lay all the day-to-day workings of a film industry that restrained easy access to that realm, and between these were the individual films that dwelt in the tension between art and business.

Nonetheless, even Patterson's most utilitarian suggestions as to the paths to cinematic art rested on a broader conception of what Art was, and to this extent we can find in her writings the rudiments of a general aesthetics of film. In her books especially, Patterson was a particularly strong advocate of the position that took film essentially to be a storytelling medium in which effective narrative unfolding relied on a logical and tripartite structure that moved by means of intervening complication from initial exposition to final resolution. In *Scenario and Screen,* she even went so far as to recommend that students read John Stuart Mill's *Logic* in order to appreciate coherence of structure in narrative construction.

Ironically, within a storytelling framework, Patterson's books exhibited a greater openness than Freeburg's to specific works that we would qualify as part of cinematic *modernism.* The irony here is that Patterson's strong sense of story as highly organized structure led her to treat modernist works from within an aesthetics of narrative clarity and of legibility. To the extent that she valorized the logic of storytelling, Patterson was able to accept modernist efforts if she could read them as essentially narrative. A film might eschew Hollywood style for, say, pictorial distortion (e.g., *The Cabinet of Dr. Caligari*) or frenetic fragmentation through montage (*Potemkin*) or a deliberately slow pace (*Sir Arne's Treasure*), as long as these stylistic choices were keyed to narrative necessity. Thus, the potentially weird and unrealistic decor of *Caligari* was, in Patterson's reading, appropriate to the film's narrative meaning rather than in excess of it. Even works that might seem pictorially or stylistically nonclassical could achieve classical status through coherent narrative construction and a harmonious unity of form and content. For all their efforts in the elaboration of cinematic form, films like *Caligari* and *Potemkin* still fit a simple narrative model in which a confrontation between the protagonist and opposing forces led to meaningful resolution. *Potemkin,* in this reading, was not just a film of vibrant montage but one in which such montage told a stirring tale. Patterson's criticism was reserved not for modernist art per se but for those works—modernist or not—that engaged in a loosening of narrative logic or a reveling in formal play for its own sake. Thus, on the one hand, she heaped great opprobrium on serial films for breaking one unified story line into a multitude of narratives, some of which petered out or went nowhere. As Patterson put it in *Cinema Craftsmanship,* "The serial can have no future as an art form. Dramatically, it is a sort of hundred-headed hydra. It has as many struggles as there are episodes, and sometimes even more. It is as easy for the serial to possess dramatic unity as it is for a sentence with fifteen subjects and fifteen predicates to possess the flavor of literary excellence. The serial is never a single entity, never an organic whole. The main road of the theme is cut by frequent cross-roads which lead to nowhere" (179). On the other hand, Patterson inveighed against the use of splashy technique in cases where she felt it had no integral, organic connection to narrative. For example, she was a vociferous critic of the use of color in film, believing that it often became a stylistic effect for its own sake and detracted from film's essential vocation of storytelling.

At the same time, Patterson would also disdain those storytellers who maintained tight narrative structure but in ways that had become tired or formulaic and therefore devoid of deeper and consequent *human* implication. More so perhaps than Freeburg, for whom the meaning of narrative emerged from its formal qualities (an end that logically responds to the beginning as in the perfect structure of the disguise plot), Patterson tended to feel that successful narratives should offer uplifting content—stories that mattered because their subject mattered. It is appropriate that she had an important role at the National Board of Review, since that reform organization took as one of its central commitments the improvement of the kinds and quality of story that the cinema offered. For Patterson, to be an art, cinema must tell stories but of a certain depth, richness, and value. Thus,

Patterson would exhibit reservations vis-à-vis D. W. Griffith, who, in her mind, offered gripping stories but ones that sacrificed profundity for mere emotional effect. For example, in *Way Down East*, suspense and excitement became the overriding goal of the narrative to such a degree that any higher purpose was lost: as she asserted in *Cinema Craftsmanship*, "'Way Down East' is another example of over-sustained suspense. . . . The laws of volume, pressure and gravitation demand her death [i.e., of Lillian Gish on the ice floe], but the happy ending demands that she be saved, and Mr. Griffith needs prolonged suspense to shore up his climax. The three are mutually contradictory. Mr. Griffith prefers to sacrifice artistry to the excitement of the moment" (*Cinema Craftsmanship*, 31). Likewise, *Broken Blossoms* "shows the touch of a master hand" (164). Nonetheless, formal play for the purposes of cheap thrills was privileged over the higher commitment to film as vehicle for deep thought: "Mr. Griffith made the story over into a surprisingly beautiful play. . . . But the play was somewhat of a commercial failure for all its marvelous techniques. It had no message. . . . [T]he photoplay accomplishes nothing. It makes us sad without holding out any strength through that sorrow, the touchingly sweet nature of the little girl is drowned in tragedy. We are overwhelmed with pity for her, and that is all" (164).

Patterson's critique of Griffith helps us identify several key points in her aesthetic of film. First, despite her relative openness to modernist cinema, Patterson had little respect for works of ambiguity, of confusion, or of that ineffable mystery that, for Freeburg, lay beyond the reality of the photographed frame and that was alluded to in filmic works of art. For Patterson, there was little value in such mystery: cinematic works must have a meaningful clarity in their narration (which, to take just one example, *Caligari* could be argued to possess, despite its weirdness of look). Whereas Freeburg most wanted films that made one marvel and wonder (and here his emphasis on pictorial beauty was of a piece with such a philosophy of art), Patterson most wanted films that made one think. As she puts it in *Cinema Craftsmanship*, "A photoplay, then, *ought* to have some sort of a message, a raison d'être, something that is ennobling, something that will awaken thought, something which will make the audience better for having seen it" (166; my emphasis). Griffith, in this context, would be branded negatively as a director of confusion, lack of unity, and an absence of salutary meaningfulness.

Second, as the notion that films *ought* to do something (in this case, have a message) suggests, Patterson's aesthetic was an evaluative one with a clear sense of what, for her, constituted proper achievement in cinematic art. Cinema had less an essence, given to it once and forever, than a potential, and the history of cinema was the development of this potential. Cinema had moved, first, from mere pictures of reality to crude if structurally sound narratives lacking in profundity, to richer narratives with the ambition to make cinema into an art of beauty and reflection. Griffith's problem, then, was that he lagged behind his times, his supposed experiments with form actually exhibiting a retrograde fascination with the armature of thrilling narrative but not pushing the cinema to do any more than offer cheap thrills in mindless fashion.

If the cinema for Patterson did not have an achieved essence, it did have an ideal to strive *toward* (and retrograde figures like Griffith served to remind the prospective scenario writer of the dangers of regress one could fall into along the way). While her philosophy of film's history did not take artistic essence as given to cinema from the start, neither did it rule out the possibility that with proper instruction filmmakers could achieve art by their efforts. This is why we can read Patterson's very practically oriented manuals for professionals as works of aesthetics too: her advice gave an indication of the paths to avoid or to follow on the way to art. In particular, the film industry needed to be understood in detail insofar as it confronted the budding writer with a set of concrete and contingent factors (such as studios' lack of respect for the profession of the screenwriter) that could either facilitate or impede cinema's progress toward its ideal. Writers must be trained in the workings of this industrial context both to steel themselves against its risks and to take advantage of its positive features. The cinematic ideal for Patterson was meaningful narrative, but nothing guaranteed in advance that this form would win out against the historical contingencies of the studio system.

Now that I have established some sense of Patterson's overall position on film art and its relationship to her concern for practice-oriented instruction in photoplay composition, we can examine more directly her course offerings themselves. As noted earlier, Patterson eventually taught three levels of Photoplay Composition, and the available syllabus usefully offers breakdowns of topics for all three. In the elementary course, there were sessions on, in order, screen values, adaptation, dramatic appeal, plot structure, plot sources (the basic plots that the narrative arts had passed down over time), scenario technique, photoplay devices, classroom discussion of plot ideas submitted by students, classroom discussion of the scenarios submitted by the students, screen comedy, final classroom discussion of student scenarios, the author's outlook, and commercial needs. Additionally, there were weekly writing assignments: a critical analysis of a current film, a synopsis of some nonfilmic narrative work, an analysis of narrative crises in that work, a synopsis of a proposed adaptation of it (along with an analysis of its narrative in terms of "premise, complication, and solution of the plot"), two ideas for original plots, the first-reel and then second-reel continuity for the adaptation, and the first- and second-reel continuity for an original plot.

In many ways, the course stands as a fairly straightforward pedagogy of script writing: the photoplay process proceeds from the inspiration of an initial premise (and, even prior to that, the influence of other arts and existing narrative formulas) to its elaboration into a narrative, and then its translation into proper photoplay format (from synopsis to detailed continuity script). There is some attention to dramatic appeal, but that tends to take a backseat to a more textually focused attention to formalities of narrative construction itself. There is a bit of concern with genres—comedy, for instance, is singled out as a narrative form requiring a pedagogy particular to its structural values. Finally, there is recognition of the concrete context of the industry and the needs of the market.

The intermediate course—which the syllabus indicates could, with the instructor's permission, be taken simultaneously with the elementary course—extends the attention to plot construction. There is now, for instance, further genre delineation, with comedies distinguished from "action plots." But the course also moves in new aesthetic directions that go beyond attention to narrative construction by placing greater emphasis on audience psychology and especially on the pictorial aspects of film. For the former concern, Hugo Münsterberg's classic *The Photoplay* is assigned, and for the latter, Lindsay's *Art of the Moving Picture* and Freeburg's *The Art of the Photoplay* are required readings (although Patterson assigns only two chapters from Freeburg). But even as the readings add attention to visual design and audience taste to the course, the trajectory of assignments still is keyed, with one exception, to instruction in *narrative* construction, from initial inspiration to final elaboration in the form of detailed continuity scripts. In contrast to the elementary course, many of these weekly assignments in narrative construction and elaboration involve Patterson assigning specific narrative premises to the students rather than their creating them on their own. For example, it is indicated in session 9 that, "At this lecture the instructor will assign a character around which every student must build a plot to be handed in [at a later session]." Such assignments appear to echo the practical experience of script production in the studios, where, after all, so much of the work would have been undertaken at the direct behest of others. In this respect, the intermediate course seems much more geared to instructing students in the procedures and constraints of the scenario-writing *business* than the elementary course, which focused more on individual expression and initiative, and which may have appeared more as a course in personal fulfillment through creative writing than one in business practices. By establishing stringent and frequent due dates in the intermediate course, it is almost as if Patterson were making the student feel the pressure of studio work, where one had to finish assignments quickly and on time.

The one exception to the practical focus of the assignments on creative work in narrative comes in week 12, where Patterson appears to have given the students a choice of assignments: "Writing a special article on photoplay subjects" or "Composition: A synopsis of the plot built around the character assigned at recitation IX." The first of these options may be in keeping with a somewhat expansive aspect of Photoplay Composition that we have already encountered: while it tended to prioritize hands-on work in photoplay writing, the course was also designed to be valuable for those students who did not intend to become photoplay writers but had simply elected to learn the intricacies of plot construction in order to become better viewers or critics of the movies. Indeed, the choice of Vachel Lindsay's and Hugo Münsterberg's nonpractical philosophical ruminations on film art as textbooks for the course might also be in keeping with a desire that this more expansive intermediate course deal directly with issues of artistic *value*.

The advanced course, finally, has a seemingly eclectic feel. For this course, limited to ten students, there was no week-by-week schedule, just a list of topics. These, the syllabus indicates, would include the following:

> The Business of Continuity Writing; The Use of Light and Color in Motion Pictures; Music and Outside Aids to Motion Pictures; Educational Films; The National Board of Review—its scope, its membership, its powers; The Use of Animals in Motion Pictures; Escapes and Disguises in Photoplay Plots; A Study of the Photoplay Market: The Producer's Point of View; The Serial in the Motion Pictures; The Field for Special Articles and Journalism; Analytical Exhibition of Films; Observation Visits to the Studios; Completion of Extended Synopsis of Three Original Photoplays.

Certainly, it seems difficult, at first glance, to deduce any general philosophy of film or any focus on plot construction—and of the ways these should be taught—from this disparate set of topics. The list starts to make more sense, however, when we take a look at Patterson's volume from 1920, *Cinema Craftsmanship*, which she used as a textbook in many of her courses. All the topics in the advanced course are, in fact, ones treated in Patterson's book. Despite the extent to which *Cinema Craftsmanship* offers, above all, a theory for the construction of resonant narratives, the book is marked in fact by a curious digressive quality in which Patterson meanders into whatever seems to preoccupy her at the moment, whether or not it bears on her central theme of narrativity. To take just one example, a discussion of color intrudes suddenly into a chapter on adaptation: in the midst of discussing Rex Ingram's *Four Horsemen of the Apocalypse* as an example of a praiseworthy adaptation, Patterson suddenly launches into a fairly long diatribe against two moments where the film switches to color and, to her mind, "violates the unity of the tonal effect" (71). At the very least, we might wonder what this has to do with a discussion of the principles of adaptation.

The sheer amount of detail in the home-study syllabus for Photoplay Composition (twenty-nine pages!)—necessary for students who would have no face-to-face contact with the instructor but would be doing their course by mail—obviously is quite useful for providing a direct sense of Patterson's pedagogy and its relation to her attempts, in a work like *Cinema Craftsmanship*, to elaborate a general aesthetics of film. For the home-study course, in fact, *Cinema Craftsmanship* was the sole textbook, although she advised students to look at other sources listed in that volume's bibliography, and the pedagogy was based on the students being directed to read selected chapters and then reflect on questions that Patterson posed about the arguments contained therein.

The home-study syllabus begins with a foreword in which Patterson sets out some central principles of her philosophy of cinema. For example, she declares, "In following the course in photoplay composition laid down in these pages the student must bear always in mind that the photoplay is fast passing through the period of transition and has already taken upon itself a technique of its own. This technique varies slightly according to the methods of the different producing companies, but there are certain standardized principles which must be learned by every aspirant to photoplay composition." On the one hand, here Patterson offers practical advice—"The student must bear always in mind," "standardized principles which must be learned"—which indicates a pedagogy that works to foster an accurate and productive assessment of the photoplay market. On the other hand, beneath the practicality one can read elements of an overall philosophy of film: cinema has, for instance, a history in which there is a "transition" through less refined forms to a contemporary situation in which the specific identity of film qua film has been achieved. As even this practice-oriented syllabus suggests, there was for Patterson a notion of the cinematic ideal—an ideal of medium specificity that film achieved as it moved through its history and cast off impure influences—for example, the influence of literature. (However, Patterson did teach the craft of adaptation, since that sort of screenwriting practice met market needs. But she tended to persist in feeling that adaptations fundamentally betrayed the independent art of film.)

In the foreword to her home-study syllabus, Patterson spoke of the lessons that could be derived from the course itself, which she says would "furnish the student with that fundamental equipment without which success in his elected profession is impossible," but she also indicated that the course alone was inadequate to give a full education in film. Part of this reservation had to do, no doubt, with her sense that a home-study course could do only so much, but it also seemed to derive from a deeper conviction that the concepts conveyed in a pedagogy needed to be grounded in a concrete contact with the actual workings of the art form. Throughout her career in film, Patterson called repeatedly for both prospective photoplay writers and general viewers interested in what cinema could do at its best to study not just the principles of film art as they might exist in the abstract but, rather, concretely in the existing range of actual cinematographic production. The student of film should view as many works as possible, as many times as possible, to understand in direct terms their material accomplishments and their failings. For her home-study course, then, she declared that to the contributions her syllabus and book could make should be added "[t]he supplementary equipment [that] must come through a careful study of the entire photoplay field: the frequenting of the motion picture theaters where representative photoplays are shown; the thoughtful analysis of these plays; the reading of all available literature on the photoplay and its allied subjects, and the daily practices of this art." As the quotation that began this chapter indicates, Patterson felt that, with proper training, the informed spectator would make of the movie theater a site of pedagogy that might even dispense with the need for classroom contact with a teacher. If Victor Freeburg could imagine a pedagogue-less pedagogy wherein viewers would use at-home projection devices to study the art of cinema on their own, so too did Patterson not assume that students needed to be in the physical presence of a professor. Hence, her willingness to teach Photoplay Composition in the home-study program. But hence, conversely, her unwillingness to let viewers imagine that any act of viewing whatsoever constituted a form of learning. As the reference to the supplementary benefit of independent spectatorial activities confirms, Patterson felt that such spectators could be left to their own devices *only if* a prior instruction, whether in the classroom or in the form of a textbook plus a twenty-nine-page manual, had prepared the way by inculcating a set of firm principles and practices.

If Patterson thus underwrote her own pedagogical role, even in cases where she was not physically present to the students, a second move in the foreword to her home-study syllabus provided further justification for her pedagogy. Here, the strategy involved her making a distinction between the student amateurs and the professionals that were already succeeding in the industry. On the one hand, Patterson warned the prospective photoplay writer that the field of film writing was a highly competitive one that might not appear to provide easy entry for the amateur. On the other hand, she advised the untrained neophyte to take heart from the fact that being an amateur ensured that one had not yet been filled up with wrongheaded knowledge about the cinema. For instance, there was every chance that the amateur had not internalized the mistaken notion that the proper way to conceive a photoplay was in terms of literary works and the laws of fiction writing. Not having been trained to think of film as a form of literature, the amateur had the advantage of not basing film on the adaptation of prior models and could instead realize it as the independent art it was ultimately capable of becoming. Patterson posited that there were a number of narrative arts, but that they were irreducible each to each other in that they each had kinds of stories and modes of narration appropriate to them. Film and literature both told stories, but each in their own way. As Patterson put it:

> His [the amateur's] advantage lies in the fact that he can learn to write directly for the screen. He can train himself to present a story through the medium of pictures alone. He can cultivate the visual appeal without being hampered by a technique with which he has become all too familiar. Not having become skilled in the narrative art [of literature] he does not have to unlearn its principles. He does not have to replace a facility for [literary] story telling by a like facility for picture telling. He is among the pioneers in a new art in which he has an opportunity to make himself a specialist. To do this he needs a pictorial mind, a sense of the dramatic, that he may create situations and crises.

Photoplay Composition, then, promised a pedagogy that avoided the mistakes of the professionals already ensconced in the studio system (a system too caught up in inappropriate or even retrograde conceptions of film such as literary adaptation) while providing a path whereby amateurs could enter into a professional realm and usher cinema into its appropriate future as medium-specific storytelling art.

Having thus asserted the indispensability and unique value of its own brand of pedagogy, the syllabus for the home-study version of Photoplay Composition could then devote the rest of its pages to the content of its instruction—what it actually took photoplay writing to entail. After a list of requirements for the course—for example, a discussion of the format in which manuscripts should be typed and the manner in which they should be submitted (namely, by mail to the home-study office)—the syllabus provided a breakdown for fifteen weeks of instruction. But before looking at some of the topics, it is worth noting one interesting aspect of the requirements. Significantly, these indicated that students would have to write criticism and film analysis as well as original photoplay creation, but that they could substitute a full scenario for critical writing. Patterson was again showing that her course targeted at least two constituencies—photoplay writers *and* critically informed spectators—and that these were not always imagined as identical.

Despite Patterson's suggestions in her books that creativity in photoplay writing would flourish most when the writer also had training in critical analysis—and despite the larger sense in which one goal of the Columbia courses was to suggest that better understanding of photoplays would lead generally to an improved cinema at the point both of consumption and of production—we can find in the idea of scenario writing being allowed to substitute for a critical writing requirement an early intimation of the division of film studies into the sorts of tracks that would remain with the discipline throughout its history: there will be those who write creative works and those who write criticism (and each will try to get out of the requirements for the other). Certainly, this division echoes Patterson's own practical sense of the varying career options open to the students who took her sort of course. But it also can be seen as a first embodiment of the diverse destinies of film pedagogy caught, as it later often would be, between practical instruction in aspects of film production and critical study geared more to analysis and evaluation of finished products and their sociocultural consumption. At the extreme, some programs set up a sharp division between creative and critical work in film: to take just one example, historically, New York University split its film courses between two separate units at the university, with various institutional barriers working against extended collaboration between them.

It is interesting nonetheless to note that Patterson did at least devote one week of the home-study syllabus to what she termed "The Critical Angle," even if she allowed budding photoplay writers to get out of critical writing assignments. It may be significant that the syllabus entry for the week on "The Critical Angle" is the only one to offer background on the topic rather than to just pose questions and assign exercises. It is as if Patterson were admitting that criticism required the particular elaboration of principles rather than just practical advice. Specifically, she explained the importance of distinguishing between destructive criticism and a more constructive mode:

> Destructive criticism may also be called negative criticism, that is, it points out the faults in a composition. . . . Constructive criticism, or positive criticism, goes a step further. It not only breaks down the structure in order to show its shortcomings, but it rebuilds it according to the best judgment of the critic. It is not sufficient to say that a certain photoplay lacks suspense. . . . [T]he critic must supply a remedy for the defect; he must offer a means whereby the needed suspense can be obtained in that particular play, for instance by introducing a certain character earlier in the plot, or by withholding certain information until later in the plot, or by eliminating certain irrelevant episodes or incident, etc., etc.

But it might be noted that this brand of constructive criticism itself has practical craft elements: the critic judges but also imagines the properly composed photoplay that could have been. Clearly, such a form of criticism could be of assistance to the creative writer. Patterson granted a special place to critical activity, while implying that criticism would often usefully lose its independent status in order to be collapsed back in the fundamental profession of photoplay creation.

For most sessions of the home-study course, the syllabus assigned this or that chapter from *Cinema Craftsmanship* and posed questions geared to it for the reader to ponder and derive practical lessons from. For example, the third week's entry, devoted to "The Principles of Adaptation" and based on chapter 5 of *Cinema Craftsmanship*, asked the student to think about questions and issues such as the following:

> What place does adaptation occupy in the art of photoplay making?
>
> In what ways does narrative material have to be altered for the screen?
>
> What is meant by making the action cinematic?
>
> Every photoplay composed for the screen ought to possess five basic values:
>
> *a.* It should have plot, i.e., a struggle, a complication, a problem which arouses suspense in the minds of the audience.
>
> *b.* It should have pantomime value, i.e., the ideas should be capable of being expressed in terms of action.
>
> *c.* It should have pictorial value, i.e., it should be capable of beauty in composition and the pictures should intensify the climactic moments of the play.
>
> *d.* It should contain dramatized physical movement, i.e., action which has been given a particular significance in the working out of the plot.

e. It should have acting value, i.e., it must offer possibilities for interesting interpretation by a good actor or actress.

Are these values present in the story you have just read? Is the story good screen material? State reasons for your decision.

Many of the sessions also offered exercises for students to engage in on their own. For example, the lesson on adaptation required students to make their own synopses of the literary work on which a film currently in release was based, then compare their synopses with the official adaptation and analyze any differences. Likewise, for a session on plot construction, students were directed to see a photoplay, leave after the first reel, imagine how the story would be resolved, and then go back to see the rest of the film in order to pinpoint how narrative unfolded as "logical complication and solution."

Patterson's home-study course covered topics such as the nature of the photoplay as creative form (with attention to the specificity of film among the arts); the critical angle; adaptation; plot; character delineation (with attention to the relationship of character types to the stars currently working in the field); setting (with particular attention to its role in the elaboration of plot); the technique of photoplay writing (with examination of specific cinematic devices and the means by which their utilization could be incorporated into a photoplay, and with practical instruction on the concrete details of manuscript format); synopsis writing; comedy and its particular traits; the photoplay market (with attention to tensions between art and commerce); copyright, plagiarism, and submission procedures (including specific information on how to mail off a photoplay); and the usefulness or not of having an agent (Patterson was against it). A final section of the syllabus offered more general lessons on overall attitudes the enterprising writer should adopt to approach the market with confidence: the photoplay writer should be courageous and strong-willed enough to not be hurt emotionally by rejection; should learn that expressions of resentment over rejections could only give one a bad reputation with the studios; and must cultivate humility in the face both of rejection and of requests for revision and resubmission.

Frances Patterson would remain the instructor for Photoplay Composition over several decades. She appears to have taken off from teaching (perhaps to go on trips to Hollywood, as several newspaper pieces about her indicated). Extension program bulletins from the early 1930s briefly list two other instructors for Photoplay Composition; in some semesters, these may have been substitutes for Patterson while she was on leave. The two additional instructors were Horace C. Coon, an English department professor who would later write the standard history of Columbia University, and Mack Gorham, a drama instructor who had had a play performed at the university. Neither of these two substitutes appear to have had any special interest in film, and they did not teach it for an extended period. One suspects that they were assigned in expedient fashion to make sure the course was offered and continued to bring in revenue. Perhaps revealingly, Coon, in his standard history of Columbia, *Columbia: Colossus on the Hudson*, made little mention of the university's extension program and did not even indicate that he taught there.[33]

My guess is that Patterson did her best to imprint Photoplay Composition with her views even when other instructors came in to teach it. But during the period of her course, there were other initiatives for film pedagogy at Columbia that went beyond Patterson herself. First, early in the 1920s, the extension program attempted to offer a course *in filmmaking*, although that enterprise does not appear to have lasted very long. Certainly, one should not give this failed venture too much attention, but in the interests of the historical record it is perhaps worth presenting what information we do have about it. A first official mention seems to have been in the "Annual Report of the Director of University Extension" of 1922, where division director James Egbert asserted that motion picture production was one "of the many special branches to which University Extension was giving its attention." As he elaborated:

> Motion pictures have assumed so important a part in the educational, industrial and dramatic world that they deserve consideration and recognition in institutions of learning. University Extension has for several years offered courses in photoplay composition. In the past two years attention has been given to the study of the operation or execution of pictures. The position of general director or that of technical or art director calls for the broadest kind of training. It is our purpose as rapidly as possible to develop both of these branches of instruction as motion pictures are destined to play an important part as a civilizing influence in the modern social world.

It is worth noting that several newspaper articles on Patterson's course suggested that she herself was attempting to have her pedagogy deal with aspects of production and hands-on areas of the film business beyond photoplay writing alone. That is, although her course was focused on the writing aspect of film creation, it increasingly gave some attention to other parts of the production process from story to screen. For example, one article, "The Rebel Cry," by Elizabeth Clark, reported that the course would include "such diverse subjects as reviewing, studio mechanics, camera angles, lighting, continuity, history, sculpture, painting, design, drama, comedy and literature."[34]

From its beginnings in Freeburg's original conception, effective photoplay composition had always been assumed to necessitate an awareness of all aspects of film production: for Freeburg, and for Patterson after him, film was a total art in which there should be concerted effort to have every aspect of production work together to create a unified, overall effect. Ideally, the photoplay writer would be the auteur of the film, composing scripts that outlined story and pictorial values together in such a way that other participants in the production process (including the director) became mere executants of the writer's plan. If the photoplay writer was indeed to be given such creative control, he or she necessarily would need to know about camera work, staging, set design, editing, special effects, and so on so that these elements could be incorporated into the photoplay from the start. In the 1920s, however, Patterson's version of Photoplay Composition seemed increasingly to recognize that not every student would go into the film business to become a writer, and that the existing mode of Hollywood production would not always allow the writer to be the total auteur. There needed, then, to be training in professional tasks that went beyond photoplay composition instruction alone. On the one hand, in gaining knowledge about diverse aspects of production, one might improve one's chance for employment in other branches of the creative process if one was not successful as a writer. On the other hand, insofar as the bosses of the industry probably would not let photoplay writers serve as total auteurs, but would use them merely as the first participants in a long chain of creative work, the photoplay writer might establish productive, collaborative relationships as a result of a more comprehensive knowledge of the entire filmmaking process. Not for nothing did Patterson's book *Scenario and Screen* (1928) include chapters on the work of the cameraman, the director, the producer, and the editor, and end with a glossary of film terms—many of which were on-set technical terms. It was as if the book were informing prospective writers that they certainly might have important roles to play in filmmaking, but that they also needed to learn their relative place in a production process that would delegate equally important roles to other kinds of talent. The "humility" that Patterson had instructed photoplay writers to cultivate vis-à-vis their own scenarios was also a humility they needed to adopt toward the other creative personnel they would likely be working with (if not under).

But even as Patterson began to incorporate a more expansive sense of the production process into her photoplay course, the film curriculum itself expanded with the broader filmmaking course that James Egbert had announced. Rowland Rogers, who had worked at the Bray Studio (animated films) and at Paramount and Goldwyn, and who more recently had been involved in areas of educational film, was assigned to teach the production class.[35] It seems that he did teach one installment in the spring of 1922, since a brief piece in the *New York Times* reported on the visit of screenwriter Rupert Hughes to his class.[36] There appears, however, to have been no catalog description for this spring 1922 course, which may have been added at the last moment to test the waters for its suitability for the extension program. The following year, the course made it into the 1923 catalog and was described as follows:

> A practical course which applies in studio and "on location" the principles which underly the production of motion pictures for entertainment, for education, and in industry. This includes planning the picture and the operation function of production by director, technical director, cameraman, title writer and editor.
>
> Students have practical experience in [the] studio and an opportunity, if they desire, to appear in a picture. They also plan and produce a single 1 reel picture each term.
>
> Experts on various subjects as direction, camera work, making raw film, developing, lenses, etc., address the class and supplement the instructor's presentation.
>
> Films produced in various studios including Famous Players-Lasky, Fox and others are shown each week. Students are invited to prerelease showings of many pictures.
>
> The aid [*sic:* "aim" is probably meant] is to have the course [be] a practical preparation to enter the motion picture profession.

The Columbia archives also include a brochure that advertised the production course and offered additional details beyond those in the extension program catalog. The brochure, for instance, referred students interested in production also to Photoplay Composition, confirming the extent to which the courses were considered paired offerings. We learn also from this brochure that the course had a thirty-two-dollar fee attached to it and, as befitted an extension course, met in the evenings (Tuesdays, from 7:45 to 9:45, in the journalism building). Interestingly, given Rogers's background in educational film, the introductory part of the brochure emphasized educational forms of filmmaking at least as much as entertainment. (Perhaps this was due also to the need to give respectability to the course and not make it seem as if it was promising easy entry to entertainment feature filmmaking). The brochure presented the course as follows:

> Motion pictures are deservedly winning a larger field of influence. As entertainment, they affect the lives, habits, and culture of millions of people who see them mostly during their leisure hours each day. As a means of expressing ideas in other fields they are rapidly proving their worth. Banks, insurance companies, railroads, public service corporations, farmers, merchants and manufacturers use them for a wide variety of uses. Daily they become more useful as a tool or agency in education, in industry, in the church, and in the home. The public schools of thirty-four cities . . . are using them for classroom instruction. The United States Government advocates their use in foreign trade. Motion pictures in the church are an accomplished fact today; movie pictures in the home will be here tomorrow.

Within a year, however, the production course disappeared from the catalog. It is hard to know why. An extensive list in the brochure of promised topics and activities suggests one very likely possibility: Rogers's course may simply have been too ambitious an undertaking, especially for an extension program attempting to cater to evening students. According to the brochure, there was to be training in location versus studio filming and in myriad areas of production, from direction and cinematography to titling and editing (and even subsidiary areas such as makeup). There would be background lectures on optics and the chemistry of film stock and developing. A variety of cameras would be studied. There would be instruction in several forms besides live-action filmmaking, such as trick photography, animation, color cinematography, and microscopic cinematography. There would be visits from filmmaking professionals, and each class session was to include screenings of both feature films and other film forms.

It may simply have become obvious that there was not enough time or resources to undertake all this. Certainly, start-up costs for a new course in film production can be expensive; this may have been an issue for the extension program, which had constantly to prove itself to the general university administration and not be a drain on resources. Note, for instance, the attitude of President Butler in a memo of June 3, 1927 (a few years after Rogers's course died, in other words), to extension director James Egbert: "Home study, important as it is, nevertheless is a department of university endeavor which can only be continued and justified if it more than pays its way." Throughout its history, the extension program seems to have been seen by the administration as a source of revenue, not as something to divert major resources to, and acquisition and maintenance of film equipment for evening students may have seemed an outlandish expense.

But it also may have been the case that this one extension program course in filmmaking was not seen as ambitious enough. In fact, as the 1920s moved on, President Butler himself began making expansive plans for film study at Columbia and imagined the possibility of a bona fide degree-granting undergraduate film curriculum in place of the series of adult education courses marginalized in the extension division. If the extension version of film production never really got going, there would soon be yet another initiative at Columbia to create a practical curriculum in filmmaking as part of the newly envisioned degree program. At the end of 1926, Butler put together a committee to investigate the possibility and desirability of creating a "School of Moving Picture Technology," and a far from insignificant effort was expended in negotiating such a school with film industry luminaries. The intent was to construct a multitrack degree program in film. The initiative seems, however, to have died early on, and, unfortunately, traces of it are sketchy.

It is not clear how the idea for a "School of Moving Picture Technology" at Columbia came about, although there is every likelihood that it got as far as it did because of the support of Will Hays at the MPPDA, who was militating during the period of the coming of sound and of the increasing rationalization of the film business for professional programs that would build on resources at select universities to give practical training in the film industry. In a letter of June 24, 1927, Hays wrote to Frank Woods, executive secretary of the Academy of Motion Picture Arts and Sciences, to report on efforts to bring professional film study into academia.[37] Hays noted he had been to Occidental College in eastern Los Angeles and had discussed with its administrators the possibility of instituting a "school, or courses, of motion picture technique" there. But he also indicated to Woods that he quite preferred the plan he had been working on with Columbia University. Columbia, he explained, had the advantage of a strong graduate program and a New York location, which meant it was near both the Hays central office and the home offices of the various production companies. He also lauded the resources of the university's library and the existing strengths of divisions that he assumed could contribute to a film curriculum, such as the departments of architecture, industrial chemistry, physics, engineering, and design. Hays was unclear whether the program of study should deal with the business of film or the manual work of production. In his words, "The subject matter soon divided itself as between men who would go into the executive and administrative parts of the industry and those who would be actively engaged in production as it is represented by the scenario departments and studios." If the former path was chosen, Hays suggested that there be courses in economics, accounting, advertising, salesmanship, business administration, corporate finance, and theater management. If the latter, Hays thought there could be concentrations in screenwriting, camera work, and architecture.

Hays undoubtedly had been in contact with President Butler about such a plan as early as 1926 and probably had floated to Butler his various ideas for diverse tracks in film practice. At some point in 1926, Butler appointed a committee to investigate the possible establishment at Columbia of the School of Motion Picture Technology, and this group submitted a report to the president on November 30. On December 29, 1926, Butler duly passed the report on to Hays. Intriguingly, the rhetoric of Butler's letter presents the idea of the program as originating elsewhere than with his university or with Will Hays: as Butler put it to Hays (quite enigmatically for our historiographical purposes), there had been the "suggestion [from whom?] that there should be established in connection with our engineering and technical schools systematic instruction and research in the field of moving picture technology" and that "[t]he matter came to our attention in so interesting a fashion that I appointed a University committee to study the matter and to report upon what might be practicable." At the same time, it is worth noting that little more than a week later—as if he had already taken charge of things—it would be Hays who hosted a luncheon for Butler, the members of the university committee, and several important figures in the film industry to discuss the initiative. In fact, by the beginning of 1927, when both he and the university had enough faith in the project for letters to be sent out to the industry for feedback, Hays's involvement was made explicit: the cover letter for this survey was in the name of both Columbia *and* the Hays Office, and *the latter* revealingly was given as the place to which feedback about the project was to be sent. Even if Columbia had come up with the idea, much of the fact gathering for it would now be conducted by the Hays Office.

One possible answer to the question of where the initiative for the Columbia program originated may be contained in the opening to the committee report that Butler had commanded: "[T]he cinema people, in general, are much interested in the establishment of such a school and would be inclined to favor it in every possible way. . . . Mr. [Adolph] Zukor believes that the time is ripe for a large number of high grade educational pictures which could be best furthered by a school connected with a great university." Perhaps Zukor, the head of Paramount, was the one who brought up the idea of a Columbia curriculum "in so interesting a fashion," as President Butler's letter to Will Hays had put it (and what was so "interesting" about it, we might surmise, was perhaps the promise of money behind the idea).

The committee report itself is rich in information about the sort of program that was being envisioned. The initial committee appears to have been composed of James Egbert from the extension program and two scientists, James P. C. Southall from physics and Daniel D. Jackson from chemical engineering. (The report, in fact, was written on Department of Chemical Engineering letterhead.) At the luncheon Will Hays hosted at the beginning of 1927, the list of professors involved had expanded to include faculty from architecture, electrical engineering, and civil engineering, and these, along with Frank D. Fackenthal, secretary of the university, became the final university committee for the project. Clearly, as the affiliations of the faculty members suggest, a primary concern for the potential curriculum was that it emphasize scientific and technical hands-on aspects of film. The report also announced a subcommittee of several important industry figures who were expected to advise the university on the project, including Zukor and William Fox. A Hays Office interdepartmental memo from February 1927 indicated that Hays himself ended up chairing this industry subcommittee.

As I suggested at the beginning of this chapter, it is perhaps noteworthy that there appears to have been no consultation with Frances Patterson in Photoplay Composition and no attempt to include her in the committee work. (Perhaps this says something about the lowly status of instructors from an extension program compared with regular professors.) Nonetheless, the report briefly mentions her courses: in outlining the current resources at the university that could be drawn upon for a new and expanded film curriculum that might include screenwriting as one of its tracks, the report noted, "We apparently have the talent for cinema writing already developed."

One assumes it was extension director James Egbert who imparted this information, and it is worth wondering why he had been assigned to the committee. After all, Columbia was now thinking of a degree program in film, one that would be very different from the random noncredit film offerings in Egbert's division. One possible reason for the inclusion of the director of the extension program in the planning of a new degree-granting curriculum is suggested in a point made by historian John Angus Burrell in his 1954 history of adult education at Columbia. Burrell notes that there were occasions where Columbia used the noncredit courses of the extension program as a sort of laboratory in which new classes and curricula that were being considered as possible additions to the regular degree-granting programs of the university could be tested out in the safe environment of noncredit pedagogy. Columbia's Business School, for example, began as a series of noncredit extension courses before becoming a regular program for degree-seeking Columbia students once it was clear that there was student demand and that business could be taught in serious fashion. Perhaps, likewise, the idea for the cinema curriculum was to start it as a nondegree program and see how it developed. Perhaps the earlier failed course by Rowland Rogers on film production had been one of these experiments. (That might explain why it was instituted without fanfare and then disappeared after a year.) In any case, Egbert must have been considered essential to the ongoing efforts to build a degree program in film: just after the January 10, 1927, luncheon hosted by Hays, Butler appointed Egbert chairman for the committee to undertake further investigation of a degree-granting cinema curriculum.

The committee report submitted at the end of 1926 had indicated that the goal was a full-fledged degree program at the undergraduate and graduate level: as the report explained, "It is the consensus of opinion that at least two years of college work should be the pre-requisite for entrance to such a school, and that two years more might be given, leading toward a bachelor's degree. There are many advanced courses in Physics, Chemistry, Architecture and Journalism which could be chosen for a year's post-graduate work, leading to the master's degree."

Within the undergraduate and master's degrees in cinema, three tracks were envisioned: cinema architecture, cinema photography, and cinema writing. The report implied that some of the decision for which tracks to implement and develop came from an assessment of existing resources at the university. In the words of the report, "In an examination of the various curricula throughout the University it has been found that only a few additional courses would be necessary to start such a school." But other factors may have led to the specific three-track structure. For instance, the writers of the report noted that in their interviews with the Hays Office the personnel there had offered advice about the three tracks: "[Hays Office administrator] Governor Milliken suggested that our School of Architecture would be of very great benefit in furnishing courses which would make better and more accurate sets, and that our courses already given in cinema writing would be useful. Mr. De Bra [Will Hays's secretary] stated that they already have in their organization quite a number of men who came from our original Signal Corps School of Photography, established at Columbia during the War, and that in spite of the short course which they had at Columbia, they had been extremely useful."

The Will Hays Papers from 1927 contain a copy of a survey to members of the film industry signed by James Egbert and Carl Milliken that offered a "tentative list of courses and subjects" for the curriculum and asked for industry feedback. The courses that Egbert and Milliken indicated seem very clearly to have taken into account existing offerings at Columbia. Proposed for the *architecture* track (which in the Egbert-Milliken survey had now been slightly renamed as "architecture and design" and included areas such as costuming) were the following courses: Elements of Design; Shades and Shadows; Architectural Drafting; the History of Ancient Architecture; Analytic Geometry and General Physics; Perspective; Cinema Set Design; Descriptive Geometry; Architecture Design and Oriental Architecture; Modeling; Theatre Design; Life Drawing and Composition; the History of Renaissance and Modern Architecture; and Costuming and Designing.

The *photography* track courses were Developing, Enlarging and Reducing; General Chemistry; Printing; Still Photography; Physics; Motion Picture Camera; Retouching and Splicing; Posing and Lighting; Cinema Studio; Photo Chemistry; Artistic Expression; Light; Composition; Optical Instruments; Physiological Optics.

Finally, the *scenario* track courses included English Composition; Comparative Drama; English Literature; Screen Adaptation; Dramatic Arts; Play Writing, Ancient and Modern; Photoplay Composition; Dramatic Criticism; History of Drama; Title Writing; Continuity Construction; Plot Construction; and Screen Syntax.

It is hard to discern whether some of the visible absences in the curriculum—such as directing, editing, acting, and music composing or scoring—were the result of the assessment of Columbia's strengths and existing resources or of industry input on areas in which it did not feel it needed university training, or of other factors or influences. In one bit of information useful to this question, Carl Milliken at the Hays Office wrote on June 24, 1927, to Frank Woods at the Academy of Motion Picture Arts and Sciences to describe the new Columbia initiative. He explained that one area where they had decided *not* to pursue courses was acting because "Here in the East this aspect of training is well provided for at Yale University."

An early draft letter to accompany the aforementioned industry survey had suggested that the questionnaire should be targeted primarily to those people in the industry actively involved in the three emphasized hands-on aspects of production: "We wish your suggestions as to the practical value training in these subjects [i.e., architecture, photography, scenario writing] would be for individuals coming into the industry for the first time. It will be particularly helpful to have suggestions from your Directors, Camera Men, Scenario Editors, Architects, Electricians and others of your professional staff, both as regards the general plan and the scope of study." At the same time, the version of the survey that ultimately ended up being sent out to the industry shows that there had been a decision to include some areas of business practice (however, these did not end up in the final articulation of the tracks). For instance, a preface to the survey described the purpose of the school as at least dual in nature: "to serve those now in the industry and to provide some technical elementary training for those who will subsequently engage in administrative departments or the studio work of the industry."

In the survey, industry respondents were asked to comment on the courses, to suggest others, and to speculate on the role film courses might have or could have had in preparing them for their own careers. Unlike the extension program course on photoplay composition, with its admission open to a general pool of motivated adults, the new motion picture school was presented as more selective: "From the first, it has been apparent that the student personnel of the school must be definitely limited. It is hoped that the curriculum and set-up may be made so attractive that a selection of only those students showing particular aptitude and with adequate educational qualifications or their equivalent in experience, will be practical." Nonetheless, the survey acknowledged a certain academic rigor that would make the program more than vocational (this, after all, was Columbia University, and there had to be some deference to liberal arts respectability): "It is our hope to organize the school on practical rather than theoretical lines. It is, however, to be a school of technology rather than a trade school. This can be accomplished if persons familiar with the various phases of production can supplement the theoretical instruction of the classroom."

In the files of the Hays Office, two responses to the survey can be found. One came from a screenwriter, Carey Wilson, at First National Productions. Wilson indicated overall support for the program of study as long as it complemented theory with practical instruction "by accepted authorities in each branch... people who have done things—and who know how to explain how they have done them." He followed this suggestion with a quite detailed, four-page outline for a possible course in scenario writing. The other letter came from the secretary of the New York office of Universal Pictures and did little more than offer an explanatory list of various positions and their duties in the business side of the firm. No other replies to the survey are to be found in the archives, and it is hard to know if this indicates lack of response to the idea at the time or poor record keeping over the years.

There appears to be no other extant material on the proposed course at Columbia, and the plan seems to have died quietly. We can only guess at the reasons. Anyone in academia is aware of the extent to which curricular initiatives often are announced, greeted with enthusiasm, and vaguely undertaken, only to disappear as scholars and administrators find other projects to devote themselves to. Individuals in the film industry may be aware of the extent to which industry officials can pay lip service to institutional support of academic ventures only to drop out when the commercial payoff becomes unclear. (In the 1980s, for instance, the American Film Institute was notorious for making overtures on a regular basis and with great fanfare to academic organizations such as the Society for Cinema Studies, only to back out of the initiatives and offer no follow-through.) Perhaps administrators at Columbia ended up feeling that they did not have sufficient resources for the program: in fact, President Butler's letter in December 1926 to Will Hays about the initiative, when it was still in the early phases of its planning, had warned, "It probably goes without saying that the University, staggering as it is under almost impossible financial burden, could not now enter upon any new field that involved even a contingent financial obligation on its part."

There is yet another possible hypothesis that, if correct, would have interesting resonances for this study. It may have been that, far from having no interest in fostering academic development of professional programs in film, the industry was so interested that it hedged its bets and simultaneously was encouraging several different initiatives at several different universities. That a number of schools were, as we will see, developing courses in film at virtually the same time may be a coincidence, or it may be a planned reaction by the industry to overall historical forces (e.g., the coming of sound certainly would have encouraged a concern for increasing professionalization of the film industry and for the training of personnel). Recall, for instance, that Hays had almost simultaneously sought out Columbia University *and* Occidental College to see if, in their proximity to the film industries on both coasts, either might be a likely venue in which to develop a professional film curriculum.

Like the proverbial Hollywood producer who puts several screenwriters to work independently on the same script and then chooses the best results from among them, Hays may have encouraged a number of universities to develop plans for film instruction at the same time and in almost parallel fashion. It is, as we will see in chapter 4, intriguing to note the resemblance of the three-track Columbia curriculum to that proposed at the same time by the team of the University of Southern California and the Academy of Motion Picture Arts and Sciences. Likewise, it is striking to realize that during the same period when negotiations were under way for the Columbia curriculum, key industry executives—a number of whom were serving on the Columbia subcommittee—were traveling to Harvard to lecture in its

1927 film course, which Will Hays also had had a key role in setting up. For instance, Universal Picture administrator Robert Cochrane had written to Hays to suggest that the Columbia program include business courses, noting that he had spoken *the previous day* at the Harvard School of Business, and it may be that his interest in business topics within a film pedagogy was concretized by his Harvard experience.

While the Columbia administration was putting some energy into its abortive but ambitious bachelor's and master's programs in film, Frances Patterson soldiered on in the shadows with her Photoplay Composition course. She retained the expansive goal of inscribing specific instruction in photoplay writing within a broader pedagogy addressing all the phases of film production, and in 1936 she and her husband, Rowland, offered a more ambitious version of the original course.[38] The new course, entitled Motion Pictures—Scenario Writing and Production, still had photoplay writing as its primary focus but linked this one craft to the rest of the filmmaking process. It was described as follows:

> An inquiry into the nature of the motion picture for the profit of those who intend to write original screen stories, to secure staff positions with the film companies, or to enter the field of motion picture reviewing. The course will follow the workshop plan, allowing for individual writing projects. There will be lectures, conferences and seminars, some of which will be conducted by representatives of the industry. Exercises will be assigned in the writing of story treatments, continuity, screen dialogue, plot building, character delineation, the dramatization of setting, and comedy methods. A library of professional scripts and stills has been assembled for the use of the class.

But just as the 1927 plan for film degree programs had kept Patterson out of the loop, she was about to be sidelined again. At the beginning of the 1930s, a new director, Dr. Russell Potter, had been appointed to head the Institute of Arts and Sciences in Columbia's extension program, and he clearly saw his enterprise as more solidly intellectual than his predecessors. (For example, he was the first director to write annual reports on the institute's cultural accomplishments.) In 1937, extension director James Egbert again got the bug for a more expansive program of offerings in film, and he and Potter established the Division of Film Study, to be run through the institute. In a 1938 report commenting on the first year's activities, Potter both explained the guiding mission for the Division of Film Study and outlined its accomplishments. The mission, he explained, had been

> to further in every possible way the development of motion picture study and appreciation—to arrange talks and illustrated lectures, to

present special showings of films, to coordinate such work in the field of the motion picture as is now being done in various parts of the University, and to act as a clearing house of information for those departments and to cooperate actively with other organizations and groups both academic and non-academic that have similar aims.

To this end, the Division of Film Study organized several activities in its first year: an evening of amateur movies, a series of six evening screenings of pre-sound American cinema, and a dinner in conjunction with the Hays Office in honor of Cecil B. DeMille at which President Butler spoke on the topic "The Motion Picture Comes of Age." It had also initiated discussion regarding an educational film rental library with national scope and a 16 mm filmmaking unit to produce educational films according to the needs of various departments on campus. Most important, the Division of Film Study had sponsored two new courses. One, entitled "Motion Picture Parade," was in keeping with the glitzy events-oriented side of the Institute of Arts and Sciences and involved a subscription-based series of film showings accompanied by a prestigious series of speakers such as Robert Edmund Jones, Gilbert Seldes, J. B. Priestly, Terry Ramsaye, Mark Van Doren, Mortimer Adler, and Paul Rotha. The other course, "Fine Arts of Motion Pictures," was, in Russell Potter's words, "an academic course limited to thirty students selected for their serious interest in and knowledge of motion pictures," who "had the privilege of hearing rather technical problems discussed by such authorities as King Vidor, David O. Selznick, Paul Rotha, [set designer] John Koenig, and others." Significantly, the course site was not at Columbia but at MoMA, where its conveners were John Abbott, director of MoMA's Film Library, and Iris Barry, the library's curator. The films for this class came from the MoMA collection (as did those for "Motion Picture Parade") and provide a clear example of how MoMA's new venture in film was clearly influencing university film pedagogy in the post-1935 period. Potter certainly was pleased with the MoMA collaboration and indicated in his report a desire "most earnestly to continue to enlarge this association." By the time of his 1939 report, Potter was hoping to develop an ambitious program of academic courses in film. As John Angus Burrell describes them in his history of the extension program, "Three courses were elaborately outlined: the first, the history and development of the motion picture; the second, present-day methods, techniques, and organization; and the third, production. In addition, there would be other courses, more specialized, in scenario writing, acting, directing, lighting, sound, cutting, montage, etc."

Ultimately, nothing came of the plan. In Burrell's explanation, "The uncertainty of the world in 1939, the outbreak of war that Fall, and then Pearl

Harbor two years later made the whole program for the time impossible. When open hostilities ceased and the University was deluged with G.I. students, there was neither time nor opportunity to organize courses and teaching staff to do a first-rate job in this field."[39]

The Division of Film Study seems to have paid little attention to the ongoing efforts of Frances Patterson to promote the art of film over the many years before MoMA came into the picture. But for an allusive mention in Potter's 1938 report that "the motion picture as a cultural and educational tool had not been ignored at the University," the plan for an expansive (and ultimately abortive) curriculum in film at Columbia at the end of the 1930s operated, like the 1927 initiative, in virtual and, it might seem, deliberate ignorance of Patterson's endeavors. She was not included, for instance, in the committee to advise Russell Potter on film study at the university.[40] Patterson continued diligently and quietly to do her job and teach her extension classes. The last records show her teaching in the adult education program as late as 1958. Perhaps she wearied of trying to do more for film than simply teaching in unassuming fashion to a nonacademic public. Throughout the 1940s and on into the 1950s, mention of her diminished in the press, and she faded from attention. It is no small irony that the last public notice of her appears to have come in her husband's *New York Times* obituary of May 25, 1954, where she was mentioned as his survivor. (No notice of her own demise seems ever to have been published.) One of the first pedagogues of film, Patterson was again relegated to the margins of a history that felt it had more important things on its mind.

2 A Brief Interlude as the Movies March On

Terry Ramsaye and the New School for Social Research

At the beginning of the 1920s, New York City's New School for Social Research shifted its emphasis from that of a Progressivist institute of scholarship concerned, as its name originally intended, with social science reflection on pressing issues of the day to a much lighter, less research-oriented extension program seeking to offer cultural diversion to the city's citizens. By the middle of the decade, the New School's pedagogical mission thus came to focus on culturally uplifting adult education in ways that led its curriculum to resemble that of Columbia's extension program—and, in particular, that university's Institute for the Arts as this was described in the previous chapter. It was in response to the increasing visibility of an adult population seeking cultural capital useful in the byways of modern urban life that the New School announced a 1926 lecture series on film history by the journalist Terry Ramsaye. Timed to coincide with the publication of his massive, anecdote-filled historical saga of cinema, *A Million and One Nights*, Ramsaye's lectures at the New School no doubt were intended to promote the two-volume study by offering a stirring condensation that, like the original, would be quite rich with diverting tales of cinema's epic past.

There is no small irony in the fact that in the 1920s the New School's curriculum had come to center so strongly on obvious cultural diversions such as Ramsaye's talks on the popular art of the movies. Entertainment and cultural uplift had, in fact, been far from the minds of the founders and original teachers of the New School. The school had derived a fundamental aspect of its mission from social critic Thorstein Veblen, who would be one of its first generation of scholars and had specifically inspired its foundational philosophy through his suspicion that commercial ventures posed a threat to the ideal of higher learning as a serious quest after knowledge for its own sake. Committed to rigorous forms of advanced scholarship, the New School had sought originally to eschew curricula of vocational training and light entertainment. Although its name identified it as a "school," it seemed to pay public pedagogy little more than lip service. In its original conception, the New School was a veritable think tank where committed researchers could probe deeply into their chosen fields, while regarding public explanation of their work as only a lesser by-product of their scholarship. The school might offer public events, even of a dilettantish cultural nature, but its primary focus was a deeply committed hard-core investigation of contemporary issues from rigorous social science positions. The mission of its scholars was to produce socially useful knowledge, and it was clear that utility was not always to be measured in terms of any pedagogy that students might encounter in classes. Utility generally involved the elaboration of public policy to be communicated to government or private agencies, and if ordinary citizens happened to get a chance to witness such elaboration in their classes, this would be only a relative aftereffect of the New School's larger policy-influencing research activities. As Peter M. Rutkoff and William B. Scott, authors of the standard history of the New School, put it unambiguously, "The New School had been founded to help reconstruct society."[1] With funding from benefactors in the private sector, the school could commit itself fully to the higher calling of research and offer itself as an alternative to the seeming surrender of mainstream universities to commercial interests.

The impetus for the New School came out of opposition to specific pecuniary compromises that Columbia University was alleged to have made and that ostensibly showed its kowtowing to nonacademic pressures: the New School was founded during the First World War by former Columbia professors who had resigned over what they perceived as that university's violation of academic freedom when, in obeisance to trustee pressure, it had fired a professor with antiwar sentiments. The New School's founding professors envisioned it as a venue in which intellectuals could conduct investigations—including ones that went against mainstream political positions—unfettered, and with little need to generate revenue by means of enrollments. Freed from the constraints of ideology and commercial accountability, New School intellectuals could devote their minds to problems that required deep engagement of research energy. In many ways, the sort of cultural entertainment that a place like Columbia University was offering through its extension program and its Institute for the Arts was *exactly* what the New School did *not* want to be associated with. It is ironic, then, that Ramsaye's New School course could easily have fit in with public entertainment and enlightenment of the very sort that the cultural forum of Columbia's Institute of the Arts had readily promoted.

Certainly, it should not be assumed that in its earliest manifestation the New School had narrowly defined the concerns of the social sciences in ways that excluded attention to cultural questions. Quite the contrary, the New School had taken an expansive approach to society, one in which culture was seen as an essential component of the social fabric. Rutkoff and Scott pinpoint, for instance, the contribution to the school's founding philosophy of the historian James Harvey Robinson, who was deeply committed to an Enlightenment sense of progress in which all human works—including the arts—reflected and interacted with the movement of social history. More generally, among the social sciences, the New School gave recognition to the specific contributions of anthropology, which through this period was fostering an expansive notion of culture that could only increase its relevance to the concerns of social analysis. Through the 1920s, for example, anthropology was taking culture to refer to the whole way of life of a society. Books like the vastly influential *Middletown* would even argue at the end of the decade for an anthropology of modernized, mass-mediated Western society, and throughout the period well-noted anthropological works like Bronislaw Malinowski's *Argonauts of the Western Pacific* (1922) or Margaret Mead's *Coming of Age in Samoa* (1928) made a point of finding parallels between "primitive" communities and modernized ones. In such cases, culture, with its concern for the symbolic, affective, and even aesthetic aspects of human interaction, was becoming accepted as an object of social science investigation. In such a context, the assertion in the 1926 catalog (where Terry Ramsaye's lecture series was announced) that a course like Waldo Frank's on modern art will "correlate what is happening with the arts with what is happening in other activities, such as science and philosophy; and will examine modern art as a potential and still very immature expression of a fundamental change in man's way of thinking and living" seems easily in keeping with the broad, interdisciplinary intent of the New School's guiding philosophy.

At the same time, however, it is clear that by the early 1920s, there were tensions already in the New School's dreams both of an expansive notion of the social sciences merging with cultural analysis and of rigorous inquiry that would be free of market needs. As Rutkoff and Scott put it, "Although personal animosities, chronic financial problems, and the waning novelty of their endeavor no doubt contributed to the mood, faculty members expressed their disillusionment in terms of institutional policy. Should the New School divest itself of its profitable adult lecture program? Should it shelve the expensive but valuable research program? Or should it try to continue to offer both?" (27). Under the tutelage of its new director, Alvin Johnson, who took over in 1922, the New School ended up moving primarily toward strengthening adult outreach through popular lectures. That is, it became essentially a venue for uplifting presentations that the New York public would pay to attend in exchange for cultural enrichment. The New School had originally decided not to grant degrees to students in accordance with the belief that research itself, rather than its dissemination in the classroom, had to be central, but now the noncredit status of the new courses fed into their appearance as diversion-rich public events—lectures to be dabbled in as quick fixes for cultural enhancement.

Entertaining the middlebrows became a major preoccupation of the New School. Instead of having a regular faculty that was funded to do research, and would be impelled to teach only when they felt that their research merited communication to a larger audience, the New School came, after 1923, to be dominated by visiting lecturers brought in as much for their showmanship as for any academic solidity. Revealingly, by 1925, Alvin Johnson had even fired Thorstein Veblen himself, a notoriously bad lecturer described by Rutkoff and Scott as having "always been contemptuous of students, believing that most sought entertainment, not learning" (36). Subsequent history reveals that, to his very great credit, Johnson never entirely gave up on the dream of a research institute, and by the 1930s, he would realize that vision in the famous University in Exile, made up in large part of major thinkers who were fleeing European fascism. This new accumulation of specialized academic researchers led eventually to the establishment in 1934 of degree-granting master's and doctoral programs at the New School through its newly formulated Graduate Faculty of Political and Social Sciences. In the 1930s, then, the New School for Social Research would more than recoup its image as a great repository of committed social reflection and rigorous scholarship. But in the mid-1920s, the dominant motif was entertainment, diversion, and cultural uplift, and this was clearly reflected in the school's curriculum, which frequently gave itself over to a cultural turn divorced from public policy and social analysis. As early as 1923, as Rutkoff and Scott observe, "Johnson, at the urging of [student and wealthy benefactor] Clara Mayer had committed the New School to several new subjects: psychology, philosophy, intellectual history, literature, and art. With . . . more offerings in philosophy and psychology, and the new cultural orientation of the courses in art and literature, the New School seemed to have adopted the human mind broadly defined, rather than social science and social work, as its dominant interest" (35–36).

Despite this desire to explore expansive notions of "the human mind broadly defined," it was increasingly tempting to try to bring in revenues through less rigorous, less academic, offerings. It likewise became increasingly easy for specific courses in the realm of art to focus on medium-specific issues without attention to larger social frameworks. It was certainly the case that by the 1920s, the synoptic view in which culture was seen as integral to the confrontation with social issues was being rivaled by a proliferation of disparate and disconnected courses in cultural areas, many of which operated with varying degrees of autonomy from any concern to link artistic accomplishment and social issues. Much of the curriculum became a potpourri of isolated bits of light entertainment.

As we will see shortly, Terry Ramsaye did have some big claims to make about the place of the movies in the history of mankind, but it is also clear that his larger ambition for his film history was counterbalanced by a sheer fascination with anecdote for its own sake. Not for nothing does the title of *A Million and One Nights* allude to the famous Arabian Nights tale in which the human capacity for storytelling becomes an unbridled machine of nonstop narrativity. One imagines that Ramsaye's series of talks at the New School functioned as much as forms of amusement as a deep pedagogy in film.

Today, the Web site for the New School's program in film and communication proudly advertises that Ramsaye's offering is "believed to be the first college course devoted to cinema," an assertion we can accept as long as we keep in mind several caveats. First, as we have seen, Columbia's extension program had been offering courses on cinema from the midteens on. Although these were nominally focused on the specialized realm of photoplay composition, it is evident that the very idea of composition was defined in such an expansive way as to go beyond the specific act of writing scenarios and to engage with the entire filmmaking process. But Freeburg's and Patterson's Photoplay Composition courses certainly did not offer the broad sweep of Ramsaye's lecture series, which promised a comprehensive look at cinema's history and present possibilities. His series, as the 1926 catalog asserted, rightly can be seen as inquiring "for the first time" in an academic setting "into the history, structure and functions of the motion picture as an art and industry."

Second, given the New School's increasing interest in the 1920s in providing adult citizens with forms of cultural entertainment and easy instruction, we need to realize that Ramsaye's offering may have been a "college *course*" in name only. There were no class assignments, and it is not clear whether the hour-and-a-half sessions included time for discussion or questions from the audience. It seems simply that listeners signed up to attend a series of lectures that brought no responsibilities with them. As noted earlier, the noncredit status of many New School courses in the 1920s brought in nonscholars and even, undoubtedly, dabblers in culture who came for undemanding infusions of eclectic bits of knowledge, and it is clear that many of the offerings required little of their audience. To be sure, some courses tried to push their clientele to engage critically with the material. For example, Waldo Frank's 1927 lecture series on modern art, which included some attention to film, invited students "to participate actively by means of questions and discussions." Certainly, too, within an institution that increasingly saw itself as ensuring the civic betterment of a broadly nonacademic public, the New School's curriculum in the 1920s did include a number of courses that entailed practical, hands-on forms of training that would have necessitated student participation. For instance, the very course listed after Terry Ramsaye's lecture series in the 1926 catalog was the directly utilitarian Technique of Vocational Guidance, geared to providing its constituency with professional training in the field of job counseling. Likewise, the next page of the 1926 catalog describes a series of "Teacher Training Courses in Adult Education," composed of four offerings. Although there were no diplomas at the New School, students who took all four teacher training courses would receive an official summary of the work they had done, and this, presumably, would aid in the students' certification as adult education teachers.

In contrast, Ramsaye's course did not lead to certification and had no directly utilitarian intent other than to offer the urban dweller a general awareness of the achievements of a new art form. This is one of the reasons the title to this chapter refers to Ramsaye's course as a "brief interlude." Despite its possible firstness within the history of the early American study of film, Ramsaye's lecture series may seem a minor moment in that history, and one perhaps should not make too much of it. Similarly, it may well be that the lecture series represented only a brief commitment of energy and attention on Ramsaye's part. There appears, for instance, to be no mention of it in his collected papers. Given the tie-in to *A Million and One Nights*, which easily contained enough fun anecdotes to more than fill a twelve-session series of lectures, it is likely that Ramsaye had little to do in his New School lecture series other than replay great stories from his rich and weighty book. Ramsaye indeed seems to have had little interest or investment in academic practice. Having worked both as a reporter and as an employee of various film concerns, Ramsaye claimed a vivid day-to-day knowledge of film that he sometimes contrasted to the dry abstractions of ivory tower knowledge. Thus, in the foreword to his book, Ramsaye inveighed against overly academic approaches to film. In his words, "The scholars, the historians, the cloistered critics of the colleges, all seeing the older arts down the cooler vistas of the ages, see them detached from their origins. Inevitably they see them all wrong."[2] Undoubtedly, Ramsaye himself would have regarded his New School "course" as an evening's nonacademic, light entertainment, not much more rigorous than the undemanding cinematic works he would be telling tales about.

If the very lightness of Ramsaye's New School series requires that we treat it with a certain degree of brevity, so does the simple fact that we know so little about it. Ramsaye left no traces of his involvement in this course, and there is no direct documentation of it other than the description printed in the 1926 New School catalog. However, given the course's status as the first comprehensive series of lectures on film in an academic institution—albeit one, admittedly, that did not offer degrees or diplomas and that was going through a period of lessening academic rigor—and given, too, Ramsaye's own legendary place in film history as one of the art's first comprehensive historians, it is worth imagining the translation of his historiographical practice into a classroom pedagogy.

In fact, much of what I offer in this chapter is decidedly speculative. Many of the topics that Ramsaye's New School course promised it would cover bear a perhaps inevitable resemblance to *A Million and One Nights,* for which the course was likely a veritable promotional activity. To that extent, we can perhaps extrapolate a guess at the course content from major themes of the book. Ramsaye's New School course The Motion Picture coincided directly with the publication of *A Million and One Nights,* ads for which appeared in New York publications as early as the first session of the course. Likewise, an essay on the history of the motion picture that Ramsaye published in a special issue of the *Annals of the American Academy of Political and Social Science* at the moment his book came out, can stand as a veritable condensation of the key points of the more than eight-hundred-page study, suggesting that Ramsaye had evolved a very definitive sense of the contours of film history and how he wanted to present them.[3] It might well be that course, essay, and book alike all presented the same material, with the first two enterprises serving as modest summaries of, and forms of publicity for, the more ambitious book.

In this extrapolation of Ramsaye's overall conception of film, we have the additional aid of one of the few critical analyses of his work, a short but sharp discussion in Robert Allen and Douglas Gomery's *Film History: Theory and Practice,* which examines *A Million and One Nights,* along with

Robert Grau's *Theatre of Science* from 1914, as examples of early film history writing that "by what they chose to include *and* exclude, and by the emphasis they placed on certain events, films, and persons, helped to determine the range of film historical subject matter for historians who wrote after them."[4] Ramsaye clearly was both representative of his historical moment and deeply influential on canons of subsequent film historiography in his cheerful attitude toward technological innovation; his complementary celebration of the accomplishment of great inventors; his concomitant acceptance of industrial enterprise as the avenue through which such invention could best be encouraged; and his consequent conclusion that there was not an incompatibility of commerce and art but a propitious flowering of the latter in the favorable soil of the former.

Born in 1885, Terry Ramsaye had first worked as an engineer, which may explain his evident ease with descriptions of scientific advances and his obvious faith in technology as causal for cultural progress. But he soon switched careers and became a newspaper reporter with an eye for the good story and an evident talent for rendering that story in vivid, if often flowery, language. From its title on, *A Million and One Nights* takes literature as its inspiration and strives for a lyricism that frequently becomes overdone. The following passage from the foreword to Ramsaye's book can serve as an example of his style at its most effusive:

> An Art is born before our eyes, just as these very movies have shown us in stop-motion the butterfly emerging from the cocoon. We see it struggle limply forth, dry its gossamer wings, and fly—with all its gay, gaudy spirit of youth, strong as youth is strong, weak as youth is weak.
> And—butterfly like, the service of this gossamer winged art of flitting shadows is mostly in pollenizing the blossoms of the Wish, be they ragweeds of commonality or roses of culture.[5]

It was perhaps this facility with style and rhetorical flourish that led to Ramsaye being hired as director of publicity for the Mutual Film Corporation (where he also produced some Chaplin comedies and newsreels). In 1920, he was put to work by *Photoplay* magazine on a series of articles on film history; these became the basis for *A Million and One Nights*. While Ramsaye himself admitted that there were vast aspects of film history he had not examined—for example, the evolution of spectator psychology—his volume soared above previous ventures in its vast scope and wealth of research materials. Ramsaye relied heavily, for instance, on court records (especially around patents litigation) and interviews with numerous pioneers from cinema history, quite a number of whom were still around when he began his research. A massive volume, *A Million and One Nights* still has legendary status as one of the key works in the critical literature of cinema studies, and it would be hard to overstate its impact on later conceptions of the movies' history. For example, it set the terms by which subsequent film history would focus on auteurs; would, more generally, imagine a history of "great men" combining science and skill to create art; would adopt a teleological structure in which cinema achieves the condition of Art by discovering narrativity; and so on.

Here, from the New School's announcement of courses for 1926–27, is the description of, and week-by-week breakdown for, Ramsaye's course The Motion Picture:

> Course No. 22. The Motion Picture—Mr. Ramsaye. Thursday, 8:20 to 9:50 P.M. (twelve lectures)
>
> This course will examine, for the first time, into the history, structure and functions of the motion picture as an art and as an industry. Various motion pictures, cinema devices and documents bearing on the rise and evolution of the films will be exhibited, as they may become available during the course. The course will cover:
>
> 1. Relations of the motion picture to the field of expression, with consideration of the common ancestries of picture, language and drama. Pre-history of the motion picture.
>
> 2. Review of the period of invention, 1870 to 1896, with an examination into causative forces and influences.
>
> 3. The growth of the new art from the novelty of 1896 to the crystallization of the narrative or photoplay form in 1903, with the incidental changes in the commercial structure and the rise of the motion picture theatre and its social conditions.
>
> 4. Publication and distribution problems of the motion picture in the beginning and their continued influence on the screen institution. The world markets, world audiences and international relations.
>
> 5. The creation and rise of the motion picture star, as a personified trademark within the industry, as a personified desire to the public. Motion picture salaries and their controls.
>
> 6. The evolution of modern photoplay structure and screen syntax—The influence of the magicians—Why D. W. Griffith became famous—The spectacle picture—Mary Pickford and melodrama.
>
> 7. The controls exerted by public taste and the box office interpretation, with consideration of sectional variations. The selection of screen material and its subsequent editorial and studio treatment. Scenario prices and the market—What the scenario schools mean—How old stories appreciate in value.

8. The relation of the screen and the printed word—Reactions of the press—The serial age and the Chicago newspaper circulation war—The art of the screen subtitle.

9. Propaganda on the screen—Its use by political parties and in national causes, from McKinley to the Prince of Wales—The screen history of the World War—Screen influences on world markets and merchandising.

10. The use of the motion picture in education—When Edison tried to make screen textbooks—Application of the motion picture to problems of research in laboratories and in industries—The film in non-theatrical circulation—The amateur motion picture.

11. The personnel of the screen institution—Film ethics and practices—Why [sic] is Will Hays and his organization—Canon William Sheafe Chase and the censorship movement.

12. The screen of tomorrow—Consideration of refinements and inventions in screen technique, including color, the talking picture and stereoscopic photography and what may be anticipated and forecast of their influences.

Not every element in this series of topics has a direct correlate in *A Million and One Nights*. In that volume, for instance, Ramsaye explicitly declared that he would concentrate on the theatrically released entertainment film, so there is little extended discussion in the book of "[t]he motion picture in education," along the lines of week 10 in the series. Likewise, as a history that terminates with the ultimate accomplishments of the present moment, Ramsaye's book appears to have more narrative closure than does the course, which in its last session deals with "the screen of tomorrow."

In fact, there is much we can say immediately about the course in and of itself—on paper at least—without reference to the book that it appears to have accompanied. First of all, for instance, it is striking how familiar, and even commonsensical, so many of the historical or aesthetic assumptions behind Ramsaye's course appear to us—in large part, no doubt, because Ramsaye set many of the terms whereby the teaching of film history has been conducted up to the present. Take, for instance, week 3 as outlined in the course description. In speaking of the "growth of the new art form" as one that goes from "novelty" to "crystallization," the description offers a quite standard notion of cinema's artistic evolution as a progressive refinement with mainstream narrative as its specific end point. At the same time, the reference to changes in commercial structure as "incidental" reiterates how the course fundamentally is offering an internal aesthetic history—the history of the evolution of specifically cinematic forms—with all other aspects of the history reduced to mere epiphenomenal forces that impact no more than contingently on the art's essential progress.

At the same time, this third class session at least appears to give some hint of an interplay of aesthetic form and commercial influence, whereas later sessions appear to isolate them from each other as autonomous realms whose natures can be analyzed in isolated purity. Thus, for instance, week 4 seems almost exclusively to concern itself with industrial and market developments, whereas week 6 returns to the internal history of film form ("the evolution of modern photoplay structure and screen syntax") even as it announces, with the first mention of proper names in the syllabus, the entrance of new forces onto the scene of film history—namely, the directorial auteur behind the screen and the actor appearing upon it. Increasingly, the structure of Ramsaye's course separates varying kinds of historical influence—commercial, formal, authorial—into their own inviolate realms.

Within Ramsaye's evolutionary schema, week 6, on the evolution of structure and syntax, is significant also in that it appears, on paper at least, as the last session (until the very final one) to be concerned primarily with issues of screen style and technique. From that point on, intervening weeks (until the wrap-up) deal more with external forces that impinge on films: public taste, market cycles, press coverage, propagandistic exploitation of film, film in education and laboratory research, censorship issues and film, and so on. It is as if the stylistic history of film stopped when it discovered narrative—or at the very latest when narrative reached its ultimate degree of refinement with D. W. Griffith. (In *A Million and One Nights*, Ramsaye presents Griffith as a veritable dividing line in the history of cinema. Up through *The Birth of a Nation*, his films concretized the virtues of narrative art, but with *Intolerance*, Griffith went beyond this salutary refinement of the form and into unbridled experimentation, and his cinema began to lose touch with popular consciousness.)

But for all the ways in which we can productively read Ramsaye's course description for its own historical argument, I think it takes on additional resonance when examined through the context of Ramsaye's writings, especially *A Million and One Nights*. For instance, the course's promise in the opening session to study the relation "of the motion picture to the field of expression, with consideration of the common ancestries of picture, language and drama" appears to indicate a fairly straightforward comparative perspective on cinema and the other arts. But when we consider the description in light of Ramsaye's own theory of artistic evolution, the comparativist perspective gains an additional and quite particular depth. For all the book's sheer fascination with details and curious anecdotes of film his-

tory, Ramsaye inscribed the narrative trajectory of *A Million and One Nights* within a very pointed and even quirky theory of art's origin and evolution.

In a prefatory section of *A Million and One Nights* entitled "The Prehistory of the Screen," Ramsaye offered an aesthetic appreciation of film within a philosophy of art history that was both regressive and progressive. On the one hand, although an art of the twentieth century, the cinema actually reached back through time to realize age-old dreams of representation. In Ramsaye's view, there was, from the dawn of humankind and driving it onward, a basic human desire to seek out pleasure, which then devolved into the wish to repeat that pleasure in the form of imaginative reconstruction and representation. From the mimicry of primitive men who tried to use their bodies to tell others of their experiences, to the cave drawings they came up with to produce less ephemeral records of those experiences, to the elaboration of language, humans endlessly strove for forms in which they could replay, and inform others of, the things in life to hunt after and the things to avoid. Human life, Ramsaye argued, was driven fundamentally by what he termed the Wish—the desire to return repeatedly to good experiences—and by the increasing realization that such repetition could be had through the ersatz forms of imaginative re-creation. A caveman could always relive the thrill of the killing of a bear by going out and killing another one, but he could also revive the frisson of the original event through the memories embodied in representational re-creation. Fundamental to the history of the arts, then, was a regressive Wish to return to primal pleasures.

On the other hand, Ramsaye's schema also was progressive in that his history of representation was one that boasted ever greater refinement of representational means. Over its history, humankind would come up with more effective means to re-create original pleasures. Thus, the painting on the cave wall might enable the painter to reproduce the best parts of an experience without the dangers and do so not only for himself but also for others, who could thereby participate vicariously in the re-creation. However, the cave image was fixed in one place and therefore limited in scope. Moreover, it was static. Language, in its abstraction from place and time, could overcome the drawbacks of the physically fixed drawing, but it could entail new limitations. For example, although language could be made vivid and visceral—through poetry and rhythm, through a vocabulary of direct action—it also had a countervailing tendency toward vagueness of reference, distance, and conceptual abstractness. At times, Ramsaye appeared to impute a bifurcation to the history of representational forms in which language veered away from the imagistic and the immediate, and in which other modes of representation had then to compensate by trying all the more directly to come back to the vivid rendition of experience. As Ramsaye put it in "The Prehistory of the Screen,"

> Let us consider written language as the off-shoot which became the greater stream for the current of ideas, leaving the now less important and obscured course of graphic art and picture making to go on its way with a diminished freight of thought. Drawing, painting, and sculpture survived and continued down the centuries, developing at times and borrowing back on occasion some refinement of ideas from the rushing new current of the written word and its abstract powers. (lxiii)

Verbal language had its own contributions to make to the history of representation, but it also entailed new problems. Specifically, insofar as words, abstracted from everyday experience, required a certain degree of translation from concept back to that experience, they could become alienating and divorce people from the world. They could lead to what T. S. Eliot, a few years before Ramsaye's book came out, had termed a "dissociation of sensibility" between word and corporeally felt experience. Language in such a case could become the province of an elite caste and cease to speak to and for the people: as Ramsaye put it, "[F]or very long periods the business of reading and writing was delegated to priests and slaves" (lxii). Dangerously, in the age of modernism, visual art was taking the abstraction of verbal communication as its model and abandoning direct representation of physical reality. In Ramsaye's words, "A vast deal of most profound foolishness about painting and sculpture has grown out of just such efforts and splashings. Every now and then we get all wet from the spray of such things as Cubism, Vorticism, and Futurism" (lxiii). Ramsaye was profoundly antimodernist and saw the experimental arts as engaging in a category error in their attempt to go beyond images to abstractions. Not for nothing did he see Griffith's attempt in *Intolerance* to experiment with large-scale arguments through editing as the point at which the once great director had begun to lose contact with his audience.

The flip side of Ramsaye's antimodernism, then, was a deeply felt populism. When it avoided the pretentious striving after the sort of conceptualism all too evident in *Intolerance,* the cinema, he argued, served as the most direct and visceral art form for the rendition of the Wish as re-creation of primary experience. The cinema came into being to provide motion and thereby fulfill the promise of the earliest of visual arts, such as the cave drawing. If it had taken centuries for the cinema to realize this fundamental Wish for representation, such delay was due merely to accidents and incidental factors—for example, the technology that would give life to images had not been available earlier. These contingent factors aside, the realization of the Wish through a great, popular art had in fact been inevitable. As Ramsaye asserted, "The motion picture was a great deal overdue many, many centuries ago" (xxxvii). But the very delay enabled it to clarify its powers while technology caught up with it. The delay, then, was propitious: "It is the very fact of the tardiness of the arrival of the screen which has resulted in this apparently miraculous growth and flowering into the magnitude which enables it [the motion picture] to claim position among the leading industries of the world" (xxxvii). Once the Wish had been installed as the driving force of humankind, everything that transpired in human history was merely contingent, merely the series of local events that sought to return to that Wish and give it potent form. The cinema was the end of that story. It was, as Ramsaye asserted emphatically, "the realization of the age-old Wish of the world" (xxxviii).

Ramsaye presented film, then, as the ultimate folk art, and he structured his history within a framework that was evolutionary in several respects. There was, first of all, the evolution of the arts out of the original primal Wish to commemorate pleasurable experience through representational means. The history of the arts was primarily the history of the improvement—for example, the addition of kinesis to static imagery—of the means of representation in order to make that commemoration all the more potent. Film bypassed the abstractions of words to offer the immediacy of images, but it also bypassed the stasis of drawings and photographs in order to make visuality come alive. In its immediacy and vitality, film could restore the sense and sensation of experience that had been alienated in the abstractions of the verbal.

But this conception of the large-scale evolution of the mission and medium of the arts, in which Ramsaye imagined cinema to be the ultimate realization of an age-old Wish, was concretized in another evolution, one as much geographic as temporal. For Ramsaye, the history of film was specifically an evolution from Europe to America (and then from the East Coast to Hollywood) as filmmakers firmly anchored in the vibrant and visceral experience of the American new land came to realize cinema's popular potential outside of European refinement. America's pioneer trajectory was replayed in the history of its film industry, which moved west to discover inspirations of land, action, direct energy, and vitality. And this westward evolution was then itself replayed in the trajectory of Ramsaye's own narrative account across the book's many pages: if early chapters of *A Million and One Nights* did give attention to European experimenters like Méliès, bit by bit these were edged out of the narrative, and the bulk of the book was given over to odes to the great American figures who realized cinema's essential popular and populist potential. It ended up offering the teleology of an essentially U.S.-governed destiny of cinema. Understandably, the advertisements for Ramsaye's book lauded it as a great contribution to "Americana."

In this respect, it is notable that the breakdown for Ramsaye's New School course likewise naturalizes a particularly American version of film history. Except for the reference in week 6 to the "influence of the magicians," which may be an acknowledgment of the early contribution of the European Méliès, among others, Ramsaye's inquiry "for the first time, into the history, structure and functions of the motion picture as an art and as an industry," as the syllabus put it, resolutely and virtually exclusively figured that history in U.S. terms.

Ramsaye's own adherence to an evolutionary schema based on historical inevitability no doubt would enable him to respond to the charge that he was offering a biased history. History, he could retort, was as it was—it had necessarily happened in this way and not another—and the historian had but to be faithful to that history as it unfolded. Revealingly, when Ramsaye made his declaration that the motion picture was "the realization of the age-old Wish of the world," he immediately followed it with the modest avowal that "[t]his is not said in glorification of the picture, but is offered *as fact* based on all of the significance of Wishing" (xxxviii; my emphasis). Ramsaye claimed to remain ever the journalist, serving simply as the literally matter-of-fact medium through which history was conveyed. As he recounted it in the last page of his preface to *A Million and One Nights*, "Twenty-one years ago Charles I. Blood, city editor of *The Kansas City Times* called me, a timid novitiate, to the desk for my first assignment. 'There has been a shooting in the West Bottoms,' he said. 'Go find out who did it, when he did it, why he did it, and who he did it to—and that will be a story.'" It was thus Ramsaye's very background as a journalist ostensibly merely reporting the facts with disinterested objectivity that allowed him to write his Americanist history. Obviously, though, Ramsaye was shaping his history in pointed fashion. For instance, one reads *A Million and One Nights* in vain for any reference to the growing currents of European modernism that suggested different options for the future of world cinema at the end of the silent period. To take just one example, Wiene's *Cabinet of Dr. Caligari* was increasingly gaining attention from an American intelligentsia interested in the ways screen experimentation might transform the cinema into an art of modernist ambition comparable to others, but there is no discussion of the film in Ramsaye's volume.

Certainly, as he closed his vast narrative, having made little mention of European film (let alone cinemas from beyond the United States and Europe) in the previous four hundred pages, Ramsaye signaled the larger global story of film with a few quick paragraphs on production trends on the Continent, or what he termed the growing "internationalization" of the film business. But, in fact, Ramsaye could speak of "internationalization" in the last pages only insofar as he had already co-opted and rewritten the process in primarily Americanist terms. Insofar as American cinema realized an essential wish that predated the emergence of the American nation, America itself was ultimately little more than a propitious vehicle for forces and energies that ultimately exceeded national provenance. The narratives in American films may have had their material origin in the national context, but they bore resonances of theme and story that went beyond that context to speak to the world. Both in the films themselves and in the background of the creative figures who made them, American cinema was, for Ramsaye, already a cinema of universal appeal and reach. As Ramsaye put it in his article for the *Annals of the American Acàdemy of Political and Social Science*, "The motion picture of the United States is international merchandise, dominating the world market, and it is under the control of the most effective race of born internationalists" (15). Not only were the moguls who came to run Hollywood a group of immigrants who possessed awareness of the cultures and values of the old country, but in the space of the new country, they set out to make works that appealed to immigrant audiences similar to them in background and old-world taste. In this fashion, their films, made in America with often decidedly indigenous American features, spoke as well to old-world concerns. Writing of the waves of immigration in the United States since the end of the nineteenth century, Ramsaye thus argued:

> Too poor to import or support their varied national arts, theatres, and literatures, and often too lowly in culture to enjoy these arts had they been available, these polyglottic aliens offered a ripe opportunity for the art of the motion picture with its simple, basic, direct and obvious narratives, embodying no linguistic difficulties and no problems of intellectualization. . . . The films were made for them, an American-born art nurtured on the tastes, codes and cultures of an imported labor population. (11)

Ironically, one can as readily imagine such words coming from the mouths of the castigators of Hollywood populism, for whom the nonintellectual and democratic appeal of the movies might have been cause for aesthetic condemnation. For example, only four years later, in "Mass Civilization and Minority Culture," the English critic F. R. Leavis would issue his call for a return of culture to an elite caste of aesthetic legislators able to promote the best that has been thought and said. For Leavis, the cinema by its very nature was a menace to art. He agreed that a dissociation of sensibility in modern times had cut high art off from the rabble, but his answer was not to bring such art back to the people but to make it ever more pure and isolated from the taint of popular reception. As Leavis saw it, the crowds who were able to find diversion in cinema were, by definition, inadequate to the demands of artistic discrimination, and true culture needed to be kept from them. It might be regrettable that modernist experimentation in art could not speak organically to the masses, but it would be all the more regrettable were such art, for purposes of mass acceptability, to be watered down, to lose its edge and be made available to the wrong people.

In contrast, it was integral to Ramsaye's affirmative philosophy of film that it be an art of *mass reproduction*, since, for him, film was an essentially *democratic* art whose vocation was to reach the maximum number of ordinary people and give vivid representation to their fundamental (and ultimately not very complicated) Wish for pleasure. Populism was an essential component of Ramsaye's evolutionary schema. For example, the history of the motion picture was, among other things, the story of the impulse to make art more accessible through increased possibilities for the widespread and large-scale viewing of images. Over the course of his book, Ramsaye's extended descriptions of the arcana of various experiments in large-screen projection might seem overly technical detours from the larger history, but they actually serve that history: in Ramsaye's account, for instance, the peephole technologies of devices like the kinetoscope were inadequate in their undemocratic restrictions of spectatorship to one viewer, and they had necessarily to give way to the motion picture's ever more democratic and inevitable advance toward large-screen projection. For Ramsaye, the motion picture's popularity, far from being a problem, was the source of its aesthetic value. Ramsaye's populism would encourage criticism of him as an apologist for the Hollywood system. For example, the European writer Paul Rotha, in his rival history *The Film Till Now,* written a few years later, would take a much more modernist-inflected position and offer biting condemnation of Ramsaye's celebration of the popular movie theater as precisely not, in Ramsaye's words, "a place of controversy, of consideration, of issues, of thinking," all of which Rotha militated for.[6]

But, as we have seen, Ramsaye's assertion of his journalistic role as merely the neutral, objective, transmitting medium for an essential, natural, and inevitable history of cinema meant that he refused the charge of apologist for Hollywood. Ramsaye was often at pains to argue that he was in no way a stooge, paid or not, for the Hollywood system. Thus, when the (generally quite favorable) *New York Times* review of *A Million and One Nights* by Evelyn Gerstein referred to him as "a wise-cracking, sentimental, undeluded child of Hollywood," Ramsaye objected strongly in a letter to the editor: "I can forgive the adjectives, but when it comes to that 'child of Hollywood,' I must observe that those are fighting words. When a stranger calls me that I want to see the smile that should go with it. If in truth I am a 'child of Hollywood' it was by immaculate conception. Anyway, I have spent but one month in Hollywood."[7] Likewise, in the preface to *A Million and One Nights*, Ramsaye made emphatic declaration of his having freed himself of all direct connections to Hollywood for the writing of the volume.

Insofar as Ramsaye's faith in history's essential teleology was naturalized in the assumption that what happened in history inevitably had to happen as it did, his analysis of the Hollywood system clearly imagined it as the necessary end point of motion picture history. Hollywood realized Art's teleology. It is noteworthy, for instance, how the end of Ramsaye's *Annals* article seemed to set up the stereotypical opposition of art and commerce only to then rewrite the seeming opposition as a case of mutual enhancement. In a first move, Ramsaye noted the extent to which industry issues dominated contemporary filmmaking: "The motion picture institution is primarily an industry. Its development as an art has been and will continue to depend on occasion, accidental and incidental experimental endeavors without important encouragement from the major interests which are operating a dividend machine" (19). In a second move, however, he clarified that while some advances in screen technique might be hampered by business conservatism, it was the current configuration of the film industry that best enabled cinema to achieve its most perfect state as popular culture: "The plain truth is that the art of the motion picture today has reached the ceiling of popular understanding, and further elaboration and refinement as a medium of expression cannot increase the screen audience in any proportion commensurate with the increased investment" (19).

Indeed, for Ramsaye, the very attempt to consciously make of cinema a high art and thereby to raise people's skills in aesthetic discrimination could only be a betrayal of film's natural vocation to speak to people as they were (such, indeed, had happened with Griffith's turn to modernism in *Intolerance*). Any conscious intention to turn the movies into Art artificially forced the motion picture away from its natural proclivities. As Ramsaye asserted in the *Annals* essay, "The production of pictures for the cognoscenti, the literati, and the illuminati, cannot be profitable in terms comparable with the pictures for the masses" (19).

Not surprisingly, then, the last pages of *A Million and One Nights* took the current political economy of Hollywood filmmaking as the logical and necessary end point of cinema history. Where some other writers of the time assumed Hollywood's practices to entail deleterious effects,[8] Ramsaye presented those practices as natural. As he declared, "The motion picture industry is controlled by entirely automatic forces of growth by which it is evolving increasingly complex specimens of the so-called vertical trust," and, again, he presented this as a process that required neither celebration nor condemnation on the part of the observer, but mere acceptance: "Everything that grows grows the same way. Nobody can do anything about it" (831). Just as the organic objects of nature contained within their genes everything they would evolve into, every new realm that the movie business set out to conquer was an inevitable part of its own organic being. Just as the "tree elaborate[d] its organic processes complete from soil to nuts," so too it was natural that the Hollywood moguls try to annex to themselves all aspects of the production-distribution-exhibition cycle and make them part of a single, controlled process. "Business," as Ramsaye bluntly put it, "is business" (831).

One has to wonder how well this narrative of American big business as the necessary conclusion to motion picture history fit the curriculum of the New School for Social Research. Ramsaye's populist, Americanist, and industry-oriented approach to film art simultaneously connects with and diverges from the philosophy of culture and education that the New School increasingly devoted itself to in the 1920s. On the one hand, the very desire to laud the ways in which an art might resonate democratically with the people fit in with the school's emphasis on popular education and on a pragmatic desire—inspired by one of its key sources of pedagogical principle, John Dewey—to reach citizens where they were situated, intellectually and emotionally. On the other hand, the New School clearly set out to be a cosmopolitan beacon that, as a New York institution, could assemble, synthesize, and radiate outward the vast dimensions of a modern thought and culture that exceeded any particular national context. In this respect, the school was especially open to currents of European experimentation and often provided venues for avant-garde artists to show off their work before an audience curious about advanced cultural endeavor. Revealingly, as noted earlier, Ramsaye's course was listed in the 1926 catalog just after one by *New Republic* intellectual Waldo Frank on modern art. With guest lectures by such pulse takers of the new spirit of the age as Edmund Wilson, Norman Bel Geddes, Alfred Stieglitz, and John Howard Lawson, among others, Frank's course promised to "examine modern art as a potential and still very immature expression of a fundamental change in man's way of thinking and living." Like Ramsaye, Frank believed that America was capable of indigenous artistry: in the teens, he had been one of the founders of the influential journal *Seven Arts,* which argued for a recognition both of homegrown American experimentation in the arts and of the need to give serious attention to the new art of cinema. Likewise, just a few years after his New School experience, he would write an influential volume entitled *The Rediscovery of America,* also a celebration of American arts, both popular and experimental. Frank, in fact, was a key participant in what cultural historians have come to label "America's coming of age," a term that refers to America's evolution of a rich, defensible culture of its own, separate from the European cultures that clearly constituted its backdrop of influence. In critics ranging from H. L. Mencken to Constance Rourke to Van Wyck Brooks to Gilbert Seldes, the search was for a usable indigenous tradition of the arts.

But Frank assumed both that such artistry would be born from creative experimentation with conventions, rather than acceptance of them, and that American creativity could only benefit from contact with European currents. (Frank was a voracious reader of European literature.) Although their emplacement one after the other on the same page was no doubt accidental, the contrast between Ramsaye's populist approach to an art he saw as overwhelmingly American and Frank's modernist approach, which viewed art as an intersection of multiple and international aesthetic currents, was pronounced. In many ways, Frank's liberal openness to modern art would have been much more in keeping with the New School's cosmopolitan leanings. Significantly, the following year, Ramsaye's course disappeared from the catalog, while Frank's offering now made explicit room for cinema in relation to both American and European traditions: in the words of the 1927–28 catalog description for his course on modern art, "Much attention will be given to the modern art of America, to preeminent American forms, such as the cinema, the photograph, jazz, commercial arts, etc.; and to the ultra aesthetic movements of Europe—constructivism, neo-classicism, surréelisme [sic], futurism, etc."

But one perhaps should not make too much of this. Whatever the fit or not of Ramsaye's pedagogy with the cosmopolitan liberalism of the New School, the very public nature of the art that his lecture series dealt with in popular fashion might have been an attraction, especially in this period where the school was clearly trying to draw a larger clientele to its programs. Ramsaye returned at least once in 1928 to give a single lecture on motion pictures, and in the winter of 1931, he again entered into plans to offer a series of twelve lectures at the school. This time, however, he was to be joined in the course by other speakers, rather than having the podium to himself.

The course catalog describes the proposed 1931 course as follows:

> Course No. 40. The Moving Picture—Mr. Ramsaye and others. Twelve lectures beginning January 8. Thursdays, 5:20–6:50 P.M. $15.00
>
> In spite of its vast popular following, the moving picture is in its infancy, both as an art and as an instrument of education. The conditions of its production have led to an excessive concentration upon a relatively small number of items of wide appeal. Nevertheless many things have been done in the movies that are highly interesting and instructive. This course represents essentially a stock-taking of achievements down to the present time, with a view to discovering the possibilities of the future. Every talk will be illustrated by actual moving picture material to give concreteness to the points of art or technique discussed.

The course appears to have been either canceled or presented by someone other than Ramsaye (the record is unclear). Several letters that Ramsaye exchanged with New School administrators as he was finalizing plans for the course provide a partial explanation.[9]

In a letter of October 2, 1930, to the New School's director, Alvin Johnson, Ramsaye indicated that he had been in touch with Will Hays and was counting on the MPPDA director for major assistance in securing guest lecturers from the film industry and in convincing them to come. Perhaps his confidence in Hays's ability to land important speakers led Ramsaye to decide to lessen his own role in the class. It seems that in early October, after his contact with Hays, he also wrote to the New School's dean, Horace Kallen, to ask permission to organize the class but *not* to lecture in it. Kallen had to insist in a tough letter of October 6, 1930, that Ramsaye "have a definite personal share in it [the course]," suggesting as a compromise that Ramsaye give the opening and closing lectures. Ambitiously, Kallen suggested also that stenographers be present at all the lectures so that a record of them could be made into a book. Clearly, for Kallen, who had long been a fan of the movies, there was hope that the lecture series might have a major and visible impact.

But the plans fell apart, and by December, Alvin Johnson was threatening to replace Ramsaye completely, a possibility the film historian appeared in fact to relish. Clearly, he wanted out. In a December 16, 1930, letter to Kallen, he was explicit: "Where I sit now, the whole project has a bilious aspect. Frankly, I am so damn tired that I would much rather go into my carpentry shop and whittle, than I would be a scintillating success in any forum circus." He argued that his current job responsibilities (he was now working for the Pathé film company) were consuming his energies, and he did not have time for the course. Most interestingly, he also referred to the "failure of the first effort towards a series of lectures on the motion picture at the New School two or three years ago," the only direct commentary we have on Ramsaye's earlier lecture series from 1927. (Kallen forwarded the letter to Johnson with a cover note explaining that Ramsaye was worried, too, that he might not get a big enough audience for the lecture series. Might this be what had happened with the 1927 course?)

On December 18, 1930, Ramsaye wrote to Will Hays to end his involvement in the saga: "Because I was unable to get the cooperation that I had hoped for from the motion picture industry in connection with the projected series of lectures at the New School for Social Research, I today decided not to give the course, and so notified Mr. Alvin Johnson, the director."

It is unclear if the course was canceled. Kallen suggested in a note to Johnson that they try to get as a replacement the critic Evelyn Gerstein (who had reviewed Ramsaye's *Million and One Nights* a few years earlier). Given Kallen and Johnson's evident interest in having a big course with famous lecturers—and given the fact that failure to land such lecturers was one of the reasons Ramsaye desisted from teaching the course—it is likely that the 1931 offering did not see the light of day. Significantly, though, the school offered another general film course only a year and a half later. In the fall semester of 1932, Marxist critic Harry Alan Potamkin began teaching his class Lands, Films and Critics. This course will be described in more detail in chapter 5, but here it is worth noting the extent to which, in academic intent at least, Potamkin would seem a much more appropriate choice for the New School than Terry Ramsaye. Having gone to Europe at an early age to study avant-garde art, Potamkin had a strong investment in cosmopolitan currents of artistic experimentation that would have fit in with the New School of the 1930s, which increasingly was home to intellectual migrants from European fascism. Likewise, Potamkin had strong leftist politics that also would have found welcome at the New School during the cultural front of the 1930s. However, Potamkin took ill and passed away in 1933 at the age of thirty-three, and his course disappeared after one semester. Film pedagogy would return to the New School only in the final years of the 1930s, when a production course and a general history course began to be offered on a regular basis. I will return briefly to these in the context of Potamkin's ill-fated venture at the school as discussed in chapter 5.

3 "Younger Art, Old College, Happy Union"

Harvard Goes into the Business and Art of the Movies

> When some future historian pens a sequel to [Terry Ramsaye's] "A Million and One Nights" we doubt if anything which he chronicles concerning the year 1927 will stand above the fact that on that date the motion picture was given official recognition as a business and as an art by the oldest university in America.
>
> NEW YORK MOTION PICTURE NEWS, April 15, 1927

On March 21, 1927, H. R. Hunt, a professor of zoology and geology at Michigan State College (and a Harvard class of 1916 graduate), addressed a letter to A. Lawrence Lowell, the current president of Harvard. Hunt inquired: "Do moving pictures and vaudeville shows in very close proximity to a college or university have the effect of tempting students to attend them to the extent that their scholarship suffers? We have never had a moving picture show in this town but one is scheduled to arrive soon. I would like to get your opinion on the matter as based on your own personal observations." On March 23, President Lowell addressed his reply: "We tried to keep a moving picture theatre away from the vicinity of the Harvard College as long as we could; but as the land could be bought, there was no possibility of doing it indefinitely, and finally one was set up here about a year ago. I do not know that the scholarship of the students has noticeably suffered, but the thing is undesirable, and a midnight performance specially designed to attract students a few weeks ago brought on a collision with the police,—the fault, I think, almost wholly of the police, but in any case regrettable."[1] The matter-of-factness of Lowell's condemnation is striking. With no evidence that moviegoing influenced student performance, and even though the late-night contretemps seems to have been the fault of the police, still he knew that the movies were "undesirable." This, we might imagine, would be a typical attitude of an Ivy League administrator to the popular art of cinema, which he would perhaps view as a corruptive assault on everything institutions of higher learning held dear.

It is somewhat ironic, then, that in the very month that Lowell was offering his advice on the dangers of the movies, his own university was sponsoring a series of lectures on the business of motion pictures. In an evident coup, Harvard alumnus Joseph P. Kennedy, who had fairly recently entered the movie business, had convinced some of its luminaries to travel to Cambridge to speak as part of a business policy course whose standard procedure was to have officials of various industries present typical problems and typical solutions they dealt with in their operations. Over a period of several weeks, such figures as Will Hays, Jesse Lasky, Adolph Zukor, Cecil B. DeMille, William Fox, Marcus Loew, and Harry M. Warner, among others, came one by one to Harvard's Graduate School of Business Administration (hereafter HSB, for Harvard School of Business) to recount their experiences growing up with the film industry and preparing it for a future as one of America's biggest businesses.

President Lowell knew about the lecture series and even met privately with Will Hays during his lecture trip to the university. But in an increasingly bureaucratized academia, a university president's involvement in any specific campus initiative was, as we have seen, becoming ever more muted, and it is perhaps not so surprising that Lowell could simultaneously welcome a lecture series in film and yet be wary of the movies in comments elsewhere. At work quite likely was a sheer ability—increasingly necessary in university administrators—to compartmentalize.

To the extent that we can grant it credence, there is a revealing example of administrative indifference to, rather than, say, high-culture dismissal of, the idea of film at Harvard in an article planted in the *Boston Transcript* in April 1927. The article was intended to publicize two aspects of the university's newfound attention to film: the recent completion of the HSB film lecture series *and* the fine arts department's creation of an annual award program to recognize twelve or so American films for their artistic accomplishments and which then commemorated them in a library-archive. Both initiatives were presented as signs of Harvard's interest in keeping up with the times—in appearing modern by dealing with a most modern form of cultural production. The article, though, depicted President Lowell as matter-of-fact about the project. Though the degree of historical rewriting is unclear, the article explained that after the professors and staff interested in the annual film award idea met for the first time and decided to proceed, they set out to gauge the administration's possible interest: "The attitude of the whole group was one of unqualified enthusiasm, but they wanted to know what President Lowell would think, so Professor Sachs and Professor Post for the Fine Arts Department saw him in a few days and he said, 'All right.'" The president's taciturnity is the point here: whether the moral of the story is his quickness at decision, his being too busy to mull things over, or his relative lack of interest one way or the other in the question, the lesson is that initiatives such as this were enacted without much oversight from the higher administration. By means of his terse "All right," Lowell could allow film as art to drop off his radar and get on with the rest of the business of university administration.

It is tempting to imagine that all of Harvard was abuzz at the prospect of its film course. In fact, however, one of the most curious aspects of the welcoming of film into the venerable ivory tower world of Harvard is that it seemed not to be curious to most people at the time. Quite the contrary, there was readiness in both the film industry and the Ivy League institution to imagine that they could indeed work together. It is revealing that in the very period that would witness the coming of sound to the American motion picture—certainly an occurrence, we might argue, of momentous occasion for the film industry—the *New York Motion Picture News*, in the epigraph to this chapter, could enthusiastically imagine the Harvard projects to be *the most noteworthy event in cinema history* for that year. For the most part, the entrance of the moguls into the hallowed halls of academia occurred smoothly and expeditiously.

Negative reaction to the idea of a film lecture series at Harvard was sparse indeed. One rare caution came in the form of a January 24, 1927, letter to Dean Donham from Mr. Eugene Webster, the principal of the University School in Boston, who had seen an announcement of the series and was protesting the morality of the film people invited to lecture. In Webster's words, "Dear Prof. Donham, No one probably objects to lectures being given at your school on Motion Pictures. But if I remember correctly, two or three of the men whose names are on the enclosed clipping were once notoriously associated with a most immoral carousing at an ill-famed 'Manor' a few years ago. If that was so, they would naturally feel honored to be invited to lecture at Harvard. Does Harvard honor herself by calling these men to her platforms?" As amusing perhaps is Donham's dry reply of January 28: "Thank you for your letter of January 24. We hope that the results of the lectures on the motion picture industry in the Harvard Graduate School of Business Administration will prove in every way satisfactory." (The letter's reference to "immoral carousing" had to do with a Massachusetts roadhouse party attended by a number of film business moguls that got out of hand, and which the moguls attempted to cover up through large money payments. Newspapers got wind of it, however, and it even got recorded for posterity in Terry Ramsaye's important history, *A Million and One Nights*.[2] It is no small irony that the party had been thrown for the actor Fatty Arbuckle, who would soon have his career destroyed at another, even more infamous wild party in San Francisco.)

If Donham could brush off Webster's reference to this event—one Harvard archivist told me the dean's reply was typical Harvard style: concede nothing, always maintain a position of superiority—far more threatening was a detailed reference to the party in a January 1929 letter to President Lowell from William Marston Seabury. A former film industry lawyer, Seabury had become dismayed by what he saw as the unethical practices of the business, and in 1926 he had published a virulent denunciation of the industry, *The Public and the Motion Picture Industry*. His letter to Lowell coincided with his initial steps to create a research enterprise to study the film business in all its detail so as to prove its perfidy: these steps were the very start of the (in)famous Payne Fund Studies of the 1930s in which major social scientists investigated the effects of movies on everyday Americans, especially children.[3]

In five vitriolic pages, Seabury attacked Harvard for daring to offer an industry-sponsored course on the film business. In his view, industry leaders had proved themselves to be unethical, deceitful, corrupt, and even criminal. Undoubtedly they were using the course as public relations propaganda. In his words, "[T]here is reason to believe that the plan, so far as the motion picture industry is concerned, is simply another means for the exploitation of individual leaders in the industry and a further opportunity to mislead the public." As Seabury saw it, the movie industry had already demonstrated its ability to lie convincingly to the public, and now it was attempting to do the same with the supposedly more perceptive members of the academic community: "The industry's effort to fog and muddle the educators of the country, as they have so successfully misled the ignorant public and uninformed public welfare societies, is of comparatively recent origin." Seabury even cited Columbia's proposed film curriculum of 1927 as an earlier sign of academia's ability to sell out its principles to the immoral leaders of the film business. Noting that Columbia president Nicholas Murray Butler had in the past voiced some criticism of cinema but had later come to support the new curriculum, Seabury asserted that the industry's sponsorship of academic film study had in that case served to buy Butler's fidelity to its corrupt principles. Based on this past record, Seabury worried for Harvard's reputation: "It would be a pity to have the prestige of Harvard as one of our greatest national institutions in its field impaired by the affrontry [sic] and pretense of this venal institution." He ended with the strong caution that the course would besmirch "Harvard's traditional dignity and intelligence."

Harvard appears to have taken Seabury's letter seriously. The university secretary, James Seymour, went to work, going through the letter paragraph by paragraph to offer a rebuttal to each of Seabury's points. Certainly, Seabury had set himself up for easy rebuttal by the sheer shrillness of his attack: for example, with implicit anti-Semitism, he had noted that the majority of industry leaders were foreign born, a point that Seymour could easily and bluntly dismiss as "irrelevant." It is clear, however, that although Seabury's rant was clearly something the university felt it had to confront, it had already decided in advance to welcome the film industry into its ranks. Seymour's point-by-point analysis of Seabury's screed conceded nothing and argued that the very purpose of the HSB course was to provide the sort of basic information on the film industry that might help confirm its rational and moral operations. For example, where Seabury had called for "intelligent and painstaking study and thorough examination of this potentially great industry by competent educators, economists, and publicists without interference or supposed aid from the industry," Seymour confidently declared, "This the course will attempt to do, but will seek the cooperation and 'aid' of all interested persons who know the facts." Where Seabury worried that Harvard might be seduced and corrupted by the film industry, Seymour contended that the great university would always be master of the situation: "If the industry as Mr. Seabury says deserves investigating, then a careful survey and study of its methods and growth by a university, with, in Mr. Seabury's words, 'Harvard's traditional dignity and intelligence' should be of value. It is with this in mind that the lectures were instituted as the beginning of a complete study of the industry."

It is unclear if Seymour's notes led to a letter of response actually sent to Seabury or if they remained an internal document by which Harvard could show itself that it knew how to dismiss the arguments of upstarts who might criticize Harvard ventures. When Seabury asserted that the "instrument [of the movies] is one of world wide importance," Seymour indicated that the point was "gladly admitted," and it seems clear that the university welcomed the chance to attend to this modern cultural form.

"Younger Art, Old College, Happy Union": I take the title for this chapter from the heading for the aforementioned plant in the *Boston Transcript* that extolled Harvard's efforts to bring attention to film into the Ivy League. Both the wording and the idea it conveys are significant in several respects. First, that the American movie business was getting attention from that most seemingly staid and established of Ivy League institutions was itself noteworthy. That Harvard could welcome the study of film stands as an intriguing event in the early intervention of academia into the pedagogy of cinema. As we saw earlier, another Ivy League school, Columbia University, had also been involved in at least two initiatives in film from the 1910s on: the ongoing extension course Photoplay Composition, an admittedly marginalized venture, and the (eventually abandoned) plan of 1926–27 to create a film school. In the case of the latter initiative and Harvard's own in the same moment, Will Hays appears to have taken a key role in the organization and implementation of the pedagogy. No doubt, Hays saw both the practical advantage of trained professionals provided to the film industry by top schools *and* the public relations benefit of associating cinema with the cultured respectability of the Ivy League.

To be sure, the Harvard initiative differed in a number of respects from that undertaken at Columbia. Above all, it offered a much less ambitious attempt to find a place for film within university curricula—not an entire major but a single course, albeit a boldly organized one with a full, and to this day still impressive, roster of film industry luminaries. It is a mark of Joseph Kennedy's growing influence within the movie business that he was able to convince so many important figures to fit the visit to Harvard into their busy schedules. In fact, in the case of the very ill Marcus Loew, president of MGM, the trip was undertaken against his doctor's advice, and he died soon afterward. As for the other executives, not merely would they have to make a special trip outside the normal pathways of their business, but a number of them would be doing so in a context in which their lack of formal education might have seemed to be on the line. Indeed, several speakers admitted they were both flattered and intimidated by the invitation to speak at perhaps the most venerable American institution of higher learning.

Like the 1926–27 Columbia curriculum, however, the Harvard initiative of 1927 did not survive the initial confluence of interests that worked to bring it into being. Although there were clear plans at Harvard to make the study of film a regular part of the HSB curriculum, the lecture series was never to be repeated, and attention to film would show up at Harvard in only sporadic ways in the years immediately after 1927.

The early Harvard initiative in cinema created no consequential legacy for film study (although the volume published from the course lectures, *The Story of the Films*, is a wonderfully rich lode of firsthand accounts of the state of the film business in 1927 by some of its most famous figures).[4] Even within Harvard, for all the openness with which administrators and faculty in the concerned departments of business and fine arts seemed to welcome film into their domains, the study of motion pictures was isolated both from the rest of the curriculum and from the intellectual mission of the university as a whole. If, eventually, the film industry in 1927 had other things (such as the coming of sound) to think about besides film at Harvard, so too did both the faculty and administrators of the School of Business and the School of Fine Arts. As has so often been true with regard to film industry overtures toward academia, a great deal of excitement at the outset seems to have been followed by a waning of enthusiasm. As with the Columbia project of 1926–27, it would appear that there was less a sudden cessation of attention to the Harvard initiative than a gradual trailing off of interest. The projects simply died out.

Here, it is important to note that one benefit Harvard University clearly hoped to gain from affiliation with film industry executives for the HSB course and the fine arts annual award concerned revenues and resources. Importantly, the lecture series came about because Joseph Kennedy promised to underwrite an HSB pedagogy in film (and related research activities). To the extent that the university assumed film pedagogy would become a regular part of the curriculum—and would thereby continue to receive funding from Kennedy (and perhaps from other studio executives)—it was no doubt easy for administrators to be enthused about course content in film. Likewise, the Fogg Art Museum plan for an annual award for best films also promised to bring resources into the university: at the very least, for example, there would be the valuable prints of films. But, as we will see, it quickly became apparent that neither Kennedy in particular nor the film industry as a whole had a long-term commitment to film at Harvard University, and little in the way of resources flowed into the university. Indeed, bit by bit during these years, Kennedy's overall commitment to film per se waned as he made a major financial killing in the industry and appears to have decided that he had gotten enough benefit from this one business and needed to turn his attentions elsewhere. Kennedy, specifically, had been instrumental in the plans that put together RKO in 1927, and he profited mightily from his efforts. That deal accomplished, he began to minimize his involvement in the film business.[5] Unfortunately, this included his not being forthcoming about moneys owed to Harvard for course expenses he had promised to cover, and the university had to keep after him into the 1930s to fulfill his commitment. In the meantime, both the Fogg Art Museum initiative and the plan to offer ongoing instruction in the business of film were left to die out.

Significantly, the phrase "Younger Art, Old College" had another, specific resonance in the case of the HSB, and here the conjunction of old and new was even more fraught. When the business school was starting out, President Lowell had to come up with a phrase to imprint on the diplomas of graduating students and decided on one that would refer to business as "the oldest of the arts and the youngest of the professions." The intention, it seems, was to emphasize that business pedagogy was not abandoning principles of liberal education for crass vocationalism but was maintaining continuity with the goals of higher learning. Certainly, the university would increasingly admit professionalism into its curriculum, but it would try to temper vocational training with an artistry and general sense of humanistic inquiry based on venerable traditions of intellectual quest. However, Lowell's attempt was met with a certain degree of derision on the part of both the business and the academic community (not the least cause of which was the fact that "the youngest of the professions" seemed an unintended inversion of "the oldest profession"—i.e., prostitution!).[6] If the program of study came off as too academic, it would run the risk of seeming irrelevant to the business community. Conversely, if the program overemphasized professional success, it risked appearing as a betrayal of the fundamental *disinterested* higher mission of the academy. Indeed, a few years after the HSB's founding, Thorstein Veblen, in his classic *Higher Learning in America* (1918), would view business schools as a particularly egregious symptom of the surrender of universities to pragmatic concerns outside their basic humanistic purview. Likewise, in his famous report on the state of higher education, *Universities: American, English, German* (1930), Abraham Flexner would single out the HSB for opprobrium as a betrayal of the modern university's mission of pure and higher research. Revealingly, Flexner turned the rhetoric of the "oldest" of institutions directly against the HSB: "The Harvard Business School raises neither ethical nor social questions. . . . This is not only to waste cultural opportunities; it is unimaginative and short-sighted from the sheer business point of view. In precisely the same base and narrow spirit does this pretentious graduate school of America's oldest and still on the whole greatest university deal with advertising 'as a tool to be used in the promotion of sales.' Does the course in advertising raise any real questions? Not at all."[7] The question of the HSB film course—how to make the cinema industry a legitimate object of study?—was to a degree a local version of the larger questions the HSB itself confronted as a school: How to teach professional and practical skills in ways that would not appear to deny the higher humanistic mission of the university?

A striking expression of the sentiment that deep humanistic education and interest in the movies might make strange bedfellows—and might indeed be rivals for the minds of modern citizens—appeared in a Harvard publication just before the HSB film course began. In the fall of 1926 (the semester, that is, before the course was offered), a Harvard alumnus, Frank Cole Babbitt, who had bachelor's, master's, and doctoral degrees, all from the university, and who was now a professor of Greek at Trinity College, Connecticut, published a short article on the dangers of the movies in the *Harvard Graduates' Magazine*. For today's film scholars enamored of French film theorist Jean-Louis Baudry's famous comparison, from 1975, of the dark of the movie theater to Plato's cave, Babbitt's little tale, entitled "Plato and the Movies," is a veritable archaeological find as he makes virtually the same comparison as Baudry and draws similar conclusions.[8] For Babbitt, film, as a visually immediate medium, has the power to insinuate itself deep into the psyche and thereby substitute seductive, misleading fantasy for a profound and meaningful engagement with reality. The movies are a menace, all the more so since they work their magic at the level of the unconscious, rather than in a rational sphere where they could be held at a distance and judged effectively. In many ways, Babbitt's condemnation of the movies seems typical of a frequent and enduring intellectual, and often specifically academic, disdain for imagistic, affective, pre- or nonrational modes of cultural production.

Hovering between fiction and autobiography, Babbitt's piece is a first-person account in which the narrator explains to his daughter Margaret why he does not attend today's moving picture shows (although he admits he went to some in the first days of cinema). As he declares, "I am spoiled because I once read Plato's account of the effect that moving pictures have on people." Taking *The Republic* down from the shelf and reading out loud the allegory of the cave, he goes on to explain, "Plato has conceived the equivalent of all these elements [lighting, photography, moving picture machine, phonograph] although, of course, his approach was pretty crude and cumbersome" (20). For Babbitt, Plato's allegory of citizens chained in darkness and forced to submit to insubstantial and unreal images that flit before them presents a case of enslavement to spectacle quite similar to the ways the cinema offers ersatz versions of life that fall far short of the real thing. As Margaret admits to her father, "Why, he got all the machinery of a movie there just as you said. I shall never go to a movie again without thinking of the theatre as a big cave" (21).

But Margaret does think she has found at least one distinction between the Platonic allegory and the specificities of moviegoing: no one, she tries to argue with her father, literally is chained at the movies, and spectators have the freedom to attend or not (indeed, her father willfully has chosen to stop going to picture shows). But once again, her father has an answer: as he explains—and here he strikingly anticipates Baudry's argument that the setup of film spectatorship is like the operations of ideology, with the physical apparatus of film projection and reception mirrored in the mental apparatus of the spectator—there are forms of enslavement other than the physical, and the movies operate by means of an emotional compulsion that weaves an inescapable spell over those weak enough to drift into its orbit. Film's spectacle ensnares the rapt spectator in a no less gripping fashion than the chains that bind Plato's viewing subjects. Margaret is convinced by the argument. "Why," she declares, "the people never take their eyes off of the screen, so perhaps it might be said that they are in bonds while the pictures are on. . . . Perhaps we are enslaved after all" (22). She concludes with a lesson that is both Platonic in its general suspicion of images and typical of the specific hierarchies of value and moral benefit that guardians of classic taste often upheld (and continue to uphold) against specifically popular arts such as cinema: "Plato means that if we could drag people away from the movies . . . [t]hey might go on to understand something about life, and people's relations and duties to one another, which they never seem to think of now except in the narrowest sort of way" (24).

Perhaps more than the willingness of, say, the Harvard fine arts division to recognize great accomplishments in film, it is the condemnation of movies from a position of classic humanism, such as Babbitt defends, that has often seemed to characterize the predictable response of intellectuals to popular culture. For someone like Frank Cole Babbitt, there was nothing positive to be said about the movies. If the early study of film is best seen as a series of episodes in which a few academics found themselves responding positively to the movies as a means to enable citizens to wend their way through the complicated cultural space of modernity, it is also necessary to remember the historical resistance to cinema—and popular culture more generally—that has also been an enduring part of the academic enterprise.

As we have seen, some early film pedagogies probably owed their very possibility of existence to their decided marginality vis-à-vis university core curricula. A course in an extension program at Columbia or in a noncredit adult lecture series at the New School existed on the fringes of academia. Likewise, that the lecture series at Harvard took place under the auspices of a professional school away from the center of the university's core efforts in humanistic uplift no doubt diminished any threat of cultural contamination. Of course, the very idea that academia might have fringes was itself anathema to some defenders of a core tradition of high humanism. For these critics, the university could not afford—whether in terms of resources or in terms of intellectual energy—to corrupt its fundamental mission. For Thorstein Veblen and Abraham Flexner, for instance, extension programs and home-study enterprises diluted the humanistic mission of the university as much as did the vocationalism of professional programs such as the newly founded schools of business. Speaking harshly of Columbia's extension program, Flexner specifically singled out "the fact that the University offers a course in 'photoplay composition.'" With evident irony and disdain, he described Frances Taylor Patterson's efforts: "[T]he ordinary photoplay has been displaced by the so-called 'talkie,' as a result of which I am informed that the course has just been abandoned and that the lady who gave the course is now at Hollywood where she is spending a year studying the 'new technique.' The University will, I assume, offer a course in 'talkies' when this young woman forsakes the alluring precincts of Hollywood and returns to the academic groves on Morningside Heights."[9]

As we have seen, Flexner also condemned the idea of a Harvard business school, but, as his own argument reveals, professional schools invited different attacks than did the extension programs, although they often overlapped. Extension programs were seen to run the risk of diluting the humanistic core by emphasizing inessential subjects—pastimes for idle persons—and surrendering rigor for mere amusement. Professional school courses were also guilty of these sins, but they additionally were to be attacked on the grounds that instead of appealing to idleness they made university learning too pragmatic, too pecuniary, and not at all disinterested. To the extent that the Harvard School of Business course dealt with the lowly art of film in a professional school context, it combined aspects both of light popular diversion (the enduring attitude that film courses are "flicks for kicks") and of overly pragmatic vocationalism. In this respect, it could easily have sparked greater outrage.

But, against critiques like Frank Cole Babbitt's of the very ontology of movies as imaginatively seductive and enslaving, the placement of the Harvard film pedagogy in a professional school might have helped to bracket out controversial issues of the cultural worth (or lack thereof) of movies, insofar as the course's concern was with film specifically within business enterprise: movies were to be treated as commodities that circulated to create pecuniary value more than aesthetic worth. However, issues of value did creep back into the course and did so, as we will see, of necessity. The unstable status of the HSB vis-à-vis the perceived mission of the "higher learning in America" (to use Veblen's phrase) meant that it might be helpful to the course's image not to dispense with questions of value altogether. Thus, the very extent to which the HSB course was conjoined by its planners with the initiative in fine arts to create awards for film based on aesthetic merit seems to have been envisioned, as we shall see, as an attempt to mediate cultural study and professional training. Both initiatives worked together to constitute film as an object worthy of respectful attention.

The original controversy around Lowell's rhetorical construction of business as both old art and new profession was indeed the controversy that business schools faced as they made their way into institutions of higher learning: on the one hand, businesspeople had to be convinced that industrial acumen could indeed be codified in teachable precepts (rather than learned experientially on the job); on the other hand, university figures had be to assured that such teaching would not besmirch academia's higher goals. The particular way in which the HSB went about its teaching of cinema can be read as an attempt to mediate these various concerns (even as it perhaps necessarily fell short of achieving this goal). For example, by presenting its own attention to film as inextricably linked with a venture in fine arts, the HSB could bracket out humanistic issues of art and aesthetic value, but only insofar as this bracketing was taken to be merely provisional and not fully exclusionary: art would indeed be dealt with, but elsewhere at the university and in a complementary fashion. The HSB would present itself as not opposed to the higher liberal arts mission of the university. In fact, it could be seen as finding its own realm in which to realize that mission. It is striking, for instance, to note the extent to which the lecturers in the course seemed to take up the task of talking about film as both business *and* source of deeper value. Even as they lectured on the *industry* of film, they endlessly insisted that the commodity their industry put into circulation differed from others insofar as it offered the intangible but higher benefits of culture, art, value, moral education, and uplifting entertainment.

Indeed, as we will see, even if the HSB course itself only rarely attended to specifically aesthetic issues of film (although it did invoke them regularly as a backdrop to its central concern with business issues), it did not leave humanistic questions behind. One way the course dealt centrally with value was through a strong concern with the issue of business *ethics.* That is, the humanistic showed up in a notion of business as a province of the moral. From the moment of the business program's foundation—when it was still a subdivision of the Faculty of Arts and Sciences and not a separate school—its administrators had emphasized that throughout its curriculum there would be necessary attention to ethical issues of business leadership. In this way, business education itself might constitute a form of higher value in its inculcation of the necessity of upright dealings between humans. Business would be studied not just in terms of financial benefit but also as a path to a higher good. In particular, the rationalization of industry that derived from university training in its byways was also a means by which business would be improved and made more morally answerable.

Certainly, some of the rhetoric of ethical conduct appears to have been lip service designed to forestall controversy over business's possible fit into higher learning, while some of it undoubtedly derived from a sincere Progressivist belief on the part of the founders of schools of business that the modern age required a transition from laissez-faire cutthroat ways of doing business to greater civic responsibility. Some of it also certainly originated in the concern of some Progressivist reformers in the area of labor relations to forestall social conflict and regulate conduct. Progressivist reform around business practices is to be seen in large part as a political activity that took up the guise of morality as a way to keep the wheels of commerce turning steadily. The emphasis on ethics could easily serve as a virtual alibi for an image and ideology of properly run business as above the crass conflicts—including class conflict—of the age. For example, the goal of emphasizing ethics in business could have as one of its targets the discouragement of behavior that was deemed irrational or unethical and that created strife in the workplace to threaten the very system of capitalist production. To the extent that business itself could be imagined as ethical in its operations, any challenge to modern business rationalism could only be seen as external and artificial—the nefarious work, for instance, of socialistic rabble-rousers. There could be no legitimate opposition to legitimate business.

Such policing by means of the rationalization of business was indeed a driving principle at the HSB—especially when ex-banker Wallace Donham became its dean in 1919. Vigorously antiunionist, Donham (along with his school) viewed reform in the workplace, and reform of the ethics of business leadership, as an ameliorative exercise that would forestall labor activism and continue to deliver a pliant labor force to big business. The film course—and Will Hays's central participation in the course itself and in preparation for it—could be useful, then, insofar as the film business might be presented as a model industry, one in which ethics increasingly was coming to dominate everyday practice and in which, for instance, institutional structures such as arbitration boards were being put into place to rewrite labor struggle as a site for intervention through adjudication and bureaucratic negotiation. Thus, in his introductory lecture for the HSB course, Hays described the early days of cinema:

> There was competition of the fiercest sort, of course. For that matter, there still is—and this is as it should be. But today the ethics of the competition are constantly higher. In earlier years the mere physical

and mechanical expansion of the industry was so swift that there was neither time nor mood to consider adequately the moral and educational responsibilities inherent in this new thing. But the old, careless, helter-skelter days are over. . . . These men who will speak to you realize that they are the responsible custodians not only of one of the greatest industries in the world, but of a most potent instrument for moral influence, inspiration, and education and of the most universal medium of art that the world has ever known. (31)

The Harvard course certainly served as a form of propaganda by which the film industry could present itself in the best moral light, while also serving the business school by emphasizing the extent to which it took as its models industrial practices that were ever more ethical—ever more humane and humanistic—in their operations. The film business, for instance, would be pictured as so rational that there could be no justification for union activity or other expressions of discontent.

To best understand the HSB lecture series on the film industry, it is necessary, then, to examine some of the governing principles of the HSB itself and their genealogy. Histories of Harvard single out the tenure of one of its presidents, Charles W. Eliot, who was in office from 1869 to 1909 and who supervised the creation of the business school, as key to Harvard's transition into a modern, increasingly professionalized university. The training of leaders who would have an effect on the culture at large had always been part of the mission of American universities and colleges; even the original pre-twentieth-century impulse of training ministers intended to produce men with impact and influence. But in the earliest days it had often been assumed that what was needed was not so much practical instruction as training in the building up of character, moral fiber, personal value, and so on: if the highest universities concentrated on an elite corps of students, this was in large part because it was assumed that such men (and they were almost exclusively men—for example, over the years the HSB repeatedly voted not to admit women) had in their fundamental being many of the seeds of moral potential from which firm principles of leadership could be cultivated. Education developed character, and in the Ivy League system especially, it also developed networks between such men of character. One goal of attendance at institutions of "higher learning" was to form bonds of friendship, trust, and devotion that would carry over into the practical world and would, indeed, substitute meaningful interaction for an alienating competition between strangers. But the growing complexity of industry—and of the tasks it faced—necessitated instruction in more than mere gentlemanly virtues. The university of the twentieth century would also teach skills, material practices, and rationalized procedures for dealing with large-scale problems. Harvard, as Roger L. Geiger shows in his classic history of the growth of American research universities, was one central participant in the move by a number of elite universities to professionalize education and think of it as practical training for high-level careers.[10]

For whatever reason, Eliot's successor, A. Lawrence Lowell, who assumed Harvard's presidency in 1909, seems not to have been much of a fan of the HSB, even though he presided over its dedication (as we have seen, he does not necessarily appear to have been much of a fan of the movies either). When, in the early 1920s, the still relatively new HSB wanted to undertake a fund drive to build a site for itself, Lowell resisted and ultimately only allowed the drive to go forward on the condition that the HSB merge its fundraising with other divisions so as not to claim too much university money for its own benefit. Fortuitously, one of the divisions with which the HSB was told to share its efforts was fine arts, and this may have either begun or concretized the association between the two programs that would culminate in 1927 in the joint enterprise of the film course and the annual film award program. As Jeffrey Cruikshank explains in his history of the HSB, "[Paul] Sachs [dean of fine arts] and Donham [dean of HSB] often traveled to and from New York together during the course of the $10-million campaign, dividing between them the prospects they hoped to meet."[11]

At the beginning of the teens, a Chicago publisher, Arch W. Shaw, had received publicity about the recently founded HSB and become involved in its projects. Shaw had been publishing, among other titles, a business journal called *System*, which emphasized practical issues of the business world, and soon would be publishing many of the school's documents (indeed, *The Story of the Films*, the book of transcripts of the Harvard film lecture series, was an A. W. Shaw item). I will return to *System* in another context later in this chapter, but at this point it is worth noting that it was concerned with recounting concrete cases dealing with typical industrial problems. For Shaw, business theory would always be balanced by an attention to practical example. *System* was very much a journal of colorful stories. It recounted the narratives of industries, industry men, and the problems they met and surmounted.

By 1911, Shaw had been invited to lecture in the HSB's course on commercial organization, and this led to an ongoing collaboration with the school. Shaw's interest in the rationalization of business led him to promote several projects at the HSB that would have direct impact on the film course. First, as a result of his concern for practical issues of marketing and distribution, Shaw encouraged the school to set up a bureau for concrete research on various businesses and collect data about them, and he offered to underwrite the initial stages of this enterprise. With Shaw's funding, this initiative ultimately led to the founding of the Bureau of Business Research. This research division began a project on the retail shoe business, and this first case of data collection initiated an ongoing concern with intensive study of specific businesses. Second—and following directly from the first—Shaw suggested that the HSB set up a course on business policy that would maintain the same overall framework from semester to semester but would look at a different sample industry each time. Business Policy would use the raw data collected by the research division to study various industries as exemplary, yet highly concrete, cases of businesses confronting and solving problems in their everyday operations.

When Dean Donham took over the HSB in 1919, the idea of a curriculum that studied specific industries resonated strongly with him. Donham had graduated from Harvard Law School in 1901 before becoming a banker with Boston's Old Colony Trust Company (a bank in which Joseph P. Kennedy had interests). Both Donham's legal education and his hands-on banking experience had fostered his belief in an education based on concrete, practical example. In particular, he appears to have been enamored of the ways that law education at Harvard had revolved around specific cases presented as problems to which solutions would be proposed. In fact, the Harvard Law School was one of the pioneers of a particularly concrete Socratic method for teaching law (given famous cinematic representation in films about Harvard such as *The Paper Chase* and *Legally Blonde*): instead of lecturing in the abstract, the professor would offer up a problem, which students would discuss among themselves (each student being asked to comment on the solution of his predecessor). From its start in 1909, the HSB modeled its pedagogy on procedures in law education (the first program description for the HSB explicitly announced an interest in case methods directly derived from the law school), and Donham clearly endorsed this direction for the school. For Donham, as he described it in an essay on the role of the case method in business pedagogy, law instruction had already gained several benefits from the approach: a practical concreteness, appeal to tradition (through the citation of precedents), and the gathering of examples that could be used repeatedly from course to course and from year to year.[12] In Business Policy, the case study approach eventually concretized into a pattern in which an invited representative spoke about his business and ended his class session with a problem to which students had to bring solutions by the next session. (When there was no guest, the professor himself would pose a question, to which the students would offer solutions in the next class meeting two days later.) In the early literature of the HSB there was some hesitation about whether to call this the "case approach" or the "problem approach." Donham pushed for the latter, believing this would demarcate the business school's methods from those of the School of Law, but nomenclature of the "case" won out.[13]

Three kinds of information were sought for the sessions of Business Policy: first, raw data—the facts and figures of the business under consideration; second, more general problems and issues of that business; and finally, narratives of solution to these problems, although in many cases it was assumed that these narratives would emerge during the lectures by guests from the industry in question. In his aforementioned essay on the case method, Donham specifically indicated a desire to make case material available for various Business Policy course offerings in some sort of published volume "containing a limited number of cases chosen by the editor because in his opinion they best illustrate or help to develop the legal principles he wishes to teach." As will be described in more detail later, data collection in film specifically seems to have led to such a volume in the form of "Motion Picture Reports" edited by an HSB professor, Howard T. Lewis.

By the end of the 1920s, there was an expressed desire at the HSB to return periodically in the Business Policy course to some key industries and study them in greater depth as more data or new problems were made available. This certainly was the case with film. As noted earlier, it is clear that, as long as funding kept coming in from a source like Joseph Kennedy, the HSB did not take the 1927 film course to be a one-shot offering but hoped for its appearance in the curriculum on a regular basis. In fact, even as the course eventually died, data collection continued. Thus, the Donham files in the HSB archives include a letter from October 7, 1929 (that is to say, almost two years after the film course was offered), in which Sidney Kent's office at Paramount authorized a case from the studio to be used by the HSB. Clearly, there was interest in data collection for the motion picture industry long after the one Business Policy offering on film had ceased.

It is not exactly clear how the original inspiration to have the Business Policy course analyze the film industry came about. The end-of-course summary in the *Boston Transcript*—clearly, a planted item—claims that Donham was having a friendly chat with Kennedy and asked him how the film business was going (Kennedy's own entry into the industry was still fairly recent); when Kennedy lauded the strength of the film business, this got Donham thinking, and within a month he asked Kennedy to consider doing a course. But other articles claim that the Harvard's secretary, James Seymour, came up with the idea as a source of publicity for the university.

If so, it is worth noting that Seymour clearly benefited from the project. Soon after the lecture series ended, he left Harvard to go to work for Joseph Kennedy's film company. (In this respect, as we will see, he is among several participants in the Harvard initiative who clearly drew direct personal advantage from the enterprise.)

Whatever the origin of the idea of the lecture series, it clearly had the potential to benefit several constituencies within both the university and the industry. Revealingly, the thank-you letters that Kennedy sent to the industry executives who spoke in the course included expression of his gratitude for "the opportunity to meet you more intimately than I might have done in many years in the business," and it is clear that Kennedy was using the course to network within a business in which he was still a novice. Certainly, too, Kennedy might have hoped to gain cultural capital from the association with Harvard: his studio, FBO, was associated primarily with lowbrow fare, and the Harvard connection would certainly have helped to elevate Kennedy's profile in the industry and the public eye. Toward this end, after the course was over, Kennedy sent copies of the published transcripts to myriad figures in the film business. There is some indication that this quest for prestige paid off. For instance, on December 1, 1927, Sam Dembow at the Publix chain of movie theaters (an influential branch of Paramount) wrote Kennedy to thank him for the volume and declared: "Please don't think that I am trying to flatter you when I say that for the short time you have been in this industry you have done more to place it on a higher plane than any one individual."

Also contributing centrally to the planning of the lecture series and hoping to benefit from it was Will Hays, who was looking for ways to promote an affirmative image of American film and the business of filmmaking. At an early stage, Hays became one of the course's primary organizers. He vetted Kennedy's choices for speakers and made choices himself, and his office helped contact the speakers and make arrangements for them. The film industry leaders agreed to speak at the course for diverse reasons—a favor to Kennedy, a chance to try out problems on newly trained students of business, the opportunity to recruit the best and the brightest, and so on—and Hays's key input added an occasion to present film as a rational and therefore ethically worthy modern American enterprise. Hays's supervision of the course was very rigorous. For instance, when Joseph Kennedy telegraphed him early on (January 14, 1927) to announce that negotiations with Harvard for the lecture series had concluded, Hays quickly put his own office staff to work on the project. Later that very day, Hays telegraphed his second-in-command, Carl Milliken, from the West Coast (where he had gone on a business trip) to offer a long list of advice and instruction. For instance, he recommended that speakers be recruited from as many companies as possible (so as not to appear to valorize one firm over another) and that the course include an actor and a director—no doubt to emphasize the affective and cultural aspects of moviemaking, as well as the economic ones. Hays wanted the course to be as ambitious as possible: as he put it in his message to Milliken with all the stream-of-consciousness breathlessness that telegrams encouraged, it should cover "every important phase of industry such as production distribution publicity exhibition general executive management studio management and if possible story adoption scenario writing etcetera."

In a previous chapter, we saw Hays engaging in efforts to foster professional training in film at Columbia University. Throughout the history of film's early entrance into higher education, Will Hays appears in fact to have been a key player in numerous moves to encourage academic institutions to offer professional instruction in film. In the case of the Harvard course, no doubt he was attracted by its promise of efficient business training for men who wanted to enter the industry. But it also seems that, independent of any direct benefit it would produce in terms of professionalized personnel, Hays also supported the lecture series as a promotional device by which the industry would gain prestige.

Hays and Kennedy worked closely together. Many of the letters that went from Harvard administrators to Joseph Kennedy were automatically forwarded to Hays, and Kennedy consulted him on all decisions about the types of speakers to be invited, the topics they should discuss, and the overall impression the series of lectures should impart regarding the current state of the American film industry. With Hays's promise of industry contact and connection, and Kennedy's pledge of financial support, case collection on the motion picture industry began during the planning phase for the 1927 course. A former HSB student, Theodore Streibert, was put in charge of the collation of cases sent by industry officials (particularly but not exclusively those who would be speaking in the course). After graduating from the HSB in 1923, Streibert had been hired as an assistant to Joseph Kennedy, and he seems to have been regarded by both Kennedy and HSB administrators as the local go-between for details of lecture series organization. Whether or not he had any particular reward in mind for having aided the course, and whether or not he had any initial input in pushing Kennedy to undertake the project, Streibert certainly appears to have benefited. On the one hand, as I will recount in greater detail later, Streibert was able to use the course as a recruiting platform for FBO and later for RKO, which he moved to when it absorbed Kennedy's company. On the other hand, the course appears to have been a way for Streibert to renew and deepen contact with his alma mater. By 1930—within three years after the course, that is—he himself would be hired by the HSB as one of its assistant deans. (He continued, though, to have a professional interest in media forms. He later served as manager of WOR Radio and, in 1953, became the first director of the United States Information Agency.)

Several documents clarify the kinds of cases that were researched and assembled for the Business Policy course on film. For example, in an undated memo, course lecturer Robert Cochrane (vice president at Universal) sent in a series of marketing challenges: How, for instance, might one promote *Uncle Tom's Cabin* in the racially fraught context of the South? How might a foreign prestige picture like *Les Misérables* be sold to average American moviegoers? In a letter of February 24, 1927, Horace Gilbert, a sometime instructor for Business Policy, wrote to upcoming lecturer Sidney Kent from Paramount, thanking him for a letter "telling of the reasons for Famous Players adding two-reel comedies, Paramount news weeklies, cartoons and miscellaneous one-reel pictures to their features and road show attractions. . . . the material will serve as the basis for a good Business School case." Similarly, a March 11, 1927, article in the *Boston Transcript*, once the course was in session, mentioned three sorts of problems it would be touching upon (1) "Methods recommended to reduce the cases for arbitration between exhibitors and distributors"; (2) "Should a firm producing feature films add miscellaneous short subjects to its line for distribution, and should it produce them in its own studio?"; (3) "Distribution of films, and the practice of block-booking."[14] Most important, as the course was ending, is correspondence from its official instructor, Nathan Isaacs, to a Boston freelance writer, William Leahy, who was helping put the course lectures into shape for publication as *The Story of the Films*. In a letter of April 8, 1927, Isaacs made reference to the way in which students for the course were guided "by means of outlines and suggestions and questions." Isaacs indicated, "This year a beginning [in an ongoing analysis of film industry problems which he imagines might be dealt with in future courses] was made by requiring them to write a report on the policy of using the so-called block-booking method." The topic of block-booking parallels the *Boston Transcript* article, where it is one of three areas of attention. It should also be noted that HSB professor Howard T. Lewis dealt with block-booking, in two Kennedy-funded volumes he prepared on the film industry, seeing the practice as a quite natural part of the operation of the film business. And, in passing, it is worth remarking that the issue of block-booking appears to have come up again in a later course at the HSB. In February 1929—two years after the lecture series on film—Neil Borden, an associate dean of the HSB, wrote to Joseph Kennedy to inform him about a class that was doing a report on the effects of block-booking. As Borden put it in a February 27 letter to Kennedy, "Already we have begun to make use of these movie cases so that our students are getting some knowledge of the problems of the industry. The marketing class, at the present time, is preparing a written report on certain phases of block booking." Nothing else is known about this course venture—was it a project of the class as a whole or of just some students? how long did it last? what was its place in the course overall?—and it appears that Borden was writing to Kennedy simply to maintain contact with their benefactor (who, by 1929, was beginning to back down on pledges of support). But it is noteworthy that the recurrent concern with block-booking appears to have derived in large part from ongoing data collection in the film business that could enable the HSB to return to this one industry and this one practice within that industry from time to time.

Through the late 1920s and early 1930s, Howard T. Lewis collected materials and coordinated a series of research efforts on film, and these had impact beyond their immediate occasion. Lewis was a professor of marketing who had been with the HSB since 1927. By 1930, he was one of the HSB's several assistant deans (and in 1936 he would become director of the school's Bureau of Business Research, thus supervising its collection of data for cases). The film industry seems to have mattered to Lewis only as one more business to be studied in a dry, rigorous fashion: typical studies of his on other areas of research around the time of his film work bear titles such as "Distribution of Hard Fiber Cordage" (a twenty-six-page publication from 1930) and *Industrial Purchasing* (a book from 1933). But he received direct financial support from Joseph Kennedy for his research on film, and for several years data collection and narrative accounts of problems and solutions in the film industry became the focus of his research.

Lewis's efforts in the examination of film are still cited in the secondary literature of film studies.[15] The first major version of his research on cases from film came in the form of a massive (almost seven hundred pages) compilation of concrete problems and proposed solutions: *Cases on the Motion Picture Industry with Commentary,* a volume of *Harvard Business Reports* from 1930 made up of sections in which Lewis reported a case from film and then offered his own analysis.[16] Typical cases in the volume include the question of a studio (Warner Bros.) creating its own trailer service; the means by which RKO's accounting system dealt with "amortization of motion picture values"; and the implications of Federal Trade Commission hearings on block-booking by the studios. In his foreword to the volume, series editor Charles I. Graff (another HSB professor, and a strong proponent of the case method) indicated that the volume presented sixty-six cases selected by Lewis from a "larger number collected under his direction." Graff intimated that another volume would be published to deal with the remaining cases in film, but no such follow-up work ever appeared.

Instead, Lewis rewrote the *Harvard Business Reports* in more synthetic, narrative form (rather than reports of isolated cases), published in 1933 as a general volume, *The Motion Picture Industry*.[17] Lewis also published shorter pieces on film seemingly in anticipation of the longer volumes. There was, for example, a general entry titled "Motion Picture Industry" written for Alvin Johnson's *Encyclopedia of the Social Sciences*, organized at the New School for Social Research. Likewise, Lewis published "Distributing Motion Pictures" in the *Harvard Business Review*'s 1928–29 volume.[18] Although there were no writings on film in the *Harvard Business Review* before this article by Lewis, two other essays on film appeared soon after: William Victor Strauss's "Foreign Distribution of American Motion Pictures" and Edward R. Beach's "Double Features in Motion-Picture Exhibiting."[19] Insofar as the *Harvard Business Review* suddenly began to publish articles on the film industry when previously it had not done so at all, one can readily surmise that a new research climate—encouraged perhaps by Lewis's efforts—was leading to a newfound focus on the business of movies. The immediate influence of Lewis's motion picture work on the research climate at Harvard shows up also in the one doctoral thesis that seems to have come out of the film research: H. C. Hawley's dissertation "Distribution as a Factor in Commercial Integration of the Motion Picture Industry," for which he was awarded a doctoral degree in commercial science in the HSB in 1930. Hawley's project was supervised by Lewis and acknowledged the use of case-study data that the HSB had been collecting. Here, Hawley noted the specific aid of three students working for the Bureau of Business Research: Amos Hiatt, H. H. Thurlby, and Leon Altstock. Lewis's *Motion Picture Industry* had also acknowledged the help of these same three student researchers, said to have provided "aid in gathering material" (v), and it is clear that they served as a regular source of data collection in relation to film projects at the HSB.

Hawley's and Lewis's acknowledgment of the data collection efforts of Harvard students who had been employed to conduct research specifically on the film industry is, for our purposes, a useful bit of information. It offers evidence, once again, that a number of figures at Harvard were working—or had been put to work—on the study of the American film industry, and it is probable that they were doing so in conjunction with the Business Policy course. That is to say, it appears more than likely that the research efforts of Lewis and the students around him were intended to provide material for a film course to be taught, it was hoped, on a regular basis at the HSB. Significantly, after working with probable funding from Joseph Kennedy, both Hiatt and Altstock ended up in positions at RKO, again suggesting the direct links between Harvard and Kennedy's business interests. (Thurlby, on the other hand, became an assistant professor at the HSB and thus also rose in the ranks.)

It is quite likely that Lewis's volumes—especially the more user-friendly *Motion Picture Industry*—were envisioned in part as textbooks for ongoing courses on the film business. The fact, however, that Lewis's volumes did not come out until the first years of the 1930s, long after the 1927 class, is intriguing. Were Lewis's books simply too late to be useful, or were they intended for the anticipated continuation of the course beyond 1927? As I have noted, there certainly were hopes at the start that the Business Policy course on the American film industry would be repeated, and it appears that some of the figures connected to it felt that a serious and scholarly textbook would be useful. It is clear, at the same time, that they did not believe that *The Story of the Films*, the published volume of transcripts of lectures from the course, could serve adequately as that volume.

Perhaps there was some awareness that, while valuable, the transcripts of the often informal talks would not fully represent the in-depth image of rigorous research in business policy that Harvard wished to convey; certainly, Lewis's *Motion Picture Industry*, published six years later, fits better the generic requirements of a volume of academic research while also employing an accessible style that would make it teachable. When *The Story of the Films* appeared, it itself also contained notice of its own inadequacy as a textbook: "It must be said in all candor that the lectures, as printed, do not constitute a textbook. They are not a classified manual of the film industry. They do not in the least suggest the work of college professors. Though carefully prepared and proceeding in every case from a fullness of practical knowledge, all but three of them were delivered extemporaneously. The reader, then, will not look for a formal, schematized presentation of the subject. What the lectures offer is material on which a textbook might be based, a starting point for systematic research" (xiv–xv). Perhaps Lewis's *Motion Picture Industry* was to have been that textbook. If so, it finally came out at a time when the HSB had all but fully abandoned its interests in cinema, and thereafter Lewis himself seems never to have worked on film-related topics again.

Even though it was no doubt obvious by 1930 that Kennedy would no longer fund HSB efforts around film, and that there would thus be no direct need for Lewis's textbook at the school, there is perhaps another reason why Lewis continued his film research for a little while longer. At the beginning of the 1930s, Lewis had discussions about his research with the moral custodians at the Payne Fund Studies, the famous large-scale research project of the Motion Picture Research Council (MPRC) to investigate (and in large part to denounce) the social impact of movies. The Reverend William Short, one of the key figures behind the Payne Fund Studies, had originally wanted one of its volumes to examine the political economy of the motion picture industry. The intent, it would seem, was to suggest that ownership practices and business strategies in the industry were so scurrilous that they had of necessity to lead to immoral product. That is, Short had wanted a study that would show that the movie business was being run in ways that encouraged the distribution of immoral movies. For example, business tactics like block-booking and double features forced low-grade films on the public and made high-quality films less available. It seems that Short went to the Social Science Research Council for underwriting, but the council said it would fund such a study only if it was anchored at a respectable business school. Short then got in touch with the HSB to see if it would be that anchor, and he was put in touch with Howard Lewis.[20]

Lewis proposed studies of both the American film industry and international trade in the industry (focusing on conditions and practices in Europe), but was turned down for funding by the SSRC and thus asked Short if the Payne Fund could directly finance his project.[21] Short demurred. At the very least, he may have been discouraged by the sheer ambitiousness of Lewis's proposed study, which the Harvard professor was envisioning as a five-year project: the MPRC was after quick results and might not have had patience for such a slow, scholarly venture. And besides the time it would take, there was always the risk that rigorous scholarship would lead to conclusions the MPRC did not expect or desire. Indeed, as film historians Garth Jowett, Ian Jarvie, and Kathryn Fuller argue in their analysis of the Payne Fund Studies, MPRC administrators such as Short decided eventually that study of the industry itself was not the best way to address issues of morality in film: in large part, Jowett, Jarvie, and Fuller suggest, Payne Fund directors feared that too explicit a critique of the industry side, as opposed to the consumer side, of the equation would bring down the wrath of the business upon them and make it harder to conduct their research.[22] There was also a reverse risk in commissioning a study of the industry: namely, that the resultant study might end up *appreciating* and *affirming* the business of film and finding in it a site of reason and proper conduct. In this respect, it is noteworthy that Lewis did tend to adhere to a rationalist teleology, visible in general at the HSB, in which twentieth-century businesses were seen as increasingly engaging in not merely efficient but socially beneficial practices.

I have noted earlier that the HSB looked to modern rationalized industries as providing models of morality, and the film business received treatment as one of these paragons of virtuous efficiency. For instance, in contrast to those who would condemn block-booking, Lewis, in "Distributing Motion Pictures," adduced arguments in "support of this practice" and concluded its legal validity. This was not a take on Hollywood business practices that the Payne Fund Studies administration would have welcomed. Revealingly, the MPRC did include Lewis as late as 1933 in a secret symposium designed to elaborate national film policies in motion pictures, but one can only imagine that his position of seeming academic neutrality (if not approbation) around a number of business practices where the MPRC wanted outright condemnation would not have made him a major ally. For example, when, at its symposium, the MPRC floated the idea of legislation to fight block-booking, blind-bidding, and other industry practices, Lewis objected: "It is somewhat inconsistent in my mind . . . to ask for an investigation and study of the motion picture industry which presumably would be impartial, and designed to get at the facts, and then *in advance* of such investigation decide that certain practices now existing are unsatisfactory."[23]

Howard Lewis represents the clearest case of an HSB scholar whose research agenda came to center on film in large part because of the 1927 course and its subvention by Kennedy, but Lewis was not the only figure at the HSB to devote himself to film study, even if for a short time. In his history of the HSB, Jeffrey L. Cruikshank notes that Dean Donham tried to enlist the help of industrial psychologist Elton Mayo in planning out the course. According to Cruikshank, Mayo had been having some problems in articulating a new research project, and it was thought that a study of the film industry might give him some direction. In Cruikshank's words, "Donham, hoping to direct Mayo's activities into a promising quarter, had asked him early in 1927 to study and report on the motion picture industry. . . . But Mayo's report harshly condemned the studio system, which struck Mayo as irresponsible and unable to learn from its mistake."[24]

To get a sense of what administrators were hoping for with film study at the HSB, it is worth looking at Mayo's report since it obviously offered an approach to the film business that was *not* what was desired by the administration. No doubt, it also would have been met with dismay by industry officials such as Will Hays and Joseph Kennedy, who wanted the course to present the best possible image of current practices in the film business. It is likely, though, that once Mayo's inflammatory analysis of the film business crossed Dean Donham's desk, it stopped there and never got to the course's sponsors in the film industry. Insofar as Mayo presented the film industry as deeply wedded to *irrational* procedures, he was moving in directions that were not acceptable for a joint HSB-industry course on film.

A key figure in the elaboration of industrial psychology, Elton Mayo is still sometimes referenced in studies of business theory and its ideologies. For Mayo, industrial psychology concentrated on improvement of worker productivity by rationalized means. A worker who felt well would be one who worked well. Mayo's specific contribution was to argue that worker well-being was as much a psychological issue as a physical or medical one. He argued for recognition of workers as beings of psychological complexity rather than as standardized cogs in the machine of production, but he himself also standardized such workers by assuming they all shared the same basic psychological makeup, one that could be scientifically studied and improved. For Mayo, it would be an impediment to industry productivity for business leaders not to learn the regularities of such psychology and subsequently cultivate proper attitudes toward work. By the 1930s, Mayo famously applied his theories of general worker psychology—of the factors that encourage or discourage pride and efficiency in work—in experiments on worker fatigue conducted at Western Electric plants. In his study of the politics of labor in America, Andrew Ross provides a succinct description of Mayo's approach:

> Elton Mayo and Fritz Roethlisberger's famous study of AT&T's Western Electric workers in the late 1920s is generally regarded as the origin of modern managerial ideas about how to boost productivity and soften conflict in the workplace by responding to the social and emotional needs of workers.... workers were more productive when they believed that managers were actually paying attention to their work conditions. They worked even harder and with more loyalty when they felt themselves to be voluntary participants in, rather than servants of, workplace goals.... Mayo's ideas were also widely embraced by corporate managers because they were a palatable alternative to socialist explanations of labor conflict.... The system of monopoly ownership, so much under the threat of government intervention, if not proletarian overthrow, in the 1930s could survive, Mayo promised, only if employees were provided with a sense of participation in the company's affairs.[25]

Presented in these terms, Mayo's approach to industry clearly was in keeping with the HSB Progressivist agenda, especially as represented by

Dean Donham, who had been instrumental in recruiting Mayo to the school. Industrial psychology became a mechanism of policing that delivered efficient workers to the system and kept them happy within the world of labor. Mayo and Donham shared an ideological belief in the necessity for the managers of successful industries to work on employer-employee relations through amelioration of work conditions. But for Mayo, one key point was that the industries undertaking this ameliorative work had to be advanced, efficient, rationalized businesses. That is, they had to have organized themselves as effective enterprises before they could undertake the complicated work of refining their labor relations. And Mayo did not feel that the film business had been rationalized in this way.

Mayo's "report" came in the form of a long, handwritten letter of May 9, 1927, addressed to Donham.[26] The letter postdates the Kennedy film course, and it is difficult to know if Mayo's thoughts had been made available to administrators before or during the course itself. (Mayo's letter alluded to previous discussions around film in which he had offered "suggestions [to industry officials?] as to selection and source of plot and story or as to the conditions governing the human appeal of a picture," but there is no existing material about this. It is amusing to speculate what this industrial psychologist so concerned with the rational operations of big business might have proposed regarding proper and effective film content.)

Significantly, Mayo noted that he had held interviews with Joseph Kennedy and actor Milton Sills (who lectured in the HSB course on film), as well as an officer in Kennedy's movie company. It is probable that Kennedy or his office (might Streibert be the Kennedy officer Mayo interviewed?) had set up these interviews for Mayo, thereby facilitating Mayo's concerted research and reflection on film as the Kennedy office had with Howard T. Lewis. But in Mayo's case, the conclusions were not favorable to the image of the film business as rational industry that Kennedy desired to establish through his subventions to Harvard. Mayo deeply doubted that the movie business was being run well. No doubt adding insult to injury, Mayo even suggested that he got his damning evidence about the fundamental irrationality of the industry from his interview with Kennedy: "I shall assume these suggestions [about the need to rationalize an intensely irrational industry] as in some degree appropriate (on Mr. Kennedy's admission) and shall proceed to indicate as best I can the consequences of the neglect of such considerations by the present random and haphazard method."

Mayo's overall contention was clear: the film industry was wallowing in inefficiency in not adhering to broadly applicable laws of industrial rationality, opting instead for a dangerous emphasis on personality at the expense of system. As he put it, "Individual excellence is made to atone for a general lack of plan and for defective understanding." For Mayo, then, it was precisely the notion of individual creative contribution that endangered the film industry. In his view, the film business was being held back, since instead of adhering to a structural understanding of work, with the employee taking up a rationalized and codified role in the system, it let itself be seduced by a much more random, haphazard cult of personal accomplishment. For instance, Mayo attacked the film director as someone whose inventive input (deriving in large part from spontaneous on-set decisions) skirted rational planning and who received too much industry encouragement for a creativity that operated outside all rules and constraints.

In Mayo's words, "My claim at this time is that, owing to defects of sheer industrial organization, there are . . . major 'leaks' in the production of pictures through which escapes each year an enormous wastage (of possibly millions) over the whole field." This idea of leakage is key to Mayo's conception of business as a system that when run well creates a veritable homoeostatic operation governed by efficiency, and invulnerable to malicious influences. In the case of the film business, the leakages occurred because of a split between managerial forces and creative ones (manifested as bureaucratic "chaos in the relation between New York and, for example, Hollywood") that led to irrationalities at several points in the process of production of films. The first leakage occurred in the nonrational way that stories were selected, which, in Mayo's view, was overly influenced "in part by the appeal of a particular story (novel or magazine source) to the representatives of the human species collected fortuitously in the office. The knowledge of what will 'picturize' was so exceedingly empiric and conventional that it must, on occasion, operate to hinder rather than aid new development. The method of assessing 'human appeal' is utterly unsystematic and random; so much so that one must believe that euphoria or malaise, fitness or indigestion, operate more than any other factors in determining choice." Moreover, even though this first phase of decision making (choice of story) was governed by irrational emotion, there was additional potential for chaos (or leakage) at subsequent stages. As Mayo noted ironically, "[I]t remains possible that sudden or drastic alteration before or during the process of picture making (apparently at the whim of the director) may alter the significance of the tale and situations entirely."

In other words, to the first irrational decision to choose this or that story were added equally irrational and equally compounding counterdecisions. As Mayo bluntly declared, "[W]him and random judgment again bulk large." Moreover, for Mayo, the cult of directorial personality was further marred by hypocrisy in its application. That is, film directors were often allowed to make creative decisions not because anyone in power really believed in directorial creativity as a source of aesthetic value but because focusing on the director as the prime figure of responsibility deflected attention from managerial irrationality elsewhere in the production process. If a film failed, the director could be blamed; if it succeeded, that success could be attributed to a fundamental artistry at work within the Hollywood system. As Mayo put it, "Individual excellence is made to atone for a general lack of plan and for defective understanding." In an interesting aside, Mayo noted that theater also was often governed by a cult of the director, but there, he suggested, irrationality was mitigated insofar as the theater was a less capital-intensive art and insofar as modification and experimentation were part of its essential mission. Creative decisions could be welcomed in theater—where no work was fixed forever but altered from one performance to the next—in a way not possible for film, where massive amounts of investment were at risk and where the end result would be a permanently fixed work (the final cut that remained the same from screening to screening no matter the flaws within it).

Mayo's conclusions were blunt and unambiguous: unless reformed, the film industry would "in the end give rise to decreasing economy if not extravagant waste of time and money—a 'bored' public and an increasing number of unsuccessful experiments." Mayo's sense of the steps necessary to avoid this was as definitive: "The motion picture industry must redeem its present chaos by subscribing to the principles of organization which govern all large-scale production." These principles included the "need for definition of function and correlation of work" and for "a species of mass-production (organizing scientists, artists and technicians)."

To be sure, in the abstract, these last principles were ones that the film industry leaders speaking at Harvard could to a large degree endorse. What demarcated their attitude from Mayo's, however, is the sentiment in their lectures that the film industry had in fact *already* put such principles into operation and was *currently* running as an efficient, rationalized industry. In other words, where Mayo called for qualities he found dangerously lacking at the present moment, it was a central aspect of the Harvard lectures to assert that the film industry was already fully operating along deeply rational lines. True, there were, as several lecturers admitted, problems still to be faced within the industry, but these tended to be presented as relatively minor. In fact, one goal of the course itself was to air any such problems through the case-study method and thereby determine if immediate solutions could be proposed for them. To the extent that there were any problems, they came to constitute little more than a basis on which ever greater, ever more efficient solutions could be built.

Take, for example, Mayo's notion that the whims of individual creativity constituted a leakage for the system of film production. Many of the lecturers admitted that there was often a tension between art and commerce in the movies, but they also argued that there could be a compatibility of industrial organization and artistic invention. Not for nothing did the latter part of the Harvard Business Policy course include lectures by director Cecil B. DeMille and actor Milton Sills—in other words, *by creative figures*. The very ordering of the lectures in this fashion suggested that once the film industry had achieved firm footing after admittedly haphazard early days, it had become strong enough to permit cultural achievement to arise from within its midst. Although, as I have noted, the course generally bracketed out issues of culture (or turned them into moral questions around the ethics of business as one of the humanities), there was still a strong sense that artistic achievement could be quite compatible with industrial efficiency and indeed would grow organically from it. The impression conveyed overall by the lectures, as collected in *The Story of the Films*, was that of an industry that had found its (rational) way and was now confident enough to venture into areas of higher aesthetic creativity.

Indeed, the image the course lecturers presented of an industry with a high degree of achieved efficiency helps explain much of the appeal *to history* in the volume—and to the personal memory of the lecturers, so many of whom had been around in the early days when the business was indeed often haphazard and irrational. By admitting that *in the past* business was conducted at best on an intuitive basis, and at worst according to an inefficient irrationality, the representatives of the film industry could offer up *the present state* of the business as the achievement of a rationality that needed no more than minor refinements here or there. This narrative in which the present was assumed to be close to perfection was quite different from Mayo's conception, which imagined the history of film up to the present as an increasing move toward irrationality insofar as the cult of the director had taken over, insofar as the East Coast–West Coast split had increased the potential for leakages, and insofar as the amounts of money poured into the business were ever greater and increased the financial risks. With such a dour assessment of present conditions, Mayo could only see the future as at best an open question: would the industry be able to right itself, or would it continue its descent into inefficiency, waste, and eventual irrelevance?

We can see, then, why Mayo's report was not what the industry or the

HSB desired. Mayo would have no further official role to play in the teaching or study of film at Harvard. However, it is worth noting, before leaving this brief and curious episode in intellectual history in which this famous sociologist encountered the popular culture of film, that in subsequent years Mayo would continue to assemble notes—offering thoughts similar to those in his 1927 report to Dean Donham—for articles on the motion picture business.[27] For example, in the later reflections, Mayo continued to maintain that Hollywood's devotion to artistic creativity led to an irrationality that he characterized as "an eccentric combination of ignorance and laziness"; that the technical potentials of film and industrial potentials of the film business were thereby retarded by the concern with artistry; that, therefore, Hollywood should give up on pretenses to art; and that its managers should devote themselves to structural issues of business. Even if Mayo was ousted from involvement with the Business Policy course, it is tempting to suppose that in his ongoing desire to write about film, we can see another productive effect of the film course on the scholarly concerns of HSB faculty. (Interestingly, for his later reflections, Mayo noted that he had conducted interviews with producers Samuel Goldwyn and Alexander Korda; his engagement in film research was evidently strong enough to impel him to seek out film business figures such as these.) Although Mayo's condemnatory take on the current state of the film business was certainly quite different from the dry (but ultimately appreciative) assessment offered by Howard Lewis, both professors serve as examples of scholars who, while not giving evidence of a career-long, consuming commitment to ongoing research on film, seemed nonetheless to have been influenced enough by the late 1920s Kennedy-sponsored activities around film at the HSB to devote an appreciable bit of their research time in the 1930s to the business of film.

A number of documents enable us to reconstruct many aspects of the actual running of the Business Policy course on film. Obviously, the most direct bit of evidence is provided by the transcripts of the lectures themselves, published as *The Story of the Films*, but we also have other sources of information at our disposal: memorandums, newspaper reports (to the extent that we can take these as more than just promotional), references in letters, and so on. Amusingly, for instance, a series of letters show that the HSB followed its standard procedure for the Business Policy course on film and sent a fifty-dollar honorarium after their talks to each of the industry leaders. Some simply returned the checks, but most donated the money to charity.

One of the most revealing documents about the lecture series is a two-page memorandum, marked "Confidential: For Private Distribution Only," that was sent to all the invited lecturers to give them a sense of the series and what might be expected of them. The memorandum explained that the Business Policy course was required for all final-year students, which meant that the enrollment figure for the class would be about three hundred. (Several newspaper pieces asserted that an additional fourteen hundred students tried to sit in on the lecture series but were turned away. It is hard to judge the accuracy of such reports, which may have been concocted for publicity purposes.)

By their final year, the confidential memorandum indicated, HSB students would have "had training in marketing, finance, factory management, statistics, and accounting" and would have begun to specialize "in such fields as banking, retail store management, sales management, foreign trade, transportation, advertising, and manufacturing." The Business Policy course was to have two goals toward helping students to make the transition into their chosen area of work: "to coordinate the knowledge gained in the other courses" and "to develop the point of view of the executive and to supplement the regular courses with other materials that must be considered by the executives in dealing with actual problems as they arise in specific trades and industries."

Indeed, the document emphasized how Business Policy centered on the analysis of real-life cases from the specific industries under consideration. One function of the memorandum, then, was to indicate to the industry visitors that they should talk about concrete matters rather than abstract issues. In this respect, the memorandum explained, the fact that so many of the leaders of the film business were there at film's beginning and were therefore "able to tell at first hand of the problems confronted at every stage of development [of the motion picture industry]" encouraged the "hope that the men who have seen this growth will be able to isolate from their experience a few typical 'cases' to present to the School with the background which they alone can furnish."

The memorandum indicated to lecturers that they did not need to make formal presentations. It explained, "What is desired is by no means formal lectures, nor, on the other hand, is it expected that those presenting various aspects of the industry will confine themselves to specific problems either solved or unsolved. A simple narrative of actual experiences, commonplace perhaps to the man who tells them, but new to his hearers, is frequently the best type of business case." In fact, many of the lecturers—especially those who were considered "pioneers" of the business—seem to have taken this advice to heart and offered somewhat anecdotal accounts of their historical trajectory through the film industry. This emphasis on the "simple narrative" had important consequences insofar as it tended to standardize the style and content of the presentations and turn disparate lectures into a somewhat unified argument about the film business. That is, despite the irreducible particularity of any one account, each lecturer tended to share with the others the very emphasis *on story*—on an understanding of the modern film industry as something one came to as an individual, while learning subsequently to adopt generalizable rules and business practices that had a supra-individual rationality to them.

Clearly, a variety of motives may have driven the lecturers, within the Ivy League context, to present their business in the most worthy way possible. For our purposes, it is enough to note that, whatever their intent, whatever their desire to construct a moral image of the industry, executives voiced such sentiments at all. Statements of moral responsibility became part of a recorded, emphatic discourse, in the form of lectures, newspaper reports, and publications, on the value of cinema, and they thereby contributed to a public relations effort by the film industry. Any inner convictions on the part of the executives ultimately matter less than the public discourse they helped to construct and promulgate. In this respect, we do not even need to imagine that the lecturers believed their own rhetoric and expressions of higher principles. It is worth assuming that many of the lecturers' speeches were ghostwritten for them. (Indeed, the Joseph P. Kennedy archives include extensive notes by a staff member at Paramount for Jesse Lasky's lecture in the series.) The American film business had long been an industry of imaginative self-fashioning, and industry executives endlessly put staff to work on fictionalizing their stories. But since we are interested here in the very image of promotion created by these lectures, it is all the more appropriate that the executives probably employed writers to craft the mythologies they would present to the HSB students.

There is some indication that supplementary material (most likely including some cases, as we have seen) was distributed to students, and there are also clues to suggest that students were involved in assignments and additional curricular activities. For example, the confidential memorandum indicated that students were given access to library materials on the film business, although it is not clear if an actual reading list was distributed. The published transcript of the course, *The Story of the Films*, included a one-page bibliography on film, and it might well be that many of the items had been obtained for the HSB library (for example, a Will Hays piece from a 1927 issue of Arch Shaw's business magazine, *System*, is cited) and were recommended and made available to the students in the Business Policy course. An even more important suggestion of how students were encouraged to conduct work beyond the confines of the lecture series came at the very end of the memorandum, where the lecturers were told that students would "also have the stimulation that comes from the requirement by the School of written reports in which the knowledge gained in this part of the course must be utilized." Unfortunately, there seems to be no documentation available on just what the assignments were: Were they directives to work out various cases or problems? Were they to be responses to the content of individual lectures? Would they involve data collection or other forms of library research?

The official length of each class session was fifty minutes, although it seems that some speakers went a bit over that time. There were stenographers at all the lectures, and there is some indication that transcripts of the talks were distributed on an ongoing basis to upcoming lecturers. Interestingly, for a course that received a fair amount of attention in the press (even if many of the items were planted), journalists were not allowed to sit in on the course itself and, in fact, were not given much access to the industry luminaries. There is the sense that, no matter how much those responsible for the course hoped its creation would receive journalistic promotion, Harvard administrators wanted the class sessions themselves to be handled like any other curricular offering, without spectacle or fanfare. At the same time, however, it is noteworthy that many of the talks were reported on in a wide range of periodicals such as the *New York Motion Picture Herald*, the *Boston Globe*, the *New York Times*, *Moving Picture World*, the *Christian Science Monitor*, and even more far-flung papers such as the *Schenectady Union*, the *Providence News*, the *San Francisco Exhibitor*, and the *Butte Miner*. Many of these articles reported on the same facts or offered the same descriptions and accounts, and a number included verbatim transcriptions of some lectures (which, given the absence of reporters in the room, makes it more than likely that the periodicals were supplied with copies of the lectures). Once again, it is clear that, even if the course itself was not attended by the press, it was very much envisioned by organizers such as Hays and Kennedy as the object of carefully planned and carefully controlled publicity efforts.

Generally, when the movie business luminaries' schedules permitted, the class met in the morning. In the afternoon, when possible, each lecturer was taken to the Fogg Museum, where, we can presume, there was discussion of the museum's plan to valorize and archive a yearly selection of the top American films and of the consequent need to receive nominations and then prints from the studios. While the higher administration of the university did not seem to seek out contact with the studio executives themselves—

there are, for example, no records of President Lowell having any of them come to his office—it is perhaps a mark of Will Hays's importance as spokesperson for this industry that the university gave him special treatment. Social events and meetings were held in his honor, and in addition to his talk in the HSB course, he had a private meeting with President Lowell and gave a university-wide lunchtime lecture in the Harvard Union that was attended by four hundred people. It was at this talk that Hays made official announcement of the annual Fogg Museum award for best films.[28]

Obviously, in a series of individual lectures by strong-willed men of industry, few of whom had had much experience with higher education, it may be risky to suggest that there was an overall theme to the instruction offered. We need to be wary of imposing too much coherence on disparate speeches. Certainly, though, the confidential instructions to the lecturers spelled out some of what was expected of them and regularized the discourse. Even more, it is clear that Hays in particular was encouraging a series of lectures that would present the film business in the best light. Indeed, there ended up being recurrent themes and presentational strategies in many of the talks and these made for a set of common concerns and goals.

First of all, as I have noted, there was a recurrent emphasis, as even the title of the published volume indicates, on "story." As Kennedy had put it in a March 3, 1927, letter to reassure one lecturer, Robert Cochrane, vice president at Universal, who had written to ask nervously if he had to give a formal speech: "All they want in the way of a talk is for you to spin a few yarns about some of the problems you've had along the lines of advertising and exploitation." Kennedy was assuring Cochrane that his talk could be informal, but it would seem there were also rhetorical benefits to be gained from this emphasis on well-told yarns.

Narrative, indeed, was central to the image of the film industry Kennedy and Hays hoped to foster. On the one hand, there was the overall narrative of an art and industry that grew up from amateur origins to become a highly rationalized and ethically directed business. On the other hand, there were the particular stories of the individual figures within that business. In fact, their tales were seen, in many ways, as both recapitulating and contributing to the larger singular story of the industry's triumph. Thus, many of the talks included anecdotes that established both how quaint the world of film once was and the extent to which that older context had been transcended by reason, efficiency, and a cooperative desire for a higher good.

Take, for instance, the story that opened Harry Warner's lecture on the film business's future developments. Warner recounted how he and his brothers began as small-time exhibitors in Newcastle, Pennsylvania, with an operation that was so bare-bones that they had to borrow their chairs from a local funeral parlor. Yet Warner was emphatic on the ways these quaint preindustrial beginnings had been left behind as the industry grew up: "Picture that theatre with those ninety-six chairs and then picture the Roxy Theatre today, and you will have an idea of the development of the motion picture industry" (319).

In conjunction with this contrast of an older, often amateurish and haphazard "mom-and-pop" operation and a grown-up industry, other recurrent motifs emerged from the talks. For example, to the extent that that contrast did indeed exist, it was assumed that there were specific concrete factors that had led to improvement in the industry and that could be pinpointed and thereby lauded. Thus, for instance, many of the speakers emphasized how a decisive change in their practice came from their realization that the application of rationalized business procedures to production and presentation of films could help the form grow up. Not merely were there older and newer forms of filmmaking, but the shift from one to the other had rationality as its primary cause. To take just one example, when William Fox was asked during the question-and-answer period after his talk if his company relied on the collection of statistics, he replied affirmatively, "A man who tries to operate any large business today without having the proper statistics compiled for him and without knowing all the facts and having them before him is groping in the dark. His competitor who uses modern methods will forge ahead of him" (316).

At the same time, as quite a number of the speakers suggested, it was not enough that the film industry be presented as an efficient operation. In keeping with Hays's particular push to paint the contemporary film industry as not merely rational but also moral, the lecturers continually emphasized the ethical nature of the movie business—ethical both in the way the business was being conducted and in the results or effects the product of the business, the films themselves, had on the public. First, the business was presented as run along lines of cooperation, of graciousness, and of gentlemanliness; no doubt, the industry figures would warily have seen each other as rivals in any other context, but in the neutral space of Harvard, they presented their realm as one of benign, mutual cooperation. For example, in his lecture, Harry Warner noted how the Fox Film Corporation was offering a sound system that rivaled Warner Bros.' own machine, but he explained to the students how the two companies were working together to enable exhibitors to have access, if need be, to both systems and to choose whichever one worked best. The image proffered was of a market in which competition existed only to give all new products their equal chance, and in which there was responsible assessment of consumer needs in determining which of the options available in the market ultimately would be chosen. To the extent that there ever had been destructive rivalry in the film business, the very emphasis of the speakers on narrative—that is, on the film business as having a history governed by maturation and amelioration of business practices—allowed simultaneously for the acknowledgment of such rivalry in the past and for its disavowal as a force continuing on in any way into the present. As Sidney Kent put it in his presentation, "Distributing the Product," "This is an age of consolidation of merchandising effort. I mean by that, that right down the line you find the bigger companies more and more providing their own show windows, their own show cases, in which to sell their merchandise. Our business at the present time is just getting over a period of fierce competition. It is still very competitive but it is competitive on a little higher basis than it was a few years ago" (228).

To be sure, some of the speakers still exhibited a degree of territoriality, but even then there was always an emphasis on the higher goals of the industry as a whole and thus on the ways that whatever territoriality still inhered in the business was necessary to its greater functioning. Thus, for instance, when short-films producer Earle W. Hammons gave his lecture on the business of shorts, he argued strongly that companies such as his, devoted to that format, should be in charge of production and distribution of such films and that the major studios should stay out of the short-film arena. Yet, even here, in the long run, a notion of a well-run industry finding its basis in cooperation would win out: as Hammons went on to explain, each type of company would be most efficient when it made the sort of films it was best equipped for—feature films for the big studios, short films for outfits such as Hammons's—and there should thus be a higher cooperation in which companies provided diverse products that could be exhibited in integrated showings made up of feature and short films alike. Every company, in its own way, could contribute to the greater good.

But if a first sense of the moral had to do with the running of the film business along ethical lines, in many of the lectures there was also the assumption—ultimately much more important—that the industry of film found its deepest moral justification in the fact that it brought a special, uplifting good to the public. Where the mere emphasis on the rational running of the business would not in itself distinguish the film industry from any other modern industry, many of the lecturers were at pains to argue that their product was indeed different from others. As they presented it, the film business produced something that was not just financial but also aesthetically valuable. Films might be the product of a business, but they were more than just an effect of figures and calculations, more than just quantity: rather, they had the distinction of *quality*. For example, a decisive step in the development in the film business came, it was suggested in several lectures, in the very recognition that film could be an important cultural form rather than low art or mere pastime. Thus, as William Fox noted in his contribution titled "Reminiscences and Observations," "The price of the story [i.e., the scenario] is no longer measured by its length but by the greatness of it and, instead of $25 for a story, as high as $250,000 is being paid for the right to reproduce a great story in motion pictures" (304).

Predictably, there were two forms of greater good that the lecturers suggested distinguish the cultural works of cinema from more utilitarian products put out on the market. First, there was what we might call the sociological good: film as a new form of education more adequate to the modern age than older pedagogies, film as a path to better communication, film as a propagandist for a better (i.e., American) way of life, and so on. Here, the lecturers would emphasize that beyond its entertainment value, American film found virtue in its presentation of valuable images and lessons of everyday life—film as visually effective instructional material. On the other hand, there was the aesthetic good: beyond its transmission of good or useful instruction and its inculcation of proper morality, film was valuable because it helped bring artistry, imagination, and creativity to the world.

A typical example of both of these qualities of film as a force for a higher good came in Harry Warner's talk on future developments in film. Predictably, given what his own company was up to in 1927, Warner's lecture centered on the implications that the coming of sound would have for the movies, and in this new technology he saw particular benefits in aesthetic appreciation and educative content alike. On the one hand, as is well known, Harry Warner's own interest in the sound film had to do with the recording not of dialogue but of music: his taste was for the music track as affective realm beyond verbal communication. As he put it in his talk, "If I myself would not have gone across the street to see or hear a talking picture, I surely could not expect the public to do it. But Music! That is another story. An organ playing to a picture was the thing that I visualized. . . . That vision came to me. So I took it up with the head of the Western Electric Company and arrived at an understanding with him" (320–21). On the other hand, Warner also presented the sound film as offering a special social good in the ways it could communicate important civic lessons on a wide scale:

We honestly believe the vitaphone is going to do more good for humanity than anything else ever invented. We all know that if you and I can talk to one another, we can understand one another. If Lincoln's Gettysburg Address could be repeated all over the world, maybe the world at large would understand what America stands for. We think that people read and know a lot of things, but when we get out into the world and see the masses of people and find out how many are working so hard to earn a living that they have not time to read, then we realize how much remains to be done in the way of bringing knowledge to them. If we can have a message of friendship or enlightenment that can be broadcast throughout the world, maybe the nations will be led to understand one another better. The vitaphone can do all that. (334–35)

Significantly, these comments on the vitaphone as a force for world communication came as part of an answer to a student's economic-based question about the cost to exhibitors of the vitaphone machines. By switching from the question of expense to that of the greater good, Warner seemed to be saying that money did not matter when something higher is at stake. Warner took a practical issue—one that was, after all, perfectly appropriate on the occasion of a course in a school of business—and turned it into a bit of moral self-promotion, of publicity for his work as part of a higher good. It almost seems as if Warner had been waiting for such a question in order to displace it into a moral realm.

I have argued that one regularity of the discourse in the lecture series had to do with narrative—a representation of the film industry as one that had moved from early arbitrariness and potential immorality to adult responsibility and rationality. I want to suggest now that in the context of the HSB the narratives of industry evolution offered by its leaders also became the story of the potential role that the professionalizing caste of business students could play in it. In other words, by coming to Harvard to tell tales of cinema's history, the industry leaders were offering students the possibility of imagining themselves as narrative agents too. Just as the case-study method made students into no-nonsense problem solvers, the narratives of industry addressed students as tough-minded men of action. I use *men* deliberately, since I want to suggest that HSB pedagogy was very much about the production of a gendered class of business leaders. Harvard's Business Policy course, restricted to men who were preparing for no-nonsense professions, offered a pedagogy that was direct, effective, and sharply practical—the world of tough problems and their tough solutions.

Here, we remember that the idea for a business policy course that would focus on concrete problems faced by industries came in large part from Arch

Shaw, publisher of an important journal of business practices, *System*. As American studies scholar John Kasson shows in a fine study of early twentieth-century modes of masculinity, *System*, for all the image its title might convey of a boring and specialized technical journal of business, is in fact readable as a direct figuration of the complications of masculine roles in the period.[29] *System* did deal, as its very title suggested, with that which was rationalized and systematic—or increasingly becoming so—in the new world of the modern business enterprise. But it also showed how a newly strengthened masculinity could avoid being lost in vast systems of business by becoming itself systematic—that is, by learning codified but personalized procedures for dealing effectively and forcefully with an increasingly instrumentalized world. To be part of the system meant learning the rules and rituals of a profession. This appealed to a masculinity that found attractive the hard realm of rational process. *System* taught about the world of business by example—specifically, by tales (both true and fictional) about men who confronted problems in the world of business and overcame them through a combination of individual character traits and general absorption of systematic rules that transcended individuality. The cases in *System* tried to maintain a delicate balance: on the one hand, too much individualization in a story and it would seem that the entrepreneur succeeded through personal talents that no one else might be imagined to share; on the other hand, too much general law and rule, and individuality would be lost in the anonymity of a demasculinizing network of abstract laws and procedures.

In its training of men in practical realms of business, the case-study method also tried to negotiate similar options. For example, the film lectures did not merely rely on a collection of problems and solutions but also, through the testimony of luminaries from the history of film, rendered that history as a set of gripping stories, narratives of clever men who surmounted adversity (and, indeed, talked eloquently of the adversities they still faced—ones in the industry or their personal lives, as was the case with Marcus Loew and his illness). In this respect, it can be argued that the film lecture series in the HSB was also about the building up of a particular kind of masculine subject. Thus, the soft realm of taste and of aesthetic appreciation would be left behind or relegated to very specific venues elsewhere (in this case, to the fine arts, where the initiative for artistic appreciation of film would find its home). The lectures would introduce young men into the modern world of a now grown-up, rationalized film industry, but it would do so through vivid example—the first-person narration of survivors from the early days of film production who by their presence would give concrete embodiment of cases but who by their stories of triumph over early adversity would dramatize entrepreneurship as a process of growth, a modernizing supersession of antiquarian, presystematic pseudo-methods. In other words, the testimony of pioneers would provide a glimpse of the old ways, no longer appropriate to the heavily industrialized world of modern businesses, but it would also suggest that anyone with enough entrepreneurship could learn to turn amateur insight into professional acumen. Necessarily, then, the HSB course not only involved instruction in contemporary up-to-date methods of the industry but made a necessary detour through film history so as to show what had been, and where, with proper rational method, it could yet go.

Through the many ways in which the HSB engaged with film, we find attempts to mediate individuality and system. Professionalized filmmaking could not occur without personal sparks of creativity, but it also could not come into being without the regulative rationality of business procedures. System and personality each became factors in the industry, each keeping the other in line, each giving the other a necessary role (and therefore raison d'être) and thereby allowing a mediation of the abstract and the individual. The new captains of industry, trained by such an institution as Harvard, would help the film industry realize its economic potential, but they would do so only because they were taking up the legacy—even as they surpassed it—of the original founding figures.

Noting that the talks that made up the motion picture series did not present "a formal, schematized presentation of the subject," the preface to *The Story of the Films* emphasized significantly how the narratives of the movie pioneers both were valuable in themselves yet constituted a stage that had to be transcended:

> The lack of stress laid on mere system by the group of founders is itself not without significance. These far-sighted pioneers did not begin with ready-made systems. They divined, as it were, the place the film would occupy in the sphere of public entertainment and applied their energies to the task of developing and promoting it. They guided a natural movement and shaped its broad outlines until the very bulk of the industry compelled the adoption of that subordination of unruly detail, that discipline and economy, which we call system. Even at this stage the human element cannot be eliminated. (xv)

For all its emphasis on system, then, narrative and personality were central to the pedagogy of the HSB in its study of enterprises such as the motion picture industry. On the one hand, to the extent that narrative represented the eccentric and unsystematic efforts of lone individuals (such as the movie pioneers), it stood as something that needed to be transcended by a modernized and rationalized system. On the other hand, there was something salutary about narrative's emphasis on the irreducibility of individual case and personal story. Narrative concretized abstract principles, humanizing them and rendering them vivid, lively, and exemplary. It suggested that business need not be a site of alienation and abstraction. As American studies scholar Esther Yogev suggests in an illuminating study on the governing ideology of the HSB in the 1920s, narrative implied that business *schooling* need not be imagined as bereft of humanistic value and moral vision. As Yogev puts it,

> This use of the symbols of American myth [i.e., narratives of pioneer spirit and the quest for success] presented the university business administration faculties as not only providers of training and academic education, but also the crucibles that formed the "conquerors of the new frontier." . . . This sort of rhetoric was rather reminiscent of the myth of success popular at the end of the last [i.e., nineteenth] century which focused on the "self-made man" who rose "from rags to riches." The new version, however, contained an additional feature: the new heroes did not "make" themselves, as portrayed in the traditional American dream, but succeeded with the help of the corporation, its skilled managers, and the channels of promotion it had established. . . . Not only did such narratives help establish the social sciences and scientific management as legitimate and indispensable to the firm, they also presented them as serving and protecting the workers, and consequently society as a whole.[30]

Insofar as the Business Policy course was intended to offer its students their own places in the narrative of industrial evolution, it is worth noting that one concrete manifestation of this practical aim came in the use of the lecture series as a recruitment enterprise. After the course was over, its instructor, Nathan Isaacs, sent the following summary to the university's information officer as background for a proposed article on the course that an unnamed Canadian journal was supposedly planning to run (the journal was most likely the *Canadian Moving Picture Digest*, which did print a number of pieces about the course):

> From the point of view of the School, the series of lectures has served several purposes remarkably well. In the first place, as was anticipated, the industry compressed within a surprisingly short period, within the experience of the men presenting the data, the typical history of a business. It did not matter, in fact it may have helped the general effect, that the men presenting the material were not conscious of the fact that it was typical. Some of them insisted that their business was unique. To

our students, however, it was remarkably clear that the early hesitation of the bankers in recognizing the industry and the peculiar consequences in its financial history—to take only one example—had parallels in many other infant industries. Quite aside from the actual information given, the opportunity to study at close range the men who had achieved outstanding success in the industry was of value to our students. They were deeply impressed with the industry, the attention to detail, the resourcefulness, and the vision of most of these men. That they were deeply interested in the possibilities and importance of the business is illustrated by the fact that about a hundred of them took advantage of the opportunity of arranging special interviews with representatives of the industry in connection with their personal problem of choosing a career. It seems that a very considerable number of the men graduating this year will be placed in business positions connected with the motion picture industry.

Perhaps the principal interest of the School in the venture has been in the establishment of a contact with an industry that has heretofore been studied too little. The foundation has been laid for further study by the School of the problems presented in this industry. It will thus take its place in business study along with a hundred other industries that are now furnishing the "cases" with which the new science of business is being created.

While Isaacs's summary was itself part of a publicity effort and must not be considered a factually reliable source of information, it is useful for the ways it both discussed aspects of what undoubtedly transpired in the course and implied some of the ongoing functions the lecture series might have been expected to perform beyond its actual stopping point in the spring of 1927. For example, as Isaac's letter bears out, one clear purpose of the film industry lecture series was to serve as a beacon for recruitment. Indeed, there is almost the indication that the specific content of the course mattered less than the networks of influence the course could open up. In this respect, the course may have been typical of much Ivy League instruction in the collegiate period of the 1920s (and beyond), where the valuable lessons to be learned had less to do with course content and the inculcation of practical skills than with personal contacts that would be fostered and cultivated. Interestingly, Yale officials came to hear about the HSB course and wrote to Kennedy to recommend students of their own to the film industry. Kennedy curtly replied that he had enough candidates from the HSB (he cited the number fifty) and wanted to keep recruitment efforts in-house.

Both the industry executives and the HSB administrators appear indeed to have envisioned the course from the start as a recruitment forum. At a minimal level, recruitment could occur on a somewhat ad hoc basis through personal recommendations. For example, in the fall after the course had been given, Paramount treasurer Ralph A. Kohn wrote to Dean Donham, asking him to send names each year of HSB students who might work well in the film industry. As he put it, "I will be in a position to place, from time to time, in minor positions, men who are graduates of universities, and who have in connection with their courses taken commercial subjects."[31] But beyond such individual initiative of this or that studio figure to engage in recruitment, it seems clear indeed that there was the desire—on the part both of the HSB and, to a certain degree, of the film industry—that the HSB serve as a *regular* source of new employees in business areas of film. For example, on November 5, 1927, Theodore Streibert wrote to Dean Donham to say that Kennedy had talked about ongoing recruitment with R. H. Cochrane at Universal, "who you will remember is Vice President and General Manager of Universal Pictures" (and who also had lectured in the course). Although it is unclear if this specific act of networking led to anything in the way of recruitment, several aspects of it are interesting. First, it is worth noting in passing the very fact that Streibert felt it necessary to remind Dean Donham of just who Cochrane was: for all the newspaper fanfare that accompanied the film course when it was offered, it did not have any great and lasting impact on the HSB or the larger Harvard administration, and it may not be surprising that things related to film had fallen off Dean Donham's radar. More important, it is noteworthy that Kennedy was recommending some sort of recruitment activity with Universal, a potential rival studio to his own FBO operation: Kennedy clearly had used the Harvard course to network and build up his standing in the industry (and, along with Will Hays, to present the film business not as one of territoriality but of a cooperativeness beneficial to all), and it seems that he was continuing to do this by cooperating with important figures at other studios. Insofar as the film industry was an oligopoly driven as much by patterns of interaction as of rivalry between studios, there could be a sharing of resources among studios. Indeed, just as the lectures themselves emphasized the industry as one in which individual firms worked together for the common good, so too could recruitment serve a function as industry self-promotion: run cooperatively, it would show how everyone got along.

In at least one instance, there seems to have been a direct recruitment success as a result of the course. On May 16, 1927 (i.e., a month and a half after his lecture), Samuel Katz, from Publix Theatres, wrote to Dean Donham, "I do want you to know how pleased we are that some of your boys are coming into our business." On May 25, he followed this up with a second letter in which he indicated that three Harvard men had just been interviewed and that he had "arranged to start them in our business." The timing of these letters—after the course had ended—would suggest that these interviews occurred not at Harvard but more likely in New York at Publix offices.

On the other hand, not all such informal modes of recruitment panned out. On June 9, 1927, Horace Gilbert, operating as an HSB assistant dean, wrote to Harry Warner to recommend two "Oriental students" who were interested, he said, in helping set up distribution for films in the Far East: "They would very much like to secure Vitaphone rights for this territory." But an undated reply from Warner was curt: "It will be quite some time before we will be in a position to do anything in the countries you mention."

Beyond individual initiative on the part of this or that student trying to contact the studios or this or that studio getting in touch with administrators at the HSB, it seems that there was also a more formal structure for recruitment. Instead of simply serving as a general announcement of the ever more pressing fact that the industry was being run along rational lines and increasingly would need professionally trained staff, the Business Policy course appears to have included an organized recruitment session (or sessions) of some sort. It seems that what Nathan Isaacs referred to in his summary of the course as "the opportunity of arranging special interviews" was handled in a somewhat formalized manner as a kind of job fair in which students were interviewed at Harvard as the film course came to a close. Evidence for this appears in a letter written by Theodore Streibert on February 9, 1929 (two years after the film course), to one of the HSB administrators. Streibert, now working at RKO, wrote to declare a willingness to continue considering HSB students for jobs in the industry. But, as he indicated, he felt there needed to be a weeding-out procedure so that not every interested student would be granted an interview: "I never want to go through another experience such as I had in interviewing men, when I talked to some fifty boys over two days just after the lectures on the motion picture industry."

It is unclear whether this newer form of formalized recruitment—a weeding-out procedure by which the HSB selected specific candidates to send on to the studios—was ever implemented in any systematic way. The few bits of correspondence in the 1930s between the HSB and studio officials would appear to indicate that the idea of recruitment—if not the more general idea of ongoing collaboration of any sort between the school and business—was on the wane. For example, as late as February 19, 1936, Dean Donham would write to an RKO officer, J. R. McDonough, to recommend for employment a student of Elton Mayo, one Russell Wallace, who had been doing film-related research as part of a project on "human behavior aspects of industry," but he received a curt reply that there were no positions available. Earlier in the period, RKO may have been able to offer positions to several of Howard T. Lewis's student researchers, but now, as one of the first studios to go into receivership because of the Depression, it could no longer be so magnanimous with Harvard's college boys.

Certainly, it is hard to know how to interpret such evidence as the curtness of reply, the trailing off of interest, and the sheer ad hoc quality of so many of the attempts to cultivate the newly established networks that had come from the course. On the one hand, it is easy to assume that once the 1927 course had been offered and received media attention, its primary function of publicizing the solidity and seriousness both of the industry and of business education would have been achieved and the course could fade away.

On the other hand, it seems clear there had been interest in continuing the course and even some expectation that this would happen. Indeed, in Joseph Kennedy's earliest telegram to Will Hays to announce the conclusion of negotiations for the lecture series with Harvard, he had indicated that the university was planning on "making it part [of] their regular curriculum." Kennedy's interest in regular ventures in film at the HSB would wane very quickly, but he does appear to have had enthusiasm for the project in its earliest stages. For instance, he orchestrated reports on the lecture series in the trade press that implied that there was every intention that the course would be offered again. Thus, on April 7, 1927, *Film Daily* noted, "Establishment of a *permanent* course in motion pictures, covering all phases of the industry, is planned by Harvard University, following successful launching of *a trial course*. Extension of the Harvard plan to other universities throughout the nation was predicted yesterday by [Joseph] Kennedy" (my emphasis). Likewise, on April 10, 1927, the *New York World* quoted Kennedy as saying that "much experience has been gained toward making it [the course] more definitive in the future." Most revealingly, an April 6, 1927, piece in the *Exhibitors Review* declared, "Following the course and the determination of the business school to make a study of the industry a part of its regular curriculum, research agents from the school will investigate the various branches of the industry this summer and next Fall the study will be inaugurated in accordance with the so-called 'case' system." This item is most interesting in that it refers both to a regular curriculum and to data collection that would feed into such a curriculum: it is tempting to think that the research team being set up for the summer involved Howard

T. Lewis and the group of graduate students he thanks in *The Motion Picture Industry*, since this would again imply that the HSB was involved in film studies on a number of interconnected fronts (with Joseph Kennedy and his studio serving as primary sponsor for the interwoven initiatives).

There probably is a series of reasons, though, why the 1927 course ended up being a one-shot occurrence. Certainly, as I have already noted, Kennedy's withdrawal of support as he pulled back from deeper involvement with the world of film probably cooled the HSB administrators to further investment in film pedagogy. In late April 1927—around the time the course was ending, in other words—Kennedy had written to Donham and offered $10,000 of support for film-related work at the HSB over the next three years. But as Kennedy's interest in film faded, he began to back down from his promise of subvention. As early as June 1927, when the Hays Office sent the final agreement for the Fogg Museum initiative to Kennedy (a series of fifteen points covered in three pages), Kennedy wrote back with his approval of the plan's content but announced that he was no longer going to be an active participant.

From this point on, relations between the HSB and Kennedy seem somewhat distant as the school tried to collect on the April 1927 pledge. Thus, the school periodically sent Kennedy announcements of events, but the intention seems to have been to remind him of his financial pledge to them. For example, two years after the film lecture series, in July 1929, Donham wrote to Kennedy, describing a special summer session for business executives and inviting Kennedy to enroll some of his employees. That this seemingly courtesy invitation was actually a subtle reminder of Kennedy's obligations appears likely; just two months later, HSB administrators came out directly and asked Kennedy to send the funds he had promised. Kennedy did send some of the money, but not all of it, and as of 1931, the HSB was still after him for his promised subvention. Finally, in the middle of that year, Kennedy paid off the last chunk of money ($10,000) and closed the books on his involvement with film at Harvard.

Whatever the desire of the HSB administrators to return from time to time to a pedagogy of film, it must be noted that the 1927 lecture series had much about it that stood as a one-shot occasion. For example, Kennedy's success in tempting the luminaries of the film business to Cambridge was not an accomplishment to be repeated easily (if at all). Not merely had some of the original arrangements been complicated (e.g., Cecil B. DeMille's talk had been difficult to schedule and came only when he was able to coordinate his visit with his required presence on the East Coast for the premiere of his film *King of Kings*). Further, not merely were some of the visits literally unrepeatable (most obviously, in the case of Marcus Loew, who died soon after his lecture), but one can only imagine that the film industry figures would have felt less impelled to return to Harvard after the accomplishments of their initial visit (especially if Kennedy was no longer involved). The first time around, they may have felt a certain pride or curiosity at being invited into the hallowed halls of the Ivy League institution, but they undoubtedly would have assumed that one visit was enough to accomplish their public relations goals (especially insofar as their talks were being preserved for posterity in *The Story of the Films*).

Additionally, the importance of film to the HSB should not be overstated. For the HSB, the very fact that the film industry was treated like all other businesses insofar as it was involved in a quite typical cycle of manufacture and consumption meant that the course did not necessarily stand out from the curriculum in any particular way. To a certain degree, this lecture series eased its way into an existing curricular framework and did not impact institutional memory. Revealingly, in the chapter on the founding and development of the HSB that he cowrote for the official history of the university, Dean Donham made no mention of the course.[32]

One can readily imagine that one series of lectures on an industry that was being studied as comparable to other industries and not singled out for its glamour or exoticism would not have garnered any heightened attention. At the end of each academic year at Harvard, a summary of the academic units' accomplishments was published as the annual bulletin, a single volume submitted to the president. Although the business school entry written by Dean Donham for the 1926–27 bulletin does include the names of the film course lecturers in an appendix listing all visiting lecturers for all courses for the year, there is no reference to the film lectures in the body of Donham's report. The only exceptional event to get special mention was the dedication ceremony for the business school's new campus in June 1927, and it is obvious that this, more than the content of any single course initiative, dominated the attention of the business school administration. In his standard history of the School, HSB Professor Melvin Copeland refers to 1927 as "a dividing point in Dean Donham's administration," and it is clear that the dean had a great deal to concern him.[33] In fact, in addition to such important HSB-related events as the dedication of the new campus, Dean Donham's wife had been seriously injured in a car accident in February and had required much care from her husband; Donham himself had started to suffer from fatigue and other ailments and was hospitalized for a renal disorder in April, and in June he would suffer a major heart attack. But one senses that even without these personal crises, the film course was not considered key in the larger scheme of things at the HSB.

Earlier in this chapter I noted that the film lecture series at the HSB was conjoined by its key players to the announcement that the university's fine arts division would sponsor an annual selection of aesthetically important American films, and it is worth examining what happened to that allied venture.[34] From the start, the fate of each enterprise was linked to the other. At the very least, there were material connections between the initiatives to offer a lecture series at the HSB and to set up an archive and annual award. For example, when the practical details of the selection were being worked out, it was suggested that the copies of the chosen films be deposited at the HSB, where space was available in the new library. Although this seems little more than an expedient resolution of a physical plant issue, it does show that there was a common assumption of cooperation between these two parts of the university.

But, as I indicated earlier, it is tempting to go further and hypothesize that an initiative like the annual fine arts selection would originally have been of interest to the HSB for the ways it could serve as an aesthetic complement or supplement to the more hard-nosed training in industry that the Business Policy course would provide. That is, by conjoining itself with an award for distinctiveness in film art, the HSB could hope to link its specific work in business practices to the connotations of a morally upright world of aesthetic uplift. If, as I have argued, schools of business had to prove that their concern with professionalism and scientific reason did not preclude questions of value, the HSB's participation in a venture that also sought aesthetic distinction might provide a way to emphasize the school's very commitment to the higher good.

In an interesting essay on the founding philosophy of *Fortune* magazine—which began publication a few years after the HSB course and was intended to be a mass-market celebration of the world of modern business—American studies scholar Michael Augspurger argues that there was an attempt by overseers of industry in the United States in the interwar years to show that business had both moved into a new realm of rationality and traded cutthroat competitiveness for a more salable image of public service and responsibility.[35] In particular, Augspurger suggests, a journal such as *Fortune* set out to extol the achievements of business in the realm of quality—not only the quality of the goods produced and marketed but also the quality of service and personal integrity that supposedly accompanied the circulation of those goods. The industrialist of the modern age would be not merely a producer and seller of commodities but a public leader through his cultivation of consumer citizenship as social benefit. This new type of businessman had to groom himself as a figure whose very life was seen to incarnate higher virtues, and this meant, among other things, a cultivation of aesthetic values. Hence, in the specific case of *Fortune*, the magazine paid much attention to lifestyle, with a particular emphasis on a training in aesthetic appreciation and the cultivation of finer tastes. For example, the journal included practical instruction in art collecting, and not only or always with an eye toward the monetary benefits of such collecting; rather, it was assumed that the ability to know which works were valuable showed not only business sagacity but also the industrialist's possession of a deeper quality of aesthetic discernment.

Augspurger argues that *Fortune* magazine was symptomatic of a larger 1920s cultivation of a new aesthetic image for business. The fine arts initiative at Harvard would fit in well in such a context. If the initiative could show that film differed from other commodities insofar as individual products of the cinema industry were differentiated by aesthetic value (rather than, say, utilitarian ones), then the HSB would be demonstrating its civic ability to cultivate business practice as something worthy in higher, cultural terms. Indeed, as we have seen, the speakers within the HSB course themselves endlessly emphasized that they were doing more than constructing a product like any other. To whatever degree of honesty, they presented the cinema as a valuable mass art: valuable both because it was an art and because it was one that reached many people. For example, as Jesse Lasky put it in his Business Policy lecture titled "Production Problems," "[W]e have a peculiar industry. I call it an industrial art or rather an art industry, for I always put the art first and I am always going to" (115). In these terms, the annual selection of high-quality films might allow a mediation of art and commerce (and by being housed in another division, it enabled the HSB to suggest that it was in no way sacrificing its own industrial commitment even as it acknowledged the need for aesthetic values). Like the art connoisseur businessman that *Fortune* magazine set out to cultivate, the Fogg initiative allowed the HSB to associate with a world of cultural distinction while continuing its fundamental work of business practice.

Of course, the fact that aesthetic distinction was being sought within the heart of the mass culture of cinema can seem somewhat contradictory. Film, after all, was not automatically considered one of the high and worthy arts. Here, Harvard's fine arts division seems to have been particularly bold in endorsing the notion that American film could deserve the title of Art. One of the key figures here appears to have been fine arts professor Chandler R.

Post, an expert in painting and a general Renaissance man (supposedly, he knew seventeen languages and taught subjects in English, French, Italian, Greek, and Russian). Post, who had written a classic twelve-volume history of Spanish painting, was also a fervent moviegoer. Indeed, his April 30, 1960, obituary in the *Harvard University Gazette* makes specific mention of his love of movies: "He became an admirer of motion pictures and was said to have been offered an advising job in Hollywood." When a list of supporters at Harvard of the fine arts initiative was drawn up in March 1927, it was indicated that Post "for the last 15 years . . . has been rating motion pictures on their artistic values including settings, artistry and acting." As figures like Post seemed to realize, if there was a risk to Harvard in seeking aesthetic distinction in the popular culture of film, there could also be a specific advantage.

Indeed, it might have mattered that film was not too fine a fine art. As Michael Augspurger suggests for the specific case of *Fortune*, and as is also suggested by the broader theorization by American studies scholar T. J. Jackson Lears of the new entrepreneurial culture of the time, there was always a set of tensions and risks in the drive to argue the higher aesthetic values of business. For example, the notion of aesthetic cultivation could lead to an impression of feminization that might sit uneasily with the sense that business required forceful figures of effective masculinity. That is, while it might be good for the businessman's image for him to associate with the refined world of aesthetic production, there was always the risk that this would damage the other necessary image of hard-hitting, nononsense maker and breaker of deals. Even as business and aesthetics benefited from their association, they also existed in tense relationship. Revealingly, although he argued for workmanship and personal investment in craft as an alternative to the alienations of mass production, Thorstein Veblen would also—in his infamous critique of "conspicuous consumption"—inveigh against craft that became too caught up in aesthetics for its own sake, one that sacrificed virile utility for useless ornament. There needed to be a careful balance between work as pragmatic and work as aesthetic: too much of the former led to crassness and an image of the market as Hobbesian battle for personal financial benefit; too much of the latter led to inefficient waste and to fears of feminine passivity in which inactive aesthetic contemplation took precedence over active doing. Speaking of *Fortune*, Michael Augspurger puts it this way, "The magazine offered businesspeople art that was neither aristocratically anticommercial nor professionally exclusive. It stressed instead experience, objectivity, and pragmatism—the values of business—and expressed each of these values in opposition both to what [*Fortune* publisher Henry] Luce called 'significant snobberies' of outmoded aristocracy and to the intellectualism and self-exclusion of academics" (436).

In this respect, the movies could have offered an alternative to effete aestheticism and its snobbery, and this might help explain why the annual film awards at Harvard centered on *American* works of cinema. Beyond the fact that industry figures like Hays may have specifically militated for prizewinners that would spotlight U.S. cultural achievement, American movies were particularly valuable because they were art but not too much so: to refer to Augspurger's terms, they too "stressed instead experience, objectivity, and pragmatism." The movies may not have been as much a form of high culture as other ventures in art (whether cinematic or otherwise), but that might have been their advantage: they avoided the associations that European art had with elitism, dilettantish connoisseurship, and even overly refined and overly civilized aestheticism. Like the case studies considered in the HSB Business Policy course—in which pragmatic solutions were sought for concrete problems—American movies offered hard-hitting narratives in which strong-willed heroes faced adversity and triumphed over it. Both movies and business practice were offered up as seductive stories of American accomplishment.

American popular film's advantage over forms of modernism and the effete high arts was that it did not bear the taint of European culture—the connotations of a supposedly decadent, effete, even corrupt culture that traded classical harmony for brooding psychologism, cynical relativism, perversity, and so on. Even as it could aspire to the quality of art, film was exempt from the most negative connotations of high modernist aestheticism. To the extent that the movies could be claimed as quintessentially American, they would serve well as a mark of the country's achievement of a valid, vital homegrown tradition. In this respect, the 1927 Business Policy course, which extolled the ability of a rationally run industry to produce valuable works rich in ethical and aesthetic public responsibility, and the Fogg initiative, which intended to single out some films from others and to do so while concentrating on a specifically American tradition, both participated in a decidedly Americanist project.

Certainly, the Fogg Museum initiative started out with much enthusiasm and ambition behind it, and with industry luminaries showing much interest. The long article in the *Boston Transcript* that came out at the end of the HSB course offered an anecdote about one such visit: "Mr. [Jesse] Lasky, visiting the Fogg Museum, observed the system of lighting and exclaimed that if the movies had understood that years ago they would have saved millions." (If Lasky did indeed say this, undoubtedly he was exaggerating for the purposes of pleasing his hosts. It is hard to believe that he would have found in museum lighting a system of illumination that would solve technical problems but that no one in the industry had been aware of up to that moment.) Clearly, the visits had a purely performative dimension: the very fact of the industry luminaries' visits could be reported on to show how a modern business enterprise was not incompatible with the venerable space of the museum. Undoubtedly, however, the university's concern to make sure the industry leaders not only gave their lectures but also visited the museum had a more far-reaching practical intent: as part of the Fogg initiative for annual film awards, it was hoped that studios would make prints available to the university—first to the judges who would do the selecting, and then to the archive where the finalists would be permanently housed. For the Harvard initiative to work, the cooperation and material generosity of the studio heads and administrators were needed. Harvard stood to gain a major collection of film, and the industry executives needed to be courted.

One of the first traces of the awards initiative comes in a January 21, 1927, letter to Will Hays by several figures in fine arts and at the Fogg Art Museum: Edward R. Forbes, director of the Fogg; Paul J. Sachs, the museum's assistant director; and George Chase, chairman of the fine arts department. This first letter—written while negotiations for the visits by industry luminaries were still under way—implies strongly that there had already been pointed discussion of the idea of an annual award linked somehow to what would be happening in the school of business around film:

> We are delighted to learn, through Mr. Joseph P. Kennedy, that you approve of the project of the Department of Fine Arts and the Fogg Art Museum of Harvard University to inaugurate here a library and archive of selected motion picture films which shall represent the best artistic achievement of the industry. We appreciate your cordial interest and willingness to cooperate in the establishment and development of such a collection.
>
> It seems to us especially fitting that this recognition of the potentialities of the youngest of arts should come first at Harvard, oldest of American universities. . . .
>
> We are preparing a plan for the project which we wish to submit to you for suggestions and criticism. It will give us much pleasure to have you lunch or dine with us and other members of the Fine Arts Department, who are especially interested in the idea, when we can discuss the whole matter in detail and secure your approval and advice. We hope that this will be possible at the time of your impending visit to Cambridge, which Dr. Kennedy tells us you plan for early March.

It is noteworthy that Will Hays's approval seemed so crucial. It is clear that from the start it was assumed that Hays would play a key role in the process. At the very least, his approval would help in getting the industry to support the initiative and make films and related materials available to the university.

Although Hays once again ended up pulling the strings behind this initiative, the official publicity of the time attributed the original idea for the Fogg collection to Harvard personnel. Specifically, several documents directly attribute the inspiration for an annual film selection to Harvard's secretary (and public relations officer), James Seymour. For example, the MPPDA files contain a description of a March 15, 1927, meeting with Joseph Kennedy and Will Hays, when they were in Cambridge for their talks. The document says explicitly that Seymour was "responsible for the suggestion of extending the activities of the University from the business field [i.e., the HSB course] into the fine arts field." Likewise, the planted article in the *Boston Transcript*, mentioned earlier, asserted that the original articulation of the project occurred at the university before being vetted by industry figures:

> James Seymour, who is secretary for publicity and alumni affairs, and who had met Kennedy through Dean Donham, proposed to Professor Paul Sachs, one of the directors of the Fogg Art Museum, the notion that if films, past and present, could be got, they might be of value to the museum and the fine art department. Dr. Sachs thought there were great possibilities, also that the plan ought to be put up to a group potentially interested which included, beside himself, Edward W. Forbes, co-director of the Fogg; Dean George H. Chase, of the Graduate School of Arts and Sciences and professor of fine arts; A. C. Coolidge, professor of history and director of the library, and Chandler Post. Here was something that deserved to be chronicled to the world: the professors of fine arts, of Greek and of history, proposed a meeting to discuss the movies which are a matter of international concern and business importance and general criticism. No one who ever knew the Yard at Harvard has ever subscribed to Harvard's fictitious failure to subscribe to the currents of the time; but this was a demonstration.

Be that as it may, it is clear that very quickly Will Hays took over much of the oversight and administration of the idea. Thus, the letter from the Harvard officials to Hays received a prompt response from him by telegram (January 29, 1927): "I am very hopeful there will be no release of the Harvard art story until I have returned [from a trip to the West Coast] and had important conference with Harvard officials. Am very hopeful of most effective results of this arrangement with Harvard and want to carefully organize it after consultation with them. Hope this will be all right." James Seymour responded the same day with approval of Hays's ideas and with an offer to come to New York to work on the project. In early February, in fact, Seymour and Paul Sachs traveled to New York and conferred with Hays. Very quickly, then, the plan had become one with very strong industry involvement, and it had now become caught up in the cogs and wheels—such as publicity efforts—of that industry.

At the beginning of March—just as the HSB course was about to begin and as Hays and Kennedy were about to travel to Cambridge for their lectures—Theodore Streibert at FBO wrote to Hays on Joseph Kennedy's behalf and forwarded a copy of the proposal the Harvard professors had come up with for the annual award and for archiving the chosen films. Streibert asked Hays to send feedback on the proposal in anticipation of meetings that Hays and Kennedy were to have together at Harvard. Hays appears to have had a quick and enthusiastic response. Within a few days, for instance, he was forwarding the proposal on to people like Cecil B. DeMille and asking for their reactions:

> Herewith is copy of memorandum prepared by the interested authorities at Harvard covering the plan as developed so far for cooperation with the motion picture industry by the Department of Fine Arts of Harvard University. I wish you would go over this so that you may be familiar with the subject matter before you make the trip up there for your lecture as some of the faculty or others may bring up the subject matter. You will note from this what the general plan is, and that it involves rather distinguished recognition by this oldest university of this newest of arts and is an emphasis on the artistic side of motion pictures in contradistinction to the business side which is emphasized in the lectures at Harvard. Too, this cooperation of the Department of Fine Arts will run indefinitely, and the Fine Arts School at Harvard is the best in this country. No announcement of this cooperation is to be made until such time as the final details are worked out at which time it will be announced by them. The memorandum is the result of several conferences with them and considerable correspondence. When the matter is divulged finally as contemplated, it ought to be a quite useful thing.

Things started moving fast at this point—in large part, it would seem, because the desire was to announce the Fogg Museum initiative as close as possible to Hays's visit to Cambridge on March 15. A meeting to finalize details was held the day of that visit with a number of Harvard professors and administrators from fine arts as well as business. The next day the details of the proposal were announced to the press.

Carrying again the phrase "Youngest of Arts Recognized by Oldest of

American Universities," the announcement of the Fine Arts initiative shows the extent to which the university was planning something ambitious and long-term. Not merely would there be an annual selection of films, but there would be some attempt to go back into the history of film and build up an archive of achievements from the past: "This collection will be formed to serve the double purpose of recording the evolution of the moving picture from its beginning to the present day and of selecting annually those films which are deemed worthy of preservation as works of art." There would be multiple criteria for selection: "It is hoped that it will be possible to use as criterion of choice the harmonious synthesis of pictorial, narrative, dramatic, and histrionic qualities."

Each year, a jury composed of Harvard faculty—most of whom would come from the original group of planners—would survey the cinematic efforts of the past twelve months and choose twelve films that seemed to best demonstrate the potentials of film art. Additionally, one clause in the document indicated that the selection committee might also make special awards from time to time: "The committee shall be at liberty to recognize special merit in production or direction on the part of individuals or individual films."

An additional clause bluntly spelled out the American bias in the selection: "For the time being, foreign films will not be considered by the committee." It was hoped in fact that Hollywood studios would make their films available to the jury: studios could nominate specific titles (but jury members could always request additional titles) or send their general output for the year. Likewise, it was expected that two copies of each of the twelve finalists would be donated to Harvard—one copy to be archived and the other to be used for screenings for the Harvard community but only, the university promised, in "no admission charged" contexts. Here, Harvard was making concessions to commercial qualms of the studios—which obviously were worried about public showings of their recent works—but it is clear also that Harvard was asking a lot of the studios in hoping to get prints both for evaluation and for permanent archiving. As the proposal notes, with an almost pleading tone, "The cooperation of the industry and of such interested organizations and individuals in bringing to the attention of the committee films for its consideration is essential." Furthermore, the proposal stated, Harvard hoped that the archive would also include related print materials about the selected films, such as press materials and reviews. Again, the expectation was that the studios would provide much of this material. Later on, the Harvard committee would even ask Hays's help in receiving trade publications on a regular basis. Thus, in a letter of May 3, 1927, to the

MPPDA, James Seymour, now serving as secretary for the Harvard committee on the annual award, asked the following of Hays: "Can you secure for the Committee two or three copies of the Film Year Book and perhaps it would be possible to secure copies of the 8 preceding annual editions to be placed with the library of films. Will you also tell us which of the film dailies and magazines we ought to plan to have in the library. . . . I hope that in order to reduce the expenses as much as possible we may be able to secure complimentary subscriptions to the magazines selected." On the one hand, the committee organizers themselves suggested they needed such material to aid in their investigations into worthy films for the selection. On the other hand, it would seem that the Harvard faculty also desired to build up a general library of materials on film—the proposal also speaks of the archive including "such literature on the art of the motion pictures as may be available and deemed worthy of preservation by the committee"—and hoped it could get some of this through the studios. The Harvard award organizers had in fact been given some promise of aid, and this may have emboldened them in their demands on the studios. Joseph Kennedy had, for instance, committed to provide two movie projectors, one to be housed at Fogg and one to be installed at the home of a jury member so that committee screenings could take place. Even more promising, Kennedy had arranged for up to four fine arts students to be given fifty-dollar-per-week summer jobs at the studios if they paid their own way out to the coast, and he had even pushed Paul Sachs to come up with names when not enough candidates initially presented themselves.

But if Harvard clearly would gain in some resources—films, student internships, documents, and so on—for an art that some of its faculty took a demonstrable interest in, there were seeming benefits of prestige for the film industry, and Hays took a very active hand in getting word about the project out to key industry figures. Thus, the day after Harvard made an official announcement of the project, a letter went out from Hays to dozens of figures in the film industry to tell them about it: the list of addressees (which obviously had been made up in advance, indicating that negotiations between Harvard and Hays had been expected to work out) included such figures as Victor Fleming, James Cruze, John Ford, Raoul Walsh, Frank Borzage, King Vidor, Harry Cohn, Jack Warner, Irving Thalberg, and Sam Goldwyn. The letter presented the Harvard initiative with great excitement (and with reference yet again to oldest university and the newest art):

> The announcement yesterday by Harvard University of the conclusion of the arrangements whereby the oldest university recognizes this, the newest of the arts, is of course of real significance. In this purpose the

organized industry is pleased to cooperate. It means much to all of us and will be of large usefulness. This usefulness from the industry's standpoint is both subjective and objective.

The fact is, of course, that the motion picture commands the greatest in art and artisanship, as well as in business, in science, in religion, in literature and in the humanities. Where the greatest artists by any other method of expression reach hundreds, through motion pictures, they reach thousands and it is the supreme challenge and calls from our artists the greatest of their art. All of this is realized by the authorities at Harvard, and it must be pleasing to us to have this recognition by them of the place the motion picture is attaining as an art.

Enclosed is a copy of the statement which the Harvard authorities made for the purpose. Attached to this—and confidential—is the memorandum which the Harvard authorities are using for its guidance of their own consideration of the matter. . . . The whole matter will, of course, be closely followed as it develops.

Hays had at least one response to this missive and thus reported to Forbes on March 30, 1927, that Inspiration Films had nominated the following films for the award: *Tol'able David, The White Sister, Romola, The Enchanted Cottage, The Bright Shawl, Classmates,* and *Shore Leave.*

The next traces of the Fogg initiative come in a May 3, 1927, letter from James Seymour to Carl Milliken at the Hays Office just as the HSB course was ending (it is not clear if there were other letters, now lost, between the March announcement and this letter). Seymour's missive provides some useful information on the internal negotiations that the Harvard committee had been engaging in during these intervening months. For example, the constitution of the committee had now been refined and currently included one professor from English (with hopes of adding a professor from philosophy), thus expanding the project beyond the original purview of fine arts alone. As perhaps befitted his explicit interest in film, Chandler Post was designated as committee chair. Seymour himself was to serve as "Acting Curator of the Library." According to his letter, the committee had already started its work and, in addition to beginning deliberation on the selection of films from 1926, had, in fact, chosen a number of films from prior to 1926 for inclusion in the film archives. As Seymour explained, the committee had picked 123 such films and wanted to think a little more about an additional 80 titles. These, it must be admitted, are big figures. A number of factors probably led to the Harvard initiative not surviving the 1920s, but one wonders if one reason was not that the university was simply asking too much of the studios in hoping for the donation of so many prints.

Yet the Hays Office itself did not appear to think that the Harvard demands were extravagant, and a few days after receiving Seymour's letter, an encouraging missive went out from Hays to the member companies of the MPPDA reporting on the developments at Harvard. Hays explained that his office would be receiving the list of selected films—both from 1926 and from the earlier years—and would act as go-between in relaying that list to the studios. But as the summer approached, it seems that difficulties in the Fogg initiative began to be apparent. Here, a June 8, 1927, letter from Carl Milliken to Joseph Kennedy to report on a dinner meeting he had had with James Seymour is revealing. Milliken noted a number of modifications in the project. Some of these revisions seem to have come from a recognition that the original plan was too ambitious. First, despite the long list of pre-1926 films that the Harvard committee had come up with, it was now the preference that the committee should "attempt first to make selections from the product of 1926, leaving consideration of the earlier pictures to be taken up later." Second, it was proposed that the committee spend the rest of the current (spring) semester refining procedures rather than actually looking at films. The committee would then review films starting in the fall semester and try to make their announcement of choices by the end of the year. Although it is hard to determine just which factors led to the eventual overall abandonment of the Harvard project, a delay in the selections for 1926 suggests both that the work of the committee was not moving along as it should and that, once completed, it would still present problems. After all, to announce at the end of 1927 the best films of 1926 would mean that, in its first awards, the Harvard committee would already be a year behind in its attention to contemporary cinema.

The last available public mention of the Fogg award seems to be from January 8, 1928, when the *Boston Herald* announced that the choices for 1927 were still being deliberated. There is no record of any follow-up. There is also an intriguing reference in an *Academy Bulletin* from the end of 1928, which indicates that the "Academy has been invited to be represented some time in January or February when the Harvard award will be bestowed for the most outstanding picture of 1926."[36] That an invitation was being extended for an event announced as a only a few months away might indicate that the awards were finally going to be given, but in fact nothing seems to have come of this imminent promise of an awards ceremony.

It would seem that the idea of an annual award never got fully implemented and then faded away. One definitive proof that the award had been dropped, and attention shifted elsewhere, came in response to a letter addressed to the HSB on April 7, 1935 (in other words, eight years after the initiative was undertaken), by a person named Virginia Ballard from Atlanta, Georgia. Referring to *The Story of the Films,* Ballard wrote, "In the book I learned that the School of Business Administration has a film library founded in 1927 at the time that the course of lectures that constitute the book were given. I wished to have a list of the best pictures of each year since the founding and the criteria by which they judge the pictures." A reply was addressed to her on April 11 by Howard T. Lewis, who was now serving as acting dean of the HSB: "Dean Donham's secretary to whom you addressed your letter of 7 April, has given me your letter since I have undoubtedly been closer to the whole film situation than anyone else in the School. The film library mentioned in 'The Story of the Films,' which Mr. Kennedy edited, has turned out to be more of a hope than an accomplishment. Our interests in the film industry have been confined almost wholly to the economic and commercial aspects of the industry. We have not undertaken to maintain a list of the best pictures each year." Lewis's letter does not really indicate why the initiative was dropped, since his "explanation" has only to do with the relative lack of interest of the HSB in specifically aesthetic issues, but it does confirm that nothing came of the venture. (It is also noteworthy, perhaps, as one more bit of evidence of Lewis's own involvement with the HSB side of the film activity in the late 1920s.)

A bit more informative is a 1933 letter from Theodore Streibert (who was once again back at the HSB after his stint at FBO/RKO) to film historian Terry Ramsaye in which Streibert wondered if the award should not be revived:

> John N. Lyle, a first year student, has been conferring with Professor Post and some of the members of the faculty of the Fine Arts Department about reviving a Harvard Committee of Award for pictures of artistic merit. You remember this started here following the lectures at the Business School along about 1926–1927 by the great leaders of the industry. It never really got going, and then sound came along to kill it completely. Their interest is reviving because they would like to have on deposit a free print of a few pictures a year which would be held available for future students in the Fine Arts Department. I sent him to you because I thought there might be some faint interest on the part of *Motion Picture Herald* in hooking up with an award to be made by Harvard. I have not put much imagination into either the feasibilities or possibilities of it, but thought you might like to play with the idea, even if it results in no more than your dropping it cold. This lad is acting as secretary to the professors who are interested in it.

Streibert may indeed be right that the coming of sound had complicated the attempt to create an archive of film. To this, we might adduce other factors that could have led to a waning of interest in the initiative. For example, as noted earlier, the sheer demands the award would have placed on the film industry for resources (such as prints) might have made practical realization of the plan seem overly ambitious. Certainly, the coming of sound would have given the film industry other things to worry about than the provision of prints to a university. Certainly, too, the plans by AMPAS to create its own annual awards program—one, moreover, that would be under direct control of the industry—would have made industry involvement in a Harvard award less attractive or pressing. And, in any case, as I have argued, the industry had gained from the very announcement of the project whether or not it ever had a chance of being put into practice.

It is worth noting, though, that an erstwhile interest in film—and even in film as potentially a form of cultural accomplishment—continued to have some life at Harvard in the latter half of the 1930s. Specifically, in 1936, several Harvard students formed the Harvard Film Society, a screening series that continues to this day. Although this enterprise originated just after the period under consideration here, and although it did not seem to have any particular impact on curriculum (e.g., it did not seem to be connected to any specific courses), the founding of the Film Society is related in several ways to the history of film pedagogy that I am recounting in these pages. First of all, as a student organization, the Film Society needed official university support, which it received in the form of sponsorship from Fogg Art Museum and fine arts department personnel such as Edward Forbes and Paul Sachs, who had also been involved in the fruitless annual awards idea.

Second, like so many other film societies and screening series that came into existence after 1935, the Harvard Film Society based its selections very closely on the recently created circulating library of the Museum of Modern Art. "You are one of their biggest customers," Edward Forbes put it in a June 2, 1939, letter in which he pushed the current student president of the society, T. Edward Ross II, to ask MoMA for permission to vary the film selections from the order proposed in the standard MoMA program. In Forbes's words, "The Museum will probably kick like a steer about giving you a program as varied as these and not selected by them, but insist." There is nothing in the records to suggest that the availability in 1935 of the MoMA series was *the* causal factor in the creation of the Film Society, but it is striking to see how the failed initiative in 1927 to create a library of important films was succeeded by the MoMA-based series, with its own promotion of an art of film. Where the 1927 Fogg initiative in film was limited by the complicated logistics of dealing with studios for resources and of creating the material infrastructure for housing and projecting films, MoMA easily enabled a readily attainable and prejudged canon to come into visibility. An April 25, 1939, note from Film Society president Ross to Edwin Forbes is, in this respect, quite ironic. Ross informs Forbes of "two programs that I worked up for presentation by the Film Society next Fall" and then continues: "They are compiled from the current catalogue of the Museum of Modern Art.... I would like to see it [the Film Society] lead to a recognized course in the university curriculum which would, I am sure, be a step in raising the standard of both educational and dramatic movies." It is unlikely that Ross knew of the HSB's attempt ten years earlier to create a pedagogy of film that would have intimate connection to a fine arts valorization of the art of cinema, but it is striking to see how the aura of the MoMA circulating series could enable a new interest in film courses to come into being.

In a 1927 review of *The Story of the Films* in the *National Board of Review Magazine,* the magazine's editor, Alfred Kuttner, seems to have been aware of the balancing act the university had been engaged in in its complicated attempt to hold together professional work in film with a humanistic concern for film as site of ethical uplift and aesthetic value: "Perhaps Harvard was merely responding to a need of modern life which the movies had been unconsciously reflecting: the fusion of the business of thinking and feeling with the business of living: art and business."[37] Kuttner praised the HSB initiative but sensed that it might not endure. In his words, "There is no reason why the idea inaugurated by this book should not continue to bear fruit. There is the problem of inertia. The great leaders of the industry will not automatically gravitate to Harvard a second time and the best pictures will not naturally find their way to the archives of the Fogg Museum. To a considerable extent, the initiative will have to come from Harvard." Kuttner's interpretation of things was both prescient and partial. On the one hand, the withdrawal of industry support led Harvard itself to cool to the idea of film-related ventures. On the other hand, that "the great leaders of the industry" might have little interest in venturing again to out-of-the-way Cambridge as a way of promoting the business of film did not mean that they had no interest in finding venues in which there could be professional training in film. Indeed, as we have seen, they tried to develop one such curriculum in the industry city of New York through their initiative at Columbia. At the same time, they turned to another capital of film, Hollywood, and looked for pedagogical possibilities there. Indeed, several luminaries spoke at Harvard and, once their talks were finished, immediately seemed to think about a Los Angeles–based curriculum. It is to the Hollywood-inflected enterprise in higher education that we now turn.

4 Between Academia and the Academy of Motion Picture Arts and Sciences

The University of Southern California Ventures into the Cinema

> If Socrates were alive today, what a godsend the talkies would be to him. He would in all probability be on the screen. . . . Yes, I think that is where Socrates would be.
> DEAN KARL WAUGH, opening-day lecture to students in the first ever film course at USC

Karl Waugh, professor of psychology and dean of the College of Arts and Sciences at the University of Southern California, came up with an interesting invention at the end of the 1920s. He had devised a sort of galvanometer, which he believed could test the extent to which people registered the sincerity of those around them. The idea was to hook test subjects up to a machine that would clock the emotional impressions being made on them by other persons. Waugh called his device the "Psycho-galvanoscope," although some newspaper articles simply referred to it as the "emotionometer." As one newspaper notice put it, the " 'emotionometer' can tell whether one's feelings are really genuine by measuring the resistance of the skin when hate, or fear or love is registered."[1] Another article from 1930 recounted that Waugh had now made the further step of linking the galvanometer to a "pneumograph," which measured respiration, and a "digital sphygmograph," which registered blood circulation. "With these three delicate inventions," Waugh asserted, "it is indirectly possible to read a person's mind. Knowing the meaning of each reaction, and checking the subject's graph, we can determine through the body, respiration, and circulation, just how a man or woman is affected by a profound question."[2]

Quickly, it seems, Waugh came to feel that the impressive ability of the nearby Hollywood studios to work their affective magic might be one such "profound question." Although his own students had served as the first test subjects for his experiments, Waugh decided to expand his horizons and hawk his gadget to the film companies, believing that Hollywood firms could use the machine to gauge the extent to which their actors were putting over their performance and were convincing to spectators. During his visits to the studios, Waugh tested his machine on actors, who were judged for their ability to put over a role but also were themselves hooked up to the emotionometer to see how their fellow thespians registered for them. Thus, the USC archives contains a publicity photo of Waugh with Buster Keaton during a visit to MGM; the caption explains that the galvanometer could get no emotional reaction one way or the other from the Great Stone Face (see frontispiece). Waugh also took time during his visit to test the intelligence of another MGM contract player, Flash the Wonder Dog, whom he declared the smartest of his species.

But Waugh had even greater ambitions: beyond registering the impact of an actor, why not use the emotionometer to study the emotional ups and downs of a film's narrative unfolding? As an Associated Press report explained on April 28, 1930, "It is planned to use this apparatus on persons in a selected audience viewing a motion picture production to register the number of thrills provided by the film. In this way the success or failure of the picture may be foretold."

One doubts that Dean Waugh got many sales for his device from the Hollywood studios. In any case, within a year, he would leave Los Angeles for Dickinson College in Pennsylvania, which had recruited him away from USC to serve as its president. But his attempt to market his device to Hollywood with the promise that it could make the difference between commercial success and failure can stand as an interesting, if admittedly quirky, marker of one of the more ambitious encounters between cinema and academia in the period covered by our history. In fact, Waugh's own contact with Hollywood was not limited to this one eccentric contact with the studios: in 1929, he was the convener for a new course, Introduction to Photoplay, that had sponsorship from the Academy of Motion Picture Arts and Sciences (AMPAS), with some likely initial push from Will Hays at the MPPDA.[3] In some documents from the 1920s, this course, a general introduction to the movies, was alternately referred to as Appreciation of the Photoplay, and the intent was to create a general course in film aesthetics that would serve as the basis for a full-blown professional curriculum in film. Although the development of that curriculum took longer than planned and although the support of the industry seems to have waned as time went on, by 1933 USC was offering the first undergraduate major in film.

Among other things, the story of Waugh's attempt to reap financial benefit from the results of his academic research reminds us of the frequent mixture of motives in academic enterprises. As the coming of sound upped the ante for technical expertise in the film business, Hollywood had a lot to gain from affiliation with a school that was nearby and could funnel newly trained professionals into the field. In this case, the goal for Hollywood was not only the symbolic prestige that came from association with academia but also the practical benefits that would accrue from outsourcing a central part of its own training to academic institutions. Likewise, USC also had much to gain: Hollywood represented a great deal of money (and certainly there was the seduction of Hollywood glamour itself), and it also represented an industry whose increasing rationalization could create a steady job market for USC grads. As state historian (and current USC professor) Kevin Starr explains in the pages on USC in his multivolume history of California, the university administration in the period when the university began its film curriculum felt poised for USC to enter the big time, and one strategy for this was to ally itself with newsworthy industries for which it could promote itself as offering instruction not available elsewhere. As Starr recounts, "The architect and demiurge behind this growth, the man who inextricably melded the fortunes of USC to the rise of Los Angeles, was its energetic president Rufus Bernhard von KleinSmid.... Only marginally a scholar by either instinct or practice, von KleinSmid understood growth primarily in terms of buildings and service programs keyed to the requirements of the developing infrastructure of Los Angeles and Southern California."[4] Soon, according to Starr, the effort paid off: "By the 1930s the USC professional schools in law, education, medicine, and dentistry dominated their fields in Southern California" (153). In similar fashion, von KleinSmid seems to have been a hearty proponent of an ambitious professional curriculum in film, and although the program may not have realized its promise as quickly as the other professional ventures, it is easy, in line with Starr's analysis, to see why a film curriculum might have appealed to the entrepreneurial president. It clearly would link the university to one of the most important industries in Southern California; it would come into existence at just the moment when new developments in that industry made training all the more necessary; and it would connect the university to an industry with lots of funding potential.

According to one story, President von KleinSmid had as a fencing partner at his private club the actor Douglas Fairbanks, who was serving as the first president of the newly founded Academy of Motion Picture Arts and Sciences, and the two got to talking about ways in which the university and the film industry could work together. In a piece in *American Weekly* from 1928 that reads like a bit of planted public relations, another story of the course's founding is provided, with von KleinSmid again pictured as a key figure. The piece offers a long quotation from the university president in which he claimed much of the credit for the idea of a film curriculum:

> What the industry has needed, and what the university can give, is men and women trained in the subjects of physics, chemistry, optics, art, architecture, English, dramatic psychology, etc., with particular application to the chemistry of the film, optics of motion picture camera work, the psychology of perception and interpretation, the art and architecture of motion picture design, stagecraft, dramatics and the elements of plot and scenario writing. A school of motion picture sciences may thus be comparable to schools of mining or civil engineering or architecture. Three years ago, I went to New York to talk over the question of such a school with Will H. Hays. My proposal met with his hearty approval. I returned to Los Angeles, mapped out the courses of study, and when the Academy of Motion Picture Arts and Sciences was organized last year, took my plans before its board of directors. As a result of the ensuing discussion, the courses were nearly entirely changed, but again I submitted them. This time they were enthusiastically received.[5]

One does not have to believe everything in this account. On numerous other occasions, von KleinSmid showed himself to be quite self-promoting and self-fictionalizing. For example, as Kevin Starr notes, although von KleinSmid did have a bachelor's and a master's degree, "All his other degrees, including the doctorate which became a fixed component of his name . . . were honorary" (151–52). In regard to the film business, where it is all too tempting to engage in legend building and personal aggrandizement, it is easy to imagine that von KleinSmid wanted to grab some of the credit for himself.

In fact, as decisive to the creation of a USC film curriculum were the efforts of a young go-getter, Lester Cowan, who was looking for a way to break into the film world and came to see the USC initiative as his first stepping-stone. Cowan had recently graduated from Stanford University (a connection that will be important later in this story) and was one of the many entrepreneurial spirits who had been drawn to the energetic world of Hollywood, with all its promise for inspired success. Through 1927, Cowan made a series of job-scouting trips from Palo Alto to Los Angeles, on one of which he managed to obtain an interview with former screenwriter and critic Frank Woods, who was now serving as secretary for the recently founded Academy of Motion Picture Arts and Sciences. Here Cowan's luck began. AMPAS was in the midst of negotiations for its pedagogical enterprise at USC, and it needed someone to help in the effort.

One of the Academy's founders, the actor Milton Sills, had been a college professor before entering Hollywood and had always maintained a deep commitment to rationalized instruction as the preparatory path to any career. Sills, in fact, had been one of the final lecturers in Joseph Kennedy's course on film in the Harvard School of Business, and he had specifically indicated a desire to foster alliances between the film world and academia. As he had put it in his lecture to the Harvard students,

> For the survival of the industry it is necessary today to draft men of finer intellectual and cultural background, of greater energy, of greater business power, and of greater poetic creativeness. I think this problem is largely one that concerns our universities. Personally I look forward to the day when in Harvard and elsewhere, schools of motion picture technique may be developed, from which we may draw our cameramen, our directors, our supervisors, our writers, and a great many of our actors. That, to my mind, would be the solution of one of the gravest problems of our industry.[6]

At Sills's instigation, a College Affairs Committee had been quickly incorporated into the initial structure of AMPAS, and Sills himself was chosen to head it. It held its first meeting just after the Harvard course finished, and it is clear that Sills had in mind a pedagogy specifically geared to professional training as the program he would like to see the Academy sponsor. The single agenda item for this first meeting of AMPAS's college committee was for its members to confer with USC's von KleinSmid about having his university offer that film pedagogy.

Whether the idea for doing something with film at USC originated with von KleinSmid or whether AMPAS had contacted him to devise a plan (the report of the meeting says that he "presented himself to the committee according to previous invitation"), it is clear that there was great enthusiasm for some sort of alliance between AMPAS and an established institution of higher learning such as USC, at that time the city's primary university. Already, the fanfare around the creation of AMPAS had brought attention from promoters of unaccredited educational ventures such as *Film Spectator* editor Welford Beaton, who kept trying to get the Academy to affiliate in some way with his proposed National Academy of Cinema Arts in Hollywood. Suspicious of such private enterprises, the AMPAS College Affairs Committee declared emphatically at its first meeting, with specific mention of Beaton's venture, that it "would not be interested in any independent school promotions but would only consider cooperative relations with established colleges and universities."[7]

Whether the idea for a USC curriculum had indeed originated with von KleinSmid, he appears to have been a passive participant in his first AMPAS meeting, as the committee essentially outlined what it hoped for in a film curriculum and he sat back and listened. As the minutes of the meeting recount, Chairman Sills

> explained the purposes of the Academy in connection with colleges and universities and pointed out that there were three lines of special instructions that could be followed: scenario writing, technical instructions in various branches, and acting. Von KleinSmid replied, outlining the hopes of his University, and explaining his desire to obtain firsthand information regarding the proper steps to take in selecting and establishing courses in college curriculum that would be desirable for motion picture training.

Members of the AMPAS College Affairs Committee had clearly been thinking hard about what they wanted from a university curriculum in professional film training, and they presented their desires at this first meeting. Technical engineer and special effects expert Roy Pomeroy pushed for courses in "higher mathematics and chemistry . . . with special reference to the peculiar demands of the motion picture industry. He was of the opinion that the college course should be at least four years starting out with cultural, literary and scientific foundation and ending with specialized subjects." Meanwhile, screenwriter Lotta Woods wanted the courses in photoplay writing to "commence with analytical study and criticism of motion pictures in the same manner that the spoken drama is taught by analysis of written play." In her view, only after such general understanding of the aesthetics of the photoplay had been established should students be given more specific practical instruction in photoplay writing. Both Pomeroy and Woods concurred, in other words, that whatever specialized areas the curriculum covered, it should start with general critical and cultural foundations and move to applied work only in a second, practical phase. Von KleinSmid readily agreed: this structure already approximated that in place at the university, where students began with a broad general education before moving into the specifics of their chosen major, and he therefore anticipated that many existing general and introductory courses could help provide the overall framework on which a specific film curriculum could build. He left the meeting with the promise to come up with a plan to present to AMPAS by the fall.

At some point in the next months, the idea of a separate acting concentration dropped out and became incorporated into a track on the photoplay (which would include acting issues related to the photoplay's dramatization). When the committee held its second meeting with von KleinSmid, on August 23, 1927, the three tracks of the program now were cinematography, photoplay, and set design, each defined broadly. Perhaps the best explanation of the tracks appeared in 1928 in the promotional piece planted in the *American Weekly:*

> There are three distinct courses of study prepared by the university. The first deals with "The Science and Technique of Cinematography." This includes, among other things, training in camera work, stagecraft, still photography and lighting effects.
>
> A second course takes up composition, literature and dramatics. This is to instruct students who want to become scenario writers, title writers, continuity writers, actors or actresses.
>
> A third course takes up architecture and fine arts, and will teach designing, modeling, decorating, mural painting, sculpturing and the like.

In the August meeting, von KleinSmid clarified how the tracks might build on the existing curriculum of the university: cinematography could take off from classes in chemistry and physics (e.g., course in optics); photoplay classes would originate in the course offerings of the English department and in dramatic arts; and set design would depend on curricula in the fine arts and architecture departments. Von Kleinsmid asked the AMPAS College Affairs Committee for permission to draft a promotional brochure for the program, one that would advertise it as "being established with the Academy in an advisory capacity." The committee approved the idea, contingent on examination of final copy, and things then moved quickly. Sometime between the committee meeting date of August 23 and the start of the USC fall semester (scheduled for September 13), a snappy-looking pamphlet appeared to announce an "Outline of Courses in the Science and Technique of Cinematography; Literature, Dramatics and Criticism; Architecture and Fine Arts."

This fancy announcement of the new program began with assertions about the value of film study that would remain part of the rhetoric of the USC planners as they refined plans for a cinema curriculum (it would remain quite literally in the discourse, since Dean Waugh directly cribbed from the 1927 brochure for his own lecture on film when one course actually got started in 1929). The brochure declared that the film industry had grown from an "experimental enterprise" to a big business to the extent that it was now "comparable with our greatest utilities," suggesting that this evolution necessitated that professional effort in the field now be undertaken "only by those who have made the most thoroughgoing and careful preparation for the work, and those who have the best practical and cultural background for the tasks to be undertaken." The model emphatically was that of a pedagogy of *practical* training with direct hands-on aspects. As the brochure bluntly stated, "A school of motion picture sciences may thus be comparable to schools of mining or civil engineering or architecture."

In passing, it is worth noting an early, somewhat critical, discussion of the USC project that showed up in a February 1928 piece in *Photo-Era Magazine* in its column on "Applied Photography."[8] The author, C. B. Neblette, from the Division of Photography at Texas A&M University, based his article on a Hays Office announcement that USC would be sponsoring the four-year course in "technical training for the motion-picture industry." Neblette's criticism had to do with the fact that he felt the specific art of cinematography might be shortchanged in such a broad curriculum. As he put it, "We are quite ready to admit that a college which is to meet the needs of the motion-picture industry must include more than the technique and science of photography and kinematography; but we do not feel that these can be left to take care of themselves and that they can be treated as a poor relation in the midst of rich and haughty autocrats of lighting, direction, costuming, staging and the like." In this respect, Neblette made the interesting point that training in cinematography for the specific needs of the commercial film industry could only ignore forms of camera work in non-Hollywood areas (he cited industrial photography and medical photography as examples); he therefore called for a course of study that would fully be devoted to camera work rather than make it just one topic studied among others. Ironically, USC had already decided to scale back its ambitious three-track curriculum by the time that promotional articles like the one Neblette was reacting to came out, so his critique was somewhat beside the point. But his recognition that a school like USC would have to take care that its proximity to Hollywood did not impel it to valorize one type of cinema (entertainment), or one type of cinematography, over others was noteworthy.

In the event, USC was not able to get its 1927 curriculum going in the few weeks between publication of the brochure and the start of the fall semester (in fact, as we will see, no course would actually get taught until 1929). But insofar as the brochure represents an early version of what both USC and AMPAS imagined for a curriculum in film, it is a significant document.

One intriguing aspect to this first proposition for a USC cinema pedagogy is that it bears a strong resemblance to the one outlined in Columbia University's proposal from 1926–27 to create a three-track curriculum divided around camera work, scenario writing, and set design. It is hard to know if the resemblance between the two projects is more than coincidental. On the one hand, as noted earlier, the USC track took on this particular three-part division only after there had been consideration of a somewhat different one that had given acting an important place (Columbia, for its part, had decided not to pursue acting because, in large part, of the unbeatable strength of Yale's drama program). On the other hand, Will Hays had been pushing for the development of respectable curricula in film, and he had exerted direct influence on the three-track program at Columbia. It might well be that Hays also had some influence in propelling AMPAS (and, by association, USC) toward offerings that resembled the program he had pushed for at Columbia. Here, we might remember that USC president von KleinSmid had talked of an early meeting with Hays to discuss a film curriculum, and the idea of tracks could have come up there. And, notably, in the aforementioned critique by C. B. Neblette of the USC plan, Neblette indicated that he had come across the USC proposal in an announcement *from the Hays Office.* This might indicate some connection, although the Hays Office sometimes gave publicity to initiatives that it had no hand in but that complemented its own work. The question of Hays's role in the USC initiative remains an open one.

In the interim moment in late 1927, when USC and AMPAS had committed to a joint venture but when it seemed clear that the announced three-track ambitious program could not be implemented right away, Lester Cowan came onto the scene. At his job-search meeting with Frank Woods, the AMPAS officer told him of the joint USC-AMPAS venture and suggested Cowan talk to Karl Waugh, who, as college dean, would be the administrator immediately in charge of a film curriculum. Waugh, it appears, had been thinking that to get off the ground, the film program needed a coordinating officer who could devote full-time effort to it. Cowan seemed to be his man, and Waugh invited him to a meeting with President von KleinSmid.

Having been filled in by Dean Waugh about the steps that had been taken thus far in the AMPAS-USC initiative, Cowan drafted a proposal entitled "What a Coordinating Officer Might Do." Noting that "[t]he University of Southern California has pledged itself to turn out young men and women equipped with the fundamental knowledge for success in the various lines of motion picture work," Cowan asserted that the university needed someone who knew the movie business and could aid in "collecting, analyzing, and classifying the facts about the industry." Although new to the field, Cowan obviously regarded himself as a fast learner and, even more, clearly wanted the post to be his. He outlined a series of responsibilities that he declared himself ready to accept. As coordinator he would provide, in his words, "Organization of courses (in cooperation with Dean Waugh and faculty members) designated in bulletin as + courses to be organized with the advisement of the Academy of Motion Picture Arts and Sciences to meet the needs of students, preparing for a career in Motion Picture Science; adaptation of courses now in curriculum to meet new requirements." (The reference here to "+ courses" related to the initial 1927 brochure, where courses already offered at USC that might fit the three-track curriculum were designated by a plus sign. Cowan was proposing to examine the current USC curriculum and see what modifications might be needed to provide appropriate training specifically in areas of filmmaking. For example, while USC had existing courses in the science of optics, they might need to be retooled to deal more with issues of lenses, moving image cinematography, and so on before they could serve in the advanced courses of the camera track.)

Additionally, Cowan promised that, as program coordinator, he would provide students with vocational guidance; secure lecturers from the industry to come address students; maintain equipment to be used in classroom film production; assemble illustrative material for courses and for visiting lecturers; and teach courses himself (in particular, he imagined teaching through USC's adult education program, where he might offer "[e]vening classes for those in industry; courses by correspondence or through medium of talking films to persons in other parts of the country desiring to 'break in'"). Perhaps the most intriguing of his suggested job responsibilities was his offer to be in charge of "[c]ollection of real problems faced and solved in the past by workers in the industry to be used in class discussion (similar to method of Harvard Graduate School of Business)." The previous chapter elaborates on how important the use of case studies had been to the Business Policy course on the movies; it is interesting to see that Cowan knew about that pedagogy (he likely had learned about this from College Affairs Committee chair Milton Sills, who, after all, had lectured in the Harvard course) and was using it to a degree as a model.

By the first quarter of 1928, Cowan had indeed been appointed the person responsible for implementing a USC pedagogy in film. At first, he was listed as a USC employee, but soon he had moved over to the AMPAS College Affairs Committee to serve as its secretary. (He in fact stayed at the Academy long after that committee disappeared. By 1931, he rose to the rank of executive secretary of AMPAS overall and left behind his concern for a general film pedagogy, as did the Academy itself more generally. During his time as executive secretary, he and AMPAS more broadly had other concerns than the universities—in particular, these were years of conflict and conciliation for a film industry beset by labor disagreements between producers and personnel—and college activities at AMPAS fell by the wayside. From 1931 to 1933, much of Cowan's time was taken up with drafting a code of ethics and proper business behavior for the film industry. But before he became executive secretary and his priorities shifted, the USC venture was pretty much his pet project, and he supervised it closely.)

Cowan's first step as college coordinator was to attempt to scale back the USC project's original ambitions. In a first formulation, Cowan proposed to Dean Waugh that there be one single course offering consisting of two semesters: Introduction to Photoplay ("a purely cultural course"), followed by Introduction to Motion Picture Production. The first semester would be open to all students, but the second semester would require special permission and was clearly imagined as a way to funnel particularly committed students toward careers in film. As Cowan described the idea in an undated draft letter to Dean Waugh and to industry officials, "The course which I have in mind will be at once cultural, practical. . . . It will give students an understanding of the photoplay as a course in the drama is designed to give them an understanding of the drama. Those interested in careers in motion picture production will get an accurate conception of motion picture production in all its branches and will lead to more intelligent decisions with regard to career."

Soon, however, the idea of a separate, second-semester course on production dropped out (some aspects of it were absorbed into Introduction to Photoplay), but it is worth describing Cowan's idea for it. His intention was not so much to create a course in hands-on filmmaking as to give students a broad overview of what transpired in big-studio production: the students would learn about the business of film and then, as Cowan put it in his letter, would "follow through a production in all its phases, having visited before." In an "Outline Program of Instruction and Study," from mid-1928, Cowan explained that the course would rely on a series of studio visits during which students would observe the actual phases of film production: management (to include such topics as budgeting and scheduling of productions), with sessions based on observation of studio executive conferences and on study of business documents (supervision by M. C. Levee, general manager at United Artists); direction, with on-set observation (sessions to be organized around shoots by D. W. Griffith and Henry King); set design, with observation of set design meetings (run by William Cameron Menzies); camera technique, with observation of shoots, of crew discussions, and of camera experiments (hosted by cinematographers Karl Struss and Oliver Marsh); and editing and cutting, based on observation (hosted by M. C. Levee and Hal C. Kern). There was some suggestion that M. C. Levee teach this course on Hollywood film production; after Waugh went to meet with him at United Artists, Levee was brought to the USC campus to give informal lectures at the student residential halls on the business of film.

Significantly, while the original, ambitious plan for a multitrack curriculum was being shelved, Cowan still assumed that there eventually would be some sort of overall, several-strand degree-granting curriculum. Introduction to Photoplay would introduce the topic, the production course would give students direct contact with the work of the film business, and then there would be more detailed courses of study (perhaps based on the three-track system) in which students could specialize. Cowan imagined the introductory classes as a way of, as he put it, "weeding out undesirables." (Cowan mentioned as a model his own alma mater, Stanford, with its elite standards of entry.) Indeed, when the Introduction to Photoplay course actually was implemented for spring 1929, it was preceded by an extensive interview process in which prospective students had to compete for slots; additionally, students who made it into the course were asked to pinpoint areas of film production they might plan to work in and in which they might need university instruction. In other words, success in the introductory class was dependent on the students' choosing already to commit to training for a career in film—even though there was in fact no curriculum yet beyond the Introduction to Photoplay course to actually give them that training.

In his draft letter, Cowan spelled out the varied purposes the introductory course would serve:

Cultural—give an understanding of newest and most popular art form, its social as well as artistic, and economic aspects.

Orientation and guidance—by giving accurate conception of motion picture production in all its branches with opportunities in each. . . .

Will make industry take new interest in project . . . make it theirs. . . .

Will establish U.S.C. as centre of motion picture education. . . .

To industry—will provide cheaper and better employees, give them prestige and will stifle much criticism. . . .

It is clear that along with these benefits to industry, university, and students alike, Cowan saw benefits to himself: in particular, such a project would provide him entry into the Hollywood milieu. With his background as a college man, Cowan may have felt it advisable to first seek employment for himself within the university world, but that is clearly not where he intended to end up. His self-salesmanship was emphatically on display when he promised that his efforts in the course would directly help Hollywood industry: "presenting this as an economy measure and am asking you gentlemen to be far-sighted. . . . You gentlemen give me your attention and I will lower your costs through standardization and development of large labor supply.... I am willing to stake my entire future on my ability to do this, providing you gentlemen really get behind me."

Cowan had big ambitions—both for himself and for the course. He ended his letter to Dean Waugh with the admission that it would "take six months to organize this course on the scale on which I want to organize it." He outlined what he would do during that time: "[F]irst job will be to Plan of procedure *[sic]*, then work out course—will write two books in collaboration with experts in industry on economic and artistic aspects of the photoplay." It seems at this point that he was planning to teach the course himself, and perhaps he needed some of the time to go through an education in cinema to bring himself up to speed.

But even the two-semester structure—one semester of introduction to cultural issues, followed by one semester of observation of production in the studios—was turning out to be too much, and by early to mid-1928 the plan had been scaled back to a single-semester offering, Introduction to Photoplay. Curiously, although the idea of a three-track curriculum clearly had been put on the back burner, it was still being lauded in the press. For example, in mid-April, one newspaper headline announced, "USC Outlines 4-Year Study on Film Work" and offered a description of the curriculum that appears unchanged from the previous fall.[9] Perhaps the university and/or AMPAS was still clinging to the hope that the broader curriculum would eventually be instituted—and that Introduction to Photoplay might serve as a means to build up interest for additional offerings in film. Perhaps either AMPAS or the university was still planting articles to continue getting mileage from the idea of a full-fledged program in film. In actuality, though, the university currently had nothing to offer budding student filmmakers but the single course, Introduction to Photoplay.

The only new piece of information in the April 1928 article was an indication that Professor W. R. MacDonald was helping to plan film study at USC. In fact, MacDonald had been designated solely to teach Introduction to Photoplay. Cowan was out as prospective teacher. It may be that university requirements mandated that a course have a regular member of the teaching staff as its instructor. Or perhaps Cowan was considered too much a neophyte (he was only twenty-three at the time). In any case, he would still control the course very closely and even determine much of its content.

A USC alumnus, William R. MacDonald was both an instructor of speech and the university play director. Prior to becoming the director for dramatic productions, he had also served as a coach in Dramatics and Stage Technique, and it is likely that he was considered for the photoplay course because of a perceived parallel between cinema and theater. With Introduction to Photoplay, he would become USC's first film teacher, and he remained with the program through 1932. MacDonald had little background in film, however, and AMPAS arranged for him to spend several summer months in 1928 working under MGM producer Harry Rapf to gain a sense of day-to-day studio operations. But the benefit of introducing MacDonald into the MGM studio was not his alone: as a specialist in issues of vocal enunciation, MacDonald was able to aid the studio as it moved increasingly into the age of the sound film. MacDonald became a sometime consultant on vocal performance for the film industry, and one imagines that he might have had more to offer film professionals than had Dean Waugh with his emotionometer.

Significantly, Lester Cowan had also wrangled a studio internship for himself. In either the spring or summer of 1928, in his capacity as coordinating officer for the AMPAS-USC project, he went to work under M. C. Levee at United Artists (Levee, as mentioned earlier, had been listed by Cowan to teach Introduction to Motion Picture Production). Cowan evidently did quite well at his work, and Levee recommended to the Academy that it hire him for editorial work on the first edition of what would be called Academy Reports—summaries of research projects or special activities that the Academy was engaged in. In this case, the project involved industry-wide study of modes of on-set illumination, and the results eventually were issued in a report titled "Incandescent Illumination," which helped set standards for lighting technology during Hollywood's transition to sound. In *The Classical Hollywood Cinema*, film scholar David Bordwell has written of this research on illumination as a turning point in the history of the Hollywood mode of production: it showed the ability of the studios to work together; it clarified that AMPAS in particular could contribute to that spirit of cooperation by serving as a centralized clearinghouse; it demonstrated the value of rationalized procedures of research and development (rather than reliance on instinct, and on random and disorganized individual initiative), and so on.[10] By helping to collate the research, Cowan was clearly establishing his own importance to the new Hollywood of the sound era. By the fall of 1928, Cowan was no longer a representative of USC but had entered fully into the employ of AMPAS.

Cowan was put in charge of the day-to-day work of the College Affairs Committee (although Sills would remain its figurehead in the position of chairman). His responsibilities still included an initiative between AMPAS and USC, but it is clear that Cowan had already begun to think beyond USC and its Introduction to Photoplay course. As early as July 24, 1928, when he had not yet officially joined the AMPAS payroll, Cowan wrote to Academy secretary, Frank Woods, both to describe his detailed plans for the USC course and to suggest projects that would surpass the one course and the one university. On the one hand, Cowan knew what he wanted from a photoplay course. It would, as he outlined in his letter to Woods, "be purely cultural":

> Technical matters will be included only insofar as necessary to bring out cultural values. The subject matter may be classified as follows:
>
> 1. The photoplay as an art form. Functions of art in life and orientation of the photoplay as a composite art form. The addition of sound and voice and its effect on the art form.
>
> 2. History and evolution of the photoplay art. . . .
>
> 3. The Modern Photoplay. The Talking Picture.
>
> 4. Social and economic aspects—Censorship.
>
> 5. Criticism of modern photoplays from their cultural aspects.

On the other hand, Cowan had begun to imagine that this one course on the photoplay might have a life beyond USC alone. If its subject matter were perfected, the course could be made available to other institutions of higher learning. Just as AMPAS was helping establish industry technical standards through such ventures as the studies in incandescent illumination, Cowan was proposing that the Academy set standards for the content of film education and offer itself as a centralized source for expert insight on film history and aesthetics. Cowan had already learned the lessons of Hollywood—for example, standardization of product—and was attempting to put them to use in the world of academia. In Cowan's words to Frank Woods:

> The Procedure suggested is to have prepared, in advisement with college leaders, the syllabus for a course called "Introduction to the Photoplay." The course will be tested by introducing it at the University of Southern California during the second half of the coming school year. The syllabus will then be revised . . . and will be sent to all universities as a publication of the Academy of Motion Picture Arts and Sciences, Bureau of College Affairs. The Authorship, which will include some of our foremost educational leaders, will insure its acceptance and introduction into the curriculum of many universities.

The reference here to "advisement with college leaders" has special significance for this study, since Cowan in fact was proposing to get in touch with, and promote the AMPAS course to, some of the very institutions that are examined throughout this book as early venues for film pedagogy. In Cowan's words to Frank Woods, "Because our universities as social institutions are, or should be, vitally concerned with the development of an art form so great in its social power as is the photoplay, we anticipate little difficulty in securing as advisors such notable persons as Chandler R. Post and W. B. Donham—Harvard, George P. Baker—Yale, Victor Freeburg—Columbia, Glenn Frank—Wisconsin, Ray Lyman Wilbur and Pedro J. Lemos—Stanford, Rufus B. von KleinSmid—University of Southern California, Kate Gordon—University of California, and Vachel Lindsey [sic]."

At some point before the fall of 1928, AMPAS in fact sent Cowan on a tour of California colleges and universities to promote the idea of a photoplay course. The results of his tour were presented to the Academy on November 3, 1928, as "Progress Report No. 1 of the College Affairs Committee." This summary of activities, written by Cowan but signed by Milton Sills, optimistically recounted Cowan's experiences at UC Berkeley, Stanford, Mills College, and UCLA, and what he promised these schools if they took on the photoplay course. In addition to offering the growing prestige of the Academy and its connection to the glamour of Hollywood, and in addition to providing a course content that would have already been tested and refined (by means of the USC offering), AMPAS would grant the academic institutions additional benefits if they signed on to the venture: mailings of Academy publications (such as the reports on research), access to the AMPAS library for faculty and students, invitation of faculty to Academy lectures, arrangement of studio visits for faculty and of meetings with selected Academy members, and speaker series by AMPAS members at the schools. One of the most intriguing parts of the package that AMPAS was offering the colleges was the possibility of filmed lectures by Academy members. That is, it would produce sound films of its photoplay lecturers and make them available to institutions, which could then dispense with any need of their own to have flesh-and-blood film instructors (an early version of the packaging of pedagogy now known as distance learning!). The Academy made one test film—a lecture on speech in film by Milton Sills—that accompanied USC's dean of the School of Speech, Ray K. Immel, when he lectured in December 1929 at the annual National Convention of Teachers of Speech. Based on the success of that first experiment in visual education, the Academy envisioned filming all the lectures in the USC course and renting them to other schools that promised to offer Introduction to Photoplay. As Sills explained in an AMPAS press release from December 13, 1928, "Several of the lectures in the course will be delivered by prominent picture people and will be permanently recorded in the same manner as my own address, for use in the perfected course. . . . Pending the equipment of all colleges for showing sound pictures, it is anticipated that class sessions may be held by arrangement in neighboring theaters." Frank Woods at AMPAS wrote to the William Fox Company, a pioneer in sound film, to ask if the company could assist in making special films of Thomas Edison and George Eastman to be circulated with the photoplay course. Fox agreed to do the filming, but, for some unknown reason, the project fell through.[11]

In return for what it was offering the colleges by means of this ready-made course, AMPAS would ask that the president at each institution "cause to be conducted within his institution a survey with the purpose of searching out those among the faculty who are, or should be, interested in a further study of the photoplay. Inventory shall be taken of the physical facilities available for carrying on study and research—projection machines, etc." All the institutions of higher learning that Cowan visited were said to have looked favorably on the idea of introducing a photoplay course into their curriculum. For example, the report claimed that the president of Mills College had created a special committee to negotiate with AMPAS. Similarly, at UCLA, "Dr. Kate Gordon, prominent psychologist and authority on esthetics has been the one designated as most likely to handle the course.[12] In the event, as will be described later, Stanford University turned out to be the only institution to actually implement Introduction to Photoplay after the course was first given at USC.

Even if increasingly there were ambitions for the photoplay course beyond USC alone, AMPAS needed it initially to be offered there as a way to test it, refine it, and record its lessons for distribution elsewhere. Through the fall of 1928, then, Cowan continued to work on the particular arrangements for a first USC offering in the 1929 spring semester of Introduction to Photoplay. Soon, a press release indicating that the course was about to happen went out to various newspapers and trade journals. One such piece, published in *Educational Screen*, provides some sense of what was planned:

> Definite announcement is made through the Academy of Motion Picture Arts and Sciences that the University of Southern California would inaugurate, as a permanent part in its curriculum, a course in the "Appreciation of Motion Pictures." The first test, which will be made before a class picked from the student body, is scheduled for February and will be in the way of an introduction to the course. Douglas Fairbanks, president of the academy, will lecture on "Photoplay Appreciation" to be followed by D. Rufus B. von KleinSmid, President of the University of Southern California, on the subject "Photoplay and the University." It is planned to make all necessary revisions, with the assistance of prominent authorities, at the close of this trial course and record them for use in the future. The course, a cultural movement to

promote the standing of the photoplay in the intellectual mind, has limitless possibilities.[13]

The university catalog described the new course as follows:

Introduction to Photoplay. A general introduction to a study of the motion picture art and industry; its mechanical foundation and history; the silent photoplay and the photoplay with sound and voice; the scenario; the actor's art; pictorial effects; commercial requirements; principles of criticism; ethical and educational features. Lectures, class discussions, assigned readings and reports. Prerequisites: 48 units of credit and special permission of dean and instructor in course.

Two units—Second Semester

Waugh, McDonald and Special Lecturers

This course description was repeated in an elegant bound pamphlet of eleven pages that announced the course and gave the schedule for classes. Printed on high-quality heavyweight paper, the brochure included photos of all the announced lecturers as well as their biographies. Notably, this glossy vehicle for publicizing the course included opening comments in which the earlier idea of a three-track curriculum was still referenced. Even though the university was doing nothing at this point to institute such a curriculum (and AMPAS, moreover, appeared to have begun to shift its college interests beyond USC), the idea of a complex three-track curriculum was still part of the promotional campaign that both USC and AMPAS were engaged in.

Introduction to Photoplay had its inaugural session on February 6, 1929, with talks by President von KleinSmid, Dean Waugh, and Milton Sills and a guest appearance by Academy president Douglas Fairbanks, who made brief remarks on behalf of AMPAS. The course planners decided to hold the first session as a highly publicized and open event, and von KleinSmid even asked all USC professors to announce the event in their own classes. After some discussion at both AMPAS and USC about keeping other sessions open, the organizers agreed, however, to restrict further attendance to those who had passed the interview process and were officially enrolled in the class. While the course had been capped originally at thirty-five students and then at fifty, the enrollment was increased a bit, and it seems ultimately that about seventy students took the first semester's offering. (Various documents report slightly divergent figures. The most reliable source of information might be a document entitled "Data on University of Southern California Appreciation class," which listed seventy-two students, divided equally along gender lines.) Space was also reserved for a select group of auditors made up of representatives from the motion picture committees of local women's clubs, faculty members, and guests of lecturers. Over the next fifteen weeks, the members of the class would hear lectures by, and address questions to, such luminaries of cinema as screenwriter Clara Beranger, actor Conrad Nagel, art director William Cameron Menzies, producer Paul Bern (substituting for director Ernst Lubitsch), producer Irving Thalberg, director William de Mille, *Los Angeles Times* critic Edwin Shallert, and AMPAS secretary and screenwriter Frank Woods (substituting for D. W. Griffith), among others. There were also academic lectures by Dean Waugh, sociology professor Emory Bogardus, and visiting philosopher J. A. Leighton.[14] In the last week of class, students were treated to a visit to the Paramount lot and to a screening of classic films at the Academy's projection facilities at its Hollywood headquarters.

Course instructor William MacDonald did not lecture in the class, but he did assume responsibility for taking the roll, running the discussions with the guest lecturers, devising reading assignments (in consultation with Lester Cowan), and grading final exams. Students who were enrolled for credit in the course had to turn in weekly writing assignments that discussed assigned readings. For these, the university began to collect a series of film books: some of the works that students were asked to read from included Hugo Münsterberg's *The Photoplay: A Psychological Study*, Victor Freeburg's *Pictorial Beauty on the Screen*, Vachel Lindsay's *Art of the Moving Picture*, Iris Barry's *Let's Go the Movies*, and the Kennedy anthology, *The Story of the Films*. Additionally, Lester Cowan had begun to prepare an extensive bibliography of short writings on film, and students were assigned readings from this list. For example, students had to look at selections from the production-oriented *Transactions of the Society of Motion Picture Engineers*, volumes of which Cowan arranged for USC to borrow from AMPAS. As their primary requirement for getting credit in the course, students were tested on the content of the lectures. For example, the final exam included such questions as the following:

> Who invented the kinetescope [sic]?—describe the kinetescope
>
> Who were the Latham Bros. and what did they do?
>
> What "art form" did Griffith bring to the moving picture industry? Describe.
>
> Who discovered and used the close up?
>
> What elements of psychology, on the part of the audience, contribute to the success of the picture?

What three handicaps face the moving picture writer?

What two aesthetic senses are necessary for enjoyment of picture forms?

Obviously, as with the Harvard lecture series, we need to be wary of imposing too much structure on the diverse speeches that made up Introduction to Photoplay. But speakers were given transcripts of prior talks and appear to have been encouraged to make reference to them as they wished. Significantly, given that one of the original reasons for AMPAS deciding that the industry required such professional training had to do with the perceived need to standardize procedures in the face of the new complexity posed by the coming of sound, a running theme of lectures became the implications of the so-called sound revolution. For example, an ongoing thread of discussion was launched with the claim by one lecturer that off-screen orchestral accompaniment to scenes destroyed realistic illusion and the counterclaim by other lecturers that film was by nature an art of convention—that is, an art based on spectators' suspension of disbelief and acceptance of dramatically effective disruptions of realism. Likewise, speakers in the course were divided on the extent to which the silent film might be able to constitute a special form of cinema that could exist alongside the increasingly dominant form, the sound film.

It is clear that AMPAS wanted there to be certain thematic regularities to the course. The course needed to give the impression that Hollywood represented a mature and rational enterprise but one that had not sacrificed the artistry of its products to anonymous standardization. Toward this end, AMPAS planning notes for the lectures grouped them into categories: first, talks that dealt with the "History and Evolution" of cinema so as to suggest that there was indeed a respectable lineage to the modern-day form and that its development was one of ever greater refinement of technique and cultural power; then, a series of talks on "Analysis," which dealt both with the art on the screen (e.g., Clara Beranger's talk on the well-prepared script) and with the artistry behind it; finally, lectures on the "Social Significance" of cinema by university professors rather than Hollywood filmmakers as if to provide the ultimate stamp of respectability to the course and its object of study.

An even greater impulse toward unity of purpose in the lectures came from Lester Cowan, who provided the speakers with advice and even directives about the content of their lectures. Indeed, many of the guests referred to the ways they had been "assigned" their topics by Cowan. Additionally, Cowan prepared bits of information on index cards and made them available to the lecturers. Thus, to take one example, he gave screenwriter Benjamin Glazer, who was lecturing on the rise of the talking picture, a series of cards that outlined divergent views of various critics on the aesthetic value of sound films, and Glazer did use these in his talk to discuss the pros and the cons of this new form of cinema. Cowan also appears to have conducted background research for the speakers. Thus, for Karl Waugh's lecture on the "Social Utility of the Photoplay," Cowan provided bibliography cards, summaries of previous lectures, articles from journals, and chapters from Edward Van Zile's *That Marvel—The Movie* and from the Joseph Kennedy volume, *The Story of the Films*, with markings to indicate the sections he felt the dean should pay special attention to. Cowan even held conferences with a number of the lecturers before their talk, and it seems he coached them on what was expected of them. A January 10, 1930, letter from Cowan to producer B. P. Schulberg, whom he tried to recruit for a lecture in the second year of Introduction to Photoplay, gives some indication of the aid Cowan might offer guests to the course: "How much of your time will it take? About ten minutes on or about April 1st for a conference to reach an understanding on the general nature of the talk so as to insure proper coordination with the other lecturers. The actual preparation should not take over one evening, especially since we expect to assist by supplying you with material, suggestions, etc." (In this particular case, the invited figure demurred: Schulberg explained, "I am a lousy lecturer except for two or three at a time and please count me out.")

Whatever Cowan's particular impact on individual lecture content, it seems clear that there evolved a shared assertion among lecturers about the need for film art to be a popular art (rather than one for an elite) and about Hollywood's special ability to create that form of publicly accessible culture. In this respect, the talk by United Artist general manager, M. C. Levee (who was to have taught the motion picture production course) offers a good condensation of many of the themes of Introduction to Photoplay. Speaking on the topic "Commercial Requirements," Levee began by referencing previous lectures that had emphasized how the cinema was an art form grounded in a strong technical infrastructure, a collaborative or cooperative means of production, and an inevitable commercial organization. While one previous speaker had suggested that rarefied cinematic experiment (the art film) could exist alongside popular film if given subvention in the form of special endowments, Levee made the case for film as a business-based enterprise that differed from arts that enjoyed the patronage of the wealthy. Cinema's patronage came from the public, and this, Levee felt, was as it should be. Special endowments for the art film could only be a waste, since the true art of film was to be found in popular appeal. In this regard, Levee offered an interesting angle on the question of whether film was a commercial product like all others. Specifically, where other defenders of film art had been at some pains to suggest that film became a vibrant cultural form by *transcending* its commercial nature, Levee argued that film achieved the status of art precisely by meeting popular needs just as other commodities did. It was when cultural work went out into the world, and met demand, that it truly acceded to the realm of art. In Levee's words,

> Every product, every commodity must satisfy a human want.... If the motion picture did not satisfy a fundamental human want, the public would not have given it the great support which it has received and which support has brought about this gigantic industry. What is the nature of this human want or need that is satisfied by the motion picture? It is the need for entertainment, for recreation, for emotional outlet; which are as fundamental to physical and mental health as the food we eat or the clothes we wear. (241)

For Levee, then, there was a natural circuit between production and consumption in which the former responded directly to virtually instinctual needs expressed in the latter. To be sure, there were potentials for disruption to the cycle. In particular, there was always the risk that producers might make mistakes about the cultural needs of consumers or, conversely, that those needs might change over time. As Levee put it, "The public is whimsical. What is 'sure-fire' today is not so tomorrow. The mood or reaction of the public cannot be accurately predicted. It is for this reason that the risk is so great in the production of motion pictures" (243). But it was precisely this unpredictability that necessitated and justified the various practices the industry engaged in to minimize risk. In Levee's words, "With the tremendous costs entailed and the uncertainty of its appeal, it is easy to realize why this art in order to exist and develop must have an industry with great financial and human resources back of it. With so great a risk attached to his investment, it is easy to understand why the producer sets up certain commercial requirements in accordance with which he wants his artists and creative technicians to work" (243). Levee's talk thus gave explicit approbation to such practices as industry consolidation and vertical integration, the star system, top-down management by producers, precise budgeting and extensive preplanning of pictures, and so on. He painted a picture of Hollywood as a well-oiled machine that delivered to the masses the culture they wanted and needed.

Levee's talk typified how the course lectures became veritable manifestos for a specifically Hollywood way of making movies. As promotion for the industry, the first year's course at USC was a success overall. A highly laudatory review of it in the *American Cinematographer* must have been gratifying to administrators at AMPAS, who had wanted the publicity value of the course (and indeed may have planted the *American Cinematographer* piece themselves).[15]

One immediate consequence of the smooth running of Introduction to Photoplay in its first semester was that it gave new impetus to Cowan's idea of marketing the course beyond USC. Throughout 1929 and 1930, AMPAS was able to report on expressions of interest in the course from venues such as Columbia University, Johns Hopkins University, Yale, Purdue, the University of Minnesota, and the University of Oregon, although none of these schools ever initiated an actual course.

There were, however, two cases in which there was concerted effort to repeat the USC pedagogy elsewhere. The first was closely linked to the original course: William MacDonald, the nominal professor for USC's version of Introduction to Photoplay, offered a replay of the course at the University of Iowa when he taught there on leave from USC in the summer of 1930.[16] Little is known about this offering, but one can imagine that it may have amounted to little more than MacDonald glossing the lectures he had listened to at USC.

The more ambitious offshoot of the USC course was an endeavor highly supported by AMPAS to have Stanford University also teach an Introduction to Photoplay course based—quite closely, as we will see—on the one at USC. Here, I offer an excursus on the Stanford venture before resuming the narrative of USC's own attempts to develop a film curriculum.

AN EXCURSUS ON AMPAS AND STANFORD UNIVERSITY

The initiative to have Stanford University add a version of Introduction to Photoplay to its curriculum seems to have been solidified around two personal networks: on the one hand, Lester Cowan, as noted, had graduated from Stanford and appeared able to exploit connections he had there; on the other hand, USC's Dean Waugh had, through his background in the field of psychology, a professional friendship with Stanford psychology professor (and department chair) Walter Miles.

The first steps by which AMPAS made its specific contact with Stanford are unclear. There is an intriguing, undated letter in the Walter Miles files in the Stanford archives from Edgar H. Yolland, a professor of political science, in which he wrote to Miles, "I heard from the Acad. of Motion Picture

Arts and Sciences you are interested to see the establishment of a College [of Arts and Sciences] course in Motion Pictures." That this professor had heard of the venture might mean that AMPAS was contacting other Stanford professors on an ad hoc basis, or that there was some specific connection between Cowan and someone like Yolland (a former professor perhaps?) and that Cowan was thereby trying to use his network of contacts to establish new links to the university.

In any case, in mid-July 1928, Frank Woods wrote from AMPAS to Miles in the psychology department, using as his pretext the university's announced upcoming ceremony in honor of the fiftieth anniversary of Eadweard Muybridge's famous experiments at Palo Alto on the photographing of horses in motion. Woods wrote to Professor Miles to say that AMPAS would like to have some strong presence at the event; soon, in fact, AMPAS had become a prime organizer of the ceremony, even setting up a delegation of industry figures (including such luminaries as Louis B. Mayer and William C. de Mille) to come to the university to honor the Muybridge experiments. Woods suggested to Miles that AMPAS could send Stanford graduate Lester Cowan to Palo Alto to help in the arrangements with the ceremony and to use that visit to initiate discussion with Stanford administrators about plans for industry-university cooperation (an allusion no doubt to the Introduction to Photoplay course idea). On September 14, 1928, Cowan himself wrote to Miles to confirm a trip to Stanford, adding, "I would like also to discuss with President Wilbur, yourself and any others who might be interested, important developments, not yet announced, in Academy College Relations." Presumably, this meant that AMPAS was ready to float the idea of a film course at Stanford University. Clearly, the Academy had begun to hope that Stanford administrators could be convinced to do more around film than just a one-day ceremony in honor of Muybridge.

On October 6, 1928, Miles himself received an invitation to speak at AMPAS at its second annual dinner, which would be held the following May *after* the Stanford-Muybridge ceremony. While Miles may have been tempted initially by the idea of visiting glamorous Hollywood, he also certainly sensed that there would be advantages, perhaps even financial, to the university as well if he allied with AMPAS. Thus, on December 5, 1928, he wrote to R. E. Swain, the acting president of the university, "The objective of the Committee [of Stanford professors working on the film idea] is twofold. First to give Mr. Stanford the honor that is justly due him for originating and carrying through, with the cooperation and skill of Mr. Muybridge, this first rate research idea. Second, to focus the attention of motion picture people on this early research and on Stanford University to the end that our university be considered a logical recipient for bequests."

As the date of the Stanford-Muybridge ceremony approached, on April 26, 1929, Miles addressed a letter to Ray Lyman Wilbur, the president of Stanford (who had taken a leave of absence to run the U.S. Department of the Interior), and again hinted at the possibility that a link to the film industry would bring benefit to the university as a whole: "We want to make it clear [in speeches during the ceremony] that the university, through teaching and research, is certain to be one of the main agencies for molding the development of the photoplay of the future and that it deserves the hearty support of the picture industry."

Even as he was finessing a partnership with AMPAS, Miles clearly had expectations that, in the area of practical film research, the university might be better placed than private enterprises (and their technical branches) to carry on some of the study necessary to industrial progress. Miles assumed that any advance in knowledge for the film industry would best come from academia and not from organizations like AMPAS. Thus, as he put it in a May 23, 1929, letter to Acting President Swain, written after the Stanford-Muybridge ceremony and after he (and several other Stanford professors) had made the AMPAS-sponsored visit to Hollywood and seen studio research facilities, "It seems evident that there is much need for research along various lines connected with these problems [i.e., of the new technology of the sound film]. I feel certain that a considerable part of this research would better be carried out in University laboratories where the workers are not striving for a particular result or end but are more open to appreciate the broad implications." In other words, while he was inviting overtures from the film industry through AMPAS, Miles was also assuming that his university could take control in areas of research and development.

But Miles also was looking out for his own academic unit, psychology, and not just the university as a whole. Even though psychology had been brought into the picture only because of the disciplinary connections of Miles and Karl Waugh at USC, Miles clearly wanted the department to play a key part in the interactions of the university with the film industry. He would even try to make the case that any film teaching at Stanford would *most appropriately* take place within the field of psychology. For example, in his letter to Swain, Miles emphasized the special role that psychology could play in the business of filmmaking: "Many of the features [of studio filmmaking] can be carried out with good efficiency but when it comes to actually making the picture, apparently so many people have to be involved in controlling the apparatus and providing for the various conditions that the actor, the highest paid individual in the whole group, has usually to do his work under extremely fatiguing demands. . . . This is only one of many problems that strike the eye of the psychologist." Likewise, as early as June 14, 1928, Miles wrote to Frank Woods to explain, and no doubt to promote, how his own personal area of research bore possible connections to film: "The field [of motion pictures] concerns vision and visual perception and therefore falls more naturally to the experimental psychology department than to any other of the ordinary university sciences." Miles was clearly lobbying for his department (and himself) to assume a key role in whatever AMPAS would do with the university.

Whether or not such strategies were evident, AMPAS was pleased by Miles's swift and encouraging response to its initial feelers. Once AMPAS received indication from Miles that he was interested, Lester Cowan picked up the correspondence from Frank Woods and, on November 27, 1928, wrote to Miles to encourage collaboration: "Naturally I am hoping that Stanford will take a prominent part in the program of the College Affairs Committee, and you seem to be the logical trail blazer" (there is a slight ambiguity in this last clause: is Cowan indicating that Miles personally [or his department] is the trailblazer, or is he making a comment about Stanford overall?). The AMPAS plans became increasingly ambitious. For example, Cowan spoke in several letters to Miles of the possibility of the university creating some sort of film institute or study center that would combine research and teaching. On February 21, 1929, for instance, he wrote to Miles of his "hope that the memorial program [i.e., the Stanford-Muybridge ceremony] would lead to the establishment of some sort of a foundation for motion picture research at Stanford," asserting that the university was "advantageously located" for such a venture. Miles was quite taken with this idea of a research center (and, especially, it would seem, with the money behind it that presumably would come from Hollywood). Thus, on May 15, 1929, he would write to Will Hays, whose organization was also sponsoring the Stanford-Muybridge commemoration, that "I trust it will seem desirable to motion picture interests to establish here at Stanford a Motion Picture Research Institute. This should not be regarded as a commercial adjunct to any one group but as a means to furthering fundamental and far-sighted research that has to do with the photoplay on the side of technique as well as that of content. . . . The University of the future must recognize the motion picture and it seems to me should be placed in a position to contribute to this important agency of civilization."

On May 8, 1929, the ceremony in honor of Muybridge and Leland Stanford took place. Articles in local newspapers show that the event also became the occasion for the public announcement of the idea of a Stanford film course. For example, under the heading "Mayer to Back Movie Course for Stanford," the *San Francisco Chronicle* reported:

> A university course in motion pictures was suggested for Stanford University today by Louis B. Mayer, vice-president of Metro-Goldwyn-Mayer motion picture producers of Culver City and in making the suggestion Mayer said he would be willing to aid materially the foundation of the course. . . . Mayer said, "Motion pictures have been neglected as a medium of education. I would be glad to contribute in a material way to the founding of a motion picture course at Stanford University. It is fitting that the industry should have further developments here at Stanford, where it received its first impetus fifty years ago [i.e., through the Muybridge experiments]. It is fitting also that the university should send professors to Hollywood and Culver City to gain first-hand knowledge of the industry in order that they may intelligently head a motion picture course, for in the motion picture industry lies a great future for the youth of today." . . . [Mayer] did not elaborate on the nature of the studies to be covered in a course on motion-pictures, but his offer to give material aid in founding such a course was warmly applauded by a large gathering in Stanford's Assembly Hall over which Acting President Robert E. Swain presided. Other speakers at the Assembly Hall exercises were Professor Walter R. Miles of the university's psychological department, and Dr. Alonzo Taylor, director of Stanford's Food Research Institute. [The latter figures in no other existing documentation about film at Stanford, so it is hard to know his connection to the event.]

The next day, an article on page 2 of the campus newspaper, the *Stanford Daily*, made clear the extent to which the onetime event of the ceremony was being thought of as a path to something more ambitious for the university:

> The talking picture, having made the production of motion pictures so much more complex, will demand the highest type of trained men and women to create it. It is to the university that all industries look for these people. . . . Stanford, as the scene of the first developments in the motion picture, should not lag in establishing courses in the field. The prominence of the motion picture industry on the Pacific Coast . . . gives the industry a much more immediate interest than it would have elsewhere. It is hoped the University will . . . take some action toward establishing courses at Stanford in this fast growing industry.

It is worth noting that the article refers, beyond the announced class for the fall, to courses in the plural. Perhaps, as at USC, the general course of Introduction to Photoplay was being envisioned as an initial offering that it was hoped would lead to an ever more specialized and advanced technical and professional curriculum. In fact, a May 24, 1929, letter from one AMPAS officer, actor Alec B. Francis, written to *Science* magazine to provide information for an article on the Stanford-Muybridge event, made explicit an ambition for an expanded curriculum that would grow from the Introduction to Photoplay course to embrace deeper professional education of movie industry workers: "I think the time has arrived when the University should give some attention to the motion picture industry by way of including it as material for instruction in art and the psychology of art and arranging for the training of a proper type of engineer to enter this industry."

Within a few days of the Stanford-Muybridge ceremony, Miles was on his way to Hollywood for the meetings he had been invited to by AMPAS, including a dinner ceremony at AMPAS in honor of its second year of operation. He was accompanied by a Stanford journalism professor, Everett W. Smith, and by a School of Engineering professor, F. G. Tickell. (USC's photoplay course, which was just finishing up its first semester, was also celebrated at the dinner, with Dean Karl Waugh giving a speech just after Miles.)

The inclusion of someone from engineering in the Stanford delegation is noteworthy. It is worth remembering that the plan initiated by Will Hays in 1926–27 for a film curriculum at Columbia University included components that touched on engineering concerns; similarly, the original three-track proposal for USC had included active participation from engineering. It is tempting to imagine that in this period there was one overall curriculum—with engineering as one of its core components—that Hays and AMPAS were promoting, whether separately or in tandem, to a variety of universities. Whatever the origin of this idea of engineering as a potential, and even perhaps essential, area of film instruction, Miles clearly was well entranced by it. For example, in a letter of May 23 to Acting President Swain in which he summed up his Hollywood trip, Miles recounted how during visits to the various studios, he had been struck by how the coming of sound raised a "whole group of problems in connection with the controlling of light and film movement for photography and of noise and sound to provide the auditory accompaniment for pictures" and saw "no special obstruction to the University entering this field." There was, as he said to Swain, "a logical necessity that the University must at last begin training a type of engineer who will be suitable for this huge industry of motion pictures." Likewise, on June 14, 1929, Miles wrote to Lester Cowan (perhaps to maintain contact during the summer break) and referred both to the overall idea of there being film instruction at Stanford and to the possibility that some major part of the curriculum might center on engineering issues: "We are continuing to discuss the general problem of University curriculum and Motion Pictures here at Stanford. Professor Tickell [the engineer who had gone with Miles to the AMPAS dinner] and I occasionally discuss the possible things along this line that may have to do with engineering."

In his speech at the AMPAS dinner in Hollywood, Miles had hinted at the importance of universities, such as his own, undertaking ambitious curricula in film. Miles referred to an "inevitable industrial cycle" in which universities developed research ideas that were then picked up by private firms as advances in industry and in turn were then complemented by the elaboration of university courses that offered rationalized instruction in precisely those new industrial practices. Just as he had indicated that the universities had specific advantages over private firms in the conducting of research, Miles was now arguing that academic research was an inevitable step that encouraged progress in business and then responded to that progress with new training curricula. As he put it in his AMPAS address:

> Out in the laboratories in the universities commences a little bit of an idea, but we don't know what to do with it. Someone outside in the world sees a big idea in it and they produce something that humanity finds interesting. Then the university begins to arrange courses, begins to do more work in that field, and begins to build up a curriculum to help make this field a more useful and more productive one. The university has just gone through this last cycle in the motion picture field. It seems to me that the motion picture industry has walled itself in—has hedged itself in. The university man has been able to learn about other industries; some he could know and understand thoroughly. But he has not been able to know the motion picture industry. . . . We have offered courses in psychology (*I think of it as human engineering*); we have offered other courses somewhat germane to your art—courses in art and the appreciation of music. Next we will introduce courses in the appreciation of the photoplay. We have never had this chance before for contact between the university and the motion picture industry. (my emphasis)

At the end of his talk, Miles announced, "Our photoplay course will be in charge of Paul Farnsworth, who has done much in the field of art and the psychology of art." Farnsworth appears to have been chosen both because he was the one professor in Miles's department with a specific interest in aesthetic issues (which would keep the course in Miles's territory and accrue benefits to his unit) and because he was an untenured professor who could be pushed to teach in this new area. Interestingly, Miles never seems to have entertained the idea of teaching the course himself. He appears to have had a certain knowledge of film—his research in psychology had focused on issues of perception, and he had done work on the filming of eye motion—and he wrote a fairly interesting and intelligent summary of the Stanford-Muybridge experiment after the ceremony. This article suggests that he well grasped technical and even philosophical aspects of photographic images in their relation to capturing temporal flux.[17] It does not suggest any particular understanding of cinema's *aesthetic* aspects, however, and Miles may have felt that he would not be adequate to the task of teaching a broad course like Introduction to Photoplay that was to have cultural issues as its primary concern. It may also simply be that his own duties as chairperson of the department precluded him from developing the course.

In his early thirties when he was assigned to teach the Stanford film course, Paul Farnsworth had received degrees in psychology from Ohio State University and had joined the Stanford faculty in 1925. The university's 1978 obituary for him explains that he was a "specialist in the psychology of music" (this was the topic of his one book, a 1969 study in musicology), but, in fact, in the late 1920s and early 1930s, he had ventured into experimental work in the visual arts as a way of extending his research.

In particular, Farnsworth was interested in the degree to which aesthetic judgment depended on contextual factors, rather than just on qualities within the work itself. Such factors included pressures on taste that came from one's membership in a social community and from prior knowledge, such as the artist's reputation and related background information about a work's history, that spectators brought to the work of art. To examine the impact of contextual knowledge on the reception of visual art, Farnsworth conducted experiments in which subjects were shown paintings with and without attribution, and with and without accompanying text, and asked to evaluate the qualities of the works. (It might be worth noting that I. A. Richards's famous experiments in the effects of contextual knowledge on literary evaluation, published as *Practical Criticism*, came from the very same historical moment—the end of the 1920s.) Farnsworth concluded that taste was fully contextual: one's social situation and one's knowledge about the work's background always influenced evaluation. There could be no pure and innocent contact with the work of art: thus, works that were presented to students without artist attribution or without explanatory text were evaluated as less artistic than those that came with such information. Farnsworth found the implications of such cultural relativism to be somewhat dismaying. As he put it, "The outlook is a disturbing one for him who believes that certain art elements are innately good." But this dire situation could be remedied by the intercession of an effective pedagogue who could manipulate contextual data to produce desired aesthetic effects: "The available data indicate that standards are relative to groups.... If, therefore, we have artistic views which we wish our children to exhibit it is up to us to stimulate them accordingly."[18] In other words, if the contextual nature of art's reception meant that there could be no objective standards, it nonetheless permitted the construction of desirable standards precisely by creation of contexts propitious for higher appreciation of the artwork.

When Miles assigned him to the film class, Farnsworth had been teaching a lower-level course in psychological aesthetics, Psychology 54—Psychology of Art, which was retooled to become the course on the photoplay. However, although among the psychology professors Farnsworth had the strongest interest in aesthetic questions, it seems that his commitment to the study of film in particular was never strong. This, at least, is the recollection of those few professors at Stanford who still remember Farnsworth or stories about him: they feel that he resented being required to teach in an area that was not really his, and that he never put much effort into the course. It is impossible to know if Farnsworth made any link between his own research on contextual factors in the reception of visual arts and the analysis of the specific cultural form of cinema. Would his recognition of cultural relativism and the instability of supposedly objective criteria for artistic judgment have led him to treat film in a positive fashion—film, in other words, as part of a new modernity in which hierarchies of art were fading away? Or would film have been one of the forms of deleterious culture that proper pedagogy could train students to eschew by establishing high-level standards of discrimination? As I note later, there is a somewhat disconnected quality in the list of topics announced in the catalog descriptions for Farnsworth's courses, which may have indicated a certain lack of interest on his part in shaping the film course to accord with his aesthetic interests in the other arts.

But AMPAS certainly tried to make it easy for Farnsworth to begin instruction in an unfamiliar area. Since Farnsworth was basically expected to copy the USC course—which had just ended—there would be little need for him to do anything but repeat the content of the talks from that earlier offering. Lester Cowan explained the procedure to Walter Miles on April 29, 1929 (about ten days before the Stanford-Muybridge ceremony), in an outline of the material support that AMPAS was prepared to offer if Stanford University agreed to offer Introduction to Photoplay:

> With further reference to the possibility of introducing a course in photoplay appreciation at Stanford University next fall. If the University, and particularly Dr. Farnsworth, is ready to go ahead, I think it would

> be very propitious to make an announcement of the course at the memorial program.
>
> As I explained to you, stenographic reports of the University of Southern California lectures will be available to Dr. Farnsworth, as well as talking picture lectures which can be reproduced by portable equipment. I think I could also arrange to have two or three of our prominent people talk at the university.
>
> If Dr. Farnsworth can spend some time in Hollywood this summer, *I will be glad to establish contact for him with some of our leading people so that he can get the necessary facts together.*
>
> Please take this matter up and if the announcement could be made in connection with the memorial program and while some of our very important people are there, we would feel deeply grateful. It would give great impetus to our plans with regard to colleges, to see another university take up the work we have started at the University of Southern California. (my emphasis)

It is easy to see that the stenographic transcripts and film recordings were being offered as a way to enable Farnsworth to crib major ideas and essentially repeat the USC instruction. In addition to making records of the USC lectures available to Farnsworth, Cowan sent copies of the syllabus to Miles and asked his opinion regarding their suitability for Farnsworth's course (Miles replied that he felt they would indeed work). Additionally, Cowan tried to arrange for William MacDonald, the nominal instructor for USC's course, to meet with Miles (and perhaps Farnsworth) when MacDonald had to come to Palo Alto for other academic business. Although the professors were not able to get together, they were able to talk by telephone, and Miles was able to report back to Cowan that USC-Stanford conversation was continuing as the fall term approached and as Farnsworth readied his course.

Whatever the accuracy of the recollections by Stanford professors regarding Farnsworth's lack of commitment to teaching the aesthetics of the photoplay, it is evident that the Photoplay version of Psychology 54 had a checkered career. The catalog description for the version of Psychology 54 retooled as the photoplay course shows both a concentration on film and a somewhat disconnected (and even schizophrenic) concern with experimental aesthetics in ways that do not seem to integrate, as if Farnsworth were simply and mechanically adding film on to his previous interests. The photoplay course was described as follows when it was first offered in the fall of 1929: "Psychology 54. Introduction to the Photoplay and Psychology of Art—History of the development and conventions of the photoplay. Aesthetic and social problems connected with motion pictures. Consideration of experimental literature of art principles, and a survey of art tests. No prerequisites." (A short notice for the course in the October 3, 1929, issue of the *Stanford Daily* provided a similar description and indicated that the enrollment for the course was limited to seventy-five students.)

It is interesting to note how the course title combines Farnsworth's own previous version of Psychology 54 and the title of the AMPAS course for USC. It is almost as if the new concern for the photoplay was being grafted artificially onto the existing course. Likewise, it is noteworthy that Farnsworth was still making reference to his previous interest in "art tests" (specifically, the tests he had conducted of the impact of context on the reception of art). Perhaps Farnsworth was suggesting that such tests be applied to film, but it is more likely that, again, his course was registering the pull he was feeling between the areas that were his real topics of concern and the new subject of film that his department chair had imposed upon him.

Virtually the same catalog entry appeared the following year, suggesting that whatever Farnsworth's possible reluctance to teach it, the film course might have been becoming a regular part of the curriculum. But there were two differences between the 1929 listing and that of 1930: first, a relatively minor one, which was that enrollment was now to be limited to fifty students; second, a more revealing one, namely, a parenthetical comment that, although listed, the course would be "[n]ot given in 1930–1931." In other words, it would seem that its place was being maintained in the curriculum although Farnsworth was not actually offering it. It is worth speculating that Farnsworth was already manifesting a resistance to film instruction. In fact, the photoplay course was not given in 1931–32 either, and Farnsworth seems to have gone back to more general teaching in aesthetics. In some of the descriptions for his later courses, film did appear, *but* only as one topic among many (one, moreover, whose integration with the rest often remained tenuous). For example, Farnsworth did not teach a photoplay version of Psychology 54 in 1932–33, but he did offer an upper division course, Psychology 152—Experimental Aesthetics, in which the motion picture was included but in mechanical, artificial, and disconnected fashion. In the words of that description, "Experimental Aesthetics.—Survey of the principles underlying the arts. Consideration of art and music tests. Aesthetic and social problems connected with motion pictures."

By 1937, Farnsworth had given up on film teaching altogether, and all mention of cinema disappeared from his course descriptions. Nonetheless, film instruction would persist at Stanford University. There is some indication that, even as Farnsworth was showing that he was not going to make film a central part of his concerns, the higher administration still had hopes for a film course and had started to look elsewhere in the university for someone to teach it. Thus, the archive files for President Wilbur contain a 1936 letter from William Dinsmore Briggs, chair of the English department, in which, in clear response to an inquiry from Wilbur, Briggs demurred from his department getting into the teaching of film: "I think it would not be wise for us to undertake this addition to our regular work. Any time that might be given to a course . . . would have to be subtracted from the at present insufficient teaching time of the English Department." Perhaps, as Farnsworth's course fell apart, the administration had been surveying potentially pertinent departments to see if they could take it over. In any case, toward the end of 1936, the *Stanford Daily* was able to announce a new course devoted to "lectures on the motion picture." Revealingly, this course would be offered in the fine arts department, not psychology, where the first course had been housed. AMPAS, it seems, had little to do with this new manifestation of film teaching at Stanford. There had been a clear transfer of the study of film into the humanities: the new course would deal with such issues as film as "graphic art," film as "dramatic vehicle," and the "aesthetics of the medium." Intriguingly, the *Daily* asserted that "this sort of a course has not been given in many universities but Minnesota and USC have recently installed courses which are similar" and offered no recognition of Farnsworth's course as an antecedent to the fine arts venture. It is likely that we have here one more example, like those encountered elsewhere in the pages of this study, of the short-term memory or lack of awareness by parts of a university of what is happening, or has already happened, elsewhere at the same institution. It is likewise noteworthy in this respect that although President Wilbur of Stanford had been kept in the loop on the 1929 course even while on leave, he seems to have exhibited typical administrator forgetfulness about the course later on. When John Abbott, the administrator of MoMA's new Film Library, wrote on February 16, 1935, to inquire if Stanford had any interest in rentals of films for courses at the university, Wilbur replied, in a letter of March 4: "So far, Stanford University has used the motion picture only in connection with certain departmental work and occasional films given in one of our assembly halls. We have not seriously taken up the question of motion pictures in education." He gave no recognition of the Farnsworth course or the broader ambitions for film study that Miles had proposed and that he himself had approved.

We can see in the fine arts reinvention of Stanford's film course after its abortive foray in the area of experimental psychology a confirmation of ever more predictable aesthetic directions that film studies would take from this period on. The new course would resemble those that later became part of the canon of film instruction. Revealingly, for our purposes, the *Stanford Daily* article noted that the new fine arts course would base itself directly on the circulating library of MoMA films. As I have noted earlier, the field of film studies changed after the founding of MoMA's film library in 1935, and Stanford provides a perfect example of this: the awkward offering in the psychology department gave way to a regular curricular item, one that pulled film away from industry promotion and placed it within the protected realm of the fine arts.

Stanford's version of Introduction to Photoplay no doubt suffered from the lack of commitment of its own instructor. But, given the fanfare with which both university figures like Walter Miles and an institution like AMPAS had initially promoted it, one can wonder why no one tried to salvage it. No doubt there are many possible answers, but the most likely one brings us back from this excursus on Stanford to the general nature of AMPAS's commitment to higher education as the 1930s began: quite simply, the Academy increasingly was getting out of the business of academia, and Stanford could no longer hope for the Hollywood benefits that it counted on originally. No doubt the Depression, which was leading to belt-tightening in the film industry, signaled a drying up of funds for ambitious academic projects.

To the extent that Miles had encouraged his university to ally itself with AMPAS's photoplay curriculum out of a hope that the contact would bring Hollywood money to the school, he, and everyone else, may have lost interest as it became increasingly clear that AMPAS intended to put no more effort or material support into the course. Both at Stanford and at USC, which had been the inspiration for Stanford's abortive first film course, any continuing curriculum in film would have to proceed on its own without AMPAS assistance.

MEANWHILE, BACK AT USC

In fact, by the end of the 1920s, with the completion of the first semester of USC's photoplay course, AMPAS had reached a crossroads around its investment in film pedagogy. At first glance, the Academy seemed to stand by its commitment. In the summer after Introduction to Photoplay had first been given, Lester Cowan called for a meeting of the College Affairs Committee at which he indicated pride in what had been achieved thus far and suggested that the future held promise for new initiatives: "The Committee now has a wide and promising field of choice in extending projects underway and responding to a variety of needs made apparent through contact with the public." Already, there were plans for there to be a second USC offering of Introduction to Photoplay, with specific administrative help from Cowan and AMPAS. This second version of the course took place in the spring semester of 1930. Some speakers from the first year, such as Milton Sills and William de Mille, returned, but there were also new visitors such as Mary Pickford, Louella Parsons, cinematographer Karl Struss, actor Hobart Bosworth, screenwriter Jane Murfin, art director Max Parker, producer William Le Baron, music director Hugo Riesenfeld, technical engineer H. G. Knox, and exhibitor Sid Grauman of Grauman's Chinese Theater fame.

Nonetheless, even before the very first semester of Introduction to Photoplay had begun, AMPAS had already started to look for ways to lessen its financial commitment to the USC course and shift the burden elsewhere. AMPAS secretary Frank Woods went in fact to Will Hays and asked his organization to take over subvention of the course. Hays raised the question, in turn, of why USC itself was not funding this curricular venture and received the reply from Woods that AMPAS had not trusted academic amateurs to run effectively a professional course of film training and had wanted to maintain its own control of course content. (In a later memo to Hays, Woods adduced as an additional point that USC funding of the course might discourage other universities from buying the lecture series, since they would have felt that another university would be getting credit for the knowledge contained therein.) It is unclear if the Hays Office provided the $3,000 that Woods was asking for in subvention of the course, but it is unlikely, since no documents, especially the publicity releases for the course, indicated MPPDA support. But the very fact that AMPAS turned to the Hays organization is a sign of the Academy's early reluctance to put too much of its own effort behind the USC course.

As quickly as AMPAS had pushed originally to get the photoplay course going at USC and elsewhere, it appeared as rapidly to get out of the college business. By September 1930, the *Academy Bulletin* indicated that Academy priorities were shifting elsewhere: "Although there is no specific present provision for the further promotion of the Academy college program, the momentum of the original work is still producing results."[19] To put it bluntly, USC was on its own. And at the beginning of 1931, the Academy folded the College Affairs Committee into its public relations division, declaring that since both were concerned with education and uplift of a broader public, there was therefore no need for separate attention to specifically college issues. Now that the course was off the ground, AMPAS's courting of academia could take a backseat to a more general enterprise of publicity and self-promotion in a variety of venues (e.g., the very public event of the annual Academy Awards).

Several weeks after the September 12, 1930, declaration in the *Academy Bulletin* that AMPAS was no longer supporting the college program, College Affairs Committee chair Milton Sills died suddenly of a heart attack. Sills had been key in AMPAS's original attempts to ally itself with academia, and one can only imagine that his passing would have served as one more argument for AMPAS to withdraw from college activities.

In fact, in reading through issues of the *Academy Bulletin* from the first years, one is struck by the extent to which the organization seemed to have many initiatives on its plate other than academic enterprise: predictably, its annual awards ceremony would soon become the primary activity that would define the Academy of Motion Picture Arts and Sciences. But additionally, in the politically complicated context of Depression America, the new decade also saw the Academy devoting more of its attention to issues of employer-employee conciliation (with Lester Cowan increasingly devoting his time to the work on an industry code). No doubt, the financially troubling situation that Hollywood was facing as the impact of the Depression fully hit home led to the sentiment that whatever resources should (still) be devoted to pedagogy would have to be more carefully controlled. There was no room for cultural courses by freethinking academics that would not necessarily issue in directly effective professional training.

Revealingly, alongside its original efforts around the USC photoplay course, AMPAS put a fair amount of energy into two other courses that would eventually be offered at USC but would not be at all academic in intent. Unlike Introduction to Photoplay, these courses were designed and designated specifically for technicians who already were working in the industry rather than for general college students who might eventually try for a film career. This venture is well described by Pierre Sands in his history of the early days of AMPAS, which is worth quoting at length:

> At the same time as the course "Introduction to Photoplay" was being organized in 1928 for college use, a different type of course was being set up for studio employees. The College Affairs Committee recommended that the Technicians Branch of the Academy cooperate with the University of Southern California in offering through the University Extension Division two courses of lectures for the benefit of Academy members and studio employees in general. The first course was to "give an understanding of the instruments and physical laws involved in the recording and reproduction of sound and voice for talking pictures."

The College Affairs Committee proposed that Professor Nye, Head of the Physics Department of the University of Southern California, handle the course with the assistance of qualified members of the Technicians' Branch. The second course was to be called "Introduction to Cinematography," and its purpose was to "give an appreciation and general understanding of the art of cinematography to persons in the studios who are interested."[20]

In the event, it was deemed a priority to devote attention to the new technologies of sound recording, and the course on cinematography dropped away. The sound course was first offered in September 1929—in other words, in the fall semester after Introduction to Photoplay had first been offered—to two sections of 125 studio technicians who followed weekly two-hour evening lectures over a ten-week period and received a certificate (but no college credit) for their efforts. It is perhaps significant, given the Academy's early attempt to involve both USC and UCLA in its general college course on the photoplay, that USC's Professor Nye taught one section of this course while the other was taught by a UCLA professor, Vern Knudsen, a specialist in acoustical physics who had recently helped MGM in the design of its soundstages.

The sound course continued into the 1930s and received acclaim from industry executives. In 1931, transcripts of class lectures were printed up as a volume, *Recording Sound for Motion Pictures*, edited by Lester Cowan.[21] Although Cowan had been instrumental in getting the general photoplay course going, he now appeared to be more interested in meeting pressing professional needs of the industry than in promoting academic study of film for potential future professionals. Just as he had parlayed his own research around incandescent illumination into a way to move from his USC internship to a more industry-connected position at AMPAS, Cowan seemed now to transfer his pedagogical commitment from the general student body to the industry-based employees of Hollywood.

To the extent that the sound course was exclusively geared to in-house professional training for personnel already employed in the film industry, it cannot really be called a USC course or even a university course at all. USC would provide its mechanisms for registering students, it would offer classroom space, and one of its faculty would be an instructor for the course. Essentially, however, USC served as little more than a subcontractor to which the industry outsourced its labor force for basic training. In that sense, the sound course is not really part of the history of the beginnings of film studies, and I mention it only to show how AMPAS's and Lester Cowan's priorities had altered.

USC would receive no more help from AMPAS for its general film pedagogy. But the university's ambition to build up a film curriculum persisted. In 1931, for instance, a second course was added to Photoplay as a screenwriter named Dorothy Yost began teaching a photoplay-writing course in the adult-education program of the university. And it was around this time that a more important figure for the future of film studies at USC came onto the scene: an eccentric old-world professor named Boris Morkovin. Over the next few years, Morkovin would expand the curriculum in cinema and would, in fact, preside over its crystallization into a degree program in film, the first ever in the United States.

Boris Morkovin is a curious, even elusive, part of the history of early film studies. He had a strong personality, but ironically it is this distinctiveness of character that makes it hard for the historian today to know what to make of him. He clearly aroused both extreme devotion and intense disdain. Thus, when I began my research and first encountered his name, some students who had gone to USC in the 1930s declared him to have had no consequential role in the development of cinema studies at the university. These students remembered him as an interloper who arrogantly tried to take over the university's efforts in film but did not have the talent to do so. At worst, he was said to be a bumbler who could not teach and who blundered around in the world of film—literally so in one anecdote according to which, as one remembrance put it, "he would take the students on visits to the studios and he'd walk in on a stage in the middle of a take, and he was clumsy about things."[22]

At best Morkovin was described as an irrelevancy—someone who did not know anything about film and who the budding film students would have to learn to ignore in order to go about their own education. Typical in this respect was the blunt comment offered by Richard Bare, who began as a USC cinematography student in 1933 and later went on to a professional career in film and television directing (e.g., he directed *Green Acres*). Bare felt Morkovin had nothing to teach him as a filmmaker: "Morkovin didn't know how to make one [a film] himself." Bare offered no further elaboration—both because the statement summed up Morkovin for him and because he felt Morkovin was a minimal presence within the film program.

Quite the contrary, Morkovin had an active and productive involvement with the movies during the years he was associated with the teaching of film at USC. As we will see, he wrote prolifically on the subject (and, beyond published work and publicly presented lectures, had plans for additional major research projects); he worked actively with the Disney studios in several capacities; he edited a national film journal; and he founded and ran a major organization on film art and public morality. Newspaper clippings show that he was an active presence in conferences and conventions on the public implications of the movies, and he seems to have been a regular at many film-betterment events in the Los Angeles area. The detailed syllabi and extensive course plans (with massive bibliographies) for his film classes belie the impression of a dabbler who did not put any effort into the teaching of film. The sense, rather, is of someone who was voraciously working on cinema and had committed to it wholeheartedly.

Yet even this seeming evidence of Morkovin's intense, almost obsessive immersion in film activities in the 1930s is itself ambiguous. At several stages of his career, Morkovin shifted his areas of interest, but each time he jumped into the new topic with extreme fervor—and abandoned his previous interests with as much energy. Thus, as will be described in more detail later, he worked in depth in such areas as comparative literature, art history, political science, film studies, pedagogy of the handicapped, and psycholinguistics (to name just a few of the fields in which he claimed expertise). Here, again, there is space for both positive and negative assessment. In the best light, Morkovin can appear as an example of that classic image of the scholar as Renaissance man, someone who possessed a general culture that enabled him (and the gendered noun seems appropriate here, since the "Renaissance man" was so often a gender privilege) to engage trenchantly and productively with a diversity of human topics. Thus, one of Morkovin's social science colleagues described him as follows in a memorial: "Boris Morkovin was a true 'citizen of the world.' He was the last of a small group close to Maxim Gorky, Thomas Mann, Jan Masaryk, and Edouard Benes. Boris was always a zealous worker, a prolific writer, and a gadfly to presumptuous students. He left behind a truly cosmopolitan group of friends."[23]

But in the worst light, Morkovin can seem a dilettante without ultimate commitments. There are moments when one sees the Renaissance man tipping over into the figure of arrogance who assumed that a little basic knowledge gave him the power to comment on anything. There was evident in Morkovin a presumption of infallible expertise that could seem virtually megalomaniacal. It is revealing how Morkovin's enthusiasms could change so abruptly: his was a career of a certain inconsistency of commitment. Once he abandoned an area of concern, he never returned to it, and there seems to have been little sense of career as meaningful trajectory, rather than as a series of discrete stages that never had a final narrative. Even if Morkovin seems to have worked incessantly and intensively on nothing but film for most of the 1930s, it is striking—and somewhat dismaying—to see the extent to which, once he left the field, he seems deliberately to have turned his back on film culture. He did not merely stop teaching, but abandoned all his other activism involving film. Thus, the journal he edited ceased publication, and the better-morals-through-film association he had founded was allowed to die. Morkovin never looked back.

This chapter has presented a number of persons who can seem veritable opportunists—Karl Waugh hawking a bizarre gizmo to the studios, Lester Cowan using USC as a stepping-stone to an industry career, Walter Miles attempting to bring Hollywood money to Stanford and to capture the university's attention to film within his own department—and it might well be that Morkovin was simply another one of these figures who knew how to be at the right place and the right time and accrue benefits to himself. In fact, early on, as an emigrant who left for the United States to begin a new life, Morkovin seems to have been infused with that American pioneer mythology that imagines the new land (and the voyage west through it) as a source for rebirth, reinvention, and self-aggrandizement. (In Morkovin's case, as even his supporters noted, this involved abandoning his wife and three children in eastern Europe and trying to start life anew without them.)[24] In the 1930s, the cinema seems to have allowed Morkovin a new identity as a film scholar and as a crusader for moral uplift through betterment of the movies. It is pertinent that this work took place in Los Angeles, where Morkovin could participate in the glamour of one of the greatest American arts to participate in this mythology of reinvention.[25]

Morkovin was born in Tashkent in 1883, but early on his family moved to Prague, where he studied at Charles University and then joined its faculty in 1912 as an instructor in journalism. Toward the end of the First World War, he worked with the Danish Red Cross as a key member of a commission on rehabilitation and repatriation of Allied prisoners. Here, in fact, we can see an early sign of Morkovin's concern with processes of human amelioration and with efforts at providing aid to the needy: while he was caught up in the specific problems brought on by war, his Red Cross activity had to do with a crusading effort to improve people's lot. From the start, a philosophy of social assistance was of central concern to Morkovin and serves indeed as the one thread that perhaps gives some unity to an otherwise dispersed career. When he eventually came to teach and engage in activism about film, it would be in large part from within the context of social reformism.

Throughout the 1920s, Morkovin exhibited an almost desperate desire to be recruited to a teaching position in the United States, and he engaged in an intense publicity campaign to get invited to speak at various venues with the obvious intent of drumming up interest toward a career in America. One flyer, for instance, which advertised "Professor Morkovin's Lecture Tour of 1926," sported testimonials from administrators of various venues in which he had lectured during previous visits to America. His proposed topics included political forces, social movements, everyday attitudes in eastern Europe, and "The Artistic Genius of the Slavs with Its Roots in Their Folk Art (with Slides)." He also, it was said, could offer a series of thirty lectures on Russian literature and fifteen illustrated lectures on "The Art of Slavic Peoples" (which would include modern performing arts), which could be shown along with a film, *The Customs, Games and Dances of Slovaks in Their National Costumes.*

It is not clear what the content of this film was—recently filmed scenes? library footage?—or if Morkovin made the film himself (if he did, it would be an early sign of his possible knowledge of at least some rudiments of filmmaking). In any case, this early self-promotion already reveals certain things about Morkovin that would eventually feed into his work on film. First, the sheer ambitiousness of the Renaissance man: politics, culture, and literature were all fodder for him. Second, the concern to understand art—including folk and popular arts—as an expression of a people; by the 1930s, when Morkovin came to film study, this would manifest itself as a reformist concern both to examine the often inadequate films people currently were being offered and to militate for a higher-quality cinema of aesthetic and moral betterment. Third, and connected to the first two points, the interest in comparative studies (in this case, the arts and politics of several eastern European countries): Morkovin did not merely claim mastery of international contexts but also saw all individual cultures as interconnecting in a shared need for verbalization and self-realization. In the 1930s, the cinema would attract Morkovin—as it earlier attracted those 1910s and 1920s figures who saw in it a universal language—as a means of expression that could cut across boundaries and divisions and offer diverse people a shared education and shared means of expression. Finally, whether or not Morkovin made *The Customs, Games and Dances of Slovaks* himself and whether or not he started out with any specific technical knowledge of filmmaking, the announcement for his lectures shows that he had a certain concern with a pedagogy by means of popular, visual media. Significant here is not only the inclusion of film and slides in the lectures but the very fact that Morkovin engaged in public relations to promote those lectures. Morkovin's salesmanship established him as one of those intellectual figures encountered regularly in this study who assumed that academic activity and the marketplace were not necessarily in conflict.

Bit by bit, Morkovin's academic self-promotion paid off. In 1926 he joined USC as an instructor in comparative literature and began work on an American doctorate. He was awarded his Ph.D. jointly in comparative literature and sociology in 1929 for a thesis titled "Incipient Revolution in Its Personality and Group Aspects: Psycho-social Study of the Latent and Overt Conflict of the Russian Intelligentsia with the Government and Conservative Society between 1825 and 1881." From this title and the published description, Morkovin's study certainly does not seem directly literary, but it did have a cultural component. Artistic works constituted for him transparent documents through which society's concerns could be read. As his dissertation description announced, "The study is based upon research into mental and social movements among the Russian intelligentsia, as reflected in the human documents (autobiographies, biographies, diaries, letters, memoirs) and literary production of Russian men of letters."

Soon after Morkovin arrived in Los Angeles, his scholarly research came to deal more and more with the cinema as a specific cultural form. As a sociologist, he predictably centered one major aspect of his work in this domain on social *effects* of motion picture *reception*. Thus, a short report in *Sociology and Social Research* (a journal edited by his colleague Emory Bogardus, who lectured in the first year of Introduction to Photoplay) summarizes a paper that Morkovin had presented on "Motion Pictures and Human Behavior" to the Social Research Society of Southern California in February 1929. As the article recounted, Morkovin "defined the role of motion pictures as a powerful accelerating and retarding agent in both cycles of social processes, the processes of social differentiation and integration.... [M]otion pictures make their mighty imprint on different forms of social maladjustment and social unrest." Themes such as the potential of film for betterment or for disruption of proper social behavior would dominate Morkovin's reformist approach to film throughout the 1930s, but it is also worth noting how this early trace of his academic work on film is also in continuity with his earlier work on national identity and cultural expression. For Morkovin, the elaboration and perfection of languages, including the specific languages of cultural and artistic forms, were the means by which societies could come to express their values and goals, and there was always a concern throughout his work to promote modes for better and broader communication. But there is also evident in his work a 1920s "League of Nations" worry that international communication could be marred by power plays in which specific cultures might overpower others. As the report in *Sociology and Social Research* goes on to say, "The people of seventy countries, speakers of more than 600 languages and dialects in the world are influenced by the actors of Hollywood. This gigantic audience has a common language. Hollywood, which furnishes 80 per cent of all motion pictures to the world, is a nucleus of radiation of the cultural patterns all over the world. The influence of America in this direction arouses great alarm in Europe and other parts of the world."

The short notice in *Sociology and Social Research* ended with two references to practical research activities on Morkovin's part that are interesting for what they suggest about his increasing engagement in the 1930s with film and his interest in establishing cinema study as a regular curriculum at the university. The report indicated, first, that Morkovin had been conducting an examination of fan mail to various actors, which gave him the opportunity to study "a striking process of the making of symbols from different stars." It is tempting to wonder about the extent of Morkovin's research on fan mail: to the degree that it was a developed research project, were the studios offering him assistance? If so, did this relate in any way to the collaboration elsewhere on campus between USC and the industry via AMPAS in the development of a film curriculum? Unfortunately, little other trace remains of the fan-mail project (and, in any case, Morkovin was good at announcing research projects that he in fact never seems to have really followed through on). Second, the short notice also referred to Morkovin's broader ambition to make film the object of regular investigation by researchers at the university: "[T]he speaker presented a plan for collective research work for the Department of Sociology of the University of Southern California, and indicated the sources of material which might be utilized by the graduate students who would participate in the suggested plan."

Morkovin does seem to have continued his research efforts into social effects of film throughout the first part of the 1930s at the very least. Thus, the *New York Herald Tribune* was able to report on one such project in a short article of December 8, 1931:

"TESTS SHOW GIRLS GET HABITS FROM THEIR
FAVORED FILM STARS"

> More than 50 per cent of the children get their mental imagery, vocabulary and manner of dress from the screen, according to Dr. Boris Morkovin, of the University of Southern California. His tests indicate that girls adopt their gait, speech, etc., from mannerisms of their film favorites. Boys, on the other hand, are tremendously influenced by aviation and other thrill pictures.[26]

But if early on Morkovin indicated a typical concern with a sociology of film *reception*, he also exhibited a less conventional interest in the sociology of *production*. Thus, on October 10, 1927, he wrote to Jason Joy at the Hays Office to ask for the MPPDA's support for a project on "The Social Psychology of the Makers of Moving Pictures." Morkovin intended to distribute a questionnaire to cinema actors to examine how their personal attitudes might show up in their film roles. In his words, his study would lead to an "impartial, objective evaluation of the immense work which goes on behind the screen with its socio-psychological analysis." The MPPDA does appear to have given some support to the project, and Morkovin drew up a long questionnaire with fifty-five questions about the psychological life of the actors. Actors were asked to write up their autobiography with special attention to "features in your previous life and experience which later formed your interests, desires, energy, character and ability or shortcomings as they helped or hindered you in your career and life." Questions included the following: What was it that particularly attracted you to moving pictures: money, glory, adventure, or other people? What obstacles did you meet in penetrating the moving picture world? Were there objections on the part of your parents or relatives? How does your work in the moving pictures affect your health? What helped you in different cases to keep or refresh your emotional powers, your enthusiasm, and your interest in life? Which were the happiest moments in your life—while in movies and before? Can you explain in concrete facts, why, in spite of success and a comfortable situation financially, so many actors and actresses in the moving pictures do not acquire inner satisfaction and are so often subject to nervous disorders?

Little appears to have come of this project, which perhaps was just another example of Morkovin's seemingly frequent announcement of programs of research that did not really develop. One mention of the questionnaires in a campus newspaper article three years later described a class lecture in which Morkovin promised to refer to replies from actors that explained "how they register the reactions of audiences to their plays or acting, and how they improve their technique on the grounds of these observations." But Morkovin's project and planned book never really coalesced. One imagines that asking actors to address fifty-five topics, including rhetorically loaded ones like the one about the lack of happiness in their lives, would not have received favorable response among the makers of the movies in Hollywood. In typical fashion, though, Morkovin promoted the project with great fanfare: it was, he said to Jason Joy, being published under the auspices of USC with plans for translation into French, German, and Bohemian languages and a print run of one hundred thousand copies! With what one comes to recognize as his habitual immodesty, he indicated that the volume was "anticipated from many sides," but the project appears to have existed in announcement only.

Throughout his career, Morkovin seems to have announced new research projects less out of deep commitment to them than as test balloons launched randomly to see which ones might merit following up on. Nonetheless, "Social Psychology of the Makers of the Moving Picture" does somewhat indicate Morkovin's shifting attention from the point of consumption to that of production. As he engaged more and more with a film curriculum at USC, Morkovin would in fact come increasingly to be fascinated by issues of film production—both the practical questions of day-to-day filmmaking and deeper questions, both aesthetic and sociological, around the activities of artistic creation. His growing interest in production issues would help orient the USC curriculum in distinctive and decisive directions.

In the fall semester of 1929 (in other words, soon after the Introduction to Photoplay course had finished up in the spring), Morkovin retooled one of his courses, Sociology 183, to become Social Aspects of Motion Pictures. Although the course was first offered in USC's evening college, it soon became part of the regular curriculum for sociology. The following is the first catalog description for the course:

SOCIAL ASPECTS OF MOTION PICTURES

The modification of personal and collective behavior through motion pictures. The motion picture as a new culture-complex in America and other countries. The socio-psychological and artistic analysis of certain motion pictures. The role of screen writers, directors, stars, and technicians in molding the mind of the public. Different picture publics, motion pictures and publicity, industry, commerce, education, and various social problems. (Illustrated with slides and films.)

Morkovin also offered to make himself available on a for-hire basis through USC's Speakers Bureau for talks based on the new film version of Sociology 183. Early announcements portrayed the course to a large degree as one typically concerned with the impact and effects of the motion pictures on its consumers:

Motion pictures have become one of the most influential social institutions, working with powerful means—by indirect suggestion and emotional appeal. How, with what processes, is this bewitching spellbinding power of motion pictures created? On what chords of human emotions do they play? What is this influence upon children and adults, upon the peoples of non-occidental civilization? . . . This is the first course of the kind given in the United States and practically in the world.

Although housed in the sociology department, the course seems a venue in which Morkovin could try out a diversity of approaches to cinema across myriad disciplines (as mentioned earlier, he was at this time a professor both of sociology and of comparative literature; in the same semester that he was teaching the motion picture version of Sociology 183, he was also offering two comparative literature courses, The Modern Continental Novel and The Modern Continental Drama). A press release in the November issue of *Educational Screen* suggests some of the topics to be covered by the course: "The course will discuss how the public dictates its shifting desires and demands to scenario writers, stars and producers. Subjects to be illustrated by films include: The mutual influence of spectator and screen, changing tastes in types of plays and players, the reign of fads and fashions, psychological trends and sociological cycles as they are reflected in films."

The concerns of Sociology 183 were in fact presented as quite varied. Students might conduct audience surveys at local theaters and examine both the attraction of specific theaters ("How long have you been coming to this theater? Why?") and the attractions on the screen ("Name the three pictures you liked best"). They might go on tours of movie palaces, like Grauman's Chinese Theater, where they would both participate in a screening and discussion of film appreciation issues and be given a lecture by the manager on practical issues of running a theater, on theater architecture, and on technical concerns of acoustics. They would also study more directly sociological questions. Thus, in a letter in the fall of 1929 to Mary Waite, executive secretary of the Institute of International Education in New York, Morkovin spoke of research his students were conducting that fit clearly with his interests in media effects: "We are carrying on a most fascinating research work with the teachers of Los Angeles in studying the influence of motion pictures on the behavior (1) of the children of the grade schools, (2) of the high schools, (3) of subnormal children, (4) of college students, and (5) of immigrants of the first and second generation."

At the same time, in another description for Social Aspects of Motion Pictures, Morkovin indicated that the course had three distinctive concerns: (1) artistic and dramatic illusion as created by scenario writers, actors, artists, and technicians; (2) evolution of the motion picture industry—talkies and television; distribution, publicity, and exhibition; and (3) personality and mass reaction of children and adults; educational, commercial, industrial, scientific, and international aspects.

At the very least, it must be said that this description gives the impression of a course that was only partially sociological. As he was attempting to develop his own approaches to cinema, Morkovin brought in whatever he could, whether or not it fit any particular rubric such as sociology. Morkovin even tried to incorporate production instruction into the course. Thus, as he explained in the first issue of the film-betterment bulletin he began to edit in the same period, students in Sociology 183 pooled their resources to buy film, worked together to build their own lighting equipment, and wrote scripts for simple narrative situations such as "Park Bench" or "The Dentist" that might allow them to hone their cinematic skills on scenes from everyday life.[27]

It is possible that Morkovin saw the sheer diversity in the course as a way to grope toward a complex analysis of film that would set out to understand the art in the interlinked ways its products moved from creation to consumption. In fact, another description for Social Aspects of Motion Pictures (which was sometimes called Social and Psychological Aspects) condensed the areas of concern into two primary ones in ways that suggest some of the linkages that Morkovin hoped to forge:

> The course is divided into the studies (1) of the technical, artistic and psychological devices used by directors, scenario writers, actors, cameramen, publicity men and others; (2) of the working of motion picture illusion upon the minds of the public and individuals, and its influence upon the human personality. Both aspects of this study will be fostered, giving the students a chance to watch the production and exhibition of pictures in studios and theaters, and to analyze the pictures with the use of a scientific criterion.

The word that mediates the two sections of the course is *illusion*. (In 1930, Morkovin gave a public lecture with the title "Cinema Illusion"; according to the announcement for the talk, he would treat cinema as "the first great art of the masses since the cathedrals of the thirteenth century.") Although he never fully let go of the idea that he had exhibited in his 1920s research on Slavonic life of culture as a transparent vehicle for ideas, in the 1930s Morkovin increasingly came to understand that film's impact derived from its construction of effective and affective cinematic illusion *through its medium-specific array of techniques and conventions*. Filmmakers had at their disposal specific "technical, artistic, and psychological devices" to create such illusion, and a full study of the power of cinema would require a careful examination of these devices. The sociology of cinema had necessarily to be linked to the aesthetic analysis of forms and structures.

Morkovin spelled out some of the dimensions of his medium-specific understanding of film in a brief article in *International Photographer* in 1933.[28] Here, again, as in his course description, Morkovin found film technique to mediate the moment of production and the sociological and psychological aspects of the moment of reception. On the one hand, film was an art form of potentially great "emotional effect upon the spectator's mind." On the other hand, in a highly competitive field, the makers of films increasingly needed, if they indeed wanted to have that effect, to think about the techniques of their art: "[T]he psychological contribution of every little detail has to be weighed with utmost care." The remainder of Morkovin's essay then set out to categorize the primary techniques of film art. First, he distinguished between those techniques that had moment-to-moment effect as a story moved along and those that came from the "cumulative and emotionally effective arrangement" of moments into a narrative structure. Then, there was also a division between formal qualities of narrative (qualities that were not medium-specific to film: some stories gained their effectiveness from "universal appeal of situations and problems") and formal qualities in the staging and filming of actors. For example, with regard to this last area, effective devices in a film included

> the popularity of stars and other actors and their casting; costumes and make-up; movement of actors within the frame; their general acting and "little" movements seen through the close-up, facial expressions, movements of different parts of the body, posture and gait; mental states of actors brought out and emphasized by outward objective means, by situation, reactions of other persons, by symbolism and insert of inanimate objects, by creation of an atmosphere with pictorial effects of background and composition, by conveying indirect suggestions as to emotional states of the character, by means of contrasted light, restless flickering, increase or decrease of light effects, high or low angle, moving camera, contrasted sound effects, their increase or decrease, music, tempo or cutting, etc.

To be sure, much of this reads as a mere list of resources of film technique, and it is not necessary to assume that Morkovin's film aesthetics was a sophisticated one. At the very least, however, the idea that the devices of cinema should not merely be enumerated at random but categorized within larger divisions (moment-to-moment devices versus story devices; extracinematic narrative devices versus medium-specific ones) did set out to give the catalog some theoretical depth. In a later essay, published in the National Board of Review's magazine, Morkovin attempted another articulation of fundamental divisions in film's aesthetic resources:

We may say that in the movies there are two main channels through which the attention of the public may be absorbed and held. One is by means of the subject matter, ideas and characters of the story, providing that these are sympathetic to the public's nerve of interest at the time they are presented. I call this the social-psychological channel of the control of the emotions. The other channel of control is the elaborate cinematic and dramatic technique employed in the making and producing of motion picture stories. This technico-artistic channel guides the attention, subconsciously playing upon the public's emotions as upon the keyboard of a piano.[29]

One curious pedagogical side effect of Morkovin's elaboration of his film aesthetic took place outside of the university, but it is worthwhile to chronicle it for the light it throws on Morkovin's developing philosophy of film. Based on his argument that filmmakers needed to be more systematic in planning out the impact on audiences of basic story elements as well as medium-specific filmic devices, Morkovin was hired by Walt Disney toward the middle of the 1930s to teach a series of courses (divided between beginning and advanced sections) in "Technique and Psychology of the Animated Cartoon" to the studio's animators.[30] Morkovin was hired not to teach drawing technique or visualization but to use his literary background to instruct animators on story line and character. Thus, his opening lecture for his beginners class offered a mini-lesson in theory of narrative and suggested that obsession with moment-to-moment cartoon effects at the expense of narrative arc was the root of the failure of some cartoons. For a successful story, Morkovin argued, it was necessary for there to be

> one basic situation carried through to a logical conclusion. . . . What is the *body* of the story? It is a series of situations by which the character experiences one difficulty after another. We will designate that as the *complications* of the story so that by the time the climax is reached, the body of the story is completed. When the middle of the story is well developed it has value plus—sometimes. Sometimes when the middle of the story is developed too much in cartooning it is dead. If there is too much plot, too many actions, too much story—if it is too formal—then it is not good because in the seven minutes allotted to our pictures you have such a little time to attract the attention of your audience. . . . Therefore, if there is too much story-action and no room to show the character as a thinking living character, it will be off balance.

Like a university class, Morkovin's Disney courses included homework for the students. For example, after the lecture about narrative arc, students were asked to come back with an analysis of selected Disney cartoons. In the words of the assignment, students were to show up at the next session ready to state in each picture whether or not it had a basic situation-predicament or if it were a situationless picture. If the picture has a basic situation, be ready to state if it had a beginning, middle and a logical ending; whether it was well developed, plausible and realistic or whether it was false, insincere, or completely impossible; whether it made room, not only for actions and mental and physical characteristics but also for feeling, thought and attitudes of the characters.

Once again, it is apparent that Morkovin was not offering a profound analysis of film, and there are accounts that his ventures into the Disney studios did not turn out well (in one version of the story, he gave Disney a narrative analysis that explained how *The Three Little Pigs* had not been as good a story as it should have been and got fired for his presumption; in another account, the animators found his attempts to explain their art to them both condescending and self-evident, and they laughed him off the lot). But the consultancy at Disney is revealing in the ways it suggests how Morkovin took his aesthetic of film as forming the base not just for a pedagogy but for one that could have direct consequences in the effective production of films. Aesthetic analysis, again, was linked to issues of creation insofar as the examination of cinematic devices could help filmmakers best exploit the resources of their art to greatest effect.

It is this seemingly commonsensical continuity between aesthetics and filmmaking that helps explain what at first glance might appear a curious and somewhat eclectic development in Morkovin's USC course Social Aspects of Motion Pictures: for the summer 1931 version of the class, Morkovin announced that the students should together produce a narrative film. For Morkovin, the move into fiction film production was logical. As he explained in an interview with the campus newspaper on June 25, 1931, "The course has been changing from a class in theory to an experimental group so that students will be able to learn the manner in which the attention of the audience is captured by creating an illusion through various technical, artistic, and psychological devices."[31]

Originally, Morkovin had assumed that the closest he could get to offering his students extended practical experience in filmmaking was to take them to studios where they could observe the day-to-day activity of production. One newspaper article (probably from the *Daily Trojan*) recounts the trips to the studios:

> Permanent passes to the Metro-Goldwyn-Mayer, Paramount, RKO, and possibly Universal studios have been obtained for students enrolled in the class. They will go every week to the movie lots, two to three in a party accompanied by Dr. Morkovin, each one to spend part of the day

observing some special phase of the industry in which they are interested. "First-hand experience and knowledge will thus be obtained," Dr. Morkovin remarked, in speaking of the course. "Once a week, the class will meet as a whole, at which time the members will give oral reports of what they observed and learned at the studios. Means used by directors to capture and maintain interest of the audience are to be given especial attention," he continued. "In motion pictures, as in any other business or art, certain devices, whether dramatic, psychological, mechanical, or artistic, are employed by those at the head of the project."

The short article ended with the announcement that the results of this on-site research into the processes of studio film production would lead the following fall to a course in film production timed to coincide with the creation of a filmmaking club on the campus. But soon Morkovin decided that the current summer course already would involve the making of a movie. A press release, picked up by a number of newspapers in the Los Angeles area and by the Hollywood trade press, provided detail on the filmmaking venture:

> Experience in filming a motion picture and educational trips to studios will be given students at University College, University of Southern California, in the summer quarter class in social psychological aspects of motion pictures conducted by Dr. Boris V. Morkovin for which registration is now being taken. . . .
>
> Scenario writers, camera men and directors will be selected from the class members, according to Doctor Morkovin. Research work is being done by prospective students to provide an authentic background for the picture which is to give an accurate portrayal of the growth of the oil industry, with a plot involving the rise of a ranch-boy to the position of an oil king who wins the hand of a Swedish beauty.
>
> At the semi-annual conference meetings of the class, parts of the film will be shown and analyzed from a social and psychological standpoint, with discussion conducted by Dr. Morkovin who has just been appointed to the advisory council of the National Committee for the Study of Social Values in Motion Pictures.

Several details of this announcement are worth remarking upon. First, the very fact that there was a press release had to do with the university's decision to open the course to the general public as part of USC's adult education program. Morkovin was very much concerned with issues of public outreach, and he even offered a broadcast version of Sociology 183 delivered as a series of radio talks over a Beverly Hills educational station, KEJK (an article in the campus newspaper claimed the lectures individually had an audience of fifty thousand listeners, but it is hard to know if one can credit that figure). Morkovin seemed particularly to encourage public school teachers to take his cinema classes out of a hope that they could bring lessons about cinema's potential into the public schools. Thus, a 1935 article in the film-betterment journal *Motion Picture and the Family* reported on a high school teacher, Miss Lillian B. Allen, who had completed Morkovin's course and now intended "to teach the student that the motion picture is an art as well as a great industry and that it must be studied the same as poetry, music and painting to appreciate its full value."[32]

A most significant detail in the press release on Social Aspects of the Motion Pictures has to do with the description it offered of the ambitious film to be made by the class: the life of an oil tycoon. In fact, one such tycoon, William E. Ramsey, head of the company that bore his name, had offered to finance the film as a promotional venture. Ramsey and his wife were even scheduled to play themselves in the film and open their Pacific Palisades mansion for on-location shooting. The provisional title of *Black Gold* was given to the production, which, as Morkovin explained in one press piece, would be an "epic of American energy, persistence and initiative."

Essentially, then, the first ever course-based effort in academic film production was planned as a privately sponsored work of industrial propaganda. In this case, however, the production seems to have not gotten off the ground. It is not clear why, although students from that time remember that there was not much in the way of filmmaking equipment available in the first film classes. Through the 1930s, cinema production at USC was sorely lacking in resources. In 1934, when Richard Bare enrolled in the USC cinema curriculum, he was able to complete the work for *The Oval Portrait*, adapted from a Poe story and the first USC film to win a prestigious award, only because he had his own camera and because he had obtained permission to shoot on the MGM lot and use its lighting equipment. As late as 1936, remembered Eleanor Hickey, a cinematography minor, some USC production classes were held at the local branch of Bell and Howell to give students access to camera equipment. One curious "film" activity that Morkovin sponsored in the first half of the 1930s might have been intended as a way of dealing with the inability to actually make films: in conjunction with the Department of Dramatic Arts, the cinema students put on what were termed either "cine-stage" performances or "filmless films," in which they acted out plays in live action but tried to make them approximate the look of films through lighting effects, rapid scene changes, actors going into slow motion, and so on. (A *Daily Trojan* article for May 10, 1935, reports on one such cine-stage production that was presided over by a student "startlingly garbed as the 'Spirit of the Cinema' with a celluloid film streaming from his hair and a weird black makeup accentuating his features.")

However, the lack of resources did not stop the ever ambitious Morkovin. In spring 1932 (the academic year after the abortive *Black Gold* project), an older student named B. K. Gillespie, who, it seems, owned a camera shop, lent his classmates camera equipment, and they completed a film for Sociology 183, a silent work entitled *Montezuma's Daughter*. (Gillespie would soon join the cinema faculty as a teaching fellow in charge of camera work for production classes.)

The academic year 1931–32 in fact showed a certain new energy around film at USC. First, in the fall, a filmmaking club was established with Morkovin as its adviser, and students were able to undertake productions by that means. Their first film was a comedy about fraternity initiation rites, *Pledge's Plight*, which began production in December 1931 and was premiered on campus in May of the following year. The film club eventually had more than one hundred members, and a second student organization splintered off from it, a writer's clinic in which students could write scripts and get feedback. Although the student organizations had no official link to the production class, it was clear that Morkovin assumed there would be inevitable connections. For example, in 1935 he asked the writing clinic to devise a collective script for the course; the outcome, a story entitled "Trojan Weekend," served as the template for the official in-class production. (The "Trojan" referred to is the USC mascot.)

As a more important register of the new interest in film in the academic year 1931–32, Morkovin increased the number of courses he offered on film topics and began to revive the idea of a broader USC film curriculum. Morkovin had in fact not been involved in the original negotiations that brought the AMPAS-sponsored Introduction to Photoplay course to the campus in 1929, although he had lectured in the course's second year's manifestation. In its third appearance, in the 1931–32 academic year, Introduction to Photoplay was still organized by William MacDonald. But now it was to be listed in a new, broader curriculum on cinematography with two new courses by Morkovin, The Art and Structure of the Screen Drama, and Fundamentals of Motion Picture Production, which were described as follows:

> 128. *The Art and Structure of the Screen Drama*. The central theme of the photoplay developed through action and characterization. Continuity and montage. Dramatic, psychological, artistic, and technical treatment as a method of animating and dovetailing the screen play. Lectures, films, slide illustrations, and excursions to studios.

129ab. Fundamentals of Motion Picture Production. Artistic standards of pictures and public demands. Selection of the story and its development into a scenario. Casting, location, property, lighting, and sets. Problems of the director, actor, cameraman, and sound recorder. Techniques used in silent and talking pictures, newsreels, scientific pictures, animated cartoons, and comedies. Lectures, films, slide illustrations, and excursions to studios.

A *Daily Trojan* piece announcing The Art and Structure of the Screen Drama suggests that the course was very much in keeping with the aesthetic approach to film that Morkovin had been developing, in which students (who included reformers and schoolteachers) learned to understand the impact of film through analysis of its devices, both medium specific and not:

> New Cinema Class is Scheduled for the Winter Quarter: In order to meet the needs of teachers and students who are interested in motion picture appreciation, and in the wider use of cinema for educational and scientific purposes, the Department of Cinematography of University College has introduced in the winter quarter course, the Art and Structure of the Screen Drama, given by Dr. Boris V. Morkovin. The class will meet every Friday evening from 7 to 9:20 beginning January 6.
>
> It is the purpose of the course to show how different technical devices of cinematography such as: camera, lighting, sound, art and composition, acting, directing and editing are used dramatically; and how these devices are combined harmoniously to build up an artistic and powerful picture.

But if The Art and Structure of the Screen Drama seems an appropriate extension of Morkovin's concerns and pedagogical style, Fundamentals of Motion Picture Production appeared to announce the move toward a highly technical, production-heavy pedagogy. Here, we can refer to notes that Morkovin collated from the first years of the course and eventually made up as a course manual by 1936.

The manual is 120 pages long and covers a number of areas. The first part, "Photography in the Field of Motion Pictures," deals with technical topics such as the science of photography, the mechanics of the motion picture camera, the technology and techniques of lighting for film, the nature of film stock (and the practices of developing), and the rise of the color film. The second part, "Effects, Process, and Techniques Used to Create Filmic Illusion," includes such topics as "Technical-Cinematic Devices Used in Obtaining the Filmic Illusion," makeup in the cinema, acting in film, costumes and film, the art of directing, props, set design, writing for the cinema (a very short section, since, presumably, other courses, such as Dorothy Yost's on screenwriting, covered much of this topic), sound recording, and personnel and production hierarchy. Much of the manual is highly technical, and sections include detailed bibliographies, key terms, study questions, illustrative drawings, and so on. For example, the section on sound offers short definitions of such concepts as frequency, pitch, tone, resonance, reverberation, and damping; explains the different kinds of microphones currently available (carbon granule, condenser, moving coil, etc.) and provides diagrams of each; explains sources of distortion in the recording process; details the variety of methods of sound recording for cinema (e.g., sound-on-disc versus sound-on-film); lists key words that students might encounter in reading about sound technology (e.g., flutter, motorboating, partials, and dubbing); provides a bibliography of almost forty books on film sound technology and recording techniques, as well as a few titles on the aesthetics of film sound; and ends with a series of study questions such as: In general, how is sound transformed from the pulsation of electric current into mechanical vibrations of the oscillator in the RCA system of sound recording? What is a variable-density sound track? What determines the number of microphones used on a set? What is sensitometry, and what is its importance in sound work?

We can draw several observations about USC film pedagogy from this production manual. First, it is striking how very technical Morkovin's production course appears to have been—how much it engaged with everyday material issues in filmmaking. In fact, Morkovin credited three men with research and organizational work for the manual, and it may be they were most responsible for devising this practical training in film. Whatever the availability or lack of equipment and resources to support film production, whatever Morkovin's own competence in the hands-on details of film creation, the course seems, on paper at least, to offer a complex instruction in exceedingly practical features of the filmmaking process. At the same time, however, it is worth noting two other aspects of the course. First, even in its technical approach, it assumed that the dominant mode toward which such filmmaking aspired was the Hollywood industry-based mode of production (hence, the concern even in the technical discussion to pinpoint who in the Hollywood system did what job and how). Students were being taught production not so they could become personal filmmakers but to prepare themselves for professional careers in the dominant entertainment cinema.

Second, even though the course was an applied one in the sciences and practices of filmmaking, Morkovin had not left his broader aesthetic concerns behind. Many sections of the manual covered not only the technical means by which one could achieve effects but the meanings and purposes of those effects. For example, the section on lighting explained, on the one hand, optics and cataloged the various technologies of lighting at use in the studios (e.g., floodlights, broadlights, spotlights). On the other hand, it also insisted on the aesthetic accomplishments that techniques and their underlying technology enabled through their elaboration of cinematic devices (light, for instance, needed not merely to be bright enough to register a scene but must be thought of in relation to dramatic and narrative effect). Even as USC film pedagogy was moving toward a specialization in material concerns of hands-on film production, there was still the desire to insist on larger purposes and meanings behind professionalized training.

With the addition of Morkovin's two new courses, interest revived in a full-fledged USC film curriculum. In the spring semester of the 1931–32 academic year, USC announced that it was creating a Department of Cinematography with the imminent intent to begin offering degrees in the field. The announcement was made at the Los Angeles branch of the MPPDA, once again suggesting the extent to which Will Hays was a presence behind the professional curricula of the day.

For the first year, 1932–33, the Department of Cinematography existed simply as an array of courses without these leading to a degree. The courses consisted of MacDonald's photoplay offering, Morkovin's two courses, and three evening college offerings by Dorothy Yost (Motion Picture Technique, Scenario Writing, and Advanced Scenario Writing), which were described as follows:

> *100. Motion Picture Technique.* Resources and contribution of set dressing, lighting, sound effects, wardrobe, camera, and directing to the work of the scenarist. Actual studio observation of these relationships as well as practice in their utilization in various ways in scenario writing.
>
> *108fs. Scenario Writing.* A beginning course in the technique of scenario as differentiated from legitimate drama. The course will consider the themes, character development, structure and manuscript form of scenario writing. Exercises will be given in original screen criticism, synopsis, adaptation, continuity-writing.
>
> *109. Advanced Scenario Writing.* Advanced work in the plot with emphasis on practical studio methods. Continuity, both in silent and "talking picture" forms. Adaptation of stage plays, novels, short stories, and training for motion picture review writing. Lectures and practice based on above topics.

For the academic year 1933–34, the Department of Cinematography actually began offering majors and minors in film. Both required that students take MacDonald's and Morkovin's courses (but not Yost's adult-education offerings), as well as a series of suggested courses from related areas in other departments, such as English, fine arts, physics, and speech. The list of these recommended courses closely approximates the sorts of classes that had been hoped for in the 1920s, when the original idea of a major had been to have three tracks in photoplay work, camera work, and set design and staging, and to rely on offerings from existing departments at USC. But the 1930s version made no specific attempt to suggest that the array of courses that students could take grouped themselves into specific tracks. The 1930s version of the cinema curriculum seems much more fluid, with students now allowed to build up their major in whatever way they desired rather than in terms of tracks. Soon, some new courses were added to the curriculum. For example, for 1934–35, R. K. Gillespie began teaching a course on the motion picture camera; studio engineer Earl Thiesen initiated a technical course, Sound Recording and Reproduction in Motion Pictures, and a drama instructor named Florence Hubbard started team-teaching a class with Morkovin, Stage and Photoplay Appreciation, and then proceeded to offer it on her own. The following are the descriptions for these offerings, which became regular parts of the cinematography curriculum:

> *126. Stage and Photoplay Appreciation.* Standards of appreciation in stage and photoplay. Nature and purpose of drama as art in relation to literature, fine arts, and music. Comparison of techniques used by stage and screen in design, lighting, acting, dialogue, directing, make-up, and costuming. Modern tendencies in the arts of stage and cinema.
>
> *180. Motion Picture Camera Technique.* Optical principles. Camera development, construction and operation. Laboratory practices. Sensitometry. Process and illusionary photography. Studio and exterior lighting. Composition. Relation of sound to camera. Make-up. Cutting and editing. Studio routine.
>
> *185. Sound Recording and Reproduction in Motion Pictures.* Principles and different methods of sound recording used in major studios. Types of recording machines and sound equipment. Tubes and light cells, their principles and use in motion pictures. Microphones and amplifiers, types and use. Recording films, exposure and development. Principles and practices of synchronization. Scoring and dubbing. Sound reproduction in the theater. Lectures, demonstrations, practices, excursions to studios.

If nothing else, this last course description suggests how far the USC program had evolved from its initial offering in 1929 of the general course Introduction to Photoplay into Hollywood studio-directed training. At the start, Introduction to Photoplay had been envisaged as a path toward professional work, but its broadly culturalist bent had given it a humanities inflection that certainly fed into Morkovin's personal desires to treat film socially and culturally, rather than technically and professionally. Now, by the mid-1930s, technical training in film production had come back with a vengeance. It is perhaps most significant that as a highly technical and practical course like Sound Recording and Reproduction in Motion Pictures made it onto the books for the cinematography major, the founding course, Introduction to Photoplay, now in fact vanished, never again to figure in the cinema curriculum. Training for industry became the norm.

Not that cultural concerns necessarily would disappear. Even as the program became more technical and professional, Morkovin was still there to insist on the aesthetics of film, and in 1935 he even began efforts to create a more critical-studies-oriented program at the graduate level. Specifically, USC announced an M.A. degree in cinema, with all courses to be taught by Morkovin. Students would write a master's thesis (presumably on a nontechnical topic) after taking two Morkovin courses: History of Cinematography as a Technique and an Art (which would deal with the history of camera technology but also concentrate aesthetically on "cinematography as a peculiar medium of expression different from the photograph"), and Seminar in Comparative Cinema Directing (which, despite the gerund in its title, was not a professional training course but an aesthetico-historical study of "theories, styles, and methods used by leading directors in France, Germany, England, Russia, and the United States").

At the end of the 1930s, however, Morkovin suddenly would leave the Department of Cinematography to go into research on speech pathology. He would abandon all concern with film studies, both his own and that of the department he had founded, and never work in the area again. Just as film had presented him with opportunities of reinvention in the New Land of Hollywood, now again he abruptly set out in new directions.

Ironically, it was a Hollywood connection that enabled him to leave film pedagogy. In one of his film classes, Morkovin had two women students who were hearing impaired, and this suggested a new research direction. In one variant of the story, he noticed that the women would remain in their seats after the bell had rung. In another, Morkovin, the vain lady's man who had abandoned his wife, noticed that the two women were attentively watching his every word and assumed that they had a crush on him. As he put it in an interview in the *Daily Trojan* in the early 1940s, "All the time I thought they were hanging rapturously on my every word, they were merely reading my lips. It was most disappointing."

Whatever the case, Morkovin decided that he would now devote himself to the study of effective pedagogy for handicapped persons, not only those with hearing impairment but also ones with disability of other senses. As an article in a local newspaper put it bluntly in its title, "Film Glamor Pales as Prof Helps Blind." As part of his new concerns, Morkovin established a research clinic at USC, the Auditory Visual Kinesthetic Clinic which, as the United States moved into the Second World War, took as one of its charges the rehabilitation of wounded soldiers.

At this point Hollywood intervened in a strange way to push Morkovin even further from film. While Spencer Tracy was devoting himself to his film career (and soon to begin his affair with Katharine Hepburn), his wife, Louise, had decided to devote her time to treatment and care for her son, John, who was hearing impaired. In 1942, Louise Tracy attended the annual convention of the National Workshop of Social Workers and Teachers of the Hard of Hearing, where one of the hearing-impaired women from Morkovin's cinema class introduced her to the USC professor. Learning of the work Morkovin was doing with soldiers at his clinic, Tracy asked him if comparable efforts could be undertaken with children. After extended and encouraging conversations, she decided to fund a children's hearing clinic, the John Tracy Clinic, which exists to this day, near the USC campus, to undertake research on and pedagogy of hearing-impaired children.[33] Although he chose not to serve as director of the clinic, Morkovin joined its staff and expanded his research on auditory ailments.

In the second half of the 1930s, Morkovin had gotten involved with the film-betterment movement, with its ideas of civic improvement both through improvement of film art and through uses of film as forms of visual education. To concretize his efforts, he had founded a civic reform organization for film, the National Cinema Appreciation League and Workshop, and created a journal which he edited, the revealingly named *Cinema Progress*, for which he wrote a number of pieces on topics such as the artistic genius of Disney (the subject of at least three Morkovin contributions). Strikingly, only a few years later, he had abandoned these activities and was now editing the *Hearing Survey Quarterly*, where he published decidedly unaesthetic essays with decidedly unaesthetic titles like "Psychotherapy and Techniques of Perceptual Reeducation of the Acoustically Impaired."

While his time in film studies had opened him to questions of cinematic specificity (the artistic devices of the form), which he now left behind, Morkovin never abandoned interest in communicative forms, such as film, as transparent vehicles for educational and moral lessons. Even as he dropped a concern with film study, he began to imagine that film might help in the sensory reeducation of impaired persons. As he put it in 1944 in the essay "Psychotherapy and Techniques of Perceptual Reeducation" in discussing soldiers who had been deafened in war, "The patient, even while still bedridden, may be given an opportunity to follow the lips of the film characters without difficulty, and realize to his great satisfaction that he can, so to speak, 'scale the wall of deafness.'"[34] It is a revealing comment on the shift in Morkovin's understanding of film that he imagined the *animated film* to have a place in reeducation of the handicapped. Where previously he had found the power of animation to lie in its ludic artistry, its cultural uplift, and its imaginative construction of fantasy universes, as in the films of Disney, he now took as his model of the valuable animated film one made specifically for training purposes. For example, he envisioned cartoons composed of slow-motion enunciation of syllables so that the hearing impaired could gain experience in lipreading.

Ironically, Morkovin was able to concretize his interest in film as visual education by calling upon the very Department of Cinematography that he had abandoned. In the mid-1950s, he commissioned the department to shoot a series of what he termed "Life Situation" films for use in his hearing clinic and elsewhere. Produced by USC film students, these films were sync-sound short anecdotes of everyday life that could be used to train hearing-impaired people to interpret ordinary situations and understand the dialogue that might typically accompany them. As one Life Situation film, *Tommy's Table Manners*, chronicled, "Tommy learns how to be polite at the dinner table, to say a table grace, and how to say, 'Please pass the bread.'"

Other institutions could rent the Life Situation films through the USC cinema department, which by the 1950s had become one of the leading distributors of educational films. From the moment of Morkovin's departure at the end of the 1930s, the department had also become a major producer of educational cinema as, first, the needs of the military training during the Second World War and, second, the push toward visual education in the postwar moment, made audiovisual production, especially in nonfiction film, a booming business. If there is an irony in the fact that Morkovin was drawn back to the very department he had so quickly forgotten, there is also irony in the fact that by the 1950s the department was so able to meet his needs. For both Morkovin and the cinema department of the 1950s, film was professional work, an instrument in the service of practical ends. The cultural and sociological study of film eventually would return to the USC program, but for the moment technical training had won out.

5 Politics as Pedagogy, Pedagogy as Politics

The Rather Brief Moment in Time of Harry Alan Potamkin

> Art has always been a victory against odds.
> HARRY ALAN POTAMKIN,
> "Motion Picture Criticism" (1931)

Ironically, one of the most legendary of early film curricula was never actually put into effect. In the papers of the influential film critic Harry Alan Potamkin—who died tragically of abdominal hemorrhaging at age thirty-three in 1933—there was found "A Proposal for a School of the Motion Picture," and this project has garnered an important reputation over the years.[1] Potamkin appears to have drafted the proposal, as Lewis Jacobs (the editor of the posthumously published volume of Potamkin's writings) explains, "when it was considered possible that a large university was interested in establishing a separate college to be instructed by a faculty of specialists, similar to existing music, medical, architecture, and business schools" (587). The proposal was published posthumously in the arts journal *Hound and Horn* and has come to symbolize a great opportunity lost through the death of the man who devised it.

In the 1940s, for example, filmmaker and writer Jay Leyda cited Potamkin's course idea as virtually the only example of worthy training in film in the U.S. context. For a series of articles by various authors on film education worldwide, Leyda was reporting on the advanced training that could be found in the Soviet Union's film schools. Against the rigor of the Soviet enterprise, Leyda lamented the fact that in America there had been no attempts by the film industry to support serious academic training about film. He had "found no evidence that any connection or mutual responsibility exists between the film teachers and the film industry." Leyda could cite the case of isolated film courses here and there in the United States—for example, he mentioned Sawyer Falk's cinema course at Syracuse University which will be treated in the next chapter—but he could find no systematic, sustained training. In this context, Leyda presented Potamkin's thwarted ambition for a film school as at best an inspiring memory: "[T]he soundest American program for a film institute has not yet been tried, thirteen years after its formulation by Harry Alan Potamkin. His 'Proposal for a School of the Motion Pictures,' though little more than a sketch, has a balance and emphasis, based on American needs, that any planner would do well to consult."[2]

That Potamkin never got to put his curriculum into practice has contributed in large part to its mythic status. Its resonance is as an opportunity missed, a potential unrealized. It is, then, an additional twist in the ironies of his case to discover that in fact Potamkin did teach a course on film, one that seems not to have been noted by the historians. In the winter of 1932, around the same time that he appears to have drafted the "Proposal for a School of the Motion Picture," Potamkin offered a course at the New School for Social Research called Lands, Films and Critics. It ran from October 3 to December 19 and was reported on, after its first session, in the *National Board of Review* magazine, to which Potamkin had been a sometime contributor. A few months after the course's end, the same journal would be running Potamkin's obituary.

To be precise, we do not absolutely know that Potamkin made it to the end of the course, but we do know that he started teaching it, and we have a description of his intended pedagogy for it. In most accounts of his demise, it is said that his illness began to take its toll in June 1933, so there is every possibility that Potamkin brought his New School lecture series to its announced close that previous December.

The National Board report offered an overview of the course and a breakdown of its scheduled topics. In its words,

> On the first Monday in October there began at the New School for Social Research, 66 West 12th Street, New York City, an unusual series of lectures that will make up what is probably the first course of its kind in this country: a critical presentation of the cinema—its history, its future; its social basis, its esthetic evolution; its forms and categories, et cetera. The lectures are being given by Harry Alan Potamkin, of the Exceptional Photoplays Committee [of the National Board of Review], a student and critic of the cinema who combines a wide and thorough knowledge of motion pictures, old and new and of all countries, with a profound understanding of people, so that to him the art of the screen is not only a live art, but one connected intimately with human living. His lectures are accompanied by illustrative film excerpts and other descriptive accessories, as well as by talks by important representatives of film bodies and activities.[3]

As we saw in a previous chapter, Terry Ramsaye had tried to come back, after teaching his 1927 course, to the New School at the beginning of 1931 to offer a new course on the motion picture. It is hard to know what transpired both to bring about the failure of Ramsaye's course (although I have made some suggestions in chapter 2) and then to have Potamkin succeed him, but it must be said that Potamkin was certainly a better fit for the New School. (USC's Boris Morkovin also tried to find a visiting position at the New School during this period. He sent a letter proposing a course either in literary study [with typical ambition he outlined five different topics, ranging across nations and genres] or in cinema. For his cinema offering, he suggested courses similar to ones he was teaching at USC: Screen Drama, Fundamentals of Motion Picture Production, or Social and Psychological Aspects of Motion Pictures. Nothing came of Morkovin's offer, and he remained in Los Angeles.)

The biographical notice that the New School bulletin ran in 1932 to accompany Potamkin's course provides some background on his career:

> Harry Alan Potamkin. B.S., New York, 1921. Director, Children's Play Village, Philadelphia, 1923–28. Managing Editor, *The Guardian*, 1924–25. Studied cinema in Europe. Foreign correspondent, National Board of Review; adviser on European films to American exhibitors, 1928–29. Elected to council of international cooperative of independent films. Sarraz, Switzerland, 1929. Correspondent, *Close Up* (London), since 1929. Contributor to general and special press here and abroad. Free lance editor of films. Member, Exceptional Photoplays Committee, National Board of Review.

Potamkin had been born at the turn of the century to an immigrant family, and through much of his life he absorbed and mediated currents of art and thought from both Europe and the United States. In the 1920s, he seemed destined for the life of the poet and used his honeymoon in 1926 to travel through Europe in hopes of meeting legendary figures of modernism and to study new literary traditions. Evidently, he discovered that much of the cutting-edge literary work of the moment took inspiration from the cinema, and he began to examine that art more systematically. He had always been an avid moviegoer, but now film became an object of close investigation. In Europe, he met with many of the important film critics and aestheticians and studied their efforts to promote the art of film not only through their writings but also through more active cultivation of film culture in ventures such as the little cinemas and the cine-clubs. Upon his return to the United States, Potamkin began to read systematically in the English-language literature on the cinema—both those works that dealt with the history and industrial structure of the Hollywood entertainment film and those that set out to theorize film's broader artistic potential. Around 1927, Potamkin himself began to write regularly on film, and there has been some speculation that at the time of his death, he was preparing a world history of cinema. As the *Nation* (for which Potamkin had been a frequent contributor) put it in its obituary for him,

> As a film correspondent in Europe for several years and as a member of the National Board of Review, Potamkin had opportunities of seeing more pictures, and a greater variety of them, than is the lot of very many people interested in the field anywhere in the world. The result was that he was in a position, just before his death, of becoming the first historian of the new art—its stumbling beginnings, transitions, experiments, and triumphs.[4]

Potamkin seems to have regarded his often quite occasional writings on film as forming the basis for such a world history: at his death, he left notes for an "Outline for a Text Book on the Movies" that collated his criticism in order to offer an assessment of worldwide cinematic experimentation in relation to the global dominance of the Hollywood model.[5]

It might well be that Potamkin's New School course was to be one venue in which he would try out ideas for this planned world history of cinema. Certainly, the broad sweep of the course, as summed up in the National Board of Review notice, suggests an attempt to deal ambitiously with cinema history as the evolution of formal devices in relation to social change, and this in an international context.

Potamkin certainly had a more cosmopolitan or internationalist perspective than Terry Ramsaye. As important, he had a strong leftist commitment that would have fit in well with an increasingly liberal, if not itself leftist, inclination of the New School, which often had seen itself in progressive terms as an intervention in social relations and knowledge.

In fact, from at least 1931 on, the New School had been one host to film screenings that the Workers Film and Photo League (WFPL), an activist organization of which Potamkin was a key member, had organized for labor education. As film historian Russell Campbell explains,

> Series were devoted to the history of Russian cinema, educational and scientific films, "the productions of independent amateurs and experimenters," "distinguished" films and so on. European directors featured by the League included Pabst, Lang, Clair, and Epstein, while Hollywood movies rescued from oblivion included *Hands Up* (with Raymond Griffith), *Beggar on Horseback* (Cruze) and *The Last Moment* (Fejos) as well as the early works of Chaplin. Frequently, speakers accompanied

the screening (Potamkin, Joshua Kunitz, or Joseph Freeman, for example, on Soviet Films).[6]

Much of the content of these screenings coincides closely with Potamkin's own screen taste (e.g., he was a big fan of early actor Raymond Griffith, whom he felt had been shunted aside by the Hollywood machinery), and it is easy to imagine that Potamkin was centrally involved in setting up the New School screenings. It would seem that he had forged close links with the school well before his course.

Few traces remain, however, of his lecture series itself. The aforementioned *National Board of Review* magazine notice offers a breakdown of topics covered, as does the New School bulletin for 1932–33, which provides a week-by-week syllabus for the course. The following provides the full breakdown of Potamkin's course as listed in that bulletin (within brackets, I have interpolated any important phrases from the National Board of Review article that show up in its breakdown for the sessions but that do not also figure in the syllabus version printed in the school's bulletin):

Course 54: Lands, Films, and Critics—Harry Alan Potamkin. 12 Lectures. Mondays, 8:20–9:50 P.M., beginning October 3. $10.00.

The lectures will be accompanied by film excerpts—selections from the National Board of Review's compilation The March of the Movies, a Soviet animated film, a "sponsored" industrial film—and notable full-length films. Speakers who are specialists in their respective fields will supplement Mr. Potamkin's lectures; among them will be G. W. Bitzer, dean of American cameramen, collaborator with Griffith on Intolerance, etc.; Wilton Barrett, executive secretary of the National Board of Review; a director; an expert in animation and others.

October 3: The I's of the movie: inventor, investor, impresario, imperialist
The relation of the mechanism to the art; economic organization; showmanship—the movie ritual; the international arena. [The film as merchandise, purveyor of other merchandise, vendor of the national idea, instrument of colonial control.]

October 10: First statements and first principles
The primitive cinema, the advent of the director, the intrusion of the star, the perfection of the scenario, the progress of cinematography [; montage].

October 17: The compound cinema
Music [and the movie], sound, color, variable screen, stereoscopy, tactilism, olfactory cinema, television.

October 24: Social energies and the national film
The early control [the first triangular competition]: France, Denmark, USA; the pinnacle of the bourgeois cinema: Sweden; the film "march to Rome": the Italian cinema; [the Latin Cinema;] the golden age of the German kino; England's belated drive; Japan—the largest producer; [the Russian film—czarist, Soviet, émigré;] minority cinemas.

October 31: The prestige of the American film
Its growth; influence; influence of other cinemas upon it; cults; its present status.

November 7: Pivotal films
A critical analysis of films like Intolerance, Caligari [—date or milestone?], Last Laugh, A Woman of Paris, Potemkin, Arsenal, Front Page, etc.

November 14: Presentation of a major silent film
With commentary.

November 21: Hollywood or Lenin Hills?
The coming of the Soviet film; Russian film before the Revolution; the world prestige of Soviet kino; objections to it; misconceptions; the two poles—their relationship.

November 28: Censorship: the control of the film
Censorship here and abroad; censorship local, national or at the [production-distribution] source; selection not censorship—National Board of Review; supervision from within—Hays; the church battle for control; the little cinema movement.

December 5: The humorous film
Slapstick [or "churlish" humor], wordly farce, comedy, satire; Sennett, Linder, [Langdon,] [Ray Griffith,] Chaplin; René Clair [and rhetoric]; [Popov, Protazonov] and others [in the USSR].

December 12: The animated film
Origins; the American animation [cartoon or "funny"]; French entr'acte film; Japanese rice paper films; [German silhouette;] puppet films; Soviet multiplication film; abstract animations, etc.

December 19: Presentation of a major talking picture
With commentary.

There is certainly much to say about this course in and of itself, but I think it takes on additional resonance when it is related to Potamkin's other energetic activities in film, from his writings to his screening programs to his militancy for the WFPL. At first glance, for instance, the December 5 and 12 sessions that help bring the course to a finale can appear to deal with issues of genre and subgenre in ways that would not necessarily be out of place in today's film teaching (although Potamkin perhaps paid more attention to varieties of animation than might be the case with any but the most specialized of topics courses today). For the most part, most current film curricula still organize their courses (especially at the undergraduate level) around a valorization of genres, treated either for their imputed formal achievements or for their ostensible social representativeness; of standout directors; of national film movements seen as combining representative types of films with nationally specific themes or issues; and of "pivotal films" (to use Potamkin's term) considered as historical markers in the evolution of screen achievement. It is clear that all these emphases were already present in Potamkin's approach to film and would seem to constitute much of his pedagogy of film.

But even as he was offering a film education that appeared to adhere to canonical models, Potamkin was also fashioning it in directions that were all his own and that bear close connection to the broader socio-aesthetic elaboration of film in his extensive writings. Potamkin's personal inflections of the standard film pedagogy start, for instance, in the very first word of the course's title, "Lands." Potamkin's approach to film often emphasized geographically local contexts from which various film movements derive. As he put it in the essay "Phases of Cinema Unity": "[I]n the unity that is the aesthetic problem of all film artists, there are the details of unity which in each land take on different necessities" (37). That is, while declaring all true film artists to share in the vocation of seeking to create works governed by unity of purpose, Potamkin contended there was no one golden path to such unity and that each national cinema would evolve its own procedures of artistic creation. At the same time, there was no inevitability that would lead each land naturally to discover its artistic richness. Potamkin was attuned to those local and specific material conditions that could foster art but also those that could inhibit it. Yet even at his most political, Potamkin never wavered from a concern for the aesthetic dimension as a sign of national well-being. The political health of a nation was reflected in the aesthetic health of its culture, and the two fed into each other dialectically. For example, for all the exciting "muscularity" (Potamkin's word) of America's narrative cinema, the very fact that it could seem to do no more than tell and retell fast-moving stories was a sign of sclerosis. The American nation had not outgrown its pioneer mythologies of conquest and aggression, and its cinema could only reflect that through its limited narratives of muscular action. In a critique of British documentary filmmaker John Grierson, Potamkin argued that faced with the lessons of American and Soviet cinema, Grierson had chosen incorrectly:

> Grierson has said he derived the *energies* of his film from the U.S.A. cinema, the *intimacies* from that of the U.S.S.R. . . . Why did Mr. Grierson not seek his energies also in the Soviet kino? Montage is an expression of the energies as well as of the intimacies. . . . I suspect that Grierson has defined energies as muscular impact. The American film is a film of muscular impact. It cannot be said to contain anything so plural as energies, for the energies—the creative expressive energies—of the U.S.A. are suppressed. The energies of a film are the energies of a land. (396)

It is important to emphasize here how Potamkin was suggesting that Grierson had a choice: Hollywood or Lenin Hills, as the title of one of his New School sessions had it. For all his belief in national identity and its embodiment in national culture, Potamkin was not a determinist who imagined that all citizens absorbed the same national impulses and in the same fashion. Against national determinism, there could be the choice, whether individual or collective, to do something different. There could be education to make the citizens of any one nation aware of the aesthetic possibilities that had been actualized elsewhere in the world. (Hence, Potamkin's self-assigned job as a film reporter: he worked to announce the accomplishments of international cinema to local audiences. On the one hand, he frequently brought news of European modernism to American readers by means of a wide variety of publications; on the other hand, he also served as U.S. correspondent for such cosmopolitan journals as the Swiss-based *Close-Up*.)

Choice and change were possible for citizens of a land because the very identity of that land was itself social and not natural. That is, a nation was formed out of history, out of material factors (even if these had coagulated into seemingly stagnant form), and history then was always something consciously made, not just mindlessly inherited.

Not for nothing did the very first session of Potamkin's New School course promise to deal with what he termed the "I's of the movie" (inventor, investor, impresario, imperialist) in connection to such issues as "[t]he relation of the mechanism to the art; economic organization; showmanship—the movie ritual; the international arena. The film as merchandise, purveyor of other merchandise, vendor of the national idea, instrument of colonial control." Although elements of a critical political economy approach to media had always been apparent in his work, Potamkin had become increasingly concerned by the 1930s by the constraints of media control on cultural production. As he put it, for example, in a 1930 essay on national cinemas and the ways each cinema "expresses with a grandiose expansiveness the economy and the politics of a land":

> As American society has become less and less diffuse, and more and more concentrated, with a corresponding concentration of the economy of the land in fewer and fewer hands, the motion picture has become less and less expressive of "independent" manipulators and more and more the merchandise and instrument of consolidated enterprises. . . . The movie is concentrated in the hands of the financial powers along with the various other media of rapid intelligence—radio and television, and, as of old, the press. There is the alignment. It expresses itself in the total impasse of American society. (151, 153)

This, then, was to say that there was no natural destiny by which a nation took on its cultural identity. That identity came from a clash of material forces—institutions, social practices, imperial gestures, and so on—and could always be configured differently. Indeed, if the movie companies had formed themselves into a cartel that fostered societal sclerosis, an alternative could be imagined: "The threat [to media domination by the cartels] can come from only one other trust: labor" (153).

In Potamkin's philosophy of national cinema creativity, then, there was little attempt to root national cultural expression in an essential and inevitable identity or a zeitgeist. It is worth noting, for instance, the extent to which the topics in Potamkin's New School course focused on *social factors* as strong influences in the evolution of national cinema: thus, he promised to give attention in his lectures to the business structure of select national cinemas, to the material play of rivalries between nations (with a recognition of Hollywood domination but also of the impact of other cinemas upon it), to institutional interference (e.g., the international impact of censorship), to national cinema history as a history of breaks as much as of organic development (e.g., Russian cinema would be dealt with in terms of the revolution that took it from pre-Soviet to Soviet models), and so on. Given the extent to which such social factors had a fully historical basis—nothing natural made them inevitable, nothing essential meant they could not be fought against—Potamkin assumed that filmic activity in any particular country was in no way *destined* for either artistry or mediocrity. Artistic accomplishment was literally something *to be accomplished*. And it would happen only if the right conditions existed and the right assessment made of those conditions by creators, critics, educators, and audiences.

Potamkin certainly saw his own various efforts as a unified intervention in the cultural front of political struggle. For example, in 1931, Potamkin issued a "Movie Call to Action!"—a veritable manifesto for the WFPL—and it is striking to see the extent to which he gave pedagogy an integral place alongside other forms of activism. Potamkin outlined twelve goals for the new organization, with education significantly framing the list as the first and last of these goals. For purposes of brevity, I will quote only enough of the twelve points to give a sense of them and of pedagogy's place among them:

1. educate the workers and others in the part the movie plays as a weapon of reaction;
2. educate the workers and others in the part the movie plays as an instrument for social purposes—in the U.S.S.R.;
3. encourage, support and sustain the left critic and the left movie maker who is documenting dramatically and persuasively the disproportion in our present economy;
4. create a chain of film audiences who would morally and financially guarantee such films;
5. publish a periodical devoted to our purposes . . .
11. re-discover and present neglected films of significance;
12. educate the critic and worker by closer contact with the worker; THE SECOND PART OF NUMBER 3 IS EVENTUALLY OUR MOST IMPORTANT PURPOSE! THIS PURPOSE IS MADE MEANINGFUL BY NUMBER 12![7]

As Potamkin himself asserted via this capitalized declaration at his polemic's finale, the fostering of propitious conditions for the work of the leftist *filmmaker* needed to be the primary mission of the WFPL, but it is more than clear that Potamkin saw education as integral to the effective realization of that mission: education of the audience (away from Hollywood lies and toward the truths of politically committed cinema; away from Hollywood trivialities and toward the aesthetic richness of world film history); education of workers (toward their own potential as documenters of the times they were struggling through); but also education of the educators—a training, that is, of critics and commentators so that they would learn to disavow their own elitism and try to find alliance with workers in everyday struggle.

Even when he was not directly addressing practical questions of schooling, pedagogical concern was never absent from Potamkin's efforts, and this helps us draw a connection between his broad criticism of culture and the specific curricular initiatives he undertook in his New School course and in his plan for a School of the Motion Picture. Take, for instance, a short review Potamkin offered in 1932 of *Shanghai Express* in the Communist paper *The Daily Masses*. For Potamkin, von Sternberg's film was a piece of meretricious reactionary ideology, and the first part of his review set out to explain how the film's content embodied counterrevolutionary sentiment in its depiction of the Chinese rebel as a corrupt bandit driven by personal urges rather than political principles. Potamkin worried that other Orientalist films attacking Chinese revolutionaries were on their way from Hollywood.

What is important for our purposes is that Potamkin, in ending his review, addressed his broader concern about a wave of Orientalism with a specific appeal *to pedagogy*. The words of his final paragraph are instructive:

> The answer lies with the audience of the movie, which D. W. Griffith called "the workingman's university." The movie tycoons are looking for a new audience. They cannot see that the new audience is the old audience with a new mind, a mind in advance of the reviewers and the producers. The audience can be directed to see the fraudulence of a film like *Shanghai Express*. Showings of films like the Soviet pictures, *A Shanghai Document* and *China Express*, profound and convincing, utilizing no "picturesqueness" and no posed frames, are themselves initial arguments against the shallowness of the American film, which has only a prejudice to inform it. The Workers Film and Photo League through bulletins on paper and screen must *instruct* the film audience in the detection of Hollywood treachery. (510; my emphasis)

Several points are worth noting here: the idea that audience response to a movie comes from forms of learning; the concomitant faith that audiences can be taught to be in advance of the assumptions that producers and critics hold about them; the activist premise that vanguard organizations (such as the WFPL) can guide the already learned response of the working-class audience in new learned directions; the belief that education in this case involves undoing the (shallow) lessons of Hollywood by contrasting them with richer lessons from Soviet cinema; and the overall implication that movies themselves are argumentative forms that militate against dominant ideological positions.

This last point—that films had pedagogical qualities themselves insofar as they constitute arguments—was central to Potamkin's theory of education. That films themselves were instructive did not mean they were explicitly didactic: even the shallowest of Hollywood films would, by its very existence, be making an argument that some people (the Hollywood producers) accepted that art should do no more than remain shallow. As we saw with Potamkin's twelve-point manifesto, he gave priority to activist filmmakers' own potential to use their creations as arguments against dominant cinema. Ideally, one could hope for an organized movement of cultural production that would itself constitute a rich aesthetic and social education. At the end of the essay "Motion Picture Criticism" Potamkin imagined, for instance, "the time when a definite social group begins to enact its social program in the motion picture" (51). But he also realized that the pedagogy contained in films themselves could only be aided by an explicit pedagogy from critics, viewers, and teachers. As he put it in the very next line, "In the meantime, it is the critic's business to help force that movement."

A formal pedagogy of film, for Potamkin, had not only to teach the art of the future but also to unteach the pseudo-culture that dominated the present. That is, a first set of lessons would have to do with breaking the spell of Hollywood escapism. Paradoxically, if all films offered lessons, the ones from Hollywood taught ignorance and the deliberate fostering of affective, nonintellective, and unreflected enthrallment to superficial story and image. It is revealing that Potamkin began his essay "The Ritual of the Movies" (1933) by examining such ritual as the way in which audiences were encouraged to become fanatics (or fans) of Hollywood cinema offered up as a veritable religion for viewers' unquestioning devotion. In ritual, Potamkin argued, "The observer has no objective attitude towards the thing that is going on" (217). As revealing, Potamkin ended the essay with an ode to movie discussion clubs as an "educational forum" in which the spell of the movies could be broken. Potamkin hinted that humans by nature wanted to reflect—wanted to learn and develop—and therefore could only end up feeling betrayed by the movies. As he argued:

> You will find it very difficult to remember motion pictures for their point, for their ideas, because they are so built as to simply assure a response from the audience at the moment and that is, by the way, to my way of thinking, one of the reasons audiences are not coming back to the movie theatres. . . . We are all, in our way, philosophers . . . we like to make deductions, and when individuals go to a movie they like those movies which seem to give them what they call an idea, a philosophy, a thought. (217)

Potamkin's philosophy of culture imagined a central role for pedagogy in several ways. First, for both filmmakers and film viewers alike, there could be training in the techniques of cinema—close study of the ways films were put together to work their effects. By understanding the precise mechanics by which cinematic devices affected audiences, an education in film technique fundamentally could help viewers break the ritualistic spell of technique. As Potamkin put it in an essay that called for film classes for children, "The concentration upon the mechanism [i.e., practical techniques of filmmaking] would lead the child to look for the mechanical base in the films he sees at the theater, thereby diluting the effect of the inimical content" (214–15). In veritable Brechtian fashion, Potamkin argued, against those who felt that analysis took all the fun out of film, that the breaking of cinematic illusion by knowledge of technique did not mean a loss of pleasure for spectators. Quite the contrary, there were new forms of pleasure to be gained for wizened spectators in achieving mastery over the superficial entertainment of the movies. It could be a source of pleasure to attend the movies with knowingness.[8]

In another essay on pedagogy for children, "The Child as Part of the Cinema Audience" (1933), Potamkin gave an example of such pleasure-filled distanciation through educated awareness of technique. He had sent children to see the Norma Talmadge film *Camille* but had instructed them to concentrate their viewing on editing tricks and photographic technique. As he recounted, "They went to see *Camille* and I asked them how they liked it. Many of them had not seen the picture because they were looking for effects, but in looking for those technical things their pleasure was enhanced through their particular experience at the motion picture theatre that day, without accentuating the sexual suggestion" (225). However, technical training and awareness of craft were not enough. There was always the danger of technique being fetishized for its own sake. Potamkin respected the Americanist tradition of workmanship, but he felt that there needed to be more than mere technical competency in the craft of any art form. Even though his politics predisposed him to an often uncritical admiration for Soviet film, it is noteworthy that Potamkin expressed reservation, in one of his last written essays, in regard to the overemphasis on technical accomplishment in the cinema of Sergei Eisenstein. With a background in engineering, Eisenstein had certainly mastered filmic form, but for Potamkin he had done so to the detriment of resonant social meaning. In Potamkin's words, Eisenstein's "montage gives the weight of the physical content, but not the meaning of the social, because the personality of the event is lacking. Yet he is the greatest living master of construction, which unfortunately is not enough. . . . There is but negligible reference to the social subject-matter, and then apart from the formalities of practice" (440).

At the extreme, craft without purpose could lead to meaningless formalism. Potamkin reserved some of his strongest criticism for European avantgardists like the Dadaists or Surrealists who put together pieces of film with brio but to no purposeful end. While Potamkin lauded the irreducible force that formal devices held as specific artistic practices, he did not want recognition of the *relative* autonomy of the aesthetic dimension to turn into a cult of art as self-contained practice cut off from society. He worried about those philosophies of film that turned it into art-for-art's sake. In his essay "Motion Picture Criticism," Potamkin wrote of the "insidious danger" of the "film-cosmogonists" who dogmatically essentialized cinema: "Footnotes become categories. The danger is accentuated by the fact that these egomaniacs seize upon currencies and appropriate them. The hope for the film and for criticism, as for the society which includes them, is in a thorough inquiry into society. Dissociated aesthetics must today be re-associated with its source. . . . Only a social ideology can supply the efficacious instrument" (50).

To make works of technical proficiency that either had nothing to say or, as in the case of the muscular Hollywood narrative, said reactionary things was to limit film's ability to resonate with its times. The filmmaker as well as the film viewer needed more than technical training. They would need to synthesize film production knowledge with broader knowledge of issues of culture and society. As Potamkin put it in regard to the director René Clair, whose cinema he had reservations about both in its Dadaist short and its feature fiction film phases, "Clair needs a re-education, not primarily in technique, but in subject matter" (409). Potamkin, notably, wanted students of film to balance their special knowledge of the craft with general education in the social issues of the day.

At the very least, such education could foster a process of distanciation not unlike the one he advocated in regard to technical training. That is, if knowledge of filmic devices could enable audiences to step back from film's formal tricks and gain pleasurable awareness of just how they worked, so too would social knowledge enable audiences to judge the lies of ideological cinema against the political truths of the world. In his essay "The Cinematized Child," Potamkin had argued that along with "training in a major contemporary [artistic] device," there needed to be "development in social (not 'moral') judgment" (215). As he explained the process,

> The content of the film should be officially recognized in courses dealing with the film as a current topic with free opportunity for the expression of opinion, reserving to the teacher the tool of Socratic stimulus—to be used in calling to the surface the ritualistic suggestions of press, fan magazines, ads, films, rumors. The relating of fact to fancy within the experience of the child would stimulate the critical judgment

of the child to a reappraisal of the misleading illusion. . . . The child would be encouraged to make his own deductions. (214–15)

In other words, trained viewers could bring to the movies worldly knowledge against which they would then judge the content of the movies. It was apparent that in such a model many Hollywood films would be discovered to be inadequate, if not misleading or even dangerous, forms of social pedagogy.

Now that we have seen some of the broader outlines of Potamkin's educational philosophy, we can return to his classroom pedagogy more specifically. Of course, one might object that much of that broader philosophy came in writings on the pedagogy *of the child* and really did not have to do with film's place *in higher education* as I have been examining it elsewhere in this book. Yet it is clear that Potamkin, author of a biography of Lenin for children, never assumed a rigorous divide between child and adult student. At the very least, the seductive lies of Hollywood posed the danger of childlike regression in which mature intellects gave up critical awareness to wallow in mindless cultism and fandom. Adults could always revert to an infantilism of an unworthy sort. Against this, Potamkin imagined maturation as a developmental process in which seeds of knowledge planted early on would bear bountiful fruit later. There was no essential or irreconcilable difference in pedagogy for children and for adults.

In this respect, it is noteworthy that one of Potamkin's rare explicit discussions of his "Proposal for a School of the Motion Picture" served as the finale to an essay entitled *"The Child* as Part of the Cinema Audience" (my emphasis). The essay opened with reference to the problem of children and the cinema (which in that period would have meant the problem of the effect of films on children), but Potamkin concluded with curricular discussion *at the university level,* as if the end of his essay was the structural answer to the beginning: a planned higher education could be a way to solve the announced problem of education *for children;* university instruction in cinema was the proper conclusion to the early and ongoing contact of the young child with the art form. Clearly, Potamkin was envisioning a film curriculum that would begin early on in the child's life and would continue logically into early adulthood. Certainly, he felt, young children could be given the social training that would enable them to judge the lies of filmic fiction against the realities of the world they were growing up in: "In the social treatment the method to pursue is to have the child relate, with assistance from the teacher, the fancies of a film to the facts of his own experience. What does he see in the picture? Can he extract from the film the truth or the falsehood? I think that can be taught" (225).

Like the film-betterment campaigners of the 1930s such as Frederic Thrasher (who will be discussed later), Potamkin wanted film awareness to be part of the early pedagogy of children (but he separated himself off from the film-betterment reformists by arguing for the need to teach film as a social, rather than moral, force). In Potamkin's words, "What are we going to do for these movie-minded young people? We must establish out of this whole educational pattern from the early days a program by which they are taught movies in the manual arts and movies in the social subjects" (226).

It is important to note, however, that along with manual training and training in social criticism, Potamkin hinted at a third essential form of pedagogy around film, one that he thought was best held back *until the child had grown up a bit.* This was aesthetic education: the teaching of sensitivity to the specific ways in which the art at its best offered imaginative extensions of social experience through formal and structural mechanisms. Despite his critique of meaningless formalism, Potamkin was not inattentive to the specific formal resources of cultural practices. Quite the contrary, many of his writings entailed a close examination of cinematic form. For Potamkin, to understand the particular force of an art form within society, there needed to be precise analysis of its specific formal resources. As noted earlier, in fact, his way of dealing with art's relative autonomy was to imagine the aesthetic dimension as in a symptomatic, homologous relationship to social life: a healthy society would be reflected in a rich and well-structured art.

As Dudley Andrew has explained in one of the few concerted writings on Potamkin's philosophy of film art:

> [W]hile the artwork is separate from reality, its life is the same as life in the world. That is, the living film is the film which has found its proper patterning and such patterning comes not from an abstract playing with form but from a close attention to the patterns of real life.... [The filmmaker's] artifact becomes formally constructed in such a way as to provide a particular contemplation of its energized theme. Nevertheless, the theme itself can unleash aesthetic energy only if it is based on a proper understanding of reality.... All of Potamkin's writing cries out for a search for a new cinematic form responding freely to a revolutionary theme producing not excitement but an intensive vision of that theme. This is a sophisticated vision of both politics and art.[9]

A full education in film would entail, then, a strong component of aesthetic education. In his essay "The Child as Part of the Cinema Audience," Potamkin had not included aesthetic education along with technical and social training, since, as he explained, "I do not stress as yet the aesthetic because children do not begin by being aesthetic in their reactions" (224). Aesthetic education was necessary to enable the well-rounded citizen to understand art's irreducibly specific place in society, but this understanding had to come in its own good time. Once children had learned basic craft and technique, and had learned how to judge the lessons of film against the experiences of the world, they could then be exposed to the third level of pedagogy, aesthetic appreciation. As Potamkin asserted, "Gradually they will take the movie up in its refinement of art" (226).

Importantly, Potamkin seemed to imply, this ultimate phase in one's film education could best happen in the university. But it might be worth noting, in passing, that Potamkin spoke of college students as "children," too. He referred to his proposed School of the Motion Picture as "a possible system where degrees will be given so that the parents may be satisfied that the children who go to the school of cinema may get an A.B. degree; may even get a Ph.D." (226). Again, for Potamkin, there was a continuum from the young child to the college student.

It is worth lingering on Potamkin's belief that a university devoted to film instruction should include a specific training in aesthetic appreciation, for it contributes a nuance to our understanding of Potamkin's politics. Some commentators have been tempted to argue a break in Potamkin's critical trajectory at the beginning of the 1930s wherein he discovered political commitment and ostensibly abandoned many of the aesthetic concerns that could have garnered him attention from historians of film art. For writers who need to imagine that an aesthetics of film can only be impoverished when it is touched by the taint of politics, the notion of a clear split allows Potamkin's early writings to be valorized and isolated from political commitment. Even some writers on the Left who cite his work give in at times to the temptation to accept this idea of a break and see Potamkin the radical as having left behind the concerns of Potamkin the aesthetician.

At the very least, Potamkin's New School course belies the idea of an easy, definitive split in his career. It is noteworthy, for instance, that the central idea of the "compound cinema," which gave its name to the posthumous volume of Potamkin writings, and which is often taken to sum up Potamkin's imputed *early formalist concern* for a specificity of cinematic art, shows up in one of the foundational sessions of the New School course (see the syllabus reproduced earlier in the chapter). In other words, *long after his ostensible definitive break from aestheticism*, Potamkin was still centrally focused on the concept that had been key to his early aesthetics. At the risk of simplifying a complicated notion, we might say that the notion of the compound involved a valorization of a planned, organic approach to film form and function: for Potamkin, a Compound Cinema was one that systematically combined its elements in an effective whole. The fact that he devoted the third week of his course to this topic shows that for Potamkin the elaboration of a sociology and social history of film was in no way incompatible with an aesthetics of film, even an aesthetics of its irreducible formal specificity and its potential organicity. For Potamkin, the aesthetic dimension (as Herbert Marcuse would later term it) symbolized a realm of human creativity above and beyond economic exchange and therefore was a necessary dimension of life that needed to be established and fought for. In Potamkin's view, the radical struggle of the 1930s included art as one of its very sites and goals.

It makes sense, then, that in his New School course Potamkin's discussion of the idea of the compound cinema came *after* an initial session on the economics and business of film and then one on the evolution of film away from its primitive days toward its present-day compounding. By beginning in the first week with issues of political economy, Potamkin was assuring that his history of the art form would not take on idealist trappings. Whatever the cinema accomplished as art, it did so within the precise historical context of material institutions, of a dominant mode of production, and of a weighty social history. As he put it in the declaration that serves as the epigraph to this chapter, "Art has always been a victory against odds," and as he went on to add, "The odds now are more vicious than ever, as we move toward a qualitative change in society" (51). Potamkin would continue to valorize an *aesthetics* of film even after his move into leftist activism, but, at the same time and necessarily, he acknowledged the material conditions in the industrial mode of production that artistic potentialities stood in relation to. The richness of what he would promote as the compound cinema could emerge only in opposition to those entrepreneurial forces that threatened to turn art into a mere matter of economics and calculation. In this respect, just as the notion of the compound cinema endured across the supposed break in Potamkin's career, it is likewise striking to note that his elaboration of the institutional odds against which cinema art had to struggle had already been initiated in the years *before* the "break." If the first session of Potamkin's course was devoted to what he termed "the I's of the movie: inventor, investor, impresario, imperialist," it is noteworthy that all but the last of these terms were already presented together in an essay from 1929. In "Music and the Movies," appearing three years before he gave his course and before the supposed break into political commitment, Potamkin declared, "If we are to see the art of the movie fulfill itself, we must do away with a number of conditions, and one is the elimination of the three i's: investor, inventor and impresario. We must recognize the independence of the movies" (99). Perhaps Potamkin's addition in 1932 of "imperialist" to the list signaled a new level of political consciousness, but the very tone in which he presented his sense of the impediments to screen expressiveness was virtually the same from 1929 to 1932. Art was always a realm of freedom, worthy of defense against the encroachments of commerce.

For Potamkin, there were many roads to creativity, many forms of compounding that could make of cinema a creative art. In fact, if Potamkin could be so severe in many of his critical writings, it was in large part because it seemed more apparent to him when something failed to be art than when it succeeded. The goal of the critic would not be to articulate the proper path to creation but to outline the overall principles by which a multiplicity of possible paths could be entertained. As Potamkin put it bluntly, "I say here that it is the creator of films who tells us how many kind of films there are, and not the critic" (33).

This is not to say that there was no function for criticism. As I have noted, it is in fact quite apparent that Potamkin took the critical function very seriously. For him, much of the role of criticism was to create a propitious space in which creative experimentation could flourish. This meant that criticism would take as its task to clear the ground of impediments to creativity: false avenues, bogus aestheticism, formulaic sclerosis, institutional blockages, and so on. Insofar as the job of the critic was in large part to cultivate a context for creative experiment, Potamkin easily saw criticism as a social activity: that is, it was not merely a description of the formal attributes of compound art but also an analysis of the best cultural conditions in which such art could grow. Potamkin was drawn to Soviet film in large part because he felt that it was working to incorporate critical attitudes into its very structures—the idea, again, that films themselves were argumentative, educational forms—but he also assumed that critical writing and the education that would emerge from it could help art make its own critical work more systematic and less reliant on myths of intuition, spontaneity, and chance. For example, in the essay "Tendencies in the Cinema" (1930), Potamkin lauded Soviet cinema for its increasing "intellectualization of the film" but also noted that its incorporation of criticism into its cinematic structures had been impeded by Soviet directors' reliance on the nonintellectual, muscular, and literal model of American cinema. In Potamkin's words, the Soviets had experienced failure "due to the employment of this reflective instrument in a non-reflective structure, the culmination of the film's first technique, the physical or American" (44). To the extent that Russian filmmaking activity maintained contact with vibrant cultural and social activity, it would gain in awareness of critical work and could begin to internalize the critical voice into its own cinematic structures. Cinema itself could eventually become a critical discourse, but only to the extent that it interacted with the critical writing (both aesthetic and social) of the day. As Potamkin put it:

> There can be no propagating art without the impulse of criticism. There can be isolations, as in France; there can be the momentarily effective, as in America; but for a cinema permanently great, strong and productive there must be criticism. The conversion of this criticism, the social theme, into its form is art, cinema. Form is the conception constantly *informing* the structure. The Russian film alone moves toward a permanent form. It is not likely that the American film, far removed from whatever critical center there is in the United States, will approximate, for some time to come, more than a style or a manner. (44–45)

Although he could be intensely opinionated in his evaluations of specific works of cinema, specific filmmakers, and specific national cinemas, and although he could be quite polemical in militating for his broader aesthetic positions, it is important to recognize the extent to which Potamkin was trying to elaborate a nondogmatic or, in his term, nonabsolutist approach to film creativity. Potamkin believed that film artists had taken upon themselves an essential, inescapable mission, but he did not feel there was any essential form in which they could or should set out to realize that mission. For example, he was unlike many modernist critics of his time in his not seeing the coming of sound as an inevitable impediment to experimentation. While it was clear to him that many employments of sound traded experimentation for mere literalism (his term for the greatest failings in cultural production, the surrender of aesthetic transfiguration to noncreative mimeticism), he also felt that sound could, in the best of cases, offer new elements for the nonmimetic compounding of form that he felt created the possibility of art. When it broke away from literal transcription of noise and voice, sound could offer the filmmaker a new resource for creative play: voice could be stylized, sound could be counterposed against silence, speech could become part of a rhythmic structure calculated according to the beats of montage, and so on.

In his article "Tendencies in the Cinema," Potamkin argued that the increasing incorporation of criticism into cinematic form necessitated a rethinking of cinematic language away from Hollywood literalism and toward complex structural compounds:

> The necessities of the critical subject-matter and the reflective processes have been evolving a new logic of cinematic construction. . . . Griffith

created the "flashback" ... but since the American film, remaining muscular, literal and sentimental, could not see the structural significance of this device, it remained as merely a part of the practice of "cutting." Russia, re-studying the film at its source, developed the Griffith technique and established montage as cinema construction. ... Beginning with this structural establishment of a device, the film could advance in its hunt for a language and get as far as the figure of speech. (45)

Such invocations of "structure" and the "structural" recurred throughout Potamkin's writings, and it would not be pushing things to treat him as a protostructuralist in anticipation of the theorists of the 1950s and 1960s. Art, for him, was not the literal representation of reality but a representation in which various artistic elements were combined into significant totalities. In the case of film, in particular, the combination of elements should lead to a rhythmic whole in which each piece worked together with every other and in which no element did not contribute to the overall aesthetic purpose. In his words, "The ideal cinema will be conceived as a ramified and rhythmic graph, a rhythmic cine-graph" (100). Potamkin was even in conformity with the assumption of structuralism that individual material signifiers do not naturally possess significance. They are not meaningful substances in and of themselves but gain their significance from the process of articulation with other elements. As Potamkin asserted in a critique of the idea in French film criticism of "photogénie" (the notion that, in his words, there is "a particular cinematic quality present in every substance"), "There is nothing intrinsically 'photogenic.' ... The cinema and not the substance determines that" (93).

To the extent that the compound is created out of structural articulation of elements, Potamkin would even go so far as to suggest that there were no such things as isolatable individual signifiers in a film, since signification arose only from the final articulated result. That is, to the extent that articulation created a meaningful totality, it would be an arbitrary and artificial exercise to extract from the work individual units and attempt to identify their contribution to the whole: there were in fact no such units of individual meaning prior to their articulation in the compound. As Potamkin asserted boldly, "*The entire film must be preconceived in anticipation of each detail.* ... The whole disciplines the detail, the detail disciplines the whole. ... No such thing as a 'shot' exists in the aesthetic sense of the cinema, whatever one may call the immediate taking of a scene" (14–15). In other words, to isolate analytically something like a shot would be to ignore that the "shot" was meaningful only in its place within the total structure.

As Potamkin continued, "Films are rhythms that commence and proceed, in which—ideally—every moment, every point, refers back to all that has proceeded and forward to all that follows. A stress or a deformation, an image or an absence of image, has a validity only if it is justified by the pattern up to that point, and if it leads again to the pattern from that point. In brief, one may not establish a camera angle unless the entire film contains the mind for *that* camera angle" (15).

While each film ideally developed its own appropriate structure and while there therefore could be no a priori notion of the one right way to create cinematic art, Potamkin's structuralism did allow him criteria for aesthetic judgment. Potamkin inveighed, on the one hand, against works of art that were too simple or literal because they lacked structuration. He did not welcome that purification of form associated with a modernist minimalism. Art was created not by the emptying out of form and its reduction to minimalist purity but by the significant articulation of elements into a complex compound. On the other hand, he also critiqued artworks that engaged in random assemblage of elements without seeking any real structural relationship among them. Thus, he was a strong adversary of surrealism and Dada (in a revealing bit of gender bias, he accused them of "effeteness"). Additionally, ever the structuralist, he maintained that only precisely delimited, discrete formal elements could serve as units within a structure: thus, he argued against such fads as the release of fragrances into movie theaters, since he felt that smell did not form itself into precisely defined signs that could be articulated in coherent fashion with other elements in the ways that sounds or images did.

In one crucial respect, Potamkin departed from some versions of structuralist thinking. In particular, he was concerned not with the elaboration of the anonymous combinatory rules of a general language of film but with those specific articulations that represented *creative use* of film form. That is, Potamkin was not out to establish a general, shared film language but to pinpoint those creative idiolects by which individual filmmakers could find their own strengths at articulating a coherent and effective cinematic expression. There was no general cinematic language, there was no ideal cinematic structure, just a series of creative experiments each associated with specific individuals who would "speak" their own particular and personally articulated filmic discourse.

Such a concern for individual contributions to the international art of cinema helps explain some of the setup for Potamkin's New School course. Once he had established, in the third session, the overall aesthetic ideals of the compound cinema, he could (1) deal in that same session with the various formal devices that either might contribute to compound structures (e.g., variability of screen size could become an element in a film's structural play) or, in contrast, might impede the structural process (hence, the monstrosity, for him, of the idea of "olfactory" cinema, since smells were not articulatable into structures); (2) examine in the following week the ways in which the history of diverse national cinemas showed them dealing variously with cinematic structure; (3) acknowledge in the fifth week the particular but undeserved privilege and prestige that American cinema had garnered by substituting literalism for complex investigation of cinematic structure; (4) segue from the acknowledgment of American domination to the recognition of pivotal works from around the world that stood out from the formulaic mass of Hollywood narrative film; and so on.

Given the extent to which Potamkin intended his "Proposal for a School of the Motion Picture" as a broader curriculum designed to offer a general overview to the student who would be, as he put it, "professionally interested in the films" (587), it is less apparent that Potamkin's plans for the school directly reflected his own pointed sociology and aesthetics of film than did his own actual course at the New School. That is, the School of the Motion Picture would not represent one teacher's pedagogy—even Potamkin's—but would offer a diversity of approaches. The very fact, too, that Potamkin's proposal appears to have come in response to a commission from an established university may have meant that he himself felt a need to tailor his own perspectives on film to the larger requirements of a venerable academic institution.

Revealingly, Potamkin referred to himself in the third person in the "Proposal for a School of the Motion Picture" by listing himself, among other names, as one possible teacher for courses (he cited himself as one of several critics who could offer "elementary lectures on the films and related arts" and as one of two persons, the other being Alexander Bakshy, who could teach History of the Films). It is as if he was suggesting that he be one voice among the array of professors and pedagogical positions that could show up in the curriculum. (In passing, it is worth noting that for his school Potamkin recommended Columbia's Frances Taylor Patterson in the area of scenario writing.)

In a number of his writings for *Movie-Makers*, the magazine of amateur filmmaking, Potamkin had evidenced a preoccupation with practical issues of film production, and he indicated a central place for filmmaking in his school proposal. At the same time, his concerns with practical issues never were disconnected from his larger aesthetic and political concerns and from his assertion that the richest sort of filmmaking could only come from artists knowledgeable of broader cultural trends and political issues of their day. In this respect, it is important to note that although Potamkin presented his "Proposal for a School of the Motion Picture" as the basis for a curriculum leading to the "equivalent of a Bachelor of Science" (i.e., an empirical, practice-oriented degree), he also clearly intended that an education in the practical work of filmmaking include attention as much to history and aesthetics of film as to hands-on training.

Potamkin envisioned the curriculum as a four-year course of study leading to the Bachelor of Science. There would be a first year of courses required of all students (some of which would also be open to the public) and then three years that broke into somewhat specialized tracks. (One exception to this separation of the curriculum was a course on the "history of the motion picture," designed specifically for would-be critics, which he proposed should be offered over the entire four-years.) The three-year, specialized part of the curriculum itself was then divided into two parts. First, a series of "Specialized Courses" that seem to approximate different tracks in professional filmmaking: Direction, Cinematography, Acting, and Scenario. Second, a group of "Seminar Courses" that honed in on increasingly specific, ever more hands-on areas and appear designed to give students actual practical experience in the professional world of filmmaking: studio production methods; on-set filmmaking; and labs in script writing, directing, and acting. Finally, Potamkin proposed that the curriculum also include invited lecturers who would come to the school to address issues of financing and distribution.

This last curricular suggestion (that the school pay attention to the business side of cinema) might give the impression that Potamkin's proposed school was envisioned primarily for the formation of not merely professional but also commercially oriented filmmakers. However, given Potamkin's own cosmopolitanism and his political and aesthetic commitments, it is easy to read between the lines for how his proposed school clearly was expected not to serve as a path to Hollywood-like film-production. For example, although the curriculum did include some courses that might seem to have a directly practical bent, many first-year courses were more general in scope and focused on the aesthetics and history of film in ways that echoed Potamkin's nondogmatic interest in the rich potentials and diversity of cinematic creativity. For example, Potamkin called for a course on aesthetic history that would focus on the development of taste and on the "sequence of styles"; one can readily imagine he took this to involve awareness of cinema in its *international* context. Likewise, Potamkin proposed that there be several courses that would lead from the study of film to comparative work with other arts: thus, one course, on "comparative literatures," would look at literary forms such as the novel, the short story, and drama; another, on design, would center on visual arts such as painting, sculpture, architecture, costume, and the decorative arts. Very rarely did Potamkin's proposed curriculum focus on the commercial business of mainstream Hollywood film.

In fact, a large part of Potamkin's proposed curriculum made no specific reference to Hollywood. Above all, he suggested that an initial part of the first-year curriculum deal with "The Forms of the Cinema." Here, what Potamkin termed the "Dramatic" form (which presumably is where Hollywood-style feature filmmaking would find its place) was listed in last place—after other forms such as Industrial, Ethnic, Educational, Abstract (absolute), and the News Film. In other words, from the start, Potamkin's school would treat narrative fiction film as only one form among many. In fact, consonant with the ways his New School course had given over an important part of its content to instruction on aspects of the animated film (one of the forms of cinema in which Potamkin took great personal interest), for his school Potamkin also clearly saw animation as having special importance, and he gave it particular attention. As a form that easily could be structurally planned for rhythmic compoundings, that could lend itself to creative interactions of sound and image, and that by its nature appeared to eschew photographic literalism, animation found favor with Potamkin in a way that the Hollywood feature film did not.

The downplaying of the mainstream Hollywood narrative film in the curriculum also showed up in another aspect of Potamkin's proposal for the cinema school. Beyond the curriculum, he envisioned a "Library of the Motion Picture," where films and supportive material ranging from books, journals, and scripts to stills and set designs would be available to students for consultation. Potamkin's plans for the library clearly show his expansive interest in a study collection that would extend far beyond the Hollywood feature film.[10] First, he made it clear that the film collection would have "two main categories": both foreign films and domestic ones, thus signaling once again that American film was to take up its (relative) place alongside other cinemas. Second, he outlined the types of film that the school library should include, and here again, the dramatic film was listed as only one option among many. In addition to the dramatic film, the collection, he argued, should include ethnological film, experimental film (divided into the two categories of abstract and absolute), educational film, industrial film, documentary, and, as always, animation.

Certainly, as his list indicated, Potamkin assumed that a "library" for the study of film should collect representative works that had "popular success," but he also expected it to attend to films that were representative of non-U.S. national trends (such as Swedish or Italian). And he called for the library to give attention to films that stood out from commercial regularization through their specific aesthetic virtues: thus, his proposed library would house films that demonstrate "[i]nnovations in style and technique" and illustrate "principles of film-making"; it should include works that highlighted specific directorial accomplishments and notable performances; and it should give special attention to "[p]ivotal masterpieces." Knowing Potamkin's cosmopolitan bent, it is easy to assume that such criteria for the library implied a collection of films only minimally devoted to dominant Hollywood-style filmmaking.

Published after his death, Potamkin's "Proposal for a School of the Motion Picture" remained a dream never directly put into practice. Significantly, Potamkin's own primary intellectual and political community of the 1930s, the Workers Film and Photo League, did take some inspiration from his plan by seeking to create a film school in his memory: the Harry Alan Potamkin Film School, which began to offer courses primarily in film production starting in late 1933. But, as Russell Campbell points out, quoting publicity material for the school, the new venture differed from Potamkin's notion of a motion picture curriculum *that would have taken place within the context of a private university*. As Campbell says, "Potamkin's outline . . . was for a four-year course of study within a university setting for 'students professionally interested in the films'; the FPL school offered training for 'workers and intellectuals who have pledged to become active participants in the work of the Film and Photo League upon completion of their studies (a five-months course).'"[11] Already at the time of the announcement of the Harry Alan Potamkin Film School, the *Nation's* film critic, William Troy, had noted the differences. Some of these differences between the WFPL school and a university curriculum might, he thought, be beneficial: "In beginning as an independent enterprise, it [the WFPL film school] will have certain advantages, the chief of which is a freedom from the restrictions of academic financial and political organization." But Troy also warned of the drawbacks of the program's isolation from a larger academic context: "[A]t the same time it may suffer from the reduced opportunity to correlate its particular field with other related fields—like literature, painting, and the dance" (all of which, we may note, Potamkin had identified as areas of study in his proposal for a university-based film curriculum).[12] In the event, the Potamkin school did not last more than a year, and so even this vague descendant of Potamkin's original pedagogy disappeared.

Likewise, there would be no new film pedagogy at the New School for a number of years after Potamkin's death, despite the evident interest of the school's administrators in having their institution address this important modern cultural form. At the end of the 1930s, film critic Sidney Kaufman began a survey course on film, based on MoMA's Film Library circulating series. Meanwhile, Jay Leyda, who later would write that Potamkin's project for a School of the Motion Picture represented one of the few real proposals for film education in America, began to team-teach a New School filmmaking workshop with Irving Lerner, who had been one of Potamkin's cohorts at the Workers Film and Photo League. Here, perhaps, some remnants of Potamkin's expansive vision of a committed film curriculum continued on in however attenuated a form.

6   Appreciations of Cinema
Syracuse Discovers Film Art

An Aristotle is needed to clear the ground for an aesthetics of the cinema.
SAWYER FALK, Cinema Appreciation lecture notes, circa 1934

The art of seeing has to be learned.
SAWYER FALK, Cinema Appreciation lecture notes, June 1, 1960

In the middle part of the 1930s, as he crafted one of the weekly film analysis assignments for the class Cinema Appreciation, Syracuse University undergraduate William Ashley found that he had to disagree with some of the aesthetic principles that the course instructor, Sawyer Falk, had so emphatically established.[1] Falk's position, so often restated as to become a veritable mantra, held that film most attained the status of Art when it exploited its essential nature as a medium of visual dynamics. For Falk, cinema was fundamentally an art of visual tonality, kinesis, and energetic graphics. Story and drama were secondary values, important only as pathways into an essential visual dynamism. The problem for Ashley was that he loved *Winterset*, a theatrical adaptation from 1936 that was the sort of dialogue-heavy, visually undynamic film that Falk hated. Despite the fact that Cinema Appreciation was offered under the rubric of drama and that Falk himself was a professor of theater arts, Falk's approach to film emphasized neither its narrative nor its representational qualities, and it certainly downplayed those aspects of dramatization that came from the sound film's ability to convey information through speech. For Falk, film should eschew the "theatrical" insofar as this term referred to characters spouting supposedly significant lines of dialogue. As Falk had said, for example, in a lecture on the Hollywood comedy *Cain and Mabel* (1936), which struck him as little more than canned theater: "If we have many films of this ilk the cinema certainly is a degenerate art.... It is just a picturization of the Saturday Evening Post. There is little in the way of cinematic value—dynamics nil; pictorialism nil; sound, gibberish and unmeaningful."

True, Falk knew that commercial cinema was inevitably geared to storytelling and that the vast majority of films centered on Hollywood stars around whom the narrative was devised and who simply performed for the camera. Falk took as one of his goals to introduce his students to other forms of cinema—for example, works of formal abstraction—but he also tried to make them focus on those aspects of mainstream film that might transcend story to achieve pure visual power. If some films aspired to art by merely offering faithful and uncinematic adaptations of respected theater or prestigious literary works, such adaptations, insofar as they made no use of specifically cinematic powers of transformation, thereby would fail at achieving independent status as film art. The cinema was not, at its best, an art of canned dialogue simply recorded and presented to audiences as such. As Falk would put it bluntly in a 1943 lecture on *Mission to Moscow*, the undynamic adaptation of Ambassador Joseph E. Davies's nonfiction memoir, "Too much talk; too little movie."

Winterset, the film that was posing such a dilemma for William Ashley, was an adaptation of Maxwell Anderson's wordy drama. It was precisely the sort of dialogue-heavy and visually uninspired work that Professor Falk felt betrayed the medium specificity of film. Ashley, however, had loved the film and thought the experience of it would stay with him for a very long time. Declaring *Winterset* to be one of his ten favorite films ever, he defended his taste: "I say this despite a consciousness of what seemed to be filmic shortcomings in light of what we have been taught so far in the course. Principally, I am referring to the lack of dynamic quality and the amount of dialogue. . . . If a picture cannot rise above its scenario [as Falk had contended in class lectures, arguing that a wordy script tended to weigh down a film's potential for visual dynamics], *Winterset* shows an example where a scenario carries its film to the heights."

It is hard to know if Ashley's "defiance" of his professor's deeply held aesthetic position turned out to be a risky one (there is no grade on the copy of his assignment found among the Falk papers). At the very least, it seems daring, since Falk's aesthetic of medium specificity was one he held to the point of virtual dogma. From 1934 to 1961, Falk taught Cinema Appreciation with little modification in his overall philosophy of film. Early on in his pedagogical efforts around the cinema, Falk honed his formalist aesthetic and then adhered tenaciously to its precepts.

Falk knew what he wanted the students to get from Cinema Appreciation. As he described the course in a 1954 memo to a journalism professor in hopes of getting him to send over some students, "[I]t is given over to the appreciation and appraisal of the film as an art form. It is not a course in film-making nor in film history. . . . Included in such an analysis are such items as: pictorialism, cinema dynamics, sound, color, scenario structure, film acting, and the social aspect of the film" (regarding this last item, we will see, in fact, that Falk's formalist position actually tended to downplay cinema's social role other than its potential *aesthetic* impact).

At worst, it might be possible to judge Falk's unwillingness to modify his initial aesthetic principles—and to revise his pedagogy—as laziness or opportunism. After all, film teaching was only a secondary part of his work as a professor primarily of drama and theater. There is some sense that he brought film into the drama curriculum at Syracuse not out of a profound commitment to cinematic ideals but for more typical pragmatic reasons of enrollment and professional needs of students. For instance, it is clear that he started teaching film in large part because he thought it would provide those students who wanted to work in theater with an additional area of professional qualification. In this respect, it might be that Falk did not vary his lectures because his heart was not in cinema, and it would have been too much work to update his teaching material. Indeed, there were evident limits to the amount of work that Falk put into his classes. For example, over the decades, the week-to-week unfolding of Cinema Appreciation was based on the viewing both of a list of cinema classics Falk had fixed on in the 1930s *and* of whatever new releases came to local Syracuse commercial venues. Screening a set list of classics meant that Falk's course reified a canon of great works that remained unchanged through the years. Sending students to whatever new releases showed up in town may have offered the course a certain freshness, since the films were always changing, but it also turned class sessions into open-ended discussions for which the professor had to do little preparation. With his aesthetic philosophy firmly in place from early on, Falk had only to go see the newest films with his class and then apply his steadfast critical principles to them.

Even the elaboration of those principles may not have required much effort on Falk's part. As his class notes from the early 1930s reveal, Falk took much of the background he needed in understanding film from one single book, the 1930 edition of Paul Rotha's *The Film Till Now*.[2] In his *On the History of Film Style*, David Bordwell has noted the extent to which *The Film Till Now* exemplifies what Bordwell terms the Basic Story of film history.[3] In Bordwell's account, the Basic Story offered an approach to film history—in both its general outlines and its specific details—that became determinant for the field and that most film scholars from then on came to adopt dogmatically. As Bordwell notes, the Basic Story was one in which, through the effort of a series of creative individuals, film developed from its beginning moment as mere entertainment or as mere unmediated representation (the actuality films of early cinema) into a richly expressive and mature art form. Typically, the Basic Story involved the valorization of a set canon of film directors that tended to remain the same no matter the individual historian writing the story. For example, Edwin Porter was a constant point of reference among the historians for moving film away from mere actuality toward narrative; as Rotha put it in *The Film Till Now,* "[I]t was not until 1903 that the first real attempt to tell a story by moving pictures was made. This event was achieved by Edwin S. Porter's sensational *The Great Train Robbery"* (70). Rotha essentially told the story of creative individuals using the specific materials of their chosen artistic medium to create a resonant vision, and this was Falk's approach as well. Both men worked, then, not only with canons of films but also with pantheons of directors, distinguishing between those who had true vision and understood the medium-specific potentials of film and those who were mere entertainers and had failed to realize cinema's particular possibilities. Moreover, as Bordwell elaborates, the adherents of the Basic Story of film tended to work, consciously or not, from a quasi-Hegelian position in which artistic production from individual national cultures was assumed to reflect national character so that film history was organized not only according to the accomplishments of creative individuals but also in terms of diversities of national spirit.

But sometimes the Basic Story also told of a failure or blockage in the development of cinema's aesthetic potential: as the Basic Story historians frequently told their tale, film had indeed been aspiring to the condition of art during the silent period, but that aesthetic progress had been disrupted and even dashed to bits by the coming of sound, which returned film to its earliest, unaesthetic days as mere recording mechanism. The Basic Story, as Bordwell explains, was often presented then as the tragic birth, maturity, and decline of a once promising art. Here, perhaps, Falk diverged somewhat from his mentor, Rotha, who voiced strong doubts about the sound film's aesthetic future. Teaching his course a few years after Rotha's book had come out and after it had become clear that the sound film was not going to go away, Falk tried to imagine means by which sound could itself become part of the aesthetic transcendence of reality. Falk certainly condemned the *dominant* use in film of sound-as-dialogue as slavish and passive recording, but, as we will see, he also thought there could be uses of sound that would be creative and not merely reproductive.

This partial act of independence aside, Falk's incorporation of Rotha's aesthetic positions into his own film pedagogy was a strong one: Falk's basic aesthetic principles, his overall understanding of the contours of film history, and even many of his aesthetic choices (e.g., hierarchies of directorial talent) all seem to echo positions that Rotha took in *The Film Till Now*. In a number of his lecture notes for Cinema Appreciation, Falk would offer an assertion and then list pages in *The Film Till Now* where similar points were made. It is tempting to imagine that Falk—a non–film expert who was teaching what was obviously an enrollment-grabber—was mostly cribbing his ideas from Rotha. However, it certainly is equally possible that Falk made the aesthetic arguments his own and simply found in Rotha a kindred and resonant ally. At the very least, Falk's method of teaching his course by organizing class sessions around the viewing of new film releases meant that there would always be room for him to move into territory all his own. That is, even if he had inherited a basic story of film from Rotha, the ongoing encounter of his course with new releases would entail Falk updating that story (which Rotha had ended at the dawn of the coming of sound) in his own fashion.

Whether or not Falk was simply parroting positions he derived from Rotha, his course appears as the most concerted effort in American academia up to that time to proselytize for an independent and integral art of cinema. Of all the courses covered in this history, Falk's was the one that most closely resembles typical approaches that would dominate film studies when it became a full-fledged university discipline: like the later curricula, Falk's course offered an elaboration of film study based on a classification of national cinemas, on auteurism, on canon history, on genre analysis, and so on. With little substantial difference, his Cinema Appreciation could substitute for many introductory film analysis classes offered in American universities even today.

Even if his own film teaching may have been somewhat opportunistic, Falk seems to have wanted Cinema Appreciation to assume an important place in his own university's curriculum. For instance, in response to reporter Chester Bahn at the *Film Daily*, who had written to inquire about film activities at Syracuse University, Falk indicated (in a letter of March 29, 1937) that he intended Cinema Appreciation to be an ongoing enterprise. But he also signaled that he was not necessarily committed to remaining the person to teach it: as he explained, "What I am after is the establishment of some kind of chair of cinema to be subsidized by those who might have the money and the inclination." In the event, such sponsorship never materialized, and Falk himself taught the course for the many remaining years of his career.

Despite its status as one of the first university offerings on film art—and certainly one of the first to resemble later traditions within the established discipline of film studies—we should not overestimate the historical importance of Falk's course. Off in the far reaches of Syracuse, Falk labored on Cinema Appreciation in relative isolation. Just as I emphasized how other early classes in film studies did not coalesce into a discipline and rarely had direct influence on later pedagogy, it is necessary to recognize that Falk's long-running course appears to have had little lasting impact on the official discipline of film studies. He wrote little and offered little of the national visibility that might have given him influence over those figures who would become the first professors in the established field of film studies. (As we will see, Falk was somewhat active in the film-betterment movement of the 1930s, but his involvement dwindled in the following decades, and he did little to make his efforts known to a later generation of film scholars.)

Nonetheless, Falk exerted one very important influence on the course of film history. One of the students in the very first semester of Cinema Appreciation, in the fall of 1934, was Maya Deren, later to become a legendarily important experimental filmmaker. (Several actors who went on to success in film and television also were students of Falk's in the drama program, although it is hard to know how many of them may have taken the Cinema Appreciation course: for example, Miriam Hopkins, William Lundigan, and, later on, Sheldon Leonard, Suzanne Pleshette, and Jerry Stiller, who appears to have been a Cinema Appreciation student in 1950).

For what it is worth, Deren received a grade of B in Cinema Appreciation. Obviously, one cannot know the extent to which Falk's aesthetic of cinematic dynamism was decisive for Deren's own attitudes toward film, but it could well be that Falk's valorization of cinematic energy and his understanding of film narrative as a mere structure for the elaboration of visual play would have resonated with Deren. Whatever his specific impact, Deren became close to Falk and seemed to take him as a mentor. Importantly, Falk was unique among early film pedagogues in his attention to forms of cinema other than the mainstream story film: early on, he screened for his students such films as *Lot in Sodom*, an avant-garde work by Melville Webber and James Sibley Watson, and he made clear the importance of an experimental tradition in film that derived from European high modernism and that moved away from narrativity toward dynamic abstraction. Later on, Falk's concern with medium-specific investigations would make him receptive to Deren's own film experiments, and he served as one of her strongest advocates: for example, he wrote an important letter of recommendation for her to the Guggenheim Foundation; he arranged for her to meet with editors of the National Board of Review's magazine so that they could screen her films for a key review they would run; and he set up a screening of her films for faculty and students at Syracuse University. (In his January 17,

1945, letter to the National Board of Review to introduce Deren's experimental films, Falk warned that "the Committee on Exceptional Photoplays [an NBR committee] will think them somewhat esoteric, but I believe, at the same time, that they may discover a kernel of talent somewhere in the midst of the footage.")[4]

Born in 1898, Falk had been recruited by Syracuse in 1927 to run the dramatic arts division in the School of Public Speech and Dramatic Arts. Founded in 1913, the school had originally been devoted just to speech and forensic skills (through the 1930s, the one degree it offered was a B.A. in "oral English"), but around the time it hired Falk, it had begun to branch out into other areas of performance. By the 1930s, students could specialize in one of several tracks, such as oral English, speech science, storytelling, and literary interpretation (which meant primarily training in the reading aloud of classic works), and dramatic arts. Falk had been brought in above all to offer practical instruction in areas of play production and presentation. Although he had obtained a master's degree in English and comparative literature from Columbia University and had served for a time there as an instructor in fields of criticism, he was much more interested in hands-on aspects of theater production such as staging and direction than in criticism or literary interpretation. Significantly, as a theater practitioner he never pursued a Ph.D., and records show that this impacted negatively on his ability to rise through the ranks at Syracuse. Intriguingly, Falk's undergraduate degree, from NYU, was in engineering: from the start, his interest was in the nuts-and-bolts craft side of things rather than in theory. Classroom teaching was only one aspect of Falk's assignment at Syracuse; in keeping with his pedagogical concentration on practical matters, he was also expected contractually to supervise the student theatrical group, Boar's Head, and to produce four plays himself per year (in addition to oversight of student-produced works). In fact, with great energy and ambition, Falk took up a series of related production projects: in addition to close supervision of Boar's Head, he established university outreach through a community theater, set up a summer theater program, created a children's theater for young people from the city, and initiated a radio drama series on the university station.

If Falk's initial courses in dramatic arts at Syracuse tended to emphasize areas of theater craft, bit by bit he began to expand the offerings to include critical analysis of dramatic texts as much as practical training in theater. Here, he seems to have been responsive to student needs and interests, and he was always willing to undertake curricular development for the relatively new track in dramatic arts. In the university's catalog for 1930, when the track was still in its infancy, Falk was listed as teaching Stagecraft, Play Production, and Play Construction. By the mid-1930s, he had added to his offerings the practical courses Training the Actor and Styles of Acting and Directing but, revealingly, also the more critically oriented Appreciation of the Drama, as well as the course that concerns us, Cinema Appreciation (known officially as Drama 136).

Intriguingly, where all the other courses that Falk taught were three-credit classes, Cinema Appreciation was worth only one credit. Perhaps Falk did not see the new course as being as important to the drama track as his other offerings. Perhaps the only way to fit this elective course into an expanding curriculum was to keep the credit units low. It is also possible that Cinema Appreciation was intended as a somewhat light alternative to allow students a break from their more serious work. Thus, it might be like the notorious "flicks for kicks" courses that so many university departments have offered as a way of boosting enrollments. Indeed, when Maya Deren's first husband, Gregory Bardacke, who had also been a student at Syracuse, was asked by her biographers if Deren had taken Cinema Appreciation course, he replied, "I don't remember that. [In fact, as noted earlier, she did in fact take it] . . . I did take that course with him in Cinema Appreciation. That was a great course. I got my *best* mark in that class. (*Laughter*) It was either the senior or junior year. All we had to do was go to movies." When asked if he remembered which movies, Bardacke answered, "Oh—not really. But it was fun."[5]

Certainly, one function of the one-unit offering might have been to increase enrollments in drama by means of an undemanding course. But despite Bardacke's own recollection of his experience, there was some perception at the time that however few units it counted for, Cinema Appreciation was a serious and demanding part of the curriculum. In this respect, it is worth noting that an article in the campus newspaper on the course's creation indicated a more respectable justification for it, one that suggests the need for at least minimal rigor. As this article from May 14, 1934, explained, "Under the State syllabus a great many high school English teachers are required to guide students toward an appreciation of the cinema or 'movies.' As a definite form of art Professor Falk declared that because of that the moving picture should consequently be studied."[6] As the headline of another newspaper piece of the time declared, "New Cinema Appreciation Course Proves No Snap."[7]

Whatever the course's degree of seriousness, there appears to have been some dismay at the university when a "movie" course was introduced. Over the years, Falk would devote part of the first session of Cinema Appreciation to recounting tales of such university skepticism. For example, there had been, as Falk put it in the notes to his opening lecture for 1954, "Reluctance of Liberal Arts Curriculum Committee [to put the course on the books]: fear of the popular, vulgar arts." Likewise, as Falk recalled, the student newspaper had published an editorial raising some concern about the new course and had declared, on May 19, 1934, "[T]here are not enough movies produced that can really be called great and worthy of study, interpretation and appreciation. If someone suggested the installation of a course in the study of literature, gleaned from most of the present day pulp paper magazines, severe criticism would be heaped upon his head. In the light of present day production of motion pictures, does not the same point apply?" Falk's ongoing rejoinder as presented over the years in his lectures was clear-cut: "All great art-forms have roots in the vulgar."[8]

One of Falk's struggles had to do with the complicated place of Cinema Appreciation in the dramatic arts curriculum. On the one hand, for bureaucratic reasons, he needed the course there; on the other hand, his own philosophy of the arts centered on a belief in medium specificity such that cinema emphatically had to be seen as *not* dependent on other arts, *including drama*. Actually, Falk did admit that, although film was an independent art form in its own right, it had performative qualities that gave it some connection to theatrical production. He resolved the dilemma of the independence and integrity of diverse performative arts by distinguishing between a restricted notion of theater as live performance and an expanded one in which theater referred to a range of visual performances, *including film*. Thus, when he encouraged Maya Deren, in a letter of March 20, 1946, to apply for grant money for her filmmaking from the National Theatre Conference, of which he was an officer, he warned her, "The only question that might be raised is whether it is theatre. As I use the term, it certainly is." Live drama and cinema were independent art forms, but insofar as both entailed performance, they could share the stage in the creation of multimedia experiences. In fact, Falk had wanted to use film sequences within some of the plays he produced at Syracuse, and there are indications that as early as 1927 he was investigating practical issues of two-reel film production toward this end. Later, Falk's desire to link drama and film in practical performance activities was indeed actualized in several cases. For example, in the mid-1930s, under his supervision, Boar's Head presented a screening of *A Time in the Sun*, the truncated version of Eisenstein's *Que Viva Mexico!*, which segued into a live production of a one-act play, *Soldadera* by Joseph Inglis, intended to fill in for missing scenes from the Eisenstein film.

By imagining the cinema in this way as a subset of theater—while maintaining the purity of cinema's difference from live performance—Falk was making a theoretical point but also thinking of the practical needs of many of his dramatic arts students who were training for careers in areas of performance. He clearly felt that his drama students could profit from instruction in film technique when they went to look for work. (Indeed, as noted earlier, several of his students did develop noteworthy careers in film and television, as well as live drama.) Although Falk himself never taught hands-on aspects of filmmaking, he always kept an eye on the practical craft aspects of the art. In the mid-1930s, for example, he tried to get a student screenplay produced and actually received national publicity in film trade journals for his effort, only to have the project fail for lack of funding.

In 1939, Falk even initiated an attempt to introduce a production course into the drama curriculum. Like Cinema Appreciation, it was offered for one unit of credit. The course, listed as Drama 141: Cinema Technique, bore the following description:

> Apparatus, methods, and technical problems involved in sound motion picture production and projection. The course deals with the motion picture camera; sound-recording on disc and on film; cutting and editing; special effects; studio and laboratory practice; newsreel practice; industrial and advertising films; motion picture projectors and their use; motion picture trade standards for apparatus. Actual motion picture equipment (35mm., 16mm., 8mm.) will be used for demonstration purposes. Films illustrative of methods and practices are shown as part of the class procedure. This study is turned directly to the business of making a film in sound on 35 mm. The cast and technical staff will be chosen from the class itself.

R. W. Stanmyre, a Syracuse technician, was hired to teach the course. Five years earlier, and probably in response to a local announcement of the new course in cinema appreciation, Stanmyre had written to Falk to offer aid in obtaining up-to-date motion picture equipment in exchange for a chance to enroll at the university and take advanced classes. Although there are no other documents in the surviving Falk papers that would help clarify Stanmyre's activities at the university and explain how the plan to have him teach production came about, it is clear that Falk had high hopes for the course. In fact, along with the new one-credit production course, he added a second, and more advanced, three-credit course to the 1939 curriculum, Drama 143: Cinema Appreciation and Analysis, which was intended to complement the production course but which he himself, rather than Stanmyre, would teach. Like the more basic Cinema Appreciation, this new course also explored broad issues of criticism. According to the catalog, it dealt with "[t]he cinema as an independent art-form; cultural and aesthetic aspects," but it also had an explicit practical intent to aid in actual film production in ways that were not evident in Cinema Appreciation. For example, whereas assignments in the introductory course centered on having the students write critical pieces on the week's screening, the advanced course emphasized writing for production rather than consumption: in the words of the course description, "Students write and organize the scenario for the film that will be made in Cinema Technique (Drama 141)." For Falk there was a clear link between the production class, Cinema Technique, and his own efforts in Cinema Appreciation and Analysis. But Cinema Technique did not last in the curriculum for reasons that are unclear: problems with Stanmyre? the coming of the war? university resistance to three-credit courses in film? the sheer difficulty of putting into operation an ambitious and potentially expensive course that had promised to teach the sound film in a 35 mm format? Cinema Technique disappeared, but Falk revamped his own more advanced film analysis course so that it did not need to link to a production class, and he taught it regularly on into the next decades.

In any event, it is the more basic Cinema Appreciation course, Drama 136, that concerns us here insofar as it represented Falk's original pedagogy on film in the first part of the 1930s. Luckily for the researcher, Falk kept many of his lecture notes from Cinema Appreciation, in large part to reuse them from year to year (thus, there are notes originally dated from the 1930s but bearing emendations from as late as the 1950s). They constitute an extensive record that allow us to reconstruct much of the form and content of the course with great detail. Usefully, too, Falk kept a number of student papers, including notebooks in which he had students outline the main points of the course as they had understood them.

We can begin to grasp the content of Cinema Appreciation by noting those aspects of film that Falk regularly announced the course would not, and should not, cover. For example, Cinema Appreciation was *not*, he would explain on the first day of class, a course in film history but an assessment of the ideal state of cinematic achievement. In fact, his aesthetic position enabled a certain idealist understanding of film's historical trajectory as the triumph of select auteurs over material constraints of their moment. This meant that history was envisioned as little more than the background against which artistic value was established once and for all. For those students who wanted a specifically historical approach, Falk would recommend secondary readings (e.g., by the 1950s, he would send them to Arthur Knight's influential *Liveliest Art*). He would also hand out a questionnaire "to find out what historical films have been seen," and this may have influenced his recurrent desire to refer to certain classics of cinema, presented as virtually timeless triumphs standing apart from the vagaries of history.

Likewise, the course was *not* concerned with the operations of the film industry "except," as he put it in lecture notes from 1961, "as its practices and policies affect the cinema's aesthetics." Here, again, the idealist side of his aesthetic position was evident: film was a creative art that had to rise above those historical-material forces, such as business practice, that threatened it with uninspired worldliness.

As for Paul Rotha before him, "Hollywood" would often serve for Falk as shorthand for these worldly pressures that menaced creativity within cinematic art. In this respect, then, it was also necessary that the course *not* deal with "gossip or trivia"—that it not turn into unscholarly and a-critical fandom. In fact, Falk's strictures against easy fascination on the part of students with Hollywood anecdotes, which obviously tended to center on stars, fit into his broader aesthetic position. Falk's philosophy of film art was one that valorized the creative work of the director, and he held strong animus against the Hollywood star system, which, he felt, enabled stars to interfere with directors' essential and fundamental creativity. Here, despite his background in drama, Falk was using his belief in medium specificity to rail against the ways in which cinema tended to overvalorize actors (and, in fact, tended to take live theater mistakenly as a model that it could emulate by mere recording of performances). Insofar as Falk felt that film could aspire to the condition of art only to the extent that it broke away from slavish fidelity to a literary and dialogue-heavy theatrical model, he tended to see the presence of professional actors in film as a violation of cinema's essence. The cult of actors, indeed, threatened to impede medium-specific artistic creation insofar as actors' histrionics tended to focalize all technique around them. In this respect, Falk could only find gossip about Hollywood stars' lives to be a misplacement of critical concerns from the preferred object of attention of critical analysis, the true artists in the matter of film—that is, the directors. Falk had great interest in forms of cinema without actors—abstract film, nonfiction film—or at least without professional actors. Thus, his lectures frequently lauded the films of Jean and Marie Epstein, which were acted by amateurs, as well as the use by Soviet filmmakers such as Eisenstein and Pudovkin of actors cast according to their visual fit with the role (what the Soviets referred to as *typage*) rather than professional acting ability. These forms of cinema did not lend themselves to "gossip or trivia."

Finally, Falk emphasized that Cinema Appreciation would *not* deal with technical aspects of film (except insofar as these fed into aesthetic potential—as when he devoted lecture time in the 1950s to newly promoted wide-screen processes), and it would not be a course in filmmaking (although he did try to push certain students toward work in film production through extracurricular film projects). Technique and technology were little more than the material paths to art's essential transcendence of the material. As Falk summarized what the course would (and would not) cover, its goal was to provide "know-why rather than know-how."

In an undated document (apparently drafted as he began in the early 1930s to think of offering Cinema Appreciation), Falk set out his overall goals for the course:

> The fundamental objective of this course is to give the student a cultural approach to the cinema (in its several manifestations) as an art form. To this purpose the film will be studied as an independent form of expression related aesthetically to the older arts but deriving its vitality and significance substantially from the conventions, limitations and potentialities of its own particular medium. This implies a study of the various forms of cinema and stress upon cinematic values per se; a ridding of the student's mind of prevalent misconceptions which have arisen through a faulty critical approach in the past; and an understanding of the actual processes involved in cinematography. Particular stress will be placed on the director's problems arising in relation to the finished product as he deals with photographic value and spatial relationships, the use of the actor, and the integration of sound; to the screen actor and the peculiar problem of cinema histrionics; and to the scenarist and the relationship of scenario to the requirements of the camera.
>
> Of necessity it will be important in passing to give attention to the history and development of the cinema and stress must be placed on social pertinency and the problems and obligations that arise thereupon.
>
> Some twenty volumes on the subject and current magazines and newspaper writings on the aesthetics of film will be used as reference material.
>
> Regular attendance upon selected films will be a periodical requirement of the course, from the point of view herein stated.
>
> The film as a valuable medium of expression rather than as a superficial entertainment; as a cultural pursuit rather than as a casual amusement.

The Cinema Appreciation catalog entry as printed in 1934 (and remaining unchanged over the years) picked up some phrases from this longer description, although it was a bit more succinct:

CINEMA APPRECIATION

The cinema as an independent art form with special stress on its cultural and esthetic aspects. Problems of the director, the scenario writer, and the actor studied in order that a standard of appreciation may be arrived at for regarding the cinema as an intelligent medium of expression rather than as casual entertainment.

For the most part, Falk's lectures in Cinema Appreciation combined abstract aesthetic principles such as those expressed in these descriptions—as he put it on the first day of class in 1961, Cinema Appreciation was "really a course in comparative aesthetics"—*and* application of those principles to specific films. First, there were films Falk showed in class or as part of the Boar's Head theatrical season. In fact, Falk had organized regular showings of films in the campus theater starting in 1933, and perhaps Cinema Appreciation came into being because the Boar's Head series had sparked student interest in a course to supplement the screenings. Thus, the *Syracuse Post-Standard* article that reported on the first semester of Cinema Appreciation asserted that the course had been created "in answer to requests for a study of the history and development of cinema art." These requests might have come from students who had participated in Boar's Head screenings and had become interested in an art of cinema.

Falk described his creation of the Boar's Head film series in a retrospective piece published in 1945 in the National Board of Review's magazine: "It was in 1933 that Syracuse University started to exhibit motion pictures on a regular-schedule basis. We decided then that our kind of theatre project was obligated to bring to the community certain films that did not reach it by the usual commercial channels. Roughly catalogued these were: foreign films, early American pictures illustrating the history and growth of this art-form; native films of proven worth which we felt needed exploitation even beyond that given by the other houses; informationals; and documentaries."[9] A number of the titles that Falk brought to Syracuse were protested on moral, political, or artistic grounds, and not only by the community at large but also within the university itself. For example, over the years, Falk would have his Cinema Appreciation students see one of his favorite films, Dreyer's *Passion of Joan of Arc*, and, with evident amusement, he would recount how in the 1930s the French department had objected to students being exposed to a film it considered inaccurate and immoral. As Falk put it in a lecture in March 1935 (i.e., in the second semester that Cinema Appreciation was offered): "French department held that this film desecrates the Joan legend and maligns the character. . . . This is a fallacy in aesthetic criticism: to use one's own personal conception as the measure of an artistic product. Every artist is entitled to his own conception of life." For Falk, the morality within an artwork's content could never be a fundamental criterion for artistic judgment, since art's very being lay in its creative reworking of content, whether moral or not, to higher ends. As he put it in another lecture, "The motion picture thus becomes an *analysis of an event, rather than the event itself.*" Thus, against the literalist, moralizing approach of the French department to a film like Dreyer's, Falk lauded and directed his students' attention to the creative techniques that transform filmed reality into aesthetic accomplishment. In the case of Dreyer's supreme masterpiece, one needed to appreciate the pictorial beauty, off-center composition, low-angle shots, stylized props, "daring use of the close-up method," montage, stylized movement, compositional lines, and so on.

At the same time, Falk was aware that, no matter their degree of creative interpretation of reality, some films would be read by the public in terms of content. Ordinary citizens had become habituated to a literalism in which they looked at films as emotion-packed dramatizations of real life. With such habits ingrained in their viewing practices and reinforced by Hollywood ideology, it was easy for films that more daringly made palpable their creative engagement with cinematic form to be deemed "bad" by ordinary viewers. Falk worried, for instance, about the potential public reaction to one of his favorite films, the experimental work *Lot in Sodom,* which he considered a work of great beauty but one that he knew would be judged for content. As he wondered rhetorically in an article in the *National Board of Review Magazine* that dealt with the public's reactions at university-sponsored film screenings, "What about the phallic symbolism, the homosexuality, the incest—abstract and stylized as these items may be?" Falk's answer was to insist on the need to concentrate on the aesthetic aspects of cinema: "It is our first business as a university to stress cultural values. Every film we choose, therefore, must without question have distinct artistic merit. . . . Our tendency at present—right or wrong as it may be—is to turn away from visual education *per se.*"[10]

Interestingly, the very fact that Falk exhibited films that he felt should be admired not for content but for their aesthetic qualities meant that, in the screenings at Boar's Head (which were open to the public as well as students), he tended to discourage the use of program notes, introductory speeches, or even post-film discussion and debate. In the open space of the public screening, he seemed to feel that any verbal discourse risked literalizing the film being viewed. At most, he allowed plot summaries to be distributed to high school classes and club groups in attendance at Boar's Head showings as a way of advertising upcoming screenings, but for the most part Falk appears to have feared that public discussion of films would fixate on issues of content and miss the artistic qualities. At the extreme, Falk felt that films themselves were their own form of education—by their very fact of existence, they offered inspiring instruction in the powers of art to add special value to the world—and to this extent, they could only be betrayed by a verbal discourse that aspired to cover over the work with often misleading thematic interpretation. As Falk put it in a 1945 reflection on the Boar's Head screenings, "It should be noted at this point that we were (and are) interested in the film as an art-form, as a medium of adult theatrical entertainment. The didactic we leave to the teachers of visual education. Indeed we are trying to teach, but in the broad sense that the arts do teach rather than in the more restricted blackboard lesson and textbook thesis. We are, in a word, interested in the art of the motion picture and in the social and cultural significance of the art."[11]

At first, Boar's Head screened films biweekly, but it seems that the needs of the weekly course on cinema appreciation led to the showing of many more titles during the semester. Thus, an undated calendar in the Falk papers shows that in one particular month, *Passion of Joan of Arc, Potemkin, Intolerance, Man of Aran, The River, The Cabinet of Dr. Caligari, The Last Laugh,* and *The Birth of a Nation* were all shown. Falk regularly returned to each of these films in his sessions of Cinema Appreciation.

In his 1936 article on the ways in which Boar's Head film shows contributed to university outreach to the larger Syracuse community, Falk provided important details on the university-sponsored screenings and, in passing, clarified some of the ways they contributed to an overall pedagogical mission in film. Soon after he had come to the university, Falk orchestrated the leasing of a theater in downtown Syracuse at some distance from campus. Here, impressively, his goal had been one of arts education for the broader community, and he saw film as part of a larger project to bring cultural forms to the public at large. At this downtown theater Falk set up programs in community theater, summer stock, children's theater, and university theater (and also subleased the site to other forward-looking production companies; for example, it was at this theater that the Federal Theatre Project would present its Syracuse productions). And it was here, too, that films were screened. As much as possible, Falk tried to connect the film screenings to other events at the theater. I have already referred to the cases in which Boar's Head productions tried directly to combine films and plays, and Falk himself seems to have tried to link specific films and plays whenever possible. For example, there might be specific seasons in which all the offerings would deal with a common topic. Thus, during one semester, a series of films and plays all presented the issues of preadulthood (here, the film screenings included Marie Epstein's *La Maternelle*, as well as the British film *The Little Friend*).

Falk saw the downtown theater as making at least one direct contribution to university pedagogy: although he supervised the theater's activities and did hire professionals for some of its operations such as bookkeeping, much of the day-to-day business of the venue was handled by students (whether for credit or not is unclear). There were no direct requirements that Cinema Appreciation students be involved in the running of screenings, but it is likely that some students from the course did help out. Most of the course's students, in fact, were theater majors who saw their cinema course work as part of their broader theatrical education, and this undoubtedly brought them to the downtown operation. It is clear, too, that the lessons gained from running an art-film series and dealing with public reaction served as a learning experience that Falk incorporated into his classroom discussions. Thus, when a particular public reacted strongly to a film, that reaction might serve as a topic in subsequent lectures (for instance, as noted earlier, he returned repeatedly to the anecdote of the French department's resistance to Dreyer's *Passion*, using it to discuss the relevance of moral criticism in the sphere of the arts). Ultimately, as Falk explicitly put it, the downtown theater served not just as a site in which to see plays and films but as "an off campus laboratory wherein we wish to evaluate the potentialities of the cinema as an art form by subjecting it to the test placed upon it by an actual theatre-going public."[12]

Interestingly, word appears to have gotten around that Syracuse University had become a major renter of nonmainstream films, and early on, a wide variety of film distributors wrote to Falk to promote their wares. Most revealingly for our purposes, in 1935, a year after Cinema Appreciation began, Falk was contacted by John Abbott, director of the MoMA Film Library, who informed him of the availability of the first installments of its new circulating series of films. But, significantly, this first series, which Abbott had described in an October 3, 1935, letter to Falk as providing "material for an outline course on the film in America, in chronological sequence, from the first Edison kinetoscope pictures through the work of Griffith, Ince, Sennett on to the coming of the talkies," ended up not meeting Falk's pedagogical needs. In his 1945 article, Falk described how they were received at Boar's Head screenings: "We had presented several programs of early American films. . . . But our audience began to tire of these. . . . It considered them quaint and gay ninety-like. . . . But quaintness and nostalgia do not alone suffice.... To the historian of the films these might be (and surely are) important items; to our movie-goers (even the more scholarly ones) they were of diminishing interest. The film apparently is an instrument of contemporaneousness that makes us alert to the present moment." At Syracuse, at least, the MoMA canon of film history did not work as an introduction to contemporary cinematic expressivity.

The point is worth remarking. Falk had a clear, consistent, and fairly articulated philosophy of film as art, but it tended not to necessitate any special appreciation of film's *history*. For Falk, indeed, film found its poetry in the present, and there was little need to look back at film's past. At best, the history of film, to the extent that Falk dealt with it at all in his class, was seen as an accumulation of standout accomplishments that rose above the mass of films and formed an ideal collection of great works. To the extent that there was a history of film, it was one in which ever greater refinement of the possibilities of the art consigned prior works to the dustbin. In his classroom presentations, Falk was fond of drawing treelike maps in which today's film art was seen as an ideal development from Porter through the early nickelodeon Westerns, Griffith, and the Italian epics of the 1910s, into the multiple strands of Soviet montage cinema, American spectacle, documentary, cine-poem, and so on. On the one hand, if the diagrams offered a history, it was one in which the past was superseded inevitably, organically. On the other hand, as diagrams, the maps spatialized history as a series of decisive accomplishments that rose above their historical times to establish an ideal and idealist canon of timeless invention. If Falk tended over the decades to return endlessly to the same 1930s classics with which he had initiated his course, this was not so much because he felt the works of the past were valuable but precisely because they were *not* of the past: in a way, film history ended with the great works of the 1930s, which thereby became eternally present references of greatness that Falk could return to in any later moment. Falk did not need MoMA's nostalgic look back at a quaint history of film.

Turning away from film's historical past, Falk directed his students to the cinematic accomplishments of the present. First, there was the canonic list of late 1920s and early 1930s films—many of which matched Paul Rotha's choices—that he taught again and again, as if film history started *and stopped* with this moment. Falk also had a fondness for some of the titles that the National Board of Review, of which he was an active member, had singled out for praise (this was the case, for example, with the Soviet films *Chapayev* and *The New Gulliver*), although he tended to emphasize less the moral qualities of such films than their aesthetic achievement, whereas the board often tried to link the two.

As an additional means of introducing his students to current work in cinema, Falk obtained from the studios scripts to recent productions so that questions of visualization could be studied in depth. In this regard, he explained in his 1937 letter to Chester Bahn at *Film Daily* that a central topic in Cinema Appreciation involved the "business of comparing scenarios and the films which are derived from them." Soon, he was regularly being offered material by major production companies. For example, in 1936, Howard Dietz, publicist (and famous lyricist) at MGM, sent him the studio's special edition volume of its adaptation of *Romeo and Juliet*. In such ways, Falk's course thus became a venue in which the ongoing efforts of film production could be tested against the seemingly timeless principles of film aesthetics. One can only imagine Falk's reaction to the MGM film, which probably would have epitomized for him the worst qualities of canned theater.

Of the myriad ways in which Falk brought his students into contact with cinema as a living cultural form, his preferred method was simply to send them to whatever new releases came to theaters in the Syracuse area and then have them test those works against the timeless principles of cinematic art at its best. This sort of assignment determined the bulk of the films for Cinema Appreciation. On the one hand, as Falk noted it in a June 11, 1956, lecture, this might mean that students would see some films that would not hold up to his aesthetic principles. As he put it, "We are not talking about masterpieces but 'the movies as they come to us.'" (Auteurists might be amused to learn that he was responding here to a film by Nicholas Ray; as he exclaimed further in a parenthetical comment on the film he had sent his class to: "Not the film at its best—*Hot Blood!!*"—a reference to Ray's gypsy drama from that year.) On the other hand, the fact that the course would have to adapt itself to the unpredictabilities of current film release patterns would put aesthetic ideals to the test and would ensure freshness and vitality: as Falk put it, "Immediacy militates against yellowed notes."

In the early years of Cinema Appreciation, Falk gave the students final exams in addition to requiring them to write analyses of current films. For example, as the *Syracuse Post-Standard* explained in its report on the course's first semester, the students were interrogated in a one-and-a-half-hour exam on the aesthetic values in select films they had seen, on issues of the specificity (or not) of screen acting compared with theater acting, on the main forms of cinema that had evolved from the beginnings of film history, and on the distinctive styles and methods of the directors who had been most studied in class. Falk's handwritten notes for the first final exam suggest the degree to which his own aesthetic principles were hardening into a dogma that he expected his students to regurgitate. For instance, in a section on "cinema values," he listed films the students had viewed—specifically, *Cleopatra, Crime without Passion, Man of Aran, Merry Widow, 14th July*—and directed them to identify for each work those "elements which place this art in its own particular medium and identifies it as such." His notes offer his own recommended answers. For example, students should say of *Cleopatra* that it was cinematic in its spectacle, its use of crowds, and its sense of detail and splendor, but that it fell short in its "lack of montage and [of] sense of 'cinema dialectics.'" On the other hand, Flaherty's *Man of Aran* should be celebrated as a "symphonic-poem" in which there was a "splendid combination of pictorialism and dynamics."

But Falk came quickly to drop the final exam and to center course requirements around the weekly screenings. Each week, students would go to Boar's Head showings and to films in current release in Syracuse cinemas, and then they would prepare short papers, usually of a page or two, on the assigned film. Falk recommended that students try to engage in "note-taking during the film," which, he asserted, would give their critical analyses a grasp of "specifics" as well as "freshness." From these notes, students would build their papers and would prepare for in-class discussion. In some cases, Falk used the occasion of a specific film as springboard to a lecture on a broad aesthetic topic. For example, the viewing of the Marx Brothers film *Room Service* (which students saw theatrically) led Falk in a late 1930s lecture to raise the issue of genre: as he put it, "the identification of species is one of the critical problems of the course—i.e., the various forms and types the screen may use." Here, significantly, the seemingly neutral issue of typology—how to classify a filmed play like that of the Marx Brothers?—tapped into Falk's overall concern with aesthetic value and medium specificity, for the question of the Marx Brothers had to do with whether or not they really were engaging in a specific art *of film*. Was their comedy cinematic, or did it merely involve the camera passively recording them in basically vaudevillian sketches? (Falk believed it was the latter.) As Falk asked in opening up class discussion, "Does the comedy of the Marx Brothers submit itself readily to film treatment or not?"

Likewise, a November 15, 1935, class on the Will Rogers vehicle *In Old Kentucky* raised, to Falk's mind, the very questions of the role of stars in film; of the related use of film as a mere recording device for essentially theatrical or stand-up performance (which he felt this film was little more than); and of the extent to which fetishizing of such stars left any room for the director's potential to transcend mere photographic realism and make film art. Here, Falk asked students such (rhetorical?) questions as "Is what he [i.e., Will Rogers] does 'acting' or what?" or "Is it the actor acting or is the director making him seem to act?" Much of the class session would set out to answer questions such as these, in relation to both Falk's general principles and the perceived fit or not of individual films with those principles.

Clearly, the classroom conversation was carefully controlled by Falk. Although a portion of Cinema Appreciation was given over to discussion, it is evident that Falk wanted the conversation to take place within the framework of general acceptance of his aesthetic principles. Indeed, what the published catalog description gently referred to as the need to arrive at "a standard of appreciation" had its more dogmatic and authoritarian side in the longer draft proposal's reference to the need for "ridding of the student's mind of prevalent misconceptions which have arisen through a faulty critical approach in the past." For Falk, such pedagogy as he could provide was needed to combat misconceptions about the movies tenaciously held by students.

For example, in a 1934 lecture on Lubitsch's *Merry Widow* (on which, as mentioned earlier, students were also tested at the end of the semester), Falk chided the students for their journal entries in which as, he put it, "class misses the point of the film altogether. Do not 'get' it at all. This is one of the best films of 1934." For Falk, the accomplishments of the film were several. First, Lubitsch had made a true "director's film" in which the resources of cinematic specificity had been exploited to full advantage for their own medium-specific sake. In particular, the film transcended its basis in the musical. Falk tended to dislike the musical genre insofar as it often seemed to take as its goal to serve as mere literal reproduction of a stage play; the film musical was, as he put it, "an 'in lieu of' type of art." What Falk wanted was for cinema to discover resources of its own—ways of reshaping reality in its own fashion—and he found these in Lubitsch's personal and particular inflection of the musical form. As Falk put it, "He has no loose ends in his picture—everything is made to count and count in terms of cinema." Here, Falk cited such qualities as the smooth continuity of editing, the narrative balance and consistency of the film, and "Lubitsch's genius for handling of black and white."

Second, Falk lauded *The Merry Widow* for its satire of everyday mores. At first glance, this valorization of satire—which Falk often spoke of as a mark of high cinematic achievement—might seem at odds with the formalist position that celebrated the director's ability to create an independent, medium-specific art. For Falk, however, satire was singled out because he saw it precisely as such a creation: satire, for him, was about an artist's conscious effort to maintain a distance from content—an effort to use medium-specific techniques to qualify and critique that content. In the case of *The Merry Widow,* Falk explained, "His genius is right here: combining satire with sentimental mood without letting the satire descend to sheer buffoonery (as the Marx Brothers) or letting his mood become too saccharine." The problem that his students' journals encapsulated was that America was an unironic nation that too often took the content of works of art literally: as Falk complained, "American people do not understand satire." In response to the student papers, he lamented, "Some of the reports handed in have even discussed the morality in this film"; that is, they had fixated on the literal content message of the film and missed the higher meaning conveyed satirically by the director's handling of the material. Falk's final admonition to the students was quite harsh and despairing: "This is not supposed to be a true picture of 1885—children!"

The role of the pedagogue, then, was simultaneously to disabuse students of misconceptions and to offer them a more appropriate—because more correct—philosophy of film. One advantage the pedagogue had over his students was a broader awareness of cultural currents that allowed him to stand beyond the narrow confines of students' knowledge and thereby point out inadequacies of their position. For instance, if, as young citizens of America, the Syracuse students tended to operate within a literalism that made them miss the complexities of satiric form, Falk had a superior knowledge of Continental traditions in which satire was fully appreciated. Thus, as he explained, *The Merry Widow* could be inscribed within a European tradition of satire whose key work, he told the students, was Swift's "Modest Proposal"—another text whose undercutting of its own pragmatic assertions he claimed Americans particularly tended to misconstrue insofar as they read the work too literally. Satire was particularly artistic in this respect because it had to do directly with a critical distance adopted toward worldly realities. For example, in a November 27, 1935, lecture on the Disney Silly Symphony films, Falk argued that these were more than playful amusement. The Disney films used animals as a satiric bestiary "to comment on human nature . . . a way to criticize human nature without making it direct."

For every William Ashley who resisted Falk's dogmatic imposition of an aesthetic, there were many more students who gave the professor what he clearly wanted. Take, for instance, the revealing use of a rhetorical question by Cinema Appreciation student Bernard S. Cohen in his highly critical

March 19, 1935, paper on *Ruggles of Red Gap:* "Didn't we decide that dialogue (conversation) was pertinent to the stage and not a good feature of cinema? I think we did!" Or Ruth Small's October 4, 1934, assignment on *The Barretts of Wimpole Street:* "Mr. Franklin [the director], instead of taking just the essence of the story and re-thinking it through in terms of movie technique, as the author of the stage play had done with the stage in mind, just *cut* an unimportant line here, an uninteresting scene there. It is just another failure because of Mr. Franklin's inability to recognize that the cinema is a new medium."

I have been suggesting some of the broad contours of the philosophy of film that Falk hoped to inculcate in his students. At this point I want to outline his aesthetics in greater detail and show how he employed it for the reading of specific films (when possible, I will concentrate on examples he dealt with in the 1930s). One useful document in this respect is a typescript text of lecture notes for a class session (probably for the beginning of the term) entitled "Cinema Is Art." Falk begins by announcing, "We shall be considering the motion picture as an art form, which is conditioned by the large audience which views it." Already, this simple declaration is revelatory. Falk's approach would be emphatically an aesthetic one, and questions of film's social functions would be bracketed out. In fact, he hinted that the social aspects of film serve as possible brakes on artistic creativity: the mention of the "large audience" that has a conditioning power over film becomes less neutral in its intent when we remember Falk's worries about the literalist misreadings that could ensue from uninformed, mass taste. Undoubtedly, Falk wanted the art of film to reach as many trained American citizens as possible; undoubtedly, too, as his approval of the Disney Silly Symphonies indicates, he believed that a folk art could also become a high art. But while Falk recognized that the cinema was a democratic cultural form—as he went on to say in the lecture notes, "Films are mass produced; of this century technologically"—he also felt that there were dangers in democratic taste: the dangers, as we have seen, of literalism, of captivation by narrative and content, and of a concomitant inability to recognize artistic medium specificity.

At its extreme, as his dismay at his students' response to *The Merry Widow* hints, Falk's goal was to save select films from crowd taste and to turn viewing into refined acts of cultural distinction. The need was to educate viewers into standards that no longer led them to accept the anonymous output of Hollywood filmmaking. Where the general public for Boar's Head screenings would be given no program notes or any other aids in the viewing of what often must have seemed works quite different from mainstream Hollywood fare, the students registered in Cinema Appreciation were subjected to Falk's explicit set of principles and judgments of individual films against those principles. Spontaneous recognition of art's transcendence of literalism may not have been for everybody, but Falk could try at least to train his university students to achieve it. Beyond the select student audience to which he would impart his aesthetic principles, Falk might have to abandon the masses to their own mass taste. Speaking in a September 29, 1937, lecture on Jacques Feyder's *Carnival in Flanders*, Falk argued that this film approached the quality of Art, but that "[b]ecause it is Molière-like, because it is civilized, because it is pure comedy, perhaps it is not meant for crowd consumption. Perhaps since the 'least common denominator' of intellect and emotion cannot here prevail, it is beyond the appreciation of the average audience."

A November 14, 1934, lecture from the course's first semester shows how Falk would interweave general principles with the close analysis of a specific film. In this case, the students had gone to see Mamoulian's *We Live Again*, but typically, no matter the specific qualities of the chosen film, it would be treated within larger conceptual frameworks such as, in this case, "The Nature of the Film," "Relation of Film to Scenario," or "The Function of the Film." Falk's lecture moved outward from the individual film in a series of seemingly logical steps. In the case of this particular film, Falk felt Mamoulian's effort did make "use of pure cinematic form," and this led him right away to compare Mamoulian to other key directors such as Lubitsch, DeMille, and Vidor. Mamoulian's aestheticizing qualities were most evident in his "use of source material" and of "acting and forms of acting"; this then occasioned a discussion of the general issue of how directors could use actors as raw material for their transformative art. Against those directors who, because of the star system, kowtowed to actors and made their films into little more than passive recordings of performances, the best directors used actors as mere elements in the construction of a greater aesthetic accomplishment. This assertion enabled Falk to make a segue into, first, a presentation of the theories of Kuleshov and Pudovkin on acting and then a broader discussion of montage as the defining characteristic of cinema per se as an art of construction and synthesis. Films, for instance, did not have to respect the integrity of a star performance but could transform it through editing. And this transformative effect of editing in the case of actors was only one example of montage's general powers. A further aspect of montage theory had to do with image-sound relations, and Falk dealt with this next. Where so many films offered a literalist match of sound and image, Falk called for a montage approach based on disjunction. He then offered examples of nonliteral employment of sound (here he cited creative use of sound, especially music, in such works as the Disney Silly Symphonies, Flaherty's *Man of Aran*, Ford's *The Informer*, and *Chapayev*). Then, moving outward from the specific example of sound-image montage, Falk returned to broader comments on film as an art that created new realities by means of editing only to then broaden the point further by arguing that editing was merely a synecdoche for the myriad techniques cinema had as its disposal to effect transformations on reality. As Falk put it bluntly, "The appreciation of the film should be based on the way it is made." This then led in the lecture to a reminder that the director was the essential creative figure behind any good film; here Falk both applauded the creative uses of montage in Griffith's rush-to-the-rescue films and in Lang's *M*, and criticized King Vidor's *Our Daily Bread* for allowing ideology and message to overpower aesthetic experimentation. All these steps in Falk's lecture had been occasioned by the local, single example of the Mamoulian film.

While many of his lectures had to deal with performance-heavy entertainment films that showed up in the theaters, Falk balanced the narrative fiction film against experimental works that he showed in class or at the Boar's Head theater, and he worked to get students to appreciate the films that were outside their normal viewing habits. At the extreme, Falk's position could lead to a valorization of a pure cinema, a cinema of abstraction, that eschewed the crowd-pleasing qualities of story and subject. Insofar as cinema was primarily an art of visual dynamics, all that was necessary was that a film capture through its medium-specific qualities some of that dynamism. Falk consistently militated for his students to open themselves up to currents of modernism, especially in their European manifestation insofar as that would help students move beyond the provincialism of their all too American investment in popular narrative entertainment. As Falk described Fernand Léger's *Ballet mécanique* in a 1934 lecture entitled "Abstract Film": "Without story or interest apart from that of true *cinema dynamics* (physical force or energy for its own sake)." But Falk could also be open to homegrown modernist experimentation. Just as he would later promote Maya Deren's works in energetic fashion, he was a strong advocate in the 1930s of such films as Webber and Watson's *Lot in Sodom*. For example, in a December 4, 1935, lecture, he situated that film in relation to "[p]ure cinema [which] uses pictorialism, dynamics of the film, and film sound. It relies on the camera and the camera's potentialities. . . . In pure cinema—abstraction results in cinema dynamics for their own sake."

In passing, it is worth noting several inflections in his film aesthetics that this lecture reveals. First, there was the affirmative attitude toward "film sound": despite Falk's clear preference for an art of pure *visual* dynamics—and despite his dislike of films that merely recorded theatrical dialogue—he shared with one of his idols, Gilbert Seldes, a hope that the sound film could discover ways to use auditory material creatively as an integral part of a film's overall formal design. Falk was quite enamored of the classic theorization of sound by Soviet filmmakers Eisenstein, Pudovkin, and Alexandrov, who a few years earlier (1928) had welcomed a nonliteral, nonsynchronized dialectical relationship of sounds to image, and he referred to it numerous times in his lectures. Falk lauded off-screen sound as a formal element that, through its divorce from the image, could enter into aesthetically constructive contrapuntal relationships with film visuals.

Significantly, while he disdained the "talking picture" (one frequent target was Marcel Pagnol), Falk was not one of those cinema purists who fully condemned the sound film. His notes are filled with analyses of the ways in which sound transcends literalism: for example, when it is off-screen; when it appears more in the form of special effects than as dialogue; when its musicality is emphasized (and here Falk welcomed dialogue when it was treated for its tonal, rather than informational, qualities). As noted earlier, he particularly admired the evocative use of music in such 1930s works as the Disney Silly Symphonies, *The Man of Aran*, *The Blue Light*, *The Informer*, and *Chapayev*, where he felt the folk songs added a poetic dimension to the work. Falk's admiration of *Chapayev*, so often thought of in film historical literature as a work of uncinematic socialist realism, is an interesting demonstration of the power of his aesthetic position: a film that most critics regard as a content-heavy work with little evident play of form became for him a work of dynamic creativity, and he repeatedly sang the film's praises over the years. Similarly, Falk lauded those directors who, he felt, managed to move toward nonliteral deployments of sound. Thus, to take just one example, his lecture condemning *The Scarlet Pimpernel* as a film in which "the exposition . . . is too novelistic and not cinematic" bore the note "Cf. *M*" and contrasted the British film unfavorably with experiments from the Continent: "Korda does not know how to use sound well, i.e., in the stupendous way that Clair and Lang do." (Elsewhere, he said of Clair that he was "[t]he first director to realize and appreciate the value of music for emphasis of the visual image.")

Similarly, Falk welcomed color into film in those cases where it was used not to reproduce the look of things as they were in real life but to creatively transcend mere recording. As he put it in an undated lecture, "It is not accurate realism of color which is desirable but the ability to be able to suggest color." Falk, for instance, regularly applauded and taught the expressionistic use of color in the 1934 short film *La Cucaracha*, which had been made to promote the new Technicolor process and had been crafted in its visual design by the legendary theater figure Robert Edmund Jones.[13]

Most interesting about Falk's lecture on *Lot in Sodom* is that, as a parenthetical comment at the top of his notes indicates, he had prepared his lecture "[b]efore seeing the film"! That Falk could so proceed results, I think, less from any sort of pedagogical laziness than from the surety and even dogmatic nature of his approach to film art. Falk began with a clear-cut set of aesthetic principles and then judged individual works against them. The philosophy of art became an evaluative template that addressed a fixed set of questions to specific films with often predictable results.

I have termed this philosophy a dogmatic one, but at moments Falk seemed to pull back from an elite perspective on the arts. In such instances, he appeared to hold out the possibility of a reconciliation of democratic folk culture and the aspirations of an art of formal transformations of everydayness. For example, in a January 5, 1942, lecture on Disney's *Dumbo*, Falk reiterated his valorization of avant-garde experimentation with the strong assertion that "[c]inema can handle all the extreme isms better than the easel arts." But the next note is revealing: "Futurism plus Surrealism—not Dali but Disney." For all the dogmatism of his tenacious belief in medium specificity, Falk resisted the extreme position that saw pure abstraction as the only viable artistic path for film. The Disney case, for example, was one in which formal experiment was tied to—and arose out of—popular narrative. If Falk vociferously advocated pure cinema, he also in a number of cases tried to emphasize the ways in which an impure cinema of theme and narrative—a popular entertainment cinema centered on storytelling—could in its best moments aspire to qualities of art and do so without sacrificing either artistic purity or democratic appeal.

Falk's October 30, 1935, lecture on *The 39 Steps*, a film he greatly admired, well shows how he could sometimes fit popular entertainment cinema into his philosophy of aesthetic transcendence. Like others, the lecture on *The 39 Steps* was situated as both a close analysis of that film and a typical extension from it into Falk's general principles. Within his overall aesthetic, Falk found much to admire in Hitchcock's films. There was, for example, pictorialism in the scene of pursuit on the moors (which Falk compared to Flaherty's *Man of Aran*), and there was dynamism in the film's depiction of movement across those moors. Further, even though the film had several key scenes set in theaters or lecture halls, it tended to use language creatively rather than as a mere vehicle of meaning (to take one example, Robert Hannay is forced to make a political speech and basically offers nothing to the crowd but gibberish). Additionally, the plot conceit of a man pursued had important formal implications, since a propitious way for the cinema to create suspense in medium-specific fashion was for it to employ techniques of editing to alternate between pursuer and pursued. And the very idea of an ordinary man suddenly finding himself caught up in mysterious intrigue was itself fundamentally artistic, since it presented the transformation of reality and the concomitant transport of the spectator along with the protagonist into a fantastic realm. Here, Falk approvingly quoted the famous declaration by G. K. Chesterton that the detective genre expressed "the poetry of modern life." As Falk explained, films such as Hitchcock's belonged to a mode of art he termed "psychological melodrama": "The psychological melodrama is in the realm of cinema-fiction because it establishes a 'dream-world'—a phantasmagoria, a nightmare. 'Dr. Caligari's Cabinet' is in this class—not documenting reality but a 'possible' reality."

In lectures such as these, then, Falk drew back from pure formalism. He tended, likewise, to disavow formal experimentation that did not seem to have an aesthetic unity beyond it: in this respect, Falk's aesthetic eschewed artistic flash, mere mannerism, and momentary flights of experimental fancy. For example, in a lecture on Alexander Korda's *Private Life of Don Juan*, Falk cautioned that although the film had great pictorial beauty, he nonetheless had to voice reservations: "Principles of linear design apply but must not destroy either the dynamics of the film or be abstracted for their own sake. Pictorial composition should be controlled by the dramatic content of the scene it expresses. Pictorial composition is not the job of the art director but the director. It is inherent in the scenario itself." In contrast, Hitchcock's films had motivated its pictorialism—the plot had found ways logically to move characters to the moors—and it had enabled fantasy to emerge naturally from its narrative by means of the premise of a man whose world quite directly is turned upside down.

As an art "of this century technologically" (as undated lecture notes from the 1930s had put it), the cinema had difficulty rendering pure abstraction, since film's technological basis was in photography, and this encouraged it to capture reality rather than directly offer abstractions from it. Falk clearly resembles those film theorists for whom cinema's photographic basis was regarded as something that had to be overcome for the transcendent qualities of art to make themselves manifest. But he did not believe that those photographic qualities could be ignored. Indeed, the challenge films faced in achieving creative transcendence of the everyday rendered those works that did achieve that transcendence all the more worthy of praise. A popular entertainment like *The 39 Steps* was almost more laudable than rigorous avant-garde works of abstraction, since it accepted photographic representation but wove complicated transformations on it.

In this respect, it is instructive to see how Falk dealt with the nonfiction film. Falk in fact liked documentaries but only insofar as they participated in, to cite documentarist John Grierson's celebrated phrase, "the creative treatment of actuality." This meant, first of all, that documentaries found value not in any inherent interest of their raw subject matter but from the ways they handled that subject matter as material for aesthetic transformation. Falk was a big fan of the documentaries of Joris Ivens, and he brought the documentarist to campus for a screening of his films toward the end of the 1930s. But what he tended to admire in filmmakers like Ivens was not a content of social consciousness but a cinematic dynamics of form. On the one hand, Ivens's films, as Falk explained in a May 7, 1936, lecture, offered "lessons in selection, organizing, cutting" insofar as they used montage to create pictorial flow. They were veritable "ciné-poems" that employed editing to create "tonal values." On the other hand, although documentary did offer a photographic record of things of the world, it could in the best of cases hone in on things that were themselves artistic or poetic when filmed in the right way. Falk maintained, for instance, that fluid movement as revealed in Ivens's best work, the aptly named *Rain*, was inherently aesthetic material and easily lent itself to dynamic rendition. Although the photographing of water simply reproduced a substance that was aesthetic in its own right, the choice of this subject matter was already a step toward the creative treatment of actuality. As Falk put it elsewhere, in a mid-1930s lecture on *Mutiny on the Bounty*, "The sea is a gorgeous thing for the cinema."

Art was not about the uninspired capturing of life. At the very least it had to involve a rendering of the poetic qualities that sometimes could shine through the ordinary objects of the world. At moments, Falk's aesthetic, for all its formalism, resembles that of, say, Siegfried Kracauer in his 1960 work of "realist" aesthetics, *Theory of Film*. Like Kracauer, Falk at times applauded the ways in which cinema's photographic basis enabled it to capture the evanescent flux of everyday life—the energy and dynamics of modernity itself. Thus, in "The Cinema as Popular Art," a 1938 lecture on divisions between experimental film and popular film (and their respective audiences) that he presented in Frederic Thrasher's NYU film course (to be discussed in the next chapter) and at the annual convention of the National Board of Review, Falk did on the one hand applaud pure cinema, since, as he said, "we even accept pictorialism and dynamism when they are presented in the abstract, for we feel that such abstraction gives another dimension to the film." On the other hand, in the same lecture, he valorized popular cinema against abstract film for those representational qualities that enabled the former to capture the feel of modernity. As he put it, the popular film, more than the work of rarefied experimentation, "keeps us alive to the contemporaneousness of the American scene." Falk offered special praise to films that captured machine-age aspects of modernity. He was, for instance, a great admirer of Fritz Lang's *Metropolis*, which he liked both for its science-fictional projections into the future and for the poetry of its photographic representation of machines in motion. At moments, Falk's odes to renditions of the machinic in film even start to seem like invocations of a fundamental ontology of cinema, as if he felt there was some essential quality by which cinema was destined to both capture and display the kinetic vibrancy of machinic technologies. As he put it in a lecture on *Transatlantic Tunnel* (1935), a vision of future scientific achievement that he felt bore the direct influence of *Metropolis*, the film participated in fantasy, but it also showed "[a]n affinity between the machine (the camera) and the machines or mechanical devices. This affinity of machine with machines is partly an abstract dynamism and pictorialism." But, as so often happened with commercial entertainment, the formal potential of cinema dynamics was marred and restrained by inadequacies in the story. In its glorious filming of technological accomplishment, *Transatlantic Tunnel* captured the feel of modernity, but the film, nonetheless, had an "[i]mperfect scenario—hindered by a hackneyed, trite and labored 'plot.'"

The goal of cinema appreciation was not to foster divisions between art and entertainment but to elevate the latter so that it could approach the condition of the former. Here, the 1938 lecture "Cinema as Popular Art" is particularly revelatory. Falk admitted that there were hierarchies of taste and value in all the arts: "Naturally, there always will be stratification of motion pictures just as novels, plays and paintings will always have relative merits and be aimed at relative tastes." But it was dangerous to allow stratification to turn into what Falk termed irremediable "breaches" among social groups—"especially," he said, "in this year of stress and strain 1938–1939 where everyone is trying to find out what is wrong." If divisions of taste and value were unbreachable, there would be no place for the pedagogue; ultimately, for all his dismay at student taste, Falk also had to hold out faith that taste could be improved and that it was the privilege of the pedagogue to enable that to happen.

One strong aspect of Falk's mission of aesthetic uplift had to do with his particular attitude toward censorship. For Falk, adults had to have access to select works of high art, even when the content of those works might invite literalist reading and condemnation. Falk saw censorship as a restrictive force that, by preventing audiences from coming into contact with daring works that pushed the limits of art in new directions, meant that they would not have the chance to grow imaginatively. Frequently, it was not some sort of inherent deficiency in mass audiences that led them to "lowest common denominator" taste. Rather, limited taste may have resulted from censorship decisions that left the masses with nothing but undemanding art with nothing adventurous about it—a debased art that prevented taste from being tested, challenged, and pushed to grow and refine itself. As Falk put it in the talk he gave in Frederic Thrasher's NYU film class, "Part of the ineffectuality and sterility of the present-day lies in its absolute subservience to the obnoxious codes [of censorship agencies]." He noted that playwrights ranging from Shakespeare to Ibsen and O'Neill—writers whose plays he had often produced at Syracuse—had dealt effectively with themes that were proscribed by the Hays Office, and he called for films that would approximate the boldness and challenge of such theatrical experiment at its best: "A producer with good taste should ignore the trivial rules of censorship and make films dealing with mature themes in a manner comparable to their treatment by the modern stage."

Contrasting the claim that immoral works would "sully" the mind to his own belief that keeping challenging works away from the people would "stultify the minds of the American motion picture public," Falk made the bold move of declaring dramatically that both the Legion of Decency and the Production Code should "be done away with as speedily as possible." When the *New York Times* reported on this proposal as part of Falk's speech at the annual convention of the National Board of Review, the newspaper's account was picked up by a number of other publications nationwide (which tended to fixate on the phrase "sullying the public mind rather than stultifying it"), and Falk became for a moment a figure of some minor notoriety in debates around film censorship. He received letters of praise as well as denunciation, and there was a caustic response to his position in *The Queen's Work* (May 1939), the Jesuit journal run by Father Daniel Lord, one of the drafters of the Production Code.

As Falk had admitted earlier in a 1934 talk on the issue of censorship given at a Syracuse Alumni Club luncheon, he was "taking the more difficult side of the question." But his devotion, he insisted, had to be to the ways good art could bring improvement to human taste, and issues of aesthetic value had to be given priority over the literalist application of moral value. As he explained to the alumni, "[My] attitude is artistic, poetic, fantastic in the interest of the development of cinema as an artistic thing and in the individual as an appreciative well-balanced adult."

For Falk, there was a fundamental human value to be derived from the act of artistic creation, and the potential for attainment of aesthetic value mattered more than any moral or immoral content in the work thereby created. Art's mission was to add new meaning to human existence. As Falk explained in the typescript notes for his lecture "Cinema Is Art," "[w]e grant certain privileges to the artist which allow him to depart from reality to make art possible," and these privileges had to include the freedom from slavishness to contents determined by current-day morality (or, rather, by misguided moral agents claiming to speak in the name of the people).

The "Cinema Is Art" lecture in Thrasher's NYU class offers Falk's philosophy of art in its most explicit form. As he declared at the outset, Art can be defined as "[n]ature reworked or restated": it is "an attempt to substitute a world of things which parallels the real world, but does not imitate it." Moreover, each art has its own specific way of creating its own imaginative universe: "Material and medium are important elements to be considered when discussing an art form." The material, Falk clarified, is "any phase of human life or activity"; it is "a composite of human experiences." The medium is "what the artist works with": "The medium will condition the kind of material the artist may use. It is of most importance that the artist define his medium in order to work with it to the most advantage."

The first goal of Cinema Appreciation, then, was to isolate precisely those qualities that are medium specific and to judge whether this or that film used them in effective, transformative ways. On the one hand, this would involve a downplaying of those qualities that often appeared in films but were not intrinsic to the medium. Some of these alien qualities that showed up awkwardly in film included histrionic acting imported from the theater (thus, as he put it, George Arliss "proves that character acting as such, no matter how adept and adroit, does not alone make a movie. Arliss's whole method is non-filmic. There is little 'cinematic' about him"); dialogue employed for simple conveyance of narrative information and not for its own formal values ("*Clive of India* is too static and dialogic"); a literalist use of film content for the transmission of social or moral messages (thus, in regard to the 1935 adaptation of *The Last Days of Pompeii*, Falk described "one of the weaknesses of this film—the photographing of a story with a 'powerful sermon' [as RKO's own publicity for the film had said] rather than the making of a cinema with imaginative use of the camera"); and narrative when not employed as a structural device in the service of cinematic dynamism (Falk had the following to say of *Gone with the Wind:* "The narrative quality is a secondary cinematic value. . . . [Director Victor Fleming] makes no attempts to be particularly cinematic . . . a literal statement with few overtones").

Films had to work to exploit primary qualities, medium-specific qualities which included pictorial values, motion, dynamism, rhythm, and so on. But it was the possibilities deriving from montage that for Falk most seemed most to define cinema's potential for medium-specific creativity. As he put it in a lecture in the first semester that Cinema Appreciation was offered, "The principle behind the aesthetics of the film is putting strips of celluloid together. Synthesis in 'theatre' is around the actor. Synthesis in screen is around the director." Beyond the invocation of montage as creative synthesis, we see here a clear adumbration of Falk's theory of the film actor, who, he felt, should be less a fount of personal creativity (the danger of the star system in acting) than a malleable tool, one more bit of raw material to be molded by cinematic technique. Falk's predictable valorization of the Soviet montage directors for their decision to downplay actor histrionics and employ actors as mere structural elements within the overall texture of their films tapped into a larger presupposition in his aesthetic (one, again, that he might have gotten in large part from Paul Rotha): namely, the assumption that the film director was the primary creative figure in the production of a film and that criticism should be directed to identification and differentiation of those specific qualities that give individual directors their distinctiveness.

Indeed, Falk's aesthetic represents a fairly early but fairly articulate and articulated version of auteurism. Strong directors, he felt, had characteristic approaches to their material, and these approaches could be carefully pinpointed, distinguished from each other, and evaluated. Falk's concern was not with recurrent *themes* that directors dealt with but with the ways they used the cinematic medium to transcend mere transmission of theme: as he put it in speaking of the contributions of Porter and Griffith, they "create filmic time as opposed to Actual Time." Each director could be judged according to his (or, in rare cases, her) realization of cinema's transformative potentials. Indeed, in the early days of Cinema Appreciation, when Falk was still giving exams, one question asked students to pinpoint the defining qualities of such filmmakers as DeMille, Eisenstein, Pabst, Lubitsch, and Mamoulian (wryly, the *Syracuse Post-Standard* article reported that several students thought Pabst "was the trade name for beer"). Remnants of Falk's own notes for the exam indicate the sorts of answers he was after, ones that identified directors with specific aesthetic accomplishments (or lacks thereof): "DeMille—spectacle, lacks artistic relevancy and lack of knowledge of cinema dialectics; Lubitsch—rhythmic montage, combination of satire and lyric; Mamoulian—dramatic (stage) qualities, self-conscious art." In class lectures, too, Falk engaged in director analysis. For example, in speaking on *Cleopatra* (1934), he asserted that DeMille "does not know what to do (cinematically) with his vast resources. He distributes them like a drunken sailor. Has little knowledge of what a film is supposed to be, and no sense of film values. Is decidedly deficient in the dialectics of the film, the language of montage. . . . He has no time-sense (a fundamental requirement)."

But if a philosophy of film authorship centered on the director was Falk's primary organizing and typologizing principle for cinema, he employed two other models to differentiate forms of film for the ways they used the medium to transform and transcend reality. First, as noted earlier in relation to Falk's comments on the Marx Brothers and their stage-derived comedy, there was the effect of genres as transpersonal and regularized means for creative transformation. Just as different directors each bore a specific relation to medium and material and thereby were deemed more or less accomplished in the attainment of cinematic specificity, so too did genres offer a means for distinguishing pure from impure forms of filmmaking. I alluded earlier to Falk's fascination with treelike chartings in which he traced the ideal evolution of cinematic forms. Significantly, each of the stages in the genealogies he drew up can be said to be manifested in dominant genres. For example, if *The Great Train Robbery* was the generative urtext for cinema history's spiritual journey, one of its values was that it inspired the genre of the Western, a key cinematic form for Falk. The Western, Falk argued, was, in the best of cases, a preeminently cinematic form: for example, it captured the pictorial poetry of life, it was fundamentally devoted to movement and dynamics, it used narrative in a structurally creative fashion, and it tended to favor nontheatrical acting or even nonacting (insofar as Western characters often fit a type, like the nonactors in the typage-based Soviet cinema). In one of his most intriguing assertions, Falk even argued that the documentary films of the 1930s derived from the Western insofar as they also tried to capture a poetry of the land and celebrate pure dynamism. But there was also the danger of a genre's degradation—of its seduction by the theatrical, the verbal, and the downright noncinematic. By the 1950s, for example, Falk had come to see recent Westerns as too stagy: thus, he felt that *The Gunfighter* had too many scenes of characters just talking to each other (what he referred to as "duo scenes") and that *Shane* tended to use the wide screen in undynamic ways simply to pit characters against each other and let them play out their drama.

Another means for typologizing creative forms came for Falk from the idea of national cinemas. He did not develop his classification of creativity according to national belonging in any consistent fashion—and much of what he did offer came in large part from Paul Rotha—but it is worth noting the extent to which Falk did assume that different cultures had different relations to creativity. On the one hand, for instance, he tended to see the British—with the possible exception of Hitchcock—as so seduced by their worthy live drama traditions that they tended to let their films be uncinematic, world-bound, and word-bound examples of canned theater. On the other hand, Falk held out great praise for French cinema as a form that recognized specifically pictorial values.

Significantly, for all his defense of medium specificity, Falk found that much of the value in French cinema derived from its debt to some of the other arts: just as he analogized film to the rhythmic art of music, his interest in pictorialism led him to applaud those aspects of French cinema that seemed inspired by painting. Noting the strong traditions of visual arts in France, Falk applauded the legacy that the country's great painters had provided for film: "great sense of design... deliberate exquisite care with every frame evidenced in [films such as] *Crime and Punishment, Carnet de bal, La Maternelle, Ballerina.*" Likewise, the satiric tradition of theater that the French had pioneered with Molière and that had culminated cinematically in trenchant comedies like *Carnival in Flanders* showed that the French had theatrical resources that avoided the literalism of conventional drama and could be used creatively: French films derived from a "great tradition of acting" but one that "insists further that screen acting has qualities unlike stage acting." Ultimately, Falk suggested that the Cartesian-inspired French possessed a fundamental and culturally specific nature that made them open to experimentation: consequently, French films "possess like the French themselves a great sense of rationality purged of all sentimentality."

In a November 2, 1938, lecture on Julien Duvivier's *Carnet de bal*, it almost seems as if the various premises in Falk's philosophy of cinema are being checked off one by one against the film. Insofar as they formed a dogma that had a priori deductive power over any specific examples it could be applied to, Falk's aesthetic principles could seem virtually mechanical. Thus, he asserted that *Carnet de bal* "comes close to being a great film" and he enumerated the reasons:

1. Because it shows a superb handling of cinematic values as embodied in the sound-film.
2. Because its scenario shows a profundity and understanding of life—thematic content.

3. Because there is a great sense of balance in the relationship of scenario parts.
4. Because of a superb feeling for design and artistic fidelity.
5. Because it uses acting to best cinema purpose.

Almost as if these typical evaluations form part of a syllogism or of a mathematical summation, Falk then announced his conclusion: "In a word, the film can be looked on as a work of art."

Twenty years later, Falk would be making similar points about another French film, one of the last works he taught: the highly experimental *Hiroshima mon amour* from 1959. Several decades after Cinema Appreciation began, one finds Falk at the end of his career using the same lecture notes, making the same critical points, even though film history had changed and now he was confronting a cinema that often fully accepted formal play with narrativity. Whatever the dogma in his critical positions, one has to acknowledge his tenaciousness and his drive to keep pushing at students to give them more awareness of culture—for example, the experimental culture of European modernism.

In 1961, in Europe for a class trip with his drama students, Falk dropped dead from a heart attack. He had been planning another session of Cinema Appreciation for the fall, and it almost seems symbolic that Falk's end came as he was continuing his pedagogical project of introducing students to the vibrant work of European modernism. As symbolically perhaps, the beginning of the 1960s was when the lineaments of an official discipline of film studies would be sketched out in terms close to ones that Falk had dogmatically imparted to his students over the years: film as an expressive art of auteurs, valorization of modernist play with space and time, genre as creative interpretation of reality, and so on. Both in the richness of films that emerged and in the culture of criticism and study that accompanied them, the 1960s would truly be an age of cinema appreciation along the lines that Falk had first begun to militate for early in the 1930s in his one-credit course off in the relative isolation of western New York State.

7 Cinematic Diversions in Sociology
Frederic Thrasher in the World of Film Appreciation

> It will present an opportunity to dispel to some extent the present popular hysteria concerning the movies and to make the public more conscious of motion pictures as a form of human expression.... I believe you will agree with me that this course will be a significant means of public education on problems and possibilities of the motion picture and will constitute an important forum for a sane and scientific discussion of motion picture problems.
> NYU PROFESSOR FREDERIC THRASHER describing his new course, The Motion Picture: Its Artistic, Educational, and Social Aspects (1934)

In his faculty biography folder in the New York University archives, there is a brief but interesting autobiographical detail offered up by Professor Frederic Thrasher (1892–1962), who taught in the School of Education from 1927 on. Under hobbies, he succinctly notes: "Motion Pictures—Gardening." The movies, indeed, seem to have had an important place in Thrasher's affections as well as a decisive impact on his career development.[1] Thus, his one single-authored book, the still-cited volume *The Gang: A Study of 1,313 Gangs in Chicago* (1927), had a short chapter on the possible causal relationship of popular culture (especially film) to urban delinquency (and the brevity, one could argue, may be more a sign of Thrasher's somewhat admiration for the movies—his desire not to see them as too blameworthy and not to give them more sociological attention than is their due—than, in contrast, a lack of interest in them).[2] Even more indicative of an ongoing fascination with movies, *Okay for Sound* (1946) a book for which he wrote the preface and which he helped edit, is a large-format *celebration* (his term) of the sound film.[3] Between these two books, Thrasher closely supervised a major research project on film and its influence on youth that his doctoral student Paul Cressey undertook at his request, and whose arguments he obviously influenced. Furthermore, Thrasher took an active role in the film reform movements of the 1930s, both as executive committee member of the influential National Board of Review (NBR) and as one of the founders and

299

administrators of the New York Metropolitan Motion Picture Council. Affiliated with the NBR, the Metropolitan Motion Picture Council was a film-betterment organization that, as its publicity materials described, had as its goals "1. to provide a means for discussion and voluntary cooperation and coordination of motion picture activities among agencies and individuals interested in the motion picture as entertainment and education" and "2. to act as a clearing house of motion picture information and the many and diverse motion picture activities within the metropolitan New York area." Representative of its efforts—and typical of an organization that operated under the auspices of the NBR—was the council's active support of the prestige picture *Pygmalion* from 1938: finding the film to be a propitious blend of uplifting story matter, quality production values, and aesthetic perfection, the council called on its members (many of whom were teachers, community organizers, and social reformers) to propagandize on the film's behalf with parents, school administrators, film exhibitors, journalists, and so on. In the 1930s, Thrasher served as technical director of the council (and by the 1940s, he would be its president), and he appears to have edited its monthly bulletin, which promoted high-quality film art and served as a source of information about works of social and cinematic value.

Most important to our concerns, Thrasher devoted pedagogical effort in the 1930s and on into the 1940s to the regular offering of a major film course. Along with his other activities in the promotion of quality cinema, his film pedagogy seems to have enabled the crystallization of his views on the movies into a veritable moral and cultural philosophy of film.

By the reference to "diversion" in the title to this chapter, I intend several things. First of all, Thrasher's scholarly concerns, which originally seemed quite bound to the discipline of urban sociology, came over the years to be diverted into an interest *in aesthetic appreciation*. In particular, film came to represent for him less an object of sociological inquiry—something to be analyzed by ostensibly scientific procedures within a position of methodological neutrality but nonetheless probably to be regarded with suspicion for its potential deleterious effects in society—than a source of cultural value to be lauded or even enthused over. Progressively, Thrasher came to serve as a promoter of film as art, and his course operated as much as an impassioned exercise in cinema appreciation as dry sociological evaluation. In this respect, then, a second sense of "diversion" came to matter: sociology would be diverted from its original path because the very nature of cinema as an entertainment form—as a diversion precisely—gave it powers that exceeded traditional sociological understanding. Thrasher was discovering that the aesthetic dimension represented what later critical discourse would refer to as art's "relative autonomy": obviously, the cinema was a force in society, but it was so insofar as it offered affective powers and imaginative projections that did not simply resemble other, more positivist factors in social life.

It is hard to know if it was inevitable that Thrasher would come to have this special and singular appreciation of the cultural realm and, in particular, of the culture of cinema. Initially, in fact, Thrasher's sociology had had an intensely scientific side to it (one that never fully dissipated over the course of his career), and he clearly had felt that the social sciences offered a mode of knowledge that was positive, empirically grounded, rigorous, and solid in ways lacking perhaps in the humanities. Indeed, in one of the few analyses of Thrasher in the current literature of film studies, cinema scholar Anne Morey treats him as representative of a techno-positivist tradition wherein social scientists imagine that the tools of their trade can help them master and contain unruly popular arts. In Morey's words, Thrasher speaks "as a technocrat searching for the right *technical* solution . . . in order to address social evils," and even she even writes of him as a Taylorist for whom social science offers forms of social management, including management of the realm of culture and of citizens' involvement with it.[4] Certainly, it is undeniable that Thrasher possessed this scientific side, and, as I note, vestiges of it remained throughout his work. For Thrasher, a science of society was possible insofar as, first, society itself was imagined to have the same characteristics as other objects of science and, second, sociology could be assumed to have the same characteristics as other, more hard sciences. In other words, he assumed that society was quite literally a *natural* object like others and therefore that the science that would seek to know it would be a natural science among others.

Thus, Thrasher's writing was filled with representations of society as an organic form, even perhaps quite literally an organism. Like other sociologists of the time, Thrasher tended to adhere to a conception of the social as an entity of natural growth that sought homoeostatic well-being. As he put in an early essay that set out a research project on the sociology of urban neighborhoods:

> The botanist concerns himself in part with plant ecology. In his field studies he marks off certain natural areas. . . . The student of human ecology likewise investigates the natural areas of the human community which come to be differentiated in the course of its development by processes (among others) of competition and segregation somewhat analogous to similar processes in the plant community. . . . The genetic approach to the study of the community needs no defense. It is a cardi-

nal method of science. The processes of growth and differentiation of parts which take place within the community are somewhat analogous in principle to those that occur in the development of an organism or of a plant community. In the human, as in the plant community, each ecological area has a history of its own.[5]

Insofar as society approximated other natural organisms in exhibiting a structured organization and a pattern of evolutionary growth that was fully teleological and not at all accidental, society became an object that could fully be known according to procedures of scientific investigation. Indeed, if the distinction of science and humanities has often been drawn around the assertion that the former is based on determinism, law, and predictability, whereas the latter deals with an area of free will, human creativity, and the unpredictable and indeterminate, Thrasher readily imagined that sociology could be a fully *predictive* science. As he put it optimistically in the next lines of the essay "The Study of the Total Situation": "The general assumption of science is that changes once understood may be predictable. It is essential, therefore, to study communities genetically and developmentally, investigating their origins and tracing the course of their development and the differentiation of their areas and structures. By this method, the natural histories of communities may be described and compared with one another in the search for general principles of community development."[6] At the same time, it must be noted, Thrasher's conception of society as homeostatic organism did not mean that he disallowed the possibility of social *dis*-functioning. Quite the contrary, Thrasher adhered to a typical, early-twentieth-century suspicion of modernity as heralding the onslaught of new forces and factors threatening to disrupt societal functioning: demographic upheavals; community uprooting; the fetish of speed, movement, and change for their own sakes; instability of identities; blurring of boundaries, and on and on. As Thrasher put it in an overview of a Boys Club study that he supervised in the early 1930s and that was the basis for his (and Paul Cressey's) film research: "An outstanding fact in contemporary America and elsewhere is the prevalence of disillusionment, uncertainty, and change in the social order. An almost universal social disorganization is accompanied by equally ubiquitous social conflict which further intensifies the disintegration. Even the casual observer cannot escape the conviction that far-reaching social changes are in progress and that further alterations in social arrangement are impending."[7]

But the disruptions with which modernity threatened organic society were not inevitable. On the one hand, strongly scientific social knowledge would be as powerful in the analysis of social upheaval as in that of social integration. Just as Thrasher's conception of a normally functioning society imagined it as a natural entity fully covered by scientific laws and fully accessible to modes of scientific knowledge, so too did he hold faith in the ability of sociology to cover and control moments of abnormality. In his words, "Optimism is justified because social disorganization is a necessary prelude to reorganization upon a more adequate basis of knowledge. Thus, disintegration presages more satisfying adjustments of social structures to functions and a more enlightened approach to the problems of social control."[8] As film scholar Mark Lynn Anderson argues in his essay "Taking Liberties: The Payne Fund Studies and the Creation of the Media Expert" (another rare writing in cinema studies today to engage with Thrasher's work), such optimism regarding the powers of sociology to deal with all aspects of society, including those forces of modernity that arise haphazardly to threaten its efficient homeostasis, served self-reflexively as a means by which Thrasher (like other sociologists) could promote his own career and delegate to himself an important professional role in his historical moment. In other words, by assuming that both normal and pathological conditions of society were ones that the trained sociologist could best know, the sociologist justified his social place, one that Anderson refers to as that of the "media expert," similar to what I have termed the "cultural mediator."[9]

Within this context of media analysis, it seems that the *cinema* increasingly came to serve in Thrasher's work not simply as one more social phenomenon among others (whether an integrative or a disintegrative one) but as a force so powerful it could take on many of the functions of social analysis that would have seemed to be the job of sociology itself. At the extreme, Thrasher came to feel that film possessed cultural resonances and values that exceeded all mere sociological frameworks. In other words, if Thrasher assigned himself the role of media expert, there was also the growing awareness in his work of film itself as offering forms of aesthetic experience and education that mere social science expertise could not hope to compete with.

In a sense, then, Thrasher was replaying a fundamental dilemma that I outlined in the introduction to this book: if film was itself a form of knowledge—if it was, for example, that effective and affective universal language as so many enthralled commentators asserted—what role but a subordinate one could be assumed by anyone who attempted to study it? Was film not a form of learning in its own right, and, if so, did it need the interventions of so-called experts to make its meanings known?

In a 1934 essay crafted with input from Thrasher, Thrasher's co-researcher and student Paul Cressey articulated these issues by analyzing cinema as a form of "informal education."[10] Cressey argued not merely that film was a potent force in society "which dispenses a great deal of informal education—general information, patterns, and not a little in the way of standards and personal ideals" (505). Beyond simply acknowledging that instructional aspect of cinema, Cressey set out to describe *specific formal and psychological means* by which film held special power for its spectators. Cinema did not just instruct but did so in a psychologically deep and complex fashion that gave it advantages over formal schooling. For example, Cressey noted the cinema's affective ability to stimulate emotional projection and identification on the part of spectators and tied these to mainstream films' employment of suspenseful narrative lines that focalized audience attention and emotional investment. In his words, "[T]he unified life situations presented in the photoplay afford a greater facility for the child of ordinary antecedents to associate himself more intimately with the life situations and characters portrayed upon the screen than is possible through a more formal agency or institution. Herein is to be found an important aspect of the educational role of the cinema. The cinema is almost unique among the agencies in a community in that it presents what are interpreted as unified segments of life" (508). In other words, by organizing its elements into the totalizing structure of a story, film appeared to offer a coherent, and therefore emotionally appealing, experience. This structured view of life gave the movies an advantage over formal schooling, since the latter was too often based on modes of knowledge broken up among different fields of study, different classes, different teachers, and so on. School did not invite a unified projection and identification. Where the movies promised a singular experience of unified emotion, the lessons of public schooling often seemed, in contrast, "a disjunctive and a repressive agent" (508–9). In the rivalry of formal schooling and the informal education of the movies, the advantage was to the latter: "In contrast to the traditional school, where motivation in learning arises extraneously, primarily through the teacher's special efforts and skill, the cinema provides for many children a means, vicariously at least, by which learning may really be a natural result of interest and activity" (509).

As we have seen, professors of film could assay any number of solutions to the dilemma of saying something salient about an art form whose powers seemed often to exceed any verbal discourse that tried to understand them. Professors could, for instance, argue that film offered a mode of knowing but one that was inarticulate and required the intercession of the trained academic to make its meanings clear. This, for example, was one solution offered by Victor Freeburg, who imagined the study of visual composition in film as making explicit what too often remained implicit and unconscious in the original act of composition and the subsequent reception of the work by untrained and unrefined spectators. Another option was to accept that film had affective advantages over verbal pedagogy but that these could be employed as means to invigorate dry, wordy education—hence, the 1930s fascination with "visual education." Cressey, for instance, ended his essay "The Motion Picture as Informal Education" with a call to use the gripping narrative art of cinema *in* the classroom: "The wider use of motion pictures in school programs and as aids in visual instruction represents a tremendous field for educational advance and coordination" (515). Professors might not be as seductive as films, but they could incorporate that cinematic seduction in their pedagogy by bringing the movies into the classroom.

In Thrasher's case, a number of options presented themselves as ways to intervene pedagogically around this art of cinema that was itself such a potent "informal education." On the one hand—and here I echo Mark Lynn Anderson's analysis—Thrasher continued to believe that scholars of a popular art like cinema could say important things about it that it itself could not say. He continued, that is, to believe that a sociology *of* the cinema was possible and possessed special explanatory powers: the media educated, but so did media experts, and they had their special role to play. On the other hand, Thrasher also came increasingly to render homage to cinema as a culture form that displayed powers that were irreducible to mere social function and that no sociological discourse could therefore adequately explain.

In passing, it is worth noting that throughout his work—from the more obviously sociological early pieces to the more culturally inflected later aesthetic invocations—Thrasher seemed to grant special power to visual analysis even as he himself had to resort to the more conventional framework of words. That is, while his role as a sociologist bound to the practices of his academic discipline was to present his arguments in *written* form, that very writing often invoked the visual as an ideal, perhaps superior, form of communication. His writings, indeed, often have a visceral and visual quality: this is certainly the case with his classic study of *The Gang*, which is filled with dynamic descriptions of urban settings and the violent actions that take place within them. Not merely does Thrasher present gang formation as assuming the form of narrative (gangs come together as an "us" that seeks to combat a "them"), but he himself tells the story of such gangs in gripping, dramatic fashion. More generally, as Thrasher at the end of the 1920s refined his research projects on delinquency (from which derived his various enterprises around film), he came to value above all what his research team termed *case study*, in which knowledge about delinquent boys was synthesized with vivid first-person testimony from them into a unified narrative mode. By these means, sociology itself became a form of lively, imagistic storytelling.

At the same time, Thrasher's writings also commented self-reflexively on the sociologist's wish to find ways to visualize knowledge, to render it in the viscerally effective form of images. In other words, he frequently appeared to long for the visual in the very language he employed. Note, for instance, the persistence of visual metaphors in his early essay "The Study of the Total Situation," a methodological reflection on neighborhood study: "It is eventually contemplated to make periodic re-studies of these local communities so that ultimately a *series of pictures* may be obtained to indicate the nature of the growth and decline of communities and the changes taking place in the various areas. Such studies will *throw light* upon the basic factors of social change in the urban and will reveal the ways in which school problems are affected by such changes. . . . Ultimately, also, the mosaic of community studies will *illumine* the processes occurring in Greater New York and in the metropolitan district as a whole."[11] Not for nothing did this essay center on the role of maps in urban sociology, since maps clearly appealed to Thrasher as a cognitive form that could represent the city by strikingly visual means. There was, it would seem, an envy for the visual in Thrasher's verbal discourse.

In this respect, I want to argue that for Thrasher the cinema came to serve as one of the ultimate forms of human accomplishment within modernity precisely because it was so viscerally visual. In militating increasingly for cinema *appreciation*, Thrasher was calling for a critical approach that would not so much attempt to *master* cinema or make it an inert object of superior social science knowledge as respect it for its own cultural role and acknowledge its powers. His late writings on film are indeed homages as much as they are analyses. Progressively, Thrasher began to articulate an aesthetics of film that appreciatively would describe cinema's powers and that would complement, and perhaps eventually supplant, mere sociological understanding of the popular art. As Thrasher argued, film's pedagogical power came not just from any particular content but from its affective force, its visual power, which stood as instructional lessons in their own right. Not for nothing did Thrasher, in the essay "Motion Pictures and Social Sciences" (1936) for the National Board of Review's monthly journal, write of the Hollywood biopic *The Story of Louis Pasteur* as "the educational talking film par excellence." The film offered a seductive informal education about the narrative thrills of scientific exploration, even though it was not faithful to the original facts of the Pasteur story: "The significance of this picture is not that it presents the accurate techniques of science, but that it is deeply touching, that it moves its audience to tears for social values that are truly significant and not the maudlin sentimentality of the 'tear-jerker.'"[12]

How did Thrasher deal with film pedagogically—that is, both as a form of pedagogy itself and as an object of study that his own instruction would attempt, perhaps enviously, to invoke through verbal analysis? The following pages set out to examine how Thrasher's class The Motion Picture: Its Artistic, Educational, and Social Aspects operated over the period of the 1930s to help him elaborate both a sociology and an aesthetics of cinema. But several caveats are necessary. First, as I have suggested by the reference to his *writings* as well as to his grassroots reform activity in such organizations as the Metropolitan Motion Picture Council, the classroom was only one among several sites in which Thrasher engaged in film. Clearly, he saw all his varied activities in film as allied efforts and endlessly brought his other work into the classroom (for instance, he used the motion picture course as a venue in which council activity could be advertised). His writings, reform activities, and classroom lectures intertwined and constituted shared testing grounds for his ideas. We need to refer to them all as part of one, singular pedagogical project.

At the same time, while Thrasher had a deep commitment to the serious study of film *and* felt that a specifically *artistic* understanding of cinema (rather than just a sociology of cinema) would increasingly matter toward that end, it would perhaps be an exaggeration to say that his NYU course offered a full-fledged cinema *aesthetics*. Thrasher seems to have left much of the work of aesthetic elaboration to others. For example, as we will see, some of the examination of cultural aspects of cinema in Thrasher's course was handled by visitors chosen to provide expert opinion on film as art. Such lecturers came to almost every session.

It is worth noting that several of the guest lecturers in The Motion Picture: Its Artistic, Educational, and Social Aspects serve as links from Thrasher's course to other pedagogical enterprises described in this volume. Although, as I have emphasized, there was no solidified *discipline* of film studies in these early days, it is clear that networks and filiations were already being established, especially in New York, and there were regular resources, including other scholars and writers, that any one pedagogue could draw upon. For example, Terry Ramsaye came to Thrasher's course several times over the years to speak on film history. USC's Boris Morkovin was invited in the late 1930s and proposed a lecture on "The Medium of the Motion Picture: Its Nature, Range, and Limitations" (although it appears that he had to cancel his presentation). Conversely, Mark Van Doren, whose film criticism forms part of the story told in the next chapter, was asked by Thrasher to lecture on "The Motion Picture as Entertainment and Creative Art" but turned the professor down in a June 12, 1937, letter of amusing curtness: "Thank you for thinking of me in connection with your very interesting course—to which my best wishes—but I must decline since, unless important personal considerations operate, I never speak for nothing."

Most notably for our purposes, Sawyer Falk from Syracuse lectured in 1938 on "The Film as Popular Entertainment" after becoming Thrasher's friend through annual conventions in New York City of the National Board of Review. In fact, Thrasher's articulated aesthetic of cinema, which found film's artistic specificity to lie in the representation of pure motion and in the creation of imaginary space and time through montage, can be seen to bear interesting parallels to Falk's own formal aesthetic of film. But while Thrasher came increasingly to value cinema for aesthetic potentials not reducible to sociologically propitious content, there was still a lingering sense in his work of film as having a necessary social, as well as aesthetic, mission. Falk, in contrast, felt that the only way in which film had social responsibility was in its powers of aesthetic transformation. In his notes on the 1935 NBR convention, which had had as one of its primary topics "Cinema as a Social Practice," Falk declared that to treat film sociologically, in terms of morally positive or negative content as did Thrasher, would be to make it "the handmaid of some social purposes." For Falk, art's only social purpose could be to confirm that there needed to be unhampered, uncensored space in society for aesthetic play and purposelessness. Falk went on in his notes to indicate how many of the sessions in Thrasher's course stressed "the educational and social aspects of film," rather than artistic ones, and he voiced worry at the annexation of film to "visual education"—to, that is, the use of film as mere vehicle for the transmission of objective lessons. As Falk wrote, "My objection to view expressed: 1. cinema cannot be objective (since it is the personal vision of the creative director); 2. who is to decide the norm of opinion?" (Falk, we might note, had criticized as "subjective" the moral objection by the Syracuse French department to his showing of *Passion of Joan of Arc*. For him, decisions about the moral effect of artistic content could only be capricious. Aesthetics alone was objective.)

Thrasher was only one voice among many in The Motion Picture: Its Artistic, Educational, and Social Aspects, and, as Falk's notes suggest, his voice was not even one that was univocally committed to a culturalist approach to film, since there remained strong traces of his original sociological impulse. Certainly, then, one should not imagine that the Motion Picture course facilitated full articulation of Thrasher's own aesthetics of film such as it was. But, as we will see, he was far from a subdued presence in the course, and the class sessions gave him a fairly propitious venue for the formulation of his own specific positions on film art.

As a final caveat in examining Thrasher's course for an overall philosophy, we must note that to the extent that he did have an articulated understanding of film as art, it was one he sometimes argued had to be opposed to the idea of a *general* aesthetic applicable to all cases of film art. In other words, Thrasher sometimes cautioned against the idea of an overall philosophy of film per se. In particular, in many of his more sociological declarations, Thrasher's approach to film appeared explicitly contextualist in ways that questioned the possibility of an essence to the art. That is, he felt that such values as film art had were only ever realized in specific contexts of consumption. Art appeared to be in the eye of the beholder. As he put it in his article "Education versus Censorship" (1940), the question of what constituted a good film or a bad one

> is confused to no end by a failure to recognize one basic principle which underlies it; viz., that there can never be objective standards for determining other than technically the essentials of a good entertainment film. The problem is a complicated one, but the value of a theater-shown motion picture in the last analysis depends upon what people like rather than upon any abstract principle of aesthetics. . . . Individual preferences for pictures vary. . . . This is less true perhaps of the technical aspects of a picture than of its theme, style, or direction, since bad photography and pure sound recording are more or less obvious to the untutored. To expect to get general agreement, however, as to what pictures are good pictures is obviously to misunderstand the whole problem. It is equally obvious that no one group can justly assume superiority over others and that it is contrary to democratic principles for any one group or combination of groups to attempt to prescribe what the general public should see. This is the basic fallacy of legal censorship.[13]

To the extent that value changed as spectator needs, desires, and judgments changed, it would, Thrasher argued, be peremptory to impose any overall aesthetic standards on the cinema audience. This is not to say, however, that Thrasher's contextualism led him to a fully relativist position on art in which there could be no universal criteria of judgment (even if the passage just quoted might give that impression). In fact, elsewhere Thrasher certainly appears to have held that there were definite hierarchies of value in art, and by the latter part of the 1930s, he did try to outline some general principles of cinematic art. One way he tried to mediate universalism and contextualism was to argue that there were indeed objective qualities to great cinematic art, but that sociological conditions of a modern, demographically divided society meant that not everyone was in contact with the same art and not everyone had been inculcated with the same talents for appreciating art according to canons of high taste. Above and beyond specific contexts there were universal values, but in the real world of social diversity it was rare for these to be materialized and made available to all citizens. For Thrasher, the separation of so many members of modern democracy from a universal situation in which they could experience and appreciate good art justified, as we will see, the role of the critically trained educator. The goal of a pedagogy in film aesthetics was not to free viewers from context but to educate them into that particular context in which they could best appreciate the highest values of cinematic form. Here, again, we see aspects of that self-promotion of the film scholar as media expert that Mark Lynn Anderson speaks of: Thrasher claimed to know what good art is and assumed that one goal of the pedagogue was to get others to accept that. As Thrasher put it in "Education versus Censorship," "[N]ew attitudes and new values must be created and education in its broadest sense is a far more effective instrument in this direction than the multiplication of restrictive laws" (291).

With these caveats in mind, we can move to a description of Thrasher's course and how it fit in with his research project. But, first, some background details are in order. Thrasher was brought to New York University's School of Education in 1927 as part of its Department of Educational Sociology, which had been founded in 1923 to engage in practical issues of social reform. As its departmental historian explains, "Throughout most of the Department's history, its major focus has been on the solution of education and other social problems with little emphasis on developing a rigorous sociological perspective on education."[14] Thrasher's particular focus was on deviancy and delinquency, and some of the courses he taught, such as Community Organization, School Children, Case Study, Leadership in the Community, Juvenile Delinquency, and Crime Prevention, are representative of his earliest pedagogical concern. At the same time, Thrasher undertook broader tasks in the department. For example, as film historians Garth Jowett, Ian Jarvie, and Kathryn Fuller recount in their study of *Boys, Movies, and City Streets*, a never-completed volume that Thrasher and Cressey researched for the Payne Fund Studies, Thrasher was hired to run a major, well-funded research project on the effects (or lack thereof) of Boys Clubs in curbing delinquency (a project that ended up including attention to film as one of its components). In the words of Jowett et al., "The study was sponsored by the Bureau of Social Hygiene (an arm of the Rockefeller

Foundation), which granted $37,500 to the project, conducted by members of the Sociology Department of New York University's School of Education."[15] Additionally, Thrasher served as associate editor of the department's publication, *Journal of Education Sociology*, which began when Thrasher arrived at NYU. Over the years, Thrasher was the guest editor for a number of issues on film, and the journal became one of the regular venues in which he (and also Cressey) elaborated a sociology and aesthetics of cinema. Thrasher also used the pages of the journal to publish the texts of some of the guest lectures from his course, although he was as likely to recommend them (especially the more aesthetically centered ones) to the National Board of Review's magazine, which he was actively involved in from at least 1933 on.

Thrasher came to New York from Chicago, where he had been a student of the vastly influential urban sociologist Robert Park. (Thrasher's 1926 dissertation on gangs was published in Park's series Studies in Urban Sociology and garnered a fair amount of academic attention.) Park had been involved in some of the initial meetings of that group of academics who would receive research moneys from the Payne Fund to investigate the potential effects of motion pictures on the public. He had signed on for two projects—with the working titles "1,000 Cases of Delinquency" and "Youth Conduct and the Movies"—that, by contrasting delinquents and college students, were supposed to examine the possible contributions of movies to youth criminal behavior. As Jowett et al. recount, "Park was an important and influential member of the Payne Fund Studies, attending the September and November 1928 meetings, but a fellowship opportunity arose for him in early 1929 to travel to China and Japan. He turned the Payne Fund project entirely over to [Herbert] Blumer" (71). Blumer, a former student and now Chicago colleague of Park in the area of social psychology, evidently became so fascinated by the accounts of film's influence that he was getting just from the college students—who originally were to serve merely as the control group to which the delinquents would be compared—that he "put the delinquency portion of his project on the back burner" (71). In 1928, Thrasher was recruited to take over the delinquency section of the Payne Fund Study.

Thrasher seemed an appropriate choice, since he had already expressed an interest in the cinema as social form and had already studied its effects on delinquency. In particular, as noted earlier, Thrasher's book *The Gang*, which brought him a certain notoriety in sociological circles, included a discussion of the influence of movies, and one imagines that its analysis might have recommended Thrasher to Blumer. Already at work on the Boys Club project—which had as one of its themes the ways in which other institutions, including popular entertainments, rivaled the clubs for urban boys' attention—Thrasher spun off the Payne Fund research project on movies and urban delinquency as a subtopic of the overall research. He put Paul Cressey in charge of this motion picture study, although it is clear that he continued to have direct input into the research and to keep close tabs on Cressey's progress. In fact, as social science historian Martin Bulmer explains in his useful study of the research community at Chicago that both Cressey and Thrasher came out of, central to its vision of scholarship was a concern for sharing and for intellectual collaboration.[16] Chicago sociologists thought of themselves as a team, and Cressey and Thrasher clearly brought this ethos with them when they both came to New York University. Their essays, for instance, frequently reference each other (in ways, specifically, that suggest an identity of basic principles). More important to our purposes, Cressey and Thrasher sometimes lectured together in Thrasher's course. In 1935, for example, they made a joint presentation on "Research into the Effects of Motion Pictures and the Payne Fund Studies." Cressey also presented by himself in the course on several occasions. For example, he lectured in the 1936–37 academic year on "Sociological Research in the Field of Motion Pictures." (The title is significant. To the extent that Cressey's work distinguished itself from Thrasher's, it is that Cressey's tended to remain more sociological, whereas Thrasher's increasingly engaged with aesthetic aspects of cinematic art.)

In 1933, Thrasher initiated his yearlong film course as he and Cressey worked on their volume for the Payne Fund Studies, and it is likely that he envisioned the classroom as a place to present and try out ideas that would aid in the formulation of the larger research project. In its initial manifestation, indeed, Thrasher's course seemed very clearly in line with the Payne Fund emphasis on media effects. Here is the 1933–34 catalog description of the first year's offering:

THE MOTION PICTURE AND EDUCATION

A scientific evaluation of the effects of the motion picture, commercialized and educational, upon children and adults, as to intellectual content, emotions, conduct and attitudes, sleep, delinquency and crime, and morality. Includes techniques for studying motion pictures and a survey of methods of control.

Here, in his initial pedagogical formulation in 1933–34, Thrasher envisioned film as something that had consequential effects—effects that were not so much artistic as societal (the movies might have, for instance, an impact on crime and morality), ones that could be examined scientifically, ones that might need to be controlled. The dry language of the social sciences matches the content of the topics to make the course seem all too purely sociological—film not as art but as a set of measurable empirical effects. The mention of the impact of movies on sleep may confirm the ways in which the course was originally being conceived within a Payne Fund–inspired framework, since the question of children's sleep (and the movies' potentially deleterious influence upon it) was a central research issue for the Payne Fund Studies.

By the following year, however, the course had a decidedly different look. Even the title had changed from the dry, seemingly discipline-bound one of The Motion Picture and Education to the more expansive, ambitious The Motion Picture: Its Artistic, Educational, and Social Aspects. In fact, at every level, the course seemed different. Indeed, a number of publications themselves declared that something new was happening. For example, a major visual education journal of the time, *Educational Screen*, announced the new version of the course in ways that easily convey the expansive concerns of its revamped manifestation:

> A unique course, entitled "The Motion Picture: Its Artistic, Educational, and Social Aspects," has been announced by New York University for the academic year of 1934–35. It is to be given under the direction of Dr. Frederic M. Thrasher, Associate Professor of Education, and will cover every phase of the motion picture including the entertainment film as well as the educational and creative production.
>
> This course is the outgrowth of the conviction, based on research, that the motion picture is one of the most tremendous educational and social forces of modern times. The tentative plan states that "the various movements now developing in the field of the artistic and creative film of the non-entertainment type as well as the enormous influence of the popular motion pictures have forced the public schools and the colleges and universities to recognize the permanence of this great educational instrument and its potentialities in all educational fields. It must be studied."
>
> Complete presentation of the technical, educational, and social aspects of the motion picture—of both the entertainment and non-entertainment types—will be illustrated by film showings. The class will visit a New York studio and see pictures in actual process of production: they will investigate the problems of exhibition at first hand; they will act as a review committee in pre-viewing a picture under the auspices of the National Board of Review; and they will study such questions as: How may motion picture appreciation be advanced by the public schools? What is the place of the motion picture in public school

programs and in the more informal types of education? How may a program of visual education, utilizing the full contribution of the motion picture, be developed?

It seems clear that the original approach to film as societal force had become more open and expansive; for example, the notion of "control" had dropped out, and there was now greater emphasis on the potentialities of films (and the very fact that they were imagined to have potentiality is itself significant). There was also now an evident concern to understand how films are made, perhaps out of a realization that it might be technical constraints of production as much as moral or ideological desires that pushed filmmakers to give their films the content and style they had. In fact, some of what the new version of the course was described as promising is not so different from that encountered in Columbia's aesthetically inclined Photoplay Composition course. Both courses appear to assume a sort of feedback loop between film production and appreciation: to learn how to better appreciate films is also to improve taste in ways that will rebound on the industry and push it to make films adequate to higher standards of appreciation. In this context, the field trip proposed in Thrasher's course to see actual production in the studios may have derived from a sense that moral custodians of film needed to know just how films were made in order to appreciate how the production context either enabled or disabled aesthetic and moral responsibility in films.

More revealing of the changes in the course is a long, detailed School of Education catalog entry for the new version. I quote most of this entry and note that its very length (compared with the dry concision in the entry for the more blunt media-effects offering of the previous year) might itself indicate that the course was seen as staking out important new directions. Certainly, by 1935–36, when the course was already a year old and had become the regular offering it was to remain until the end of the 1930s, the description could once again be succinct. As this shorter presentation of the new course reads, "This course, which presents the artistic, educational, and social aspects of the motion picture, puts particular emphasis on the contribution of the motion picture to education and other phases of contemporary life. It is richly illustrated by the showing of both sound and silent films. Lectures are given by many persons eminent in the motion-picture field. It includes field trips to studios, and other opportunities to gain a first-hand knowledge of the motion picture." With minor variation, that description would remain over the following years. But when the new course was announced for the first time in the catalog, the presentation was more extensive. Here, then, is that longer transitional catalog description from 1934–35:

THE MOTION PICTURE: ITS ARTISTIC, EDUCATIONAL, AND SOCIAL ASPECTS.

This course is given with the cooperation of the National Board of Review.

Research has established the fact that the motion picture is one of the most tremendous educational forces of modern times. The motion-picture audience in the United States is composed normally of about 70,000,000 people each week. More than one third of this immense group, receiving vivid impressions from the screen, is made up of children and adolescents. It has been demonstrated that the films, even of the purely entertainment type, are far-reaching instruments of popular education, unwittingly imparting information to all kinds of persons more effectively than other types of learning which have been experimentally measured. It has been shown that the pictures powerfully affect the emotions and that they may unconsciously change the attitude of their audience on important public questions such as race, nationality, war, and peace.

The various movements now developing in the field of the artistic and creative film of the nonentertainment type, as well as the enormous influence of the popular motion pictures, have forced the public schools and the colleges and universities to recognize the permanence of this great educational instrument and its potentialities in all educational fields—formal and informal, juvenile and adult. Education can no longer neglect the motion picture. It must be studied. [Parts of these last lines also appear in the previously quoted notice in *Educational Screen*, suggesting that the journal's report had been planted.] Its problems must be understood by the public and the educational expert alike. Its potentialities must be appreciated and developed. The artistic, educational, and social values implicit in the motion picture, of both the entertainment and creative types, must be understood.

This course will present in compact form many of the important aspects of the motion picture and its problems, illustrating most of them by showings of actual films, both silent and sound. What is the organization of the industry and what are its problems? How are motion pictures produced and what are the problems involved? What is good photography both from a commercial and from an experimental standpoint? What is good direction? What are the critical standards by which one may judge the artistic excellence of an entertainment film? What are the special problems of acting for the cinema? What are the recent trends and experiments in the development of the cinema as a new art form?

The course will also give a complete presentation of the educational and social aspects of the motion picture, of both the entertainment and nonentertainment types, also illustrated by film showings. What methods have been proposed for the social control of the pictures? What are the pros and cons of censorship? What is the work of the Board of Review? How are motion pictures reviewed and what are the standards set up for recommending them? How may the films be used for purposes of social education? How may motion-picture appreciation be advanced by the public schools? What is the place of the motion picture as a mode of visual instruction in public-school programs and in the more informal types of education? How may a program of visual education, utilizing the full contribution of the motion picture, be developed? [Again, these last lines appear in almost identical form in the piece in *The Educational Screen*.] The various topics will be presented by recognized leaders and authorities.

Revealingly, in 1933–34, Motion Picture and Education had been presented within the specialized division of educational sociology (the department that Thrasher was appointed to) and seems to have been envisioned as meeting specialized needs around training in practical matters; for example, it was listed among other practically oriented courses such as Education in Health or Nature and Needs of the Child in the Social Life. It would appear that initially Motion Picture and Education was to lead to practical activity on the part of educators: at the very least, they would conduct research on the movies' effects; at most, with the results of that research in hand, they would act to curb and control any possible deleterious effects of the motion picture. In contrast, the following year, the new course was offered as part of the School of Education's General Education program, rather than in the specialized area of Educational Sociology. General Education within the School of Education was a program intended to move beyond those divisional courses that aided in career specialization and to deal with broader concerns across the specialities of education. The 1934–35 bulletin of the School of Education captures some of this expansiveness in its very definition of General Education courses: they will be "of interest to students of education in general, or to special students without regard to departmental affiliation. These courses will be accepted as free electives in all undergraduate curricula and some distribution requirements." The new course, then, was no longer just about training in a specific field but about the raising of problems general enough to be of relevance to several fields in education.

Describing the new course, The Motion Picture: Its Artistic, Educational, and Social Aspects, in an August 26, 1934, letter to Ralph Pickett, NYU's secretary, whom he was probably trying to enlist in promotional activities for the course, Thrasher explained that the class constituency logically included "citizens and non-academic people." As one ad for the new version of

Thrasher's course clarified, the class "may be taken by any adult whether college credit is sought or not." In fact, taking certain courses at the School of Education could qualify a public school educator for a salary increment from the New York City Board of Education; Thrasher's new version of the film course was designated as one of those that helped educational professionals rise in the salary ranks of the public schools. The course also seems to have garnered some enrollment from employees of the city government itself, specifically from those branches concerned with social and civic improvement. For instance, it appears that some workers in the New York Department of Public Welfare attended the course.

On paper at least the new manifestation of the course seems quite different from the media-effects study offered only a year earlier. NYU's and the NBR's notices for the revamped version advertised it explicitly as a *new* course and eliminated any reference to the earlier Motion Picture and Education version (even though the new offering had the same course number and occupied the same time slot). Where The Motion Picture and Education had sought scientifically to study the effects of movies, the new course assumed those effects as given: hence, such phrases as "It has been demonstrated" or "It has been shown" in the catalog's references to the impact of cinema. To the extent that the movies' effects had in this way been demonstrated, scholarship could move beyond effects study to new areas of concern. The overall question (and it is worth noting how much the new catalog description employed the question form to suggest the open-endedness of the project) now was, Given that movies have been shown to have effects, how do we evaluate those? It is clear that the answer was far from condemnatory. Movies were not described as unambiguously negative, and the very fact that they were depicted early on in the catalog description as "one of the most tremendous educational forces of modern times" can almost seem affirmative of their powers. Taken out of its immediate context and removed from a curriculum in education, the paragraph that begins "This course will present in compact form" could easily come from any number of film appreciation classes on the books today. Certainly, its emphasis on a goodness that is presented in purely aesthetic terms (as, for example, in the question "What is good photography both from a commercial and from an experimental standpoint?") could appear to be recognizing qualities (or potentialities) of the cinema that were not merely sociological and did not easily fit the rubric of The Motion Picture and Education.

Why had there been such a dramatic change? Here, in moving toward an answer, it is essential to note one consequential change from 1933–34's offering of The Motion Picture and Education that the 1934–35 catalog description signaled: the new rendition of Thrasher's course had the support of the immensely influential reform organization, the National Board of Review. No doubt some impetus for the cultural turn that led to the new manifestation of the course came from NBR sponsorship.[17]

Defining "goodness" in terms both moral and aesthetic, the NBR spread information to the public about films it deemed salutary and hoped that such singling out of worthy titles would be reflected in the box office and thereby encourage producers to make more such works of merit. Thrasher himself offered a paean to the organization in his essay "Education versus Censorship," claiming that the NBR "more than any other force in American life has spread the idea of the education of the public to appreciate and demand good movies rather than the negative approach of forbidding bad ones."[18] Where the framers of the Payne Fund Studies, such as the Reverend William Short, had intended to uncover enough proof of the immoral practices of Hollywood filmmakers and of the deleterious movies that ensued from those practices so that the government could be pushed to enact legislation against movies and the movie business, the NBR took a more reformist approach to moral problems of film. At every phase of the cycle of production, distribution, exhibition, and consumption, this Progressivist philosophy was an optimistic one that imagined change was possible and that improvements in any one sphere could only rebound on the rest of the cycle.

There is no doubt that the NBR appreciated the singular contributions that Thrasher made to The Motion Picture: Its Artistic, Educational, and Social Aspects. It might also be that the NBR administrators considered him little more than a figurehead whose role it was to introduce guest lecturers and disseminate NBR information to students. For example, although an NBR advertisement for the course did list Thrasher as the person to whom inquiries about the course should be addressed, nothing in the notice indicated that he was the course's leader. Quite the contrary, prospective attendees were told simply that, "under the joint auspices of the National Board of Review and New York University," the course would include "many outside speakers who are authorities on their subject." So much did the NBR seem to regard Thrasher as little more than a convener for the class that they pushed in 1937 to have the course recreated in New Haven, Connecticut, with a nonacademic, Evelyn Gerstein, in charge. Gerstein, who had been a film critic for the *Boston Herald* and then the *Boston Evening Transcript*, had lectured in Thrasher's course René Clair and the Social Problem Film. (As noted earlier, her name was also bandied about when Terry Ramsaye demurred from returning to the New School to teach film at the beginning of the 1930s.) In his history of early American film criticism, Myron Lounsbury describes Gerstein as "one of the earliest American critics to write of the motion picture's visual appeal in dynamic, as opposed to purely pictorial, terms."[19] Unfortunately, no information appears to exist on how she might have run her version of Thrasher's course in New Haven, but the very idea that the course could be re-created in toto in different contexts may indicate the extent to which the NBR regarded Thrasher to a large degree as a mere factotum.[20]

Undoubtedly, the perception that Thrasher was in large part a facilitator for the course is not inaccurate. Clearly, much of what he did in the course was to serve at the bidding of the NBR and to take on the role of mere disseminator of information. Additionally, one should not expect that a course that included screenings, general announcements, guest lectures, and so on would give its convener much chance to use the classroom as a site for the articulation of his own ideas. In this respect, it is worth noting that the Motion Picture class ran one day per week from 8:15 to 10:00 P.M., which certainly did not give Thrasher much time, especially when screenings of full-length films are factored in (sometimes, though, the class was allowed to go to 11:00 P.M.).

At the same time, Thrasher's own contribution to the course should not be underestimated. At the very least, he took his role as host for the lectures as that of providing, as he put it, "continuity and synthesis of the diverse materials presented in the course." And he made his own direct contribution by lecturing a number of times in the course: over the years, his topics included ones that predictably fit his earlier background, such as "Social Aspects of Motion Pictures," but he also increasingly used the classroom as a venue for testing out a more purely aesthetic valuation of film through such topics as "The Motion Picture as an Instrument of Cultural Transmission" or "The Exceptional Photoplay." Through such culturally inflected topics, Thrasher was able to open up his own work in new directions.

Around the time that Thrasher began offering The Motion Picture: Its Artistic, Educational, and Social Aspects, he became an active participant in the Executive Committee of the NBR, and it is clear that he came to share more in the NBR's emphasis on film betterment (including aesthetic betterment) than in the denunciatory and more sociological approach of the Payne Fund. Certainly, other participants of the Payne Fund Studies seemed to perceive that Thrasher was moving away from the sociological critique of cinema as deleterious low form. For instance, on December 24, 1935, Payne Fund researcher Edgar Dale wrote to Thrasher to caution, "Whether you wish it or not, you are now definitely labeled as being pro-industry and pro-Hays . . . you cannot escape being considered as a spokesman for the motion picture industry in your present set-up." In their study of Thrasher's and Cressey's aborted volume for the Payne Fund Studies, film historians Jowett, Jarvie, and Fuller hypothesize that one of the reasons for nonpublication was the apparent lack of fit between the philosophy of the Payne Fund administrators—who wanted a study that would see the movies as directly causal of delinquency—and the research conclusions that Cressey and Thrasher were coming to: namely, that only in some contexts were the effects of film deleterious and that in other contexts the movies' impact could be quite salutary.

Whether it was the NBR that sought out Thrasher or the reverse, the NBR clearly came to see Thrasher's course The Motion Picture: Its Artistic, Educational, and Social Aspects as a venture that well represented and advanced its own reformist program. It was to its advantage to promote the course to as many people as possible and to have as many worthy citizens as possible enroll in it. For the NBR, clearly it was a great public relations coup to have this affiliation with academia, and NBR missives expressed the desire for there to be press and radio coverage of the course, although nothing appears to have come of this.

At the NBR's encouragement, the course was advertised to the general public, and it does seem that it attracted strong enrollments. Letters, publicity flyers, and other documents suggest that anywhere from 100 to 500 people attended the individual sessions. Thrasher himself wrote to NBR executive secretary Wilton Barrett about a month into the first semester of its first year to say that 120 students were enrolled in the course, and they had just taken a field trip to the Vitagraph studio. An intriguing confirmation of the course's popularity appears in one of the handouts that were distributed weekly to the students: it cautioned that some interlopers had forged the names of enrolled students in order to sneak into the class for individual sessions!

While Thrasher's course was offered for credit to students in the School of Education, the NBR also wanted it to reach people of influence in the metropolitan community, such as teachers, activists, and reformers. For example, NBR members were given special notice of a course lecture on "Music in Films"; perhaps the NBR administration felt that the society patrons who made up a large part of the reformist constituency of the NBR would find particular appeal in a topic so evidently about aesthetic uplift. Likewise, Thrasher had the NBR provide him with mailing lists (e.g., of those Women's Clubs the board was affiliated with) for NYU to use in sending out materials. He even convinced the board to try to recruit for the course among film studio staff on the East Coast. Thus, on September 25, 1934, Thrasher sent a note to Wilton Barrett at the NBR, suggesting that Barrett write to producers to "find out if any members of their staff or organization would be interested in taking the Motion Picture course." Barrett agreed to do so and got at least one response: Leon J. Bamberger at RKO wrote back to Barrett on October 2 that he was distributing the announcement of the course to "every executive and department head at this office, asking them to bring it to the attention of all their employees. . . . we trust that many of the employees will take advantage of this course."

Although there seems to have been no direct subvention to Thrasher from the NBR, it is clear that it provided various forms of material support, and he regularly sent in reports on the course as if to acknowledge its contribution. Much of the NBR's aid seemed to come in the form of contacts the board had with film-related circles. Thrasher had acquaintances in the academic community to draw upon as lecturers for his course, but the NBR clearly had the clout and connections to recruit important and often prestigious speakers from the film industry. For example, on September 17, 1934, Wilton Barrett invited Harry Warner to speak on "The Problems of Motion Picture Production," explaining in his letter to the mogul, "It is encouraging to find that the medium of the motion picture has at last received at the hands of a great eastern University the recognition it deserves as a subject for serious study, and the National Board of Review is happy to have had a prominent part in bringing this about and in organizing the study course." (It must be said, however, that nothing in the available records confirms whether Warner did in fact come to the class.)

Barrett used his influence to negotiate reduced rental fees for the films Thrasher showed over the years. Some of the 1930s screenings included *Lot in Sodom* (1933), *The Cabinet of Dr. Caligari* (1920), *Shattered* (1921), *The Passion of Joan of Arc* (1928), *The Blood of a Poet* (1930), *The Road to Life* (1931), *Potemkin* (1925), and *The Mechanics of the Brain* (1926). Many of these films represent canonical works of adventurous film art and confirm the extent to which Thrasher's course was serving as an important venue for the introduction of a wide audience to important experiments in cinematic experimentation. Moreover, in their avant-garde status, these works had rarely, if ever, been part of a sociological discourse on film; in this respect, it would seem that the screening choices confirm the sense of Thrasher's course as one increasingly devoted to an *art* of cinema no longer enclosed within questions of sociological pertinence. (Nonetheless, some of the films may have pushed the envelope of acceptability for some audience members who came with an agenda more geared to issues of film morality. In 1940, two college teachers were upset by a screening of Buñuel and Dali's *Un Chien Andalou*, and Thrasher had to offer an apology to the NBR.)

The course also became a venue for previews of uplifting or aesthetically accomplished narrative films of the sort the NBR advocated. For example, the quality feature films *Sequoia* and *Les Misérables* both were screened in Thrasher's class before their theatrical release. Likewise, Barrett was able to arrange a special screening of the Hungarian film *Spring Shower*, by Paul Fejos (whose American film *Lonesome* was a darling of the film-betterment crowd), and Thrasher based a course assignment on that screening, requiring students to write one-page reviews of Fejos's film.

Most important, Thrasher relied on the NBR to help broaden his own knowledge of film. Movies may have been a "hobby" for him, but he had not worked through either the history of film (especially nonmainstream film) or its critical literature in any systematic way, and he would write to Wilton Barrett for enlightenment on particular topics. For example, when a distributor confirmed that he could not get Cocteau's *Blood of a Poet* in time for guest lecturer Julien Levy's talk on the "The Motion Picture as an Instrument of Creative Art," Thrasher quickly sent off a missive to Barrett on January 9, 1935, noting, "I think you suggested one entitled 'Potemkin.' I am not familiar with that film, however." Clearly, he would learn his lesson well, since by the end of the 1930s he was celebrating *Potemkin* as one of the great works of independent cinematic art. Likewise, on February 28, 1935, Thrasher wrote to Barrett that he had a student who wanted to study photoplay structure, and he needed to know what books to recommend; Barrett's answer was to suggest NBR member Frances Taylor Patterson's *Scenario and Screen*.

There were also material benefits for the NBR in its association with Thrasher. Thrasher used the course, for instance, as a venue in which to advertise NBR activities. For example, he handed out invitations to the students to the annual NBR conventions, typically held in New York City; in fact, Thrasher sometimes arranged for course sessions to take place concurrently with convention events so that interested parties could attend both. He assigned select issues of the NBR's journal as required reading and even used the course to recruit new members to the organization: anyone who took both semesters of The Motion Picture: Its Artistic, Educational, and Social Aspects was eligible to join the general membership of the NBR.

More pointedly, Thrasher used his course to instruct his students about film in ways that clearly complemented and fed into the NBR philosophy of film. For example, in keeping with the NBR interest in dissemination of news about valuable film experiences, each week Thrasher gave his students long, informative handouts. Predictably, these included program notes on the evening's screenings and biography of the speaker for that session, but the handouts—which would often reach five pages or more—also offered news about film activities in the larger metropolitan area. For instance, the handouts provided recommendations of films for the students to see (and, if they were public school teachers, to recommend to their own students; for example, one handout said of the 1936 film *The Robber Symphony* that "teachers will find it an excellent photoplay to delight their classes"). There also were notices of theaters for which arrangements had been made for reduced ticket prices for artistic films that the NBR had decided to promote (e.g., one theater promised a reduction if twenty-five or more class members attended any single showing of MGM's *Romeo and Juliet*). In an effort to inform students of those films that critics deemed "Best," the handouts reprinted "Ten Best" lists from various publications, including, predictably, the NBR's own magazine, the *New York Daily Post, Film Daily, Hollywood Spectator,* and, interestingly, the Communist Party publication the *Worker* (later known as the *Daily Worker*). The handouts also included notices of employment opportunities related to reform work, arts education, or both. Thus, one week's handout advertised for a movie reviewer for the children's publication of the Religious Motion Picture Foundation. There were also announcements of uplifting events in the allied arts: for instance, one handout lauded a shadow play at the Hudson Guild Theater. Finally, the handouts encouraged students to patronize the little movie theaters that specialized in art cinema, such as the 8th Street Playhouse, the 55th Street Playhouse, the Cinema de Paris, the Filmarte, devoted, as the handout put it, to "distinguished foreign films," and "the several small cinema houses which frequently revive distinguished films." In this way, the handouts did not merely deal with film as visual education in the schools but clearly also militated for a notion of film as salutary fine art. Students in Thrasher's course were being taught about uses of film in the classroom, but they were also being given a more general arts education, one that presented film as part of the vibrant experimental culture of the metropolis.

Importantly, in keeping with a primary NBR activity, Thrasher's course devoted time to encouraging those of its students who were (or were studying to be) teachers in the public school system, or who worked with youth agencies, to create Scholastic Photoplay Clubs. Such clubs, also known as 4-Star clubs, were one of the central activities of film-betterment organizations like the NBR in the 1930s, and Thrasher's course was a fundamental venue for explaining to public school personnel and youth agency organizers how such clubs could be formed and how they would function. Briefly, the clubs were intended to create extracurricular groups in which children and adolescents would engage with the movies.[21] Under the supervision of trained advisers/teachers, young people would learn to appreciate the finer aspects of movies—both in consumption through training in refined film viewing *and* in production through training in filmmaking. For example, in his *Photoplay Appreciation in American High Schools*, which served as the veritable manual for teachers desirous of organizing clubs at the high school level, William Lewin, the chair of the photoplay appreciation committee of the National Council of Teachers of English, suggested that in the photoplay clubs students could hone their skills in the consumption of films by reading established critics, by seeing and discussing movies, by writing journals on the role of movies in everyday life, and so on. Likewise, students could come to appreciate the power of movies by making movies themselves: the photoplay clubs would encourage group filmmaking projects in which students would learn and apply techniques of film production and postproduction.[22]

Thrasher's course militated for photoplay clubs by a variety of means. First, he handed out descriptions of how such clubs worked and how public school teachers and youth agency personnel might go about creating them. Second, Thrasher regularly began his class with guest presentations (usually around three minutes in length) by "junior reviewers"—students from the public schools who would either recount how photoplay clubs had worked in their schools or give practical examples of their work by reading their film criticism or even by projecting a film their club had made. Third, and perhaps most important, Thrasher listed the creation of a photoplay club as one of the ways students in The Motion Picture: Its Artistic, Educational, and Social Aspects could meet the course's requirements (I will return to the other options in a moment). As the syllabus put it:

> Students working in connection with settlements or other social agencies, teachers, or principals, may find it interesting to organize and conduct a photoplay club. In case there are members in the class who are already conducting such clubs the term project will consist of a careful account of the activities of the club during the term and is to be written up in full and handed in at the end of the term. In the case of students who organize and conduct a photoplay club, a complete account of the organization and activities of the club and its problems is to be handed in at the end of the term. Hints as to how to organize and conduct a photoplay club in schools and elsewhere may be obtained from the ma-

terials on 4-Star Clubs distributed to members of the class. Additional information as to how such clubs carry on their activities may be obtained by addressing a letter or a postcard to Dr. Thrasher.

Part of a broader, concerted 1930s valorization of such activities on the part of a wide array of educators, civic activists, and social reformers, Thrasher's classroom promotion of the photoplay clubs is indicative of the interconnected ways his course was reconceiving film, in line with NBR philosophy, as a practice both social and cultural. Obviously, for instance, the emphasis on training young people in the techniques of refined film criticism fit the model of moral amelioration through aesthetic training espoused by reform organizations like the NBR. Likewise, the emphasis on training in the practical techniques of an art fed back into that general valorization of craft and workmanship so central to American ideologies of valued human activity. Whatever the fruits of their labor, junior filmmakers would benefit from the sheer accomplishment of having crafted something they could look back on with pride. (No doubt, many Americans still remember the arts-and-crafts objects they fashioned for their parents, which were considered valuable simply for the effort that had gone into them. The pedagogical philosophy at work here is one that imagines it is good to craft things, whatever the aesthetic value of the results.)

Certainly, however, it would be even more salutary were the efforts of a junior filmmaker to lead to the production of works that had value beyond the mere pride that comes from personal craftsmanship. On the one hand, in keeping with the tenets of a visual education that imagined a film to be worthy insofar as it offered instruction about the world, many photoplay clubs were encouraged to make films of a documentary sort. A typical topic was life in the school or the local neighborhood. Reports on such efforts in the NBR magazine and in Thrasher's own Metropolitan Motion Picture Council newsletter frequently recounted how such films were successfully shown to parent groups or in class assemblies. Here was a direct rendition of the interconnections of the motion picture and education. On the other hand, it is clear that just as exercises in the clubs in photoplay appreciation and in refined consumption took the fiction film as their primary object, so too did production work in the clubs frequently concern itself with the well-made artistic film of fiction. Students were instructed in an array of artistic topics, ranging from good cinematography (lighting, composition, rules for establishing continuity, and so on) to effective plot construction. Movies did not always have to instruct about the school or community: it would be as valuable to make films that could bring higher entertainment in fiction form to that school or community.

In this way, the photoplay clubs supported an expansive notion of film's role in education, and it is clear that Thrasher's course centrally promoted this more affirmative and cultural understanding of film as educational force. Film was valued as a form of visual education but also as aesthetic accomplishment. Indeed, other term-paper requirements for the course suggest how Thrasher's course was being conceived as engaging with the affective and cultural powers of film. (Each semester also ended with a short-answer exam composed of two hundred questions. One handout from 1935–36 wryly reports on the first semester's exam: "It was generally conceded by students in the Motion Picture course that the final examination for the first term of 1935–36 pretty well covered the work of the term. Students who took the examination provided a good deal of interesting information to the instructor. Among other things, four students credited Alexander Dumas with writing 'Anna Karenina'. . . . One student referred to a picture which he called 'The Lot of Sodom,' and another optimistic soul declared that the editor of the Motion Picture Herald was Frederic M. Thrasher.")

For the final assignment, students could choose from among five kinds of term projects. In addition to organizing a photoplay club in which public school children might make films, students in Thrasher's course were given the option of making a film themselves to meet class requirements. Here, again, the objective of such practical work ran the gamut from the directly educational to the more elusively cultural. We can see the variety of goals in the syllabus description:

> *Make your own movie.* Students having motion picture cameras may make a movie. In this case the scenario must be in the hands of Dr. Thrasher before the actual shooting begins. In case this alternative is chosen, it is recommended that the student take out a membership in the Amateur Cinema League . . . and avail himself of the excellent service and advice offered to amateur movie-makers.
>
> Students planning to make their own movies should purchase and study Arthur L. Gale's new and interesting volume, *How to Write a Movie*. . . . In this book the basic principles of film planning are presented in simple terms for new movie makers and are illustrated with numerous examples of movie episodes. . . . Plot and scenario writing for amateur photoplays, industrial and publicity films are explained in simple, understandable terms. Planning films for lecture use, presentation with music and sound effects and for sound on film post-

synchronization is covered in detail. Simple methods for getting entertaining pictures with amateur sound cameras are given. . . . Fundamentals of talkie scenario writing are presented clearly and are illustrated with sample talkie scripts.

Most notable perhaps in this presentation of the filmmaking option is the extent to which it did not assume that a film course in a school of education necessarily should instruct in the making of traditional *instructional* or *educational* films. The production of such films certainly was held out as an option—as we see in the mention of "films for lecture use"—but the reigning assumption was that any number of types of film were worthy of production and could have values of uplift and betterment, including, for instance, the scripted fictional film. As much as the assignment was concerned with the purely educational film, it was also geared to the making of what it termed simply "entertaining pictures."

Another assignment option encouraged the students to build a scrapbook of movie reviews and articles they came across in the mainstream press. As the syllabus explained,

> The scrapbook should contain one review of a motion picture for each day of the course and any other articles of interest which pertain to motion pictures. 100 clippings are considered a minimum requirement for this work. Neatness should be observed but the selection and arrangement of the clippings are considered more important than the artistic appearance of the scrapbook. Every item included in the book *must be accompanied by a notation as to its source and date*.

The scrapbook seems an option that fully treated film in aesthetic terms. This option—which evidently supposed that the work of professional film critics might serve as models by which the students could refine and articulate their own aesthetic understanding of film art—was very similar to one frequently practiced in the photoplay clubs of the public schools. There, in similar fashion, young people were encouraged to keep scrapbooks of reviews and study them in terms of their aesthetic precepts and presuppositions. In his book on photoplay appreciation in the high schools, William Lewin (a regular lecturer in Thrasher's course) assumed that such an assignment would appeal more to girls than to boys, and it is worth contemplating that Thrasher's course may have supposed the same gender split among his own students at the college and adult level. Certainly, the reference to "neatness" has a patronizing quaintness.

Another course option even more directly connects Thrasher's course to the film appreciation courses that still fill the curricula of so many universities today. Quite simply, students were offered the possibility of writing term papers, and many of the suggested topics encouraged a cultural or aesthetic approach to the movies. Of the fifty-eight suggested topics, at least the first twenty-four were geared to understanding the cinema as an independent cultural form. Here, it is helpful to cite some of these:

History of the Motion Picture. To be a general study of the development of the motion picture from its beginnings to its present status.

The Art of Motion Picture Photography. To be a study of what constitutes good photography—perspective, the close-up, distance shots, montage, lighting, balance and focus, blends, double exposure, treatment of action, film editing, etc.

Development of the Entertainment Film. To be a study of the evaluation of the entertainment film from its simple beginnings to the varied types of films presented currently in the theater.

The Motion Picture as an Art Form. To be a study of the relative contributions of photography, montage, color, sound, motion, symbolism, etc. and to include a discussion of the realistic, imaginative and abstract trends in the films, and the experimental film. What is pure cinema?

The Directing of Photoplays. To be a study of the function of the director in producing motion pictures. Who are the great directors and what have their special contributions been?

Foreign Films. To be a comparative study of the entertainment films of the foreign countries with special emphasis upon England, Germany, France, and Russia.

Color in the Motion Picture. To be a comparative study of color processes and their effectiveness together with a discussion of general contribution of color and its future potentialities.

Here, again, we appear to be quite far from the 1933–34 Motion Picture and Education course, with its emphasis, as described earlier, on "scientific evaluation of the effects of the motion picture, commercialized and educational, upon children and adults, as to intellectual content, emotions, conduct and attitudes, sleep, delinquency and crime, and morality." The discourse now was as much a humanities-style one of great directors, important national traditions, potentialities of artistic processes, generic diversity, aesthetic purity and ideal form, valuations of the good, history of the medium as increasing refinement and complexification, and so on.

To be sure, the sociological bent had not disappeared from the course. The list of suggested topics for the term paper also included more social science–friendly topics as "Medical and Clinical Films," "Researches as to the Social and Educational Aspects of Entertainment Films," "The Imitation of

Movie Patterns," "The Motion Picture as an Instrument of Visual Instruction," and "The Place of the Motion Picture in Relation to Other Visual Aids and the Course of Study." Likewise, another final assignment option for the course connected back to one of Thrasher's earliest research interests and shows that he had not left sociology behind. Here, students were given the possibility of writing what the syllabus referred to as their "motion picture life history." From his background in the streetwise sociology of the Chicago school and from his own down-and-dirty investigations of gangs, Thrasher had come to have great faith in autobiographical accounts as a source of sociological information. Today, it might seem commonsensical to incorporate such accounts into sociological investigation, but in the early days of urban sociology, as Robert L. Whitley, one of Thrasher's researchers on the Boys Club study, explained, many mainstream sociologists felt that accounts by participants could only be subjective and biased, too particularistic, too impressionistic, and so on.[23] Thrasher admitted that other kinds of data such as statistical renderings were also essential to a full sociological investigation, but he insisted that there was a place for personal narrative within the research project. His own book on gangs in Chicago had relied heavily on interviews and testimony. When he and Cressey spun off their Payne Fund movie research project from the Boys Club study, they built much of their own materials from delinquent boys who were asked to recount movies they had seen, scenes they remembered, life lessons they had thereby garnered, and so on.[24]

For his Motion Picture course, Thrasher imported interview methods—and even specific questions—from the movie portion of the Boys Club study.[25] A five-page handout explained the steps the student should take in preparing a "motion picture life history." In the handout's words, the overall point was as follows:

> The most interesting subject in the world for most of us is ourselves. Yet it is a subject we know little about. . . . We are asking you to think about the influences which motion pictures have had upon you, your likes and dislikes, your ideas on life and your beliefs. Writing your motion picture life history will not only be a fine experience for you, but will also be valuable in helping to understand movies. One way to find out how people are influenced by motion pictures is to ask them. Each person is asked to write the story of their motion picture experience, beginning with their earliest recollection and carrying the story down to the present time.

The assignment was divided into parts. In the first, students were asked to recount generally the influences in their lives (what sort of family and neighborhood they had grown up in, what forms of entertainment and culture they had experienced, and so on) and how they had internalized these influences (as the assignment declares, "Some people always see the world through 'rose-colored glasses' and think everything is O.K. Others are always gloomy, always sure things are going to get worse. . . . Just what kind of person are you? Are you a gloom, or do you believe everything is all right? How come you got that way?")

In the second part, students were asked to talk about the specific impact of motion pictures. Here they were instructed to deal with the role of movies in seven different spheres (in the following list, quotations are taken from the assignment and are followed by my commentary):

1. "Write about your childhood experiences with the movies": students were to talk about their earliest movie memories, their first likes and dislikes, the stars they connected to, the people they went to the movies with, their comportment at the theater, and the influence of the movies on their childhood play.
2. "Describe how motion pictures have affected your ambitions and moods": students were instructed to recount both the emotions they felt during and after screenings of films *and* their ability rationally to control those feelings.
3. "Write as full and accurate an account as you can of what you have consciously imitated from the screen and added to the different ways you act."
4. "Describe your experience with pictures of love and romance": students were asked to describe how stars came to serve as romantic ideals and thereby influence how they might interact with real-life romantic partners.
5. "Talk of any ambitions and temptations which you received from the movies": in this section, students were to comment on the hopes and dreams, both good and bad, that movies had instilled in them. For example, "Have the movies ever caused you to rebel, or want to rebel against your parents? Did you get ideas of how much freedom you should have from the way in which children, young men and young women are given privileges in motion pictures?"
6. "Describe as completely as you can any movie experiences which have given you ideals or strengthened those which you already had." This section is in keeping with Thrasher's and Cressey's ideas of film as a form of "informal education." Against the intent of the original framers of the Payne Fund Studies who wanted evidence that films caused bad behavior, Thrasher and Cressey came to focus more on how films either reinforced

or challenged existing attitudes. For example, one question asked, "Have you seen any pictures which you felt broke down any narrow-mindedness in you?" Films might not always be the primary source of social ideas, although they could reinforce ideas that citizens already possessed.

7. "Trace the development of your notions concerning the reality of motion pictures": Here, students were directed to examine the ways in which the fictions on-screen could be confused with reality. For example, questions asked: "Do you believe in the life shown on the screen? Have you believed that to be true of real life as well as life in the movies? Does a picture which turns out sadly have any effects upon you?"

The life story assignment seems very much in keeping with media-effects aspects of the original Motion Picture course that were still in play even after Thrasher's pedagogy had opened itself to a very strong culturalist inflection. Film here was treated not as stylistic or formal practice but as a vehicle for representations and misrepresentations of life. Significantly, when the last section of the assignment directed students to compare movies and reality, the assumption appears to have been that a lack of faithfulness of art to life was a potential danger—a potential source of misleading ideas—rather than a mark of art's accomplishment in creating imaginative universes with no obligation to offer a realistic copy of life. As significantly, however, other assignment choices—for example, the moviemaking option, with its emphasis on style for its own sake, or the term papers, in which, among others, one topic had promoted an idea of "pure cinema"—construct an image of the course as much more emphatically concerned with questions of culture and artistic value.

At times, the course almost can seem an exercise in schizophrenia in its attempts to reconcile its original sociological intent with the cultural turn that Thrasher seemed to be opening up to. In fact, Thrasher's course The Motion Picture set out to deal with conflicting identities for film—mere empirical force among others in society? art form that took a relative autonomy from any identity as mere social practice?—*by splitting its curriculum in two*. Each semester of the yearlong course had a clear and distinctive focus, with the first emphasizing cinema's cultural identity and the second constituting film as an object of the social sciences. (Students could enroll for both semesters or just one or the other.) In a short survey of mid-1930s courses devoted to film, the National Board of Review's magazine offered a good description of the split between semesters in Thrasher's pedagogy: "The first term will be devoted largely to the evolution of the motion picture and its technical and artistic problems. The second term will deal more largely with the educational and social aspects of the movies."[26]

To be sure, the division was not absolutely clear-cut. In part, there may have needed to be some flexibility around the availability of the various visiting lecturers. For the most part, though, the course clearly divided into a first semester that dealt with the ways movies were made and with the qualities that established cinema as an art, *and* a second semester that dealt with sociological issues of the movies' impact and influence on behavior. In this respect, the second semester more directly approximated the media-effects concerns of the course in its original Motion Picture and Education manifestation.

A number of syllabi exist from 1935 on that provide a fairly explicit sense of the division between semesters and the content of each. For example, the first semester of the 1935–36 academic year included lectures by, among others, Terry Ramsaye on the "march of the movies" (with a "special screening of an unusual film"); Society of Motion Picture Engineers member Russell Clark on "The Technical Development of the Motion Picture"; Wilton Barrett from the NBR on "The Experimental Film" (with a screening of Webber and Watson films "to illustrate the art of motion picture photography"); Columbia music professor Douglas Moore on "Music in Motion Pictures"; French filmmaker Jean Benoît-Levy on "The Production and Direction of Photoplays" ("illustrated by special showing of his own 'La Maternelle'"); Fred Waller (the inventor, later, of Cinerama) on "The Short Subject and the Animated Cartoon"; Roy W. Winton, director of the Amateur Cinema League, on "Personal Motion Pictures"; Stanford University professor of English Henry David Gray on "The Author and the Motion Picture"; American Civil Liberties Union director Arthur Garfield Hays on "Motion Picture Censorship"; MoMA curator Iris Barry on "The Art of the Motion Picture"; and attorney Louis Nizer on "Trade Practices in the Motion Picture Industry." Many of the guests returned over the years to speak on the same topics, but there were also notable new lecturers in subsequent sessions: for example, in the following year, the course included lectures by Pare Lorenz on "The Documentary Film," noted composer George Antheil on film music, and Max Fleischer on film animation.

Such an array of speakers and topics certainly does not resemble a course on motion pictures and education; even more, it seems quite far from the media-effects emphasis all too visible in the first (1933–34) manifestation of Thrasher's film teaching. Film was now presented as having a resonant history (in Terry Ramsaye's image, the movies "march" through time); as dividing into significant genres, many of which went beyond Hollywood entertainment (e.g., the personal film, the experimental film, the animated film, and, more generally, the overall rubric of the artistic film); and as deriving from a labor-intensive production process but also from a context of personal authorship. To the extent that the course dealt with industrial and economic issues—as in Arthur Garfield Hays's talk on censorship or Louis Nizer's on industry practices—it is more than likely that these were seen within the context of a cultural appreciation of cinema. In other words, in keeping with NBR philosophy, cinema was imagined to be a resonant cultural form, one that should be allowed to have full rein of expression (hence, no censorship) and that would best be served by efficient, rational, and moral business practices arising from within the film industry (rather than imposed by legislation).

On the other hand, the second semester for the course more typically resembled one in which cinema would be treated *as a sociological object* that had empirical and emphatically nonaesthetic or extra-aesthetic effects in society. In the 1935–36 academic year, for instance, lecturers included Robert A. Kissack Jr., a noted analyst of visual education, on "Motion Pictures in College Education"; famed psychiatrist A. A. Brill (later an important figure in the NBR) on "Psychiatric Aspects of Motion Pictures"; Dr. William Snow, director of the American Social Hygiene Association, on "The Motion Picture and Social Hygiene" ("illustrated by a private showing of a film originally banned by the New York State Board of Censors"); Dr. Joseph F. Montague of the New York Intestinal Sanatorium on "Medical and Clinical Films"; Dr. V. C. Anspiger of ERPI Pictures on "The Educational Talking Picture"; Arthur Gale of *Movie Makers Magazine* on "Industrial Films"; and Dr. Raymond Ditmars, curator of mammals and reptiles for the New York Zoological Park, along with Grace Fisher Ramsey, associate curator at the American Museum of Natural History, on "Scientific Films and the Role of the Museum in Visual Education."

Obviously, there is a greater sense here than in the first semester of a course for committed specialists and professionals, even to the extent of including a private screening of a banned film that it was assumed the viewers would be professional enough to view without deleterious effect. Very few of the topics have a specifically cultural component, and even the ones that do seem to deal as much with social issues. Very clearly, film was treated as an object of social science analysis and examined for the ways it took up a place alongside other anodyne practices of everyday social life.

I have referred to the course's structure as schizophrenic, and here it is perhaps necessary to unpack that metaphor. On the one hand, it is certainly possible to read the inflection of the course away from its 1933–34 media-effects orientation as a dramatic *break* in which a sociologist such as Thrasher came to realize the limits of a purely social science understanding of cinema as a source of everyday empirical effects. Such indeed seems to be the position of Jowett et al. in their study of Cressey's and Thrasher's failure to produce a study that fit the denunciatory framework that had originally driven the Payne Fund Studies. In their book, they pointedly assert that Cressey "had an intellectual epiphany in the fall of 1932" that led to a "180-degree turnabout" in the film research he and Thrasher were undertaking.[27] Jowett et al. argue that from an earlier monocausal understanding of film as having a singular and special role in sparking delinquency, Cressey (and Thrasher) now came to understand society as a complex mesh of diverse forces and influences, such that no one social practice—in this case, the movies—could be considered to be inevitably and exclusively determinant of social behavior.

On the other hand, it may well be that for Thrasher the opening up of the sociological model was not so punctual and complete as the notion of "epiphany" implies. It is clear, for instance, that the film-betterment philosophy of the 1930s that Thrasher adopted through affiliation with the NBR did not draw a sharp distinction between cinema as a social phenomenon and an aesthetic one. For example, betterment might come from a film's transmission of a beneficial content (film, in other words, as an aesthetically neutral vehicle of informal visual education), but it might equally derive from aesthetic qualities that added artistry to a culturally impoverished society (film, in other words, as something "good" in its aesthetic qualities). The motion picture course may have broken into two parts, but opening with a semester on film's formal qualities, medium specificity, aesthetic powers, and so on may have led the more exclusively sociological understanding of film offered in the second semester to be understood *within* a larger context that started from an essential recognition of film's primary status as cultural form. As Thrasher described the structure of his course in the short essay "The Sociological Approach to Motion Pictures in Relation to Education" (1938), the first goal was to offer students "a broad background of knowledge *and appreciation* of motion pictures. . . . *After* this ground-work of understanding of fundamental motion problems is laid, the student is next introduced to the educational and social aspects of the film and the various ways in which the schools can relate themselves advantageously to motion pictures."[28]

There is, however, another possible way to understand the relationship between the sociological and the aesthetic in regard to the split in Thrasher's course, and it is this other possible articulation of their relationship that I now want to posit. Specifically, I want to suggest that Thrasher's own writings on film posit that film's status *in some contexts* is primarily sociological and *in other contexts* is primarily aesthetic.

Earlier, I implied some of the dimensions of this bifurcated understanding of film on Thrasher's part when I noted how he combined a relativist understanding of film's value as deriving from particular cases of its consumption by specific social groups with a universalist faith that beyond any such context-specific acts of consumption there were still general standards of what a good film should be. An expansive philosophy of film—one that dealt both with film's relative reception by specific social constituencies and with the regulative ideal of universal aesthetic judgment—was necessary to deal with all the ways films work in our world.

In particular, Thrasher appeared to assume that for *youth* audiences film's effects would be primarily sociological, while an adult spectator might possess the necessary distance from mere emotional investment, simple character identification, and confusion of life and art to be able to appreciate film as an aesthetic object. We might remember, for instance, how the motion picture life stories that Thrasher allowed as one option for his course's final assignment asked students about moments from their life history in which they had mistaken movies for reality. The temptation to confuse the two was always a risk for children and adolescents, and for that sort of audience Thrasher seems to have accepted the necessary intervention of sociology. But he also assumed that adults had the potential to be able to discount film's reality effect. With such discernment in hand, adults could appreciate movies as the purely aesthetic forms they deeply were. This is one reason why, for instance, in "Education versus Censorship," Thrasher opposed censorship: while there needed to be concern about the effects of film on youth, censorship ran the risk of making unavailable those quality works of film art that would be valuable to adults able to appreciate their aesthetic virtues. Here, Thrasher's position approximated that of the film-betterment movement, which sometimes advocated separate forms of cinema for children and adults—separate screenings, separate kinds of film, and so on—so that adults could enjoy the mature art while children's morally fraught forms of moviegoing could be controlled.

And if movies could be aesthetically salutary for adults, they were not necessarily bad for children either. For Thrasher and Cressey, film was only one of many influences on youth, and it was far from always a deleterious one. In fact, both Thrasher and Cressey frequently contended that films possessed consequential social influences in specific contexts of children's or adolescents' viewing only to the extent that the countervailing influences of other social or cultural institutions were absent. For instance, for Cressey, films came most to constitute "informal education" in those intense cases where schooling, the family, and uplifting leisure were inadequate or lacking to the child and were therefore unavailable as countervailing forces.

Even for the delinquent child or adolescent, there were so many other vivid temptations in city life that film's impact could pale by comparison. Even more than Cressey's, Thrasher's work on delinquents frequently showed them as uninterested in aspects of moviegoing that seemed to them to involve passivity (the spectator rapt before the screen). One factor that allowed Thrasher, from his earliest work on gangs onward, to underplay any major deleterious effect of motion picture narratives on the lives of children and adolescents was that he imagined those lives themselves to frequently take on narrative forms so dramatic and exciting as to render the fictional narratives offered by film as, by comparison, meager and relatively lacking in impact. That is, urban life was such a source of gripping stories that the tales projected on the movie screen frequently seemed inconsequential or ersatz. From the start of *The Gang*, city experience itself is figured in vibrant narrative form. For example, on the third page, Thrasher tells us, "It is in such regions as the gang inhabits that we find much of the romance and mystery of a great city. Here are comedy and tragedy. Here is melodrama which excels the recurrent 'thrillers' at the downtown theaters."[29] That life for city-dwelling gang members itself took on the generic forms of fiction meant that those top-down narratives presented to them by such forms as the movies could only appear distant, minor, even irrelevant. Thus, to the extent that gang members set out to engage in leisure activity, they might often choose to eschew the passive experience of moviegoing, where they would simply be watching distant stories presented for passive absorption, for more participatory narratives in which they themselves would be active players. For example, Thrasher contended that for the gang member, a hands-on activity like football was "of intense interest because the conflict it involves is personal, direct, and dangerous" (100).

Thrasher suggested that gang activity itself was an exciting narrative that often surpassed the mere passive entertainment of the movies. The gang itself evolved in dramatic form. In a first, prenarrative stage, the gang came into being when a group of young people found their interests coinciding but could initially evolve no definite plan of action. As the group coalesced and formulated projects, going around aimlessly in circles gave way to linearity: the group advanced into the world and made claims on it. That world, made up of other gangs, forces of authority, and the ordinary citizens of the city, reacted (usually negatively), and the gang's worldly engagement would turn combative. Thrasher saw the us-them moment in which the gang warred with others as a decisive moment in the drama. The gang's conflict with the world would issue either in temporary victory and consolidation of the gang's position or, more likely, in defeat and dispersion as gang members drifted off (or grew up and accepted adult responsibility). But before the moment of defeat and dissolution, the gang's trajectory resembled nothing so much as a well-made narrative in which there is an initial state, followed by confrontation and crisis, and, finally, dramatic resolution. For the gang member, this was an exciting story indeed.

The narratives presented on the screens of the moving picture houses would often seem lesser by comparison. When gang members did mention moviegoing in *The Gang*, they tended to do so only in passing and without reference to any specific titles: movies frequently were incidental and fairly forgettable in the larger narrative of personal everyday life activity. Thus, rare citation of a specific movie title in *The Gang* came when Thrasher recounted how he tried to take one gang member to something other than an action film—in this case, a local offering entitled *Enemies of Women*—only to have the boy declare that he hated that kind of romantic picture and run off (103).[30]

For Thrasher, it was at most only certain kinds of films (namely, films of pounding action) that in certain contexts only—ones in which there was the absence of effective countervailing social institutions such as family or school—would have a morally worrisome impact on a certain kind of spectator: namely, the gang boy. By implication, then, if there were improvements in any of these elements—the type of film, the efficacy of countervailing context, a differently trained spectator—the entire situation would change, and a different impact of the movies might be gained. It is in this respect, for instance, that Thrasher so militated for the photoplay clubs and film appreciation classes, since their goal was to show schoolchildren how to appreciate an ostensibly finer sort of cinema that could substitute for visceral action pictures. As he put it in his essay "The Sociological Approach to Motion Pictures in Relation to Education," schools should implement the "introduction of motion picture appreciation courses as units of study. This is highly important in order that children may learn to discriminate between worthless pictures and those which are socially valid and artistically adequate. Such discrimination naturally registers at the box office and encourages producers to make more acceptable pictures."[31]

Gang boys, Thrasher argued, were vulnerable to the emotional appeals of mass culture and to a confusion of life and images only as "a consequence of the disorganized state of their social milieu and their own lack of contact with organizing influences" (*The Gang*, 115). The sociologist's goal was to fight against negative influences of mass culture, but one central way to do this was to be precise about what culture at its best could be: not a deleterious emotional seduction, not a misleading substitute for life, but an independent art form in its own right to be enjoyed as nonutilitarian aesthetic object. To be sure, Thrasher did not assume that children and adolescents could fully be taught to distinguish art and life and thereby develop their own independent aesthetics of cinema; to the extent that there would always remain some temptation for young viewers to accept films as realistic representation, the sociologist as much as the aesthetician had an essential role to play in children's and adolescents' viewing experiences.

But the *adult* spectator could be taught the art of film, and to this extent, Thrasher provided lineaments of an aesthetics of film alongside his sociology. Thrasher's aesthetic may not seem particularly deep, especially by the standards of today's film theory, yet it does stand as a concerted effort to elaborate an appreciation of the independent status of cinema as an art form. Strikingly, the essays in which Thrasher elaborated this independent aesthetic made little or no mention of sociology; if one did not know Thrasher's background, one might easily take his writings on film as culture as the work of an art critic attempting to come to grips with a powerful new aesthetic form in modernity.

Two texts from the end of the 1930s stand as the most explicit of Thrasher's articulations of a film aesthetics. The first of these writings is a short article that Thrasher offered for a forum in the National Board of Review's magazine on "What Is a Good Movie?" It is striking that for this journal of film betterment, Thrasher offered an answer that was fully aesthetic and made no mention of sociological responsibility for the art of cinema. It now appeared that cinema would achieve its value in a society simply when it perfected its qualities *as art*.[32]

Thrasher argued that three qualities constituted goodness in film: in his own words, they were technical excellence, artistic worth, and adequate use of cinematic resources. The first of these was a minimal requirement: a film must be put together with proficiency. As he explained, technical excellence "involves the highest standards of mechanical efficiency; in a word, good photography combined with proper sound reproduction [as well as] application of the principles of composition to the scene; the proper and effective synchronization of sound and photography; good continuity and editing; well planned and appropriate scenery, props, and costumes; and authenticity of background; events and characters in films which need to be historically and sociologically correct" (12).

Technical excellence, as Thrasher described it, was a standard, predictable achievement of the film industry; it came, as he said, from "the highest degree of training of numerous technicians." But if such technical perfection was a minimal requirement for art and derived from the regular but anonymous functioning of the moviemaking system, the second level of goodness in films came from "the finest artistry of creative minds"—that is, from individual figures who went beyond the basic proficiency of the film industry to offer something more. In Thrasher's words, "The major artist, however, is the director and upon his skill in weaving the various elements of the production together depends the total impression and artistic worth of the film" (12).

Although such artistry assumed the director's specific abilities to give value to story, plot, and scenario—which Thrasher declared to be "major factors which are necessary to achieve artistic excellence"—Thrasher's third criterion of goodness seems to do with more than just effective dramatization of a scenario. He posited, "There is a third essential, however, that must not be overlooked; that is, the necessity of utilizing the resources which are peculiar to the cinematic medium and which are usually not available to other forms of art." Just as Thrasher's course had given attention to "pure film," here he valorized a notion of medium specificity that did not necessarily have to do with narrative or subject matter. As Thrasher put it, "The essence of pure cinema is movement through space, because the film represents the only art form which can so well express motion. The resources of the camera make it possible for this motion to transcend the limitations imposed on the legitimate stage. . . . For this reason the motion picture is peculiarly able to present certain types of subject matter which are difficult for other art forms—such as the conquest of the air, warfare on land and sea, the chase, the horse race, and other types of movement" (6).

Thrasher noted, moreover, that to the mere filming of vibrant motion the cinema added forms of motion that came from its own medium-specific qualities. For example, "The close-up, the camera angle, the moving camera which moves the audience instead of the setting are all vital mechanisms which the director may use to make the movie more interesting and compelling." Additionally, montage had a central role in transcending the photographic single shot to create a resonant movement that is irreducibly cinematic. And even the photographic image could be altered by "double exposure, dissolves, animation and other photographic tricks," which would make it "possible to liberate the creative imagination of the artist who can now achieve effects hitherto undreamed of in any art form" (7).

The second writing in which Thrasher outlined his aesthetics of film was a set of notes for a lecture he gave in his motion picture course on "The Nature, Range, and Scope of the Motion Picture." (Thrasher may have drafted this presentation in order to fill in for USC's Boris Morkovin, who had announced a 1939 lecture with a similar title but appears to have canceled his visit to Thrasher's course.) In some ways, the notes simply expanded on the short discussion of "qualities peculiar to the cinema" in the earlier "What Is a Good Movie?" piece. By this time Thrasher had concretized his aesthetic, which would persist unchanged as a set of critical assumptions he could regularly refer to. (For example, in 1941, Thrasher presented the William Dieterle film *All That Money Can Buy* to his class and fairly mechanically applied each of the three categories of his "What Is a Good Movie?" meditation to the film.)

Beginning with the assertion that "[t]he cinema may make a unique contribution to art that cannot be made in any other medium of human expression," Thrasher's lecture notes identified film's importance as lying in its ability to create a separate reality through cinematic technique. Again, as in "What Is Good Cinema?" Thrasher took the epitome of cinematic specificity to lie in its creation of forms of motion all its own. Thrasher then proceeded to provide examples of numerous films in numerous genres that emphasized motion: for instance, the Western, the war film, the chase and horse race film, films of crowd motion such as *Potemkin* (a film, we remember, that he had not even heard of a few years earlier), aviation films, films of nature's cataclysms, and so on. All these films, Thrasher said, "have elements in them which no other form of art can catch and transmit, elements which represent the peculiar province of the motion picture." The rest of the lecture reiterated the specific techniques that the "What Is a Good Movie?" piece had listed, although it added others such as the flashback and animation (where "the imagination of the artist is given free rein to carry his audience into the utmost realm of fantasy and absurdity"). Even more than the published essay, the lecture emphasized that, through its techniques, film could create a fantasy universe that must not be judged according to sociological criteria of earthly reality: "It is possible in the cinema," he says, "to transcend the material into realms of fantasy which other forms of art find it much more difficult to present. . . . In motion pictures a man can leave his body and travel far afield over the earth or into a land of dreams."

As I have indicated, Thrasher's aesthetic of film was not theoretically profound. But without making too much of these short writings, it can nonetheless be noted that they do not merely ignore the sociology of cinema's effects but even may reverse certain of its fundamental suppositions.

For example, where *The Gang* had worried that action pictures might dangerously and seductively break through delinquents' frequent lack of interest in a cinema deemed to be a passive entertainment form, Thrasher's invocation of movement as the essence of cinema valorized precisely those genres of action (e.g., the thundering Western) that the early book had seen as potentially deleterious for younger spectators. Likewise, where Thrasher earlier had voiced concern that children and adolescents might be vulnerable to a confusion in which they did not distinguish movie fantasy from social reality and might therefore fall for the lies on screen, Thrasher now lauded cinema's ability to create fictions—to construct imaginary universes. The difference, of course, was that the trained spectator would appreciate such fictions in their own right, would not confuse them for life, and consequently would not try to take usable life lessons away from them. Maturity of mind enabled one to put film in its proper and, in fact, quite exalted space.

It is noteworthy to see someone like Thrasher, who originally had been so enmeshed in a sociology of film—to the extent of constructing a media-effects course like the one offered in 1933–34 and of agreeing to work with the Payne Fund Studies in their interrogation of cinema's worth—so firmly coming to adopt a fully aesthetic discourse for the appreciation of film. One final assertion of Thrasher's essay "What Is a Good Movie?" is particularly striking in its explicitness in this respect: "In my opinion a film does not have to be socially significant to be good."[33] Between sociology and aesthetics, the role of education, then, was to enable spectators to grow up: if a pedagogy like Thrasher's helped them do so, film would cease to be a sometimes dangerous social force and realize instead its potentialities as cultural form in all its radiant particularity and medium specificity.

NYU EPILOGUE

Although it goes beyond my time frame, it is worth noting some developments in film pedagogy that ensued at NYU in the latter part of the 1930s after Thrasher had already been offering his course for a while. One new class came about as a direct consequence of Thrasher's course: in 1936, Thrasher himself proposed that NYU offer a course on amateur moviemaking. The course would be supervised by the Amateur Cinema League (whose director, as mentioned earlier, lectured in Thrasher's class), although Thrasher's suggestion that the course be scheduled in the two hours before his own class The Motion Picture: Its Artistic, Educational, and Social Aspects might well indicate that he planned to be present at the filmmaking class and saw the two offerings as directly linked. Thrasher's interest in a production class was in keeping both with a desire to instruct teachers in means of visual education—film as neutral vehicle for the transmission of useful lessons—and with a film-betterment belief that filmmaking in and of itself was a beneficial activity insofar as it taught a concerted form of craftsmanship that was valuable in its own right. As his proposal for the course put it, "This course is designed particularly for teachers who wish to become sponsors of school photoplay clubs or are interested in teaching photoplay appreciation. It will appeal also to persons who wish to learn the techniques of movie making, using 16 mm. and 8 mm. film, in order to carry on educational work in connection with settlements, churches, and other social institutions." In the event, the course was not established until the 1939–40 academic year, when it was listed as a yearlong nondepartmental course in the School of Education. The course seems to have disappeared quite quickly, perhaps because of the material difficulties that equipment-dependent production courses always have faced (difficulties that might have been compounded by the onset of world war).

Another NYU initiative in the latter part of the 1930s was more consequential for the future history of film studies. Starting in the academic year 1935–36, an English department professor, Robert Gessner, began offering a course on screenwriting in NYU's adult-education extension program. Soon after, he organized an evening lecture series for the extension program, based on films from the Museum of Modern Art, on "History and Appreciation of the Cinema," which by the end of the 1930s mutated into a for-credit course in the English department, "The Cinema as Literary Art." Despite its title (which might imply a course on adaptations), the course treated the history of narrative film as an independent art form in its own right through an approach that approximates the basic courses on film one could find decades later in many universities and colleges:

THE CINEMA AS LITERARY ART

The historical and aesthetic development of both the silent and sound film is presented through lectures, illustrated by excerpts from some of the most notable productions, and by class discussion. The narrative development is traced from the early days of Edison and Lumière, through the development of plot in the "Western" period, through the early technical and psychological maturity of D. W. Griffith, and concluding with the contemporary period of foreign and Hollywood films. The development of comedy is traced from Méliès through Sennett, Chaplin, Lloyd, and the contemporaries. The sound film is studied in its relationship to the new narrative, descriptive, and expository problems which it created. The animated cartoon is analyzed in its relationship to fantasy and the fairy tale. Colored films as a problem in description are exhibited and studied. The documented film as related to exposition in the newsreels and social travelogues is also seen and analyzed.

Soon, Gessner's ambitions for film studies at NYU expanded as he began to envision a degree program in the discipline. In a January 30, 1940, letter to Nigel Dennis at the NBR, he expressed the desire for such a curriculum and acknowledged that NYU's interest in film studies had originated with the efforts of Frederic Thrasher, "the pioneer teacher at NYU with his general course, unique and valuable." A snazzy brochure of September 1941 outlined the proposed four-year curriculum in Motion Picture Writing and Production. Thrasher's School of Education course was listed among the electives for this program.

But an ambitious program that was announced just two months before the United States went to war probably did not have much chance of getting off the ground. The program disappeared, and Gessner had to struggle to keep film studies alive at NYU. At the end of the 1950s, however, he was instrumental in founding the professional organization that would help establish film studies as a regularized part of modern university curricula, the then-named Society of Cinematologists (eventually to become the Society for Cinema and Media Studies). Gessner would serve as the organization's first president. He thus formed an important link between the sporadic attempts to create film education that dotted American academia through the 1930s and the successful flourishing of programs in the new media explosions of the 1960s.

8 Middlebrow Translations of Highbrow Philosophy

The Film Fandom of the 1930s Great Books Intellectuals

> One cannot live in a democracy and despise the popular arts.
> MORTIMER J. ADLER, *Art and Prudence*, 1937

An anecdote: In the mid-1990s, I was asked to be part of the external evaluation committee for an English department, with a strong film component, at a midwestern university. The arts and sciences division had recently acquired a new dean who had come from the hard sciences. The English professors, especially those who concentrated on cinema, wondered not just about his view of the humanities but of popular culture curricula within the humanities. They expressed the hope that in my meeting with the dean I might get some sense of his attitude—positive or negative—toward their program's devotion to mass cultural forms such as cinema. During my meeting, I asked him directly how he felt about film being taught at his university. Immediately, and with great enthusiasm, he said he welcomed the idea. "After all," he said, "we're not St. John's"—a reference to the Annapolis college that since the late 1930s has taught a single and singular curriculum based on the so-called Great Books of the Western World. The dean's contrast of two types of curricula—one restricted to great books, and one open to new contents, including the popular arts—was understandable: through the 1980s and 1990s, especially as the ravages of the "culture wars" had ramped up battles over what universities should be teaching, it was easy to imagine that study of popular culture was by nature opposed to the study of high tradition. This dean at least assumed the opposition did not have to come at the expense of popular culture: he felt that for different academic institutions, there could be different curricula, each with its own justification. For neoconservatives, in contrast, popular culture could only constitute an absolute enemy, the very threat of a destruction of reason.

For example, for Hilton Kramer, writing in the 1980s on the fate of humanistic inquiry, film study was likened to natural disaster:

The courses that now substitute Hollywood movies for classic texts, that scrap the study of Western civilization for a whole variety of politicized ethnic, racial, and gender studies . . . news of these developments reaches us every day in accelerating numbers, and all too often we follow these news reports with the same kind of sinking feeling, and feelings of helplessness, that we experience in following the news of devastating hurricanes and volcanic eruptions. We know very well what kind of destruction follows in the wake of these disasters.[1]

Quickly, Kramer's fear of popular culture moved from natural disaster of a local sort (the hurricane, the volcano) to apocalypse. On the very next page, Kramer would declare that "it is our civilization that we believe to be at stake in this struggle." In this ultimate battle for the survival of humanity, and not just the humanities, action was demanded:

> I want to begin with a modest but radical proposal: that we get the movies out of the liberal arts classroom. We've simply got to throw them out. There is no good reason for the movies to be there, and there is every good reason to get rid of them. . . . Students are going to go to the movies anyway, and to bring them into the classroom—either as objects of study or as aids to study—is to blur and destroy precisely the kind of distinction—the distinction between high culture and popular culture—that it is now one of the functions of a sound liberal education to give our students. Following from this, I believe that all forms of popular culture should be banned from courses in the arts and humanities. Typically today students arrive on college campuses already besotted with the trash of popular culture, and it must now be one of the goals of a sound liberal education to wean them away from it. (4)

For Kramer, like so many of his confreres, higher education should devote itself to higher purposes, and these could only be degraded by attention to everyday culture. In such context, the Great Books could easily be assumed to represent the form of deep learning that had to be pitted, but also defended, against the ravages and assaults of a degraded and degrading popular culture. Predictably, St. John's College itself would be referenced as one of the bastions of a great tradition defending itself against the corruptive assaults of popular culture on academia's higher mission. At the height of the culture wars, for instance, when neoconservatives were running St. John's, a promotional packet for the college proudly included a reprint of a *Washington Post* article in which the headline proclaimed St. John's to be "The College of Political Incorrectness." The article even treated as inevitable the opposition of the world of St. John's to popular culture: "[I]t is possible to spend a week at St. John's and never once see a Sony Walkman. . . . you're more likely at St. John's to hear students talking about Tacitus or Hegel than about the latest and most ephemeral rock band." Here, offered as self-evident was a rhetoric of mutual incompatibility between the Great Books and an everyday life infected by popular media: to defend the higher life of the mind, one must choose irrevocably for great enduring classics over a nonculture of evanescent triviality.

Kramer's neoconservative rhetoric of imminent crisis might seem to bear an antecedent in an assertion from the work of another dogmatic defender of the Great Books tradition, Mortimer J. Adler, in his *Art and Prudence* (1937): "If the society in which we live is not already demoralized by the progressive corruption in our universities during the last half century, it will happen unless the tide is turned." But it is sobering to realize that Adler was saying this in the context of an almost-seven-hundred-page ode to the mass art of cinema.[2] Far from a low object onto which opprobrium should be heaped, "The motion picture theatre," Adler declared, "is the theatre of democracy, and the motion picture is its most popular poetry" (118).

Strikingly, along with Adler, many of the key figures in the original push for Great Books curricula for American colleges in the first part of the twentieth century welcomed popular culture. At the very least, they imagined everyday life to be composed of a diversity of experiences and values: forms of culture were not so much in opposition as located along a continuum, where each had its possible contribution to make to overall well-being. For example, in *Art and Prudence,* Adler did, on the one hand, assume there should be privileged moments of intellectuality in which the philosophically inclined person could devote attention to higher ideas and ideals. But Adler also admitted that not all of us in all instances could be so pure. A recent convert to Catholicism, Adler saw humans as less than angels, and he assumed they could not always devote themselves to great works of transcendental profundity. Humans sometimes needed mere relaxation, and this the world of popular culture amply could provide.

But often, Adler and his contemporary Great Books proponents would move beyond this minimal and benign program for popular culture as temporary respite to a much bolder position. Often, the Great Books enthusiasts would endorse the popular arts as worthy forms of great culture *in their own right*. It might surprise both the midwestern dean and the neoconservatives alike to learn that film study was in fact strongly promoted as an integral and even necessary part of the original plan for St. John's as a Great Books college.[3]

In 1937, a friend of Adler's, a philosophy professor named Scott Buchanan, had left the University of Virginia to take up a new post as dean of the revamped St. John's College in Annapolis. Through the 1930s, St.

John's fate had been typical of the small liberal arts college in the United States. For instance, it had increasingly come to be dominated by a fragmented curriculum in which students could choose from a variety of majors tailored to their individual needs and complemented by a wide array of nonmajor electives. The idea that students could fashion their own course of study had been gaining in strength in higher education in the period as a result of a number of influences: for example, the pattern set early on by Harvard University, where the influential Charles W. Eliot had pushed for personalized majors rather than a set curriculum for all, and, more recently, John Dewey's pragmatist philosophy of education in which students were encouraged to structure study according to personal needs and talents.

Unfortunately, the very extent to which St. John's curriculum was typical of pragmatic trends in higher education meant that it did not necessarily stand out in any way from its competitors. With so many colleges with so many open curricula to select from, there was no particular need for a student to choose the undistinguished St. John's. By the 1930s, enrollments were in decline. Moreover, the dire context of the Depression had increased the college's economic woes: in particular, the school's administrators had let themselves be seduced into joining an expensive citywide colonial restoration campaign undertaken to rival the recently established tourist attraction of colonial Williamsburg in Virginia (started in 1926), and now the consequences of that financial folly were also coming due.

By turning to Buchanan and his Virginia colleague Stringfellow Barr, who would become president of the revamped St. John's, the trustees of the college boldly were setting out to remake St. John's from the ground up. The plan was to establish one single curriculum in which all students would, in the same order and at the same moment, read so-called Great Books of the Western World. Through the 1930s, Buchanan and a cohort of colleagues and friends had been pushing for various institutions of higher learning to develop singular curricula based on the Great Books. For example, at the end of the 1920s, Mortimer Adler had been brought to the University of Chicago by its president, Robert M. Hutchins, with the specific charge of militating for a Great Books curriculum for all undergraduates. At Chicago, the admittedly abrasive Adler had run up against all sorts of resistance. For example, social scientists (several of whom, incidentally, were involved with the Payne Fund Studies into the effects of motion pictures) had reacted violently against Adler's attempts to argue that humanistic tradition had epistemological priority over scientific knowledge of society. Adler was able to insinuate Great Books learning into only a small part of the Chicago curriculum under the auspices of a limited-enrollment honors seminar for select humanities majors.

Likewise, Buchanan himself had tried to push for a required Great Books curriculum at the University of Virginia. A short essay Buchanan had written in 1935 for one of the university's publications stood as a veritable manifesto for his desire to institute Great Books learning there.[4] Significantly, Buchanan's reflections came in the context of a discussion of the value of Great Books for the university's *adult education* program. For Buchanan, the necessity for Great Books education derived directly from an essential populism: like the neoconservatives who by the 1980s would be running St. John's, Buchanan certainly believed in the indispensability of the Great Books, but rather than these being cloistered off in the elite space of the university, he imagined them moving out into the world, interacting with ordinary people in the context of their everyday interests and needs. Moreover, he assumed the role of Great Books was not to supplant people's everyday culture but to interact with it—to serve laudably alongside it in dialectical fashion. Central to Buchanan's philosophy of culture, and supporting his deep commitment to adult education, in fact, was a faith in the activity of what he termed *translation:* different parts of life were not so much to be contrasted to each other—so that, for instance, defense of Great Books education required a concomitant rejection of popular culture—as imagined to exist in a fluid and beneficial process of influence and interchange with conduits of translation between them. Dialectic was one name for the activity of translation in which different compartments of human life—both high and low—could all find acceptance. As Buchanan put it in his essay, "Dialectic is the art of sorting out the lingos we are mixing, and discovering the ideal dimension in which we move when we use them" (31).

Even as it set out to justify the establishment of the privileged venue of St. John's College for the study of Great Books, a long report that Buchanan drew up in 1937 to justify the new curriculum continued to rely on democratic rhetoric and on faith in a possible dialogue or translation between Great Books and everyday popular culture. True, the very fact that Great Books education would now find a home in a specific academic institution might imply a certain cloistering in which it could be imagined that Great Books study would flourish in a pure environment against the debasing influences of the ordinary world. Indeed, Buchanan's report, entitled "In Search of a Liberal College: A Program for the Recovery of the Classics and the Liberal Arts," began with a long section on the "monastic ideal" in which Buchanan nostalgically looked back to the medieval monastery as the privileged site in which humankind "withdrew from the wilder and less workable regions of nature [and] relied on reason to construct an intelligible human world from which with virtue and skill and understanding, the modern conquest of nature might proceed."[5]

But even Buchanan's invocation of the monastery was not as elitist as it might first appear. As the very reference to "the modern conquest of nature" intended, Buchanan assumed that the cultivation of reason within the confines of the monastery or the cloistered college was not to be undertaken for its own sake as idle reflection with no impact on the world beyond. Humankind certainly required sanctuary in which to hone its reasoning skills—and to study those great works that best encouraged reason—*but* there also needed to be a corresponding move outward from the cloister so that reason could issue in everyday practice, one now informed by higher ideals. Where his more polemically inclined friend Mortimer Adler would rail virulently against American pragmatism (incarnated by his Chicago nemesis John Dewey), Buchanan adhered to an expansive philosophy in which the pragmatist interest in action and accomplishment was to be appreciated: as he declared emphatically toward the end of "In Search of a Liberal College," "knowing without doing is empty." Even as he looked back with nostalgia for a place apart in which learning could flourish, Buchanan was also updating the monastic ideal in decidedly American ways to enable knowledge to take its effective place in the go-getter context of modernity.

But as Buchanan also cautioned, "Doing without knowing is blind." An Aristotelian by training, Buchanan saw humankind as distinguished by poesis, defined not only as the mechanical act of making but as the simultaneous activity of reasoning that accompanied mechanical effort. Human acts of making were not merely manual but symbolic: even at its most seemingly mechanical, human labor was expressive of humanist meanings. As Buchanan put it, "The whole world may wisely be seen as an arsenal of tools and instruments for man as long as he has his ends forced upon his attention. . . . It is well that he train his eyes and hands to fit the tools and instruments, if only that some day, when his imagination moves, it may act as the bridge and coordinator of tools and intellect." The quintessentially American fetish of direct action in the world necessarily was to be complemented and tempered by a European-inspired faith in the powers of reason to give sense to action. American pragmatism was in dialectical relationship with European philosophical abstraction. In Buchanan's words, "Imaginatively and intellectually, we have to get over our provincial patriotism. This calls for a special concerted effort to expand and liberate our imaginative and intellectual powers. Pragmatism and instrumentalism are good honest American provincial doctrines, and we have learned our lessons well; in fact it is because we have learned them well that we are at present articulately conscious of their shortcomings for the next step in our civilization. . . . Discipline starts with hand and eye and with age moves to thought and spirit, still not forgetting that the child is father to the man."

Buchanan noted, in fact, that the original monastic ideal had emphasized both mental and manual arts. The medieval monks spent much of their time in reflection and study, certainly, but they also worked the land and maintained their habitat (and sometimes went out into the world to do good deeds). The manual arts were a necessary part of the cycle of life, something the monks committed to with devotion. Buchanan pictured, then, the monastery as a model for the desired unity of thought and practice.

Consequently, Buchanan's plan for St. John's diverged somewhat from Robert Maynard Hutchins's (and Adler's) Great Books project at Chicago insofar as Buchanan felt that a humanistic curriculum centered on Great Books needed to be complemented by practical work in the sciences and by hands-on training in fine arts. At St. John's, students would do more than just read Great Books. Buchanan outlined some of their other intended activities in the last section of his document "The Laboratory Arts," which forms a significant symmetry with the opening section on the monastic ideal. It is in this last section that Buchanan made a bold—even, I dare say, startling—suggestion.

Buchanan's primary impetus in the final section was to explain the essential value of a Great Books school also giving attention to practical activity: for example, studio arts, hands-on scientific research, physical endeavor, manual application, and concrete experiment. Liberal education in the reading of the Great Books was from the start always to be conjoined with pragmatic research and laboratory endeavor.

Within this context—one connected to that broader early twentieth-century concern with "craftsmanship" that we have encountered elsewhere—Buchanan launched in his final section into praise of practical research in relation to abstract reflection undertaken for its own sake. Although the emphasis on intensive undergraduate Great Books education required that St. John's be a college without a research-oriented graduate track, Buchanan lamented the separation in higher learning of concerted research from studious reflection (and, with this lament, he differed greatly from Hutchins, who wanted to defend undergraduate Great Books education against technical, applied research). To counter the rupture of mental and manual, Buchanan had a bold proposal:

We want research that will actually contribute to teaching.... There must be a medium within which genuine understanding and efficient communication can be brought about. The proposal for St. John's is that there be an Institute of Cinematics, a full-fledged graduate research institute ... where everything from the raw material, both animate and inanimate, to the finished movie performance is studied from both theoretical and practical standpoints. This is not a proposal to turn St. John's into a Hollywood but rather to follow the professional movement which is now going on in certain other unprofessionalized fields, notably business. The movies are in their Hollywood stage, are in the raw commercialized art state without benefit of either the fine or liberal arts; on the other hand it is being recognized increasingly that their genuine function has these academic and liberal dimensions.

Buchanan was attributing a variety of functions or values to the cinema. First, there was the role of film as a generalized medium of communication—film as a discursive form that dialectically enabled translation between disparate areas of human life. Buchanan was here offering a late version of that notion prevalent in the 1910s and 1920s of film as universal speech, a fully effective Esperanto, that could serve as a force of transmission for myriad forms of knowledge. As Buchanan asserted,

[T]he training we are giving in our studies of the liberal arts [i.e., the Great Books curriculum] would gain greatly from the pointed practical utilities of the moving picture array of literary and histrionic arts. Both the college and the institute should improve in each other's company. The classics would receive another translation into both distant and diverse mediums, and the translation would or could make the tradition come to an obvious present utility, which is in turn a gathering and focus of all the other utilities in modern life.

Second, Buchanan's invocation of the ways the new recording technology of film could bring a great tradition of thought up to date and give it "present utility" complemented his pragmatically Americanist assumption that ways needed to be found to make the essentially European tradition of Great Books relevant to the new American context. Contrary to later defenders of the Great Books as timeless entities of objective and unchanging value, Buchanan felt that the Great Books always needed to be updated and tested against their times, and he felt that the cinema could help in this process of review, revision, and rejuvenation of tradition. Where later Great Books proponents in the moment of the culture wars could often only dread any attempt to translate tradition into modern idiom, Buchanan's expansive philosophy of Great Books education viewed tradition not as a set of immutable ideas but as a potentially usable past that could and would be updated to the specific interests of new and contemporary contexts.

Third, in Buchanan's very emphasis on the film *profession* (even if distinguished from a specifically Hollywood version), there was strong acknowledgment of the educational benefits of immersion in a craft, of mastery of art as act of making. The very extent to which cinema was a labor-intensive art (both fine art and practical art, in fact) meant that student exposure to filmmaking practices would constitute a supreme form of instruction in poesis. The making that was inherent in film*making* established cinema as a site of workmanship—the outcome of a concerted and skilled training that could only be beneficial for body and mind. (In passing, it is worth noting that, in the quoted passage, Buchanan also seemed to feel that business was increasingly being professionalized in ways that moved it toward the liberal arts. Business practice was, for Buchanan, also a creative activity, which gained in value as its practitioners gained in discipline and in a symbolic understanding of the higher purposes of their craft. Where just a few years later, Abraham Flexner would pit the great tradition *against* schools of business and condemn the latter as a betrayal of the spiritual mission of higher learning, Buchanan was arguing that the worldly professions could themselves be spiritual. Human beings were creatures of labor, but at its best labor was itself poesis: inspired and reflected transformation of the world by mind and body alike. Far from seeing craftsmanship in the modern age as an inevitable betrayal of higher spirit as exemplified in great works that would resist crass worldliness, Buchanan applauded modernity's creativity.)[6]

For our purposes, the most important aspect of Buchanan's ode to the movies has to do with his suggestion that the processes of filmmaking could be studied *theoretically* as well as practically and that such study might make essential contributions to the elaboration of a philosophy of liberal education centered on the Great Books. While Buchanan's Institute of Cinematics clearly was focused on production, he also was calling strongly for the *critical study* of the art of film. In later passages of his proposal, he continued the claim that a worthy liberal education would find its veritable dialectical culmination in the humanistic study of film. Cinema, he argued, was the contemporary age's only truly totalizing art, an eminent Gesamtkunstwerk (total artwork) that would bring all the arts together—not just the fine arts, not just the manual arts, but the liberal arts too. The movies, he asserted, "call for and focus practically all the leading parts of contemporary culture; they have the largest following of any of the arts partly because they put all the arts together." Indeed, for Buchanan, the movies so served as a synthesis of poetic activity that he even proposed that the Institute of Cinematics take over direction of St. John's creative pedagogy; as he argued, "Music, literature, dramatics, painting, sculpture, architecture, workshop, and even athletics, would gain an integrating end and achieve just that degree of detachment and practical responsibility that college activities should have."

But the value of cinema for liberal arts education came not just from its power to synthesize and orient creativity in the individual *arts.* So powerful were the movies, in his view, that Buchanan asserted they could unify the diverse fields *of liberal knowledge* overall. For instance, as both technology and creative activity, the cinema helped bridge the perennial gap between the two cultures of science and humanistic inquiry. Buchanan felt that the cinema's technological infrastructure meant that its study necessarily expanded scientific learning. As he put it, the movies' "need for mechanical, electrical, optical, chemical, and even biological science is obvious; their laboratories would present an encyclopedia of modern empirical science." Directly inspired by Lewis Mumford's *Technics and Civilization* (1934), which presented the technologies of the machine age as symbols of essential human creativity, Buchanan felt that study of the cinema brought the laboratory arts together in ways that realized their potentiality and forged their dialectical link with the higher liberal arts.

The conclusion that Buchanan drew from this special ability of the movies to bring together the arts and the sciences was far-reaching: "In all respects, [the movies] offer the microcosm of the modern cosmos in a manner and compass appropriate to the university and even to the college. In some sense they offer the only major activity of modern civilization which properly and exhaustively mirrors the liberal college. They are increasingly calling on all the cultural resources that we can recover, including even the classics in the sense that we are using them."

If Buchanan assumed that the examination of cinema should take place in a graduate institute that would not be part of the regular Great Books curriculum, this was not because he somehow felt that such an institute was extraneous to the primary work of liberal arts study. Quite the contrary, he clearly saw the Institute of Cinematics as the effective culmination of the four years of Great Books study. He was not calling for cinema to be part of the regular undergraduate curriculum because "that would merely add another professional burden upon the liberal college." In other words, with so many books to read, there was no room for required film study in the undergraduate curriculum. Buchanan worried that adding film to the Great Books curriculum would bring the charge of "dilettantism." Better that the creative impact of film filter down from the laboratory, and that students be exposed to cinema through extracurricular activity in the fine arts. Nonetheless, cinema was essential, Buchanan imagined, to the ways Great Books study would be configured at St. John's. In the last lines of his proposal, he imagined the college as realizing its mission in the synthesis of two forms of background education: "for the past the Benedictine monastery with its useful, liberal, and divine arts and their rotating daily schedule; for the future the cinematic institute where mathematical physics finds a liberal home and progressively finds the synthesis for what may be a twentieth century renaissance of the same useful, liberal, and fine arts."

Buchanan emphatically believed that the cultural centrality and value of the movies to the modern age had been established, and that the cinema constituted a force to be built upon in liberal education. He even cited a usable tradition of critical works from which serious reflection on the cinema could take inspiration: the valorization of popular culture in the writings of critic Gilbert Seldes; the massive study of film that his friend Mortimer Adler had written entitled *Art and Prudence;* and the more general discussion of art, technology, and the modern age to be found in Mumford's *Technics and Civilization*.[7]

Nothing came of Scott Buchanan's plan for an Institute of Cinematics at St. John's, and it would be easy to dismiss it as an eccentric idea that never would have integrated well with a Great Books program. Nevertheless, I find the very fact that Buchanan could even imagine the possibility of a film initiative for St. John's significant and quite fascinating. To the extent that, as Michel Foucault argued, the discourse of any field of knowledge is constrained by historical conditions of rarity—at each instance in the history of a discipline there are limits to what is considered sayable, legitimate, and acceptable[8]—there is something noteworthy in the very fact that in the moment of the 1930s Buchanan could even consider film study as compatible with great liberal arts study. And he was not alone in this. The popular culture of film had a much greater favorable reception among 1930s proponents of the Great Books tradition than the neoconservative defenders in a later period would have us believe. For example, as Buchanan was articulating his ideas for St. John's, two close friends of his who also strongly contended that Great Books study was the best curriculum to shake higher education from its lethargy were writing each other to applaud the idea of the cinematics institute. Letters between philosopher Mortimer Adler and poet and critic Mark Van Doren, employed at that time as film critic for the *Nation*, lauded the movies and discussed the curricular plan for cinema study their friend Buchanan had come up with. Neither Adler nor Van Doren saw anything strange in Buchanan's project. Neither viewed it as a betrayal of the ideal of Great Books education. Quite the contrary. In fact, their own reflections on film had fed into Buchanan's valorization of cinema and had formed its necessary background. Van Doren even imagined that the oftentimes dogmatic Adler might be a great director of such an institute.[9]

I find Buchanan's dream of cinema, shared by his friends Van Doren and Adler, a revealing conclusion to this study. Their engagement with cinema came out of a strong populist impulse that inscribes these Great Books intellectuals squarely within the tradition of middlebrow cultural mediation that it has been much of my goal to chronicle. For all their defense of a great tradition, these humanists imagined that high culture existed alongside, and even gained in richness from contact with, everyday popular arts.

Some recent scholarship has helped revise the image of the original Great Books intellectuals as vociferous opponents of everyday democratic culture along the lines of a Hilton Kramer or an Allan Bloom. For example, in *The Romance of Commerce and Culture,* James Sloan Allen describes the efforts of Mortimer Adler literally to *sell* the Great Books beyond the confines of academic curriculum. In the 1950s, as Sloan Allen shows, Adler became a veritable salesman for the Great Books, helping Encyclopaedia Britannica put together a special edition of the texts and encouraging members of the Chicago business community to fund and participate in annual conversations on great ideas (the Aspen Institute for Humanistic Studies).[10] Likewise, in *The Making of Middlebrow Culture,* Joan Shelley Rubin includes several of the Great Books proponents among the middlebrow intellectuals who, she argues, set out to provide a social centrality for themselves in modern, mass America by seeking ways to make their high culture accessible to American middlebrow audiences.[11] Rubin's subjects are a select group of genteel intellectuals who, instead of retreating into the ivory tower of academia or into the quiet of the private study, entered into the new public sphere of mediatized America to turn new media culture to their own benefit. Above all, a primary lesson of Rubin's research has to do with the extent to which, with astounding regularity, a number of high humanists in America came to grips with mass culture and saw it as a positive force: they tried to gauge its effects for democratic liberal education, and they sought to exploit the seductions of such mass forms for the transmission and cultivation of high humanist ideals. Rubin discusses, for instance, such Great Books cultural mediators as Mortimer Adler taking up common techniques of marketing to hawk the Encyclopaedia Britannica edition of Great Books; St. John's College's first president, Stringfellow Barr, who initiated a popular radio show about great ideas called "Invitation to Learning"; and Mark

Van Doren, who often appeared on that show. (In passing, given that I have been arguing throughout this study about the ways in which a number of high-culture intellectuals entered, often quite willingly, into the orbit of popular culture, it might be worth noting that Mark was the father of Charles Van Doren, who in the 1950s would have his own infamous encounter with mass culture through his ill-fated quiz show adventure, where he began as the intellectual darling of television only to end up a symbol of the betrayal of mind by mammon and media.)

Where, at the height of the culture wars, Allan Bloom could refer to the "closing" of the American mind in positive fashion as the necessity for defenders of great tradition to close themselves (and their students) off from the imputed dangers of ordinary everyday culture, the 1930s Great Books intellectuals offered a significant and salutary openness. For all their defense of an ostensible great tradition that, in our stereotypes, we imagine they fetishized as the province of a cultural elite, these intellectuals had a significant Progressivist commitment to cultural democracy. Whatever the questions we can raise about the very notion of a canon of great works, these high humanists felt, first, that it was a central duty of the intellectual to make that canon available to as many people as possible, and, second, that in furtherance of their mission, they could turn to forms of popular culture for the transmission *and extension* of the lessons of the great tradition. It is this latter goal, for instance, that inspired Buchanan's notion of film as a medium of *translation:* insofar as film might serve as a vehicle by which great ideas could be made available to people in widespread fashion, it was not in opposition to high humanism but could be a propitious medium for its widespread transmission. Moreover, at the extreme, film was not merely a medium for translation of great ideas but an embodiment of greatness in its own qualities as art. It could have its own integrity as a laudable form of culture.

One useful way to provide context for the Great Books intellectuals of the 1930s is to say a bit about their mentor, Columbia University English professor John Erskine.[12] It was Erskine who did the most to bring Great Books study into the American university in the first decades of the twentieth century, and it was as section leaders for his Western Civilization course at Columbia that a number of the 1930s Great Books proponents derived their initial enthusiasm for the high humanism of Great Books education. A generation older than Scott Buchanan, Mortimer Adler, or Mark Van Doren, Erskine offered a link between the earlier gentlemanly tradition of classical humanists and the newer traditions of modernizing middlebrows like Buchanan or Adler who sought to adapt canons of knowledge to the demands of a new technological, commercial, mass world. Strikingly, Erskine's own career trajectory involved at several points a quite salutary engagement with the realm of popular culture.

Erskine's efforts to build a Great Books curriculum in fact had a decidedly worldly aspect. During the First World War, Erskine had gone from his position as professor at Columbia to serve overseas as chair of the Army Educational Commission. With the armistice, he stayed in France in the role of academic director for the American Army University (AAU) at Beaune. Recruiting more than ten thousand students for courses in all sorts of areas (from the theoretical to the practical), the AAU offered college courses (with transferable credits) to soldiers who would be returning home.

As with Scott Buchanan's work in adult education (and Mortimer Adler's also, as we will see), the AAU saw itself as reaching beyond the traditionally defined college student to offer democratic education to a broader and older population. One required course, Citizenship, included readings in classic texts, since Erskine asserted that study of the Western tradition had a special contribution to make to the constitution of citizens going out into the everyday world of modernity. As with Buchanan's attempt to mediate pragmatism and high humanism, Erskine's desire was to find a pedagogy appropriate to contemporary American needs, no matter how classic and traditional the content of that pedagogy might be.

Erskine's notion that classics had pertinence to the ordinary citizens of American modernity relied on an assumption that well shows how he imagined Great Books as in a continuum with everyday commercial culture. Specifically, in contrast to some neoconservative proponents of Great Books education who feel that the classics wear their value on their sleeves and that therefore their quality will be recognized by those refined and educated enough to discern it, Erskine assumed that the idea of the Great Books had to be "sold" to people. The Great Books would have pertinence to the age only if their value and their attractiveness for that age were demonstrated. In this respect, rather than oppose the Great Books to other forms of cultural expression, Erskine argued their similarity. He posited, for instance, that Great Books were not necessarily different in appeal than popular books and should be "promoted" just as works of the mass market were. As he put it, in describing how he tried to sell the idea of a Great Books curriculum to other faculty members: "I reminded my colleagues that the *Iliad* and most other epics were shorter than the average novel, and many of our students read at least one popular novel every seven days. Having read a new book, which their dormitory mates were also reading, they would then engage in a hot discussion about it. Why not treat the *Iliad*, the *Odyssey*, and other masterpieces as though they were recent publications, calling for immediate investigation and discussion?"[13]

One immediate consequence of Erskine's wartime curricular efforts around Great Books was his creation, when he returned to Columbia University, of a course called War Values, intended to inspire proper citizenship through education in classic works of high culture. The title of the course came from Erskine's sentiment that the war had posed new challenges to civilization that could be best addressed by study of the finest that had been thought and written in the Western tradition. It was this course that would mutate into Erskine's Great Books honors seminar. Erskine originally had argued that the civic importance of core learning in the great tradition was so great that *all* Columbia students should take the Great Books course. Other members of the faculty resisted the general reform, however, and the course became but an honors seminar for advanced students.

The honors course consisted of a number of individual sections, each made up of between twenty-five and thirty students, in which an entire book from the Great Books program was discussed (the same one for all sections). Like the seminars later instituted at St. John's, each section was run not by one but by two graduate students. The idea for the pairing was to provide undergraduates with direct experience of dialectics insofar as a learned conversation was expected to occur between the two graduate leaders (and then, by extension, the students). Mortimer Adler and Mark Van Doren served as one such pair.

Their joint Great Books teaching, inspired deeply by Erskine's model, serves as the next link in our story. But before leaving Erskine, it is worth noting that his career continued to revolve around encounters with American popular culture and democratic life. For all his commitment to fostering a core curriculum of classic works within the elite space of the Ivy League seminar room, Erskine was no less driven by a desire to make knowledge easily available to the public at large. In addition to his seminar, Erskine promoted the democratic spread of Great Books through adult education, through heavily advertised publishing ventures, and through other forms of consumer outreach.

At the beginning of the 1920s, after establishing Great Books at Columbia, Erskine might have seemed destined to remain in the cloistered life of an academic high humanist. But he had trouble finishing a contracted scholarly manuscript on Milton and asked his publisher if instead he could offer a popular novel he had been percolating. The publishing house accepted, and the novel, *The Private Life of Helen of Troy*, became a number one best seller in 1921. After a few more successful novels, Erskine left academia. By rendering Greek history in seductive form in his Helen of Troy book, Erskine had confirmed his sense of the values of popularization, and he now concretized his faith in publicly accessible presentation of ideas by undertaking an additional career as an energetic and active public lecturer. Traveling around the country and giving informative talks on a variety of subjects to a variety of groups, Erskine became one of the age's cherished public speakers.

His travels even brought him to Hollywood. There he took up with people in the world of cinema, which he claimed later in his autobiography to have admired as "the most influential medium of expression which mankind enjoys, criticizes, or envies" (226). In Hollywood, he stayed with his old classmate, William C. de Mille, the successful producer-director, and tasted the good life: when not hanging out at de Mille's luxurious estate, he frequently borrowed de Mille's car and chauffeur and spent his evenings partying. He tried his hand at screenwriting, chummed with the Marx Brothers (and appeared on variety shows with Groucho), and seems even to have been considered a potential successor to Will Hays as czar of the film industry.

Meanwhile, as Erskine was voyaging far from academia in the service of new forms for the popularization of knowledge, back in New York a number of his former Great Books teaching assistants were about to be invited by Scott Buchanan to participate in another project to democratize the high tradition through adult education and democratic outreach.

In the mid-1920s, Buchanan was working as assistant director of New York's People Institute, a civic organization of public outreach and education, and eventually served as director of its School of Philosophy. Buchanan's work at the People's Institute seems a decisive step in the solidification of a conception of Great Books pedagogy as a potentially democratic, progressive training that eschewed elite conceptions of education for a pragmatic attempt to make classical humanism pertinent to modern needs. Buchanan wanted the People's Institute philosophy program to include Great Books seminars like those he had heard about at Columbia through Mortimer Adler, and he turned to Adler and fellow former teaching assistants to direct some of the classes.

The People's Institute had been founded in 1897 by a former Columbia literature professor, the aristocratic Charles Sprague Smith. In the moment of turn-of-the-century urbanization (and especially the concerns, political and cultural, raised by increased immigration), the institute was part of a notable Progressivist mission to deal with new political and cultural configurations of multicultural (and class-divided) urbanism through programs of uplift and reform.[14] Unlike the Mechanics Institutes and American Lyceums of previous decades, whose primary concern had been with technical vocationalism, the People's Institute centered its philosophy on a belief that the people needed a broad humanistic core education as much as training in everyday skills. From the start, education in great works was central to the institute. As Robert Fisher says in his history of the organization, "Through the work of the Institute, Smith desired to educate the people in a cultural tradition, a system of values and ideals, foreign not only to the immigrants but to the majority of Americans as well. This was the cultural tradition of men of Smith's background, of the American 'aristocracy.' The People's Institute was organized to educate the people in this tradition—a tradition redefined in the context of an urban, industrialized, technological civilization" (23).

Although this is not directly part of our story, it is worth noting that the People's Institute had earlier played a major role in uplift of American film.[15] In 1909, a number of reformist civic groups in New York came together under the umbrella of the institute to fight for movie reform after the mayor had shut down all the movie houses for their supposed risks to public health (and morals). Out of their efforts arose the National Board of Censorship, later to become the National Board of Review, whose role in fostering the teaching of cinema appreciation we have encountered at several points. Despite its original title, the Board of Censorship was not so much out to block movies as to push for amelioration in quality for those movies that did reached the screens (and for a complementary improvement of the physical conditions in the theaters where these movies would be shown). With that brand of Progressivism now familiar to us that was fundamentally optimistic about the function and effect of film in contemporary society, the National Board of Censorship started from the assumption that film could be a worthy cultural form even if specific films fell short of that goal. Under the leadership of the People's Institute, the board worked to put into practice its guiding assumption that better films fostered better citizens.

In the late 1910s, an assistant director of the People's Institute, Everett Dean Martin, served also as chairman of the National Board of Review, but he left the latter position to become the full director of the institute. In his history, Robert Fisher sees a break between the earlier period of the People's Institute and the Everett Dean Martin years, where the institute's focus shifted from direct city reform (neighborhood projects, formation of social clubs, interventions in elementary and high schools, and so on) to a concern with high humanistic education for working-class city dwellers. Earlier, the institute had tried to change social conditions in directly material ways; now the emphasis was on fostering ameliorative change through education and uplift of the minds of people living within those conditions. As Fisher puts it, by the 1920s, the institute's "goal of developing a scientific, efficient urban environment was replaced with a more individualistic, intellectual aim—the creation of an educated, rational, humanist adult population" (355).

A Unitarian minister who felt that the moral purity of ordinary citizens was always in danger of being corrupted, Martin saw the human self as defined by, and finding its essential resistance to corruptive influences in, reason. While there could be intervention at the level of material conditions, Martin argued also for reform efforts at the point of personal consciousness—the spirit of citizens who could be educated in such a way as to ward off misreason.

Of all reform activities, Martin had special faith in pedagogy, especially one based on fundamental issues as incarnated in the great humanistic tradition of Western thought. Ever the believer in the primacy of education, Martin himself lectured endlessly at the institute (Fisher estimates that from the time Martin came to the institute, he himself delivered one-third of its big public lectures). Symptomatic of his pedagogy was a series of talks titled "What Is Worth Knowing—A Course on the Meaning of a Liberal Education," presented the year Scott Buchanan became his assistant director. Martin's concern for broad liberal education for ordinary citizens formed the basis for his book *The Meaning of a Liberal Education* (1926), in which, in the words of the *Dictionary of American Biography*, Martin "condemned what he considered the utilitarian emphasis of contemporary schooling and advocated a humanist education as the bulwark of liberal democracy, believing that it inoculated individuals against infection by the irrational behavior of crowds."[16]

In 1917, Martin created an evening lecture series that he initially intended to use to foreground his own speeches but which he eventually expanded to include regular talks by a wide range of guests. In an outreach effort, the events were frequently held away from the institute headquarters in such venues as libraries, settlement houses, and local schools. However, where other Progressive reform programs often centered their talks on subjects of directly practical import such as vocational training, Martin pushed for his lecture series to deal with broad questions of culture and society. Aptly, his evening program was named the School of Philosophy.

As Robert Fisher explains, "only instructors with a 'humanist point of view,' that is, classical and critical in their conception of subject matter, were invited" (400). Many famous public intellectuals of the moment came to speak. For example, one series, on Sunday evenings, dealt with "Ethical Factors in the Problem of Social Justice" and included such names as Frederick Lewis Allen, Clifton Fadiman, Robert Lynd, and Lewis Mumford. Great Books advocate John Erskine lectured in 1931 and, according to Fisher, "praised the audience for its intelligence and seriousness" (389).

The initial courses appear to have been a success. Fisher estimates that there were almost one hundred lecture topics in the first half of the 1920s, with an overall attendance of about five thousand students. Flush with success, the program gained new allies and patrons. In 1925, with funding from the Carnegie Foundation and the support of the American Association for Adult Education (a spin-off from the foundation), the People's Institute began a series of adult education courses specifically focused on Great Books. Scott Buchanan was put in charge of this series (and eventually became director of the School of Philosophy under Everett Dean Martin). Fifteen such Great Books courses were offered in various venues throughout the city.

In many ways, the courses formed a link between the earlier Erskine seminar at Columbia and the later activities of St. John's College. Often referred to as "General Honors," like Erskine's seminar, the People's Institute's Great Books classes set out to facilitate direct contact with, and discussion of, major works from the humanist tradition. Buchanan brought in a number of Erskine's current or former General Honors teaching assistants to run sessions, and he would later invite many of these teachers to lecture at St. John's. Among the Erskine acolytes who appeared at the People's Institute seminars in Great Books were such figures as Whittaker Chambers, Richard McKeon, Rex Tugwell (later a major player in Franklin Roosevelt's "brain trust"), and Mortimer Adler. Lionel Trilling, a young Columbia professor, who later would take up the mantle of liberal humanism at the university, evidently applied for a teaching position at the institute but was rejected.

The structure of the institute's Great Books courses, officially named the Reader Roundtable Discussion Groups, was very similar to the one that had been used for Erskine's seminar and later would inspire St. John's practice: organized as seminars for ten to fifteen students, the classes offered Socratic discussions launched by initial questions from either of two seminar leaders (generally, one a specialist in literature and the other a specialist in philosophy). Buchanan and Adler constituted one such team and taught a seminar in Great Books at the Manhattan Trade School, becoming close friends.

Their alliance was solidified in 1927 when their dissertations, for which they had exchanged ideas, were published in the same series, the prestigious International Library of Psychology, Philosophy, and Scientific Method, edited by C. K. Ogden.

Superficially, the People's Institute version of Great Books learning might appear to differ from the pedagogical procedures that St. John's would later adopt. Whereas St. John's would ask its students to spend four years moving chronologically through Great Books of the Western World that everybody read in the same order, institute courses were organized by topics and pulled individual texts out of chronological sequence to group them thematically. Some groupings concentrated on specific historical subsets of the larger Western tradition, while others dealt with issues through the books that engaged them explicitly. For example, several seminars in 1929 concentrated on the specific topic of "Art and the Machine," with selected readings from the Great Books that it was felt shed some light on this particular issue. No doubt some of this honing down of the broader list seemed necessary because, as seminars for working adults, the courses could not demand the comprehensiveness that would soon be put into play in St. John's four-year curriculum. Fisher notes that assignments for individual sessions demanded between two and eight hours of reading a week; one can only imagine that to get adult students with full-time jobs to engage with even more of the Great Books tradition would have been a quite difficult task.

But Fisher also suggests that the thematic and selective, rather than comprehensive and chronological, orientation of the institute's Great Books courses had to do with more than just expediency. From the start, pedagogy at the School of Philosophy had been assumed to have practical implication: even as students studied the classics of the Western tradition, they were doing so in order to address contemporary problems. The Great Books were to be studied not in themselves as works of antiquarian interest or as ones that addressed timeless themes. Quite the contrary, it was assumed that the classics of the Western tradition could be employed directly in the analysis *of present-day issues.* Thus, for example, as Fisher recounts, when Adler and Buchanan returned to the institute in 1933–34 to run a seminar on "Experiments in Socratic Discussion," the course turned out not to be some sort of venture in abstract philosophic reflection but a practical exercise "devoted to discussions on current problems with an eye to examining the gap between political and economic theory and practice" (415).

This concern to always test the eternal verities of the Great Books against the historically contingent issues of the day was central to these Great Books proponents' Americanist desire to bring the great works up to date and to instrumentalize them as tools in the solution of everyday problems of modernity. Here, again, we see these intellectuals' middlebrowism, their pragmatism, at work: ideas had to prove themselves by demonstrating their worth and efficacy in the arena of ordinary social life. John Erskine himself had always imagined that the value of the Great Books was relative to a context of consumption: a great book that did not live for its readers was relatively worthless, no matter the timelessness of the ideas it contained. In a pragmatic assertion in his autobiography that undoubtedly would have horrified later neoconservatives, Erskine offered this pointed definition of a great book: "A great book is one that has meaning and continues to have meaning, for a variety of persons over a long period of time. The world chooses its great books by a social process" (168–69). Significantly, in his plan for St. John's, Scott Buchanan would adopt this sociological approach as among the criteria for establishing the identity of a great book: "[A] great book is one that has been read by the largest number of persons. . . . The second criterion is also apparently numerical: a great book has the largest number of possible interpretations." In fact, at the very moment that he was advocating a return to Great Books tradition, Buchanan could be seen as subverting the very notion of that tradition as existing outside the flux of historical contingency.

Perhaps the most striking of Buchanan's claims that great works are made in the act of reading came in a late chapter of his book *Possibility* (1927), pointedly titled "Apology for Historical Piracy." Here, Buchanan outlined the attitude contemporary readers should adopt vis-à-vis "the representatives of the greater philosophical tradition [i.e., Great Books]."[17] The works of this tradition should be read, Buchanan argued, not to recapture an original, eternal meaning but to construct meanings *for the present.* Readers were "pirates" or, to use the language of today's cultural studies, "poachers," who took from the great texts according to current needs. As Buchanan says,

> Suppose we call in Kant and Aristotle and tell them what their doctrines mean in our terms and bring points from their own writings to support our contention. If it appears in the end that we have exploited their meaning, we may apologize, but we need not admit that we have been refuted merely because we have misunderstood or misused the classics. . . . The realism that demands what Kant and Aristotle really meant when they said certain things is quite irrelevant to our purpose, and we shall not be frightened by it as much as by the necessity of our own intellectual problem. (111)

Buchanan so accepted the idea that consumption of Great Books literally is an act of consuming that he even argued that reading was an inevitable and salutary killing of the work's original meaning for the purposes of making it take on new life in a new world. In Buchanan's vivid terms regarding what should be done in the pirating of great works of the past for present purposes, "before we go at this business of grave-opening we may as well state the wicked intention we have. We are going to select quite unscrupulously what we can use to advantage.... Such intellectual necromancy may carry its own vitality with it" (111–12).

When he was hired to save St. John's, then, Buchanan came to the task with a complicated, even critical attitude toward the notion of Great Books as a somehow timeless store of higher wisdom. He added to this the further inflection of admiration for the popular art of cinema. Here, he benefited from the similar admiration on the part of his friends Mark Van Doren and Mortimer Adler. In particular, Adler's massive *Art and Prudence* gave to Buchanan the concept of "cinematics," which referred to film's medium-specific artistic potential and demonstrated more generally that one could attend to Great Books and mass culture alike.

It is necessary here to address the pedagogical implications of Adler's book, since it was evidently so foundational for the film appreciation of these 1930s Great Books intellectuals. For example, in one of his few elaborations of general principles of criticism for film, Mark Van Doren—ever the film populist—worried that too much of a scholarly approach might interfere with everyday appreciation of the movies, but he singled out *Art and Prudence* as a rare academic exception insofar as the knowledge it offered deepened appreciation, rather than intellectualizing it away:

> Our movie-goer will educate himself in the history and theory of the art at his own risk. If he holds on to the original and fundamental principles there will be no risk and he will enjoy what he sees all the more for having some wisdom about it. He may, for instance, proceed to read the excellent analysis of the movie which Mortimer Adler has provided in the closing section of his long volume, *Art and Prudence*, and thereby enrich his understanding of the processes involved in the collaboration of many experts to produce any film at all, let alone a good one; which, indeed, will then seem even more than before a marvel in his eyes.[18]

Art and Prudence is, it must be noted, a baggy monster filled with meanderings, dogma, vicious polemics, overly fastidious distinctions, and arcane philosophizing. Parts of it, I dare say, are close to unreadable. My comments on it will be inevitably reductive, all the more so since I want to concentrate on its *pedagogical* implications: what enabled Great Books proponent Adler to accept that film could be a worthy object of philosophical attention, and what did this imply for the ways in which film might be approached as an object of *study* as well as of *appreciation*?

Adler, more philosophically conservative than his friend Buchanan, probably would have resisted the notion of "historical piracy" in which great ideas are refashioned to present needs. But he certainly was no less committed to the belief that such ideas had to be tested in concrete contexts and their relevance thereby reaffirmed. Unlike Buchanan, Adler took the great works to embody absolute truths, but these remained absolute only insofar as they continued to show their worthiness in answering new questions posed in human history's unfolding. Furthermore, any individual great idea might embody some, but not all, truth. No one great work covered all aspects of human life, especially as that life mutated over the centuries up to modernity. There thus needed to be what Adler later would refer to as "the great conversation" among ideas, in which each would establish its part of the truth and then be complemented and completed by other ideas (this dialectical notion would culminate in Adler's creation, for the Encyclopaedia Britannica edition of the Great Books, of his famous Syntopicon, which indexed 102 great ideas and then mapped out links among them). In the case of *Art and Prudence*, Adler adopted a fundamentally Aristotelian philosophy as his essential and unalterable dogma but then argued that Aristotle needed to be complemented and brought up to date by Christian doctrine of fallibility and by Deweyan recognition of the specifically modern problems posed by mass communication.

From Aristotle, Adler took as given a definition of poetic art (a category within which he included film) as offering spectators fictions that were mimetic enough of real life to invite audience interest but different enough to encourage distance and contemplation, with the result that the audience would be led to engage in beneficial catharsis. Christianity was necessary to explain the one aspect of Aristotelian poetics that had always remained especially shadowy: Why did art need to provide such catharsis? Why were people not born into the life of contemplation (as Plato had suggested philosophers were—an assertion that allowed him to call for art's banishment from the Republic, since it could not do what philosophers did)? Christianity—particularly the Thomism that Adler had adopted in his conversion to Catholicism—clarified that humans lived in a fallen state: not merely were none of them angels, but few of them were philosophers. While the elite caste of the philosophers might live from the start in pure contemplation and thereby not need art (Plato's position), Christianity and Aristotle together explained why everyone else—the nonphilosopher citizens—needed art and how it would raise them up to the realm of contemplation. Dewey added to this great conversation the recognition that since modern democracies had increased the size and scope of society, the possibility of an art that could speak to the masses wherever they were, and at whatever level of intelligence they possessed, required new reflection on means of communication and their technological infrastructure. (Adler, ever skeptical of the relativism of Deweyan pragmatism, was not altering his view here: rather than endorsing Deweyan relativism, he was simply taking from Dewey that one part of his work that dealt with communication in the modern world. Here Dewey, in Adler's view, was not a relativist: Dewey objectively had recognized that the modern world presented a complexity of peoples and diversities of intelligence that needed to be addressed in systematic ways.)

For Adler, it would seem, all great philosophies had some essential rightness to them. But the rightness of each philosophy might be restricted to limited spheres of applicability. That is to say, philosophers might be right, but only for certain cases, situations, or contexts. For example, even Plato, generally the philosophical nemesis in *Art and Prudence*, was right that philosophers in particular might not need art's fostering of contemplation, since by definition they lived already in the mode of contemplation; elitism, however, had made Plato not see that everyone else required the less-direct path to the contemplative life provided specifically by works of art. Plato's insight about art in society was, even in its time, of limited value, and it became all the less valuable with the coming of democratic culture.

In this respect, the movies served as a means for Adler both to test the verities of great ideas—to uncover the places in which they need to be complemented by other great ideas—and to make those ideas live in the everyday context of present-day modernity. As he said on the first pages of his study:

> In the field of practical philosophy there is always the general problem and the special case. Action is taken in singular situations under particular circumstances. Thinking about action must, therefore, take account of many contingencies, but it must no less rely upon principles of great generality. . . . There is merit, therefore, in considering the general problem and a special case at the same time. . . . On the one hand, discussion of the principles illuminates the particular case. . . . On the other hand, consideration of the special case tests the adequacy of theoretical formulations; more than that, in imposing the obligations of casuistry upon the philosopher it puts him, sympathetically at least, in the position of the man of action. The *rapprochement* of the philoso-

pher and the man of action is certainly a consummation devoutly to be wished. (vii–viii)

Again, the rhetoric here radiates a strikingly American faith in action tempered by European abstract philosophizing. It is the cinema specifically that would serve as the mediating force for this rapprochement of general and specific, theoretical and practical, and contemplative and active. The philosophical questions of *Art and Prudence* were, What is the function of art for humankind, and can art be judged according to the same criteria applied typically to nonartistic social practices? Did art require special protection from such nonaesthetic forms of evaluation (e.g., was critique of the morality in a work of art's content pertinent to critique of the artwork qua art)? The movies grounded these questions in the specific contingent historical context of today's world: Were the movies in particular a form of art? Did they represent life in ways both similar to and different from everyday reality such that distance, contemplation, and catharsis would occur? If perhaps they were art in only some contexts, should they be condemned when dangerous in other contexts where they might be received nonartistically? For example, it might be admitted that movies could serve as art for adults, but for children, who potentially were less able to maintain a contemplative distance from the emotional distance on the screen, movies might risk raising the emotions without leading to catharsis. Should the aesthetic benefit of film art for adults outweigh banishment because of movies' danger to children?

For Adler, the answer was that movies were indeed a form of art and as such had their necessary place in society. As art, the movies bore an irreducible specificity, which meant that they could *not* be judged according to nonaesthetic criteria (such as the morality of content). The last part of his massive work, a section entitled "Cinematics," set out to explain precisely how art worked and how the movies found aesthetic identity through their specific formal properties and techniques. Before elaborating his own aesthetics of film, however, Adler devoted the bulk of *Art and Prudence* to a critique of approaches, from Plato on, that misunderstood the specific social role of art, attempting to judge it as if it were just like other social practices.

In fact, the immediate context for *Art and Prudence* was a commission by the Hays Office for Adler, who previously had written against censorship of the arts, to write a critique of the Payne Fund Studies and their social science analysis of the movies as a source of risks to health and public morality. Adler took his assignment very seriously and spent much of middle part of the 1930s compiling notes on the history of censorship and reading widely in the literature on condemnation of the arts and on governance of children. A research assistant prepared a list of works in film aesthetics, summarized the bulk of them, and singled out specific texts that he felt Adler should look at (namely, the writings of V. I. Pudovkin, Gilbert Seldes, Hugo Münsterberg, and to a lesser degree Raymond Spottiswoode, Rudolph Arnheim, and Allardyce Nicoll, all of which ended up as central references in Adler's book).

Adler's critique of the Payne Fund Studies' attempt to reduce cinema's complexity to the morality of its content extended over several hundred pages in which Adler went over the premises, procedures, and conclusions of the Payne Fund researchers with a fine-tooth comb, dissecting every detail, and every argument, at ploddingly great length. Basically (to reduce the several-hundred-page screed to its fundamental points), Adler concluded that the Payne Fund researchers generally engaged in bad social science: they violated fundamental rules about control groups when they did experiments, they allowed their own personal morality to predetermine their results, they ignored data that did not fit these anticipated results, they offered opinion as knowledge, and on and on. In fact, Adler's not so veiled suggestion was that even if they had done their science well, the Payne Fund researchers could not have said much of value about art. Behind *Art and Prudence* lay a broad polemic about the humanities versus the social sciences and, in particular, about the inability of social sciences to say anything pertinent about the specific realm of the arts. (There was also a more specific polemic about the humanities versus the social sciences at the University of Chicago in particular, since a number of the Payne Fund researchers working there had been adversaries of Adler on various occasions.) A long footnote in which Adler set out to justify why he had to spend so many pages on the inadequacy of the social sciences in appreciation of art offers some sense of the dimensions of the polemic:

> It is not only in the service of prudence that a critical survey of this sort should be made. It should be done, and even more thoroughly, for the sake of universities, from which most of this work emanates. They harbor and support such research. Can their good name, and even more their intellectual integrity, survive if they permit empirical psychology and the social sciences, as well as the kind of "philosophy" with which these are associated, to continue in their present temper; if they do not recognize and fight the appalling intellectual confusions which spread from these fields into all the educational and scholarly efforts of the academic community; if they do not require their professors to be educated men, cultivated by sound philosophy whatever be their field of teaching or research? Investigations of the Payne Fund variety . . . are

probably the worst example of the kind of work that is done today in psychology and the social sciences.... The existence of such research in our universities, and of ever so much more that is essentially similar, calls upon anyone who has the impulse to reform things for man's greater good to direct such efforts to the improvement of universities, as much as, if not more so than, to the regulation of the arts. (699)

While early pages of Adler's book had chronicled a long history of moral condemnation of the arts, the Payne Fund Studies stood out insofar as they showed a specifically academic co-optation of such practice: now the social sciences were going to annex evaluation of the arts as their province. Adler's lengthy critique in *Art and Prudence* of the Payne Fund Studies had implications for film appreciation as much as did the later section on "Cinematics," where Adler finally presented his own aesthetics of film. In other words, both his own argument for the art of film and his clearing away of rival methodologies were to be read as part of the same process of aesthetic reflection.

Likewise, "The Movies, the People, and the Critics," a short reflection on film that Adler presented at the National Board of Review conference soon after the publication of *Art and Prudence*, offered in condensed form a demonstration of the interconnectedness of the negative and positive moments—sweeping away rivals versus articulation of one's own philosophy—in Adler's affirmation of aesthetics.[19] As Adler stated, "I believe that the cinema should be considered primarily as a work of art, and, hence, a source of entertainment" (5). This seemingly simple declaration required, however, that one work both to define philosophically the nature of art and to eliminate the interference to such philosophizing that came when art was misconstrued as something else (e.g., a source of moral instruction). Art came into being through the transformation of content, whether moral or not, by style (defined as "the manner in which the subject-matter is presented: how the plot is developed, how the theme is handled" [6]). "Style," Adler went on to assert, "is the important factor in judging a work," and this meant that aesthetics had to theorize the specific operations of style and its concrete embodiment in techniques. The problem, though, was that moralists had taught the public precisely to value content over form in a "reversal of the right order of importance" (7). Average moviegoers had come to believe that what should be appreciated in movies were aspects such as "[t]he content of the story rather than the style. How it is told narratively rather than filmically ... the propaganda, the lesson, the message, and the comment on current affairs" (6).

The goal of the aesthetician, then, would be the pedagogical one of reversing the reversal: teaching people to stop understanding art in terms of represented content and to come to appreciate instead how style gave art its special imaginative status in society. Cinema study had as its goal to increase "the number of those who can appreciate the higher levels of cinematic art," and this required both a critique of existing content-oriented modes of criticism *and* careful, concerted analysis of cinema's intrinsic qualities. Concerted study was necessary because appreciation of artistic form did not come easy and was in fact always in danger of being reoriented toward content criticism. As Adler explained, "[T]here is the simple fact that it is easier to *enjoy* the cinema than to *study* it. Study of cinematic style requires many repetitions and careful witnessing" (7).

At one point in the essay, Adler suggested, "It is such figures as Mickey Mouse who can best make the movie theater a school for the imagination" (5). It might seem at first that this idea of movies *as themselves* a pedagogy goes against the idea that movies as art are not about the content or message. The important qualification in the statement, however, is the idea of a schooling "for the imagination." For Adler, to the extent that the movies educated, they did so not by transmitting a content but by enabling spectators to contemplate and appreciate cinematic form's imaginative transcendence of content. Art's training occurred in the province of taste and imagination, not concept. Art was not philosophy.

Conversely, philosophy was not art. The goal of philosophy was to respect the specificity of art as imagination and to clear the ground of bad analyses so that that specificity could be pinpointed and appreciated. As Adler put it in *Art and Prudence*, "[T]aste has reasons, and the technical analysis of art is able to provide taste with rational illumination" (458). In an ideal world (although for the Christian Adler, the worldly sphere was never ideal, since humans always lived in degrees of separation from grace), it might be possible to stand directly before the work of art and intuitively experience its value, but in the everyday real world of ordinary people with varying degrees of aesthetic cultivation, that immediate experience was unlikely. Aesthetic education was needed to bring citizens to the level at which they could have valuable appreciation of art. In a footnote, Adler quoted the declaration of his aesthetic idol, Jacques Maritan, that "if the act of perception of the beautiful takes place without speech or any effort of abstraction, conceptual discourse can nevertheless play an immense part in the *preparation* for that act" and clarified that "preparation" was another word for education and instruction. As Adler went on to say, "The cultivation of critical discriminations with regard to the cinema—necessarily in the light of analysis and a knowledge of its rules—is a condition of good taste here as anywhere in the field of art.... The spectator must be trained to see *how* the story is told as, in the field of literature, he must be taught to see *how* it is written" (675–76).

Art was one thing, and philosophy, which could train the appreciation of art, was another. To simplify, we can say basically that Adler assumed humankind to be distinguished by a number of separate faculties or capacities. Each faculty had its essential area of concern and its specific way of being in the world. In *Art and Prudence*, the highest human capacity was the faculty of philosophizing. The lowest was carnality, the animal appetite for immediate sensation. Between them were faculties such as the *arts*, geared to fabrication of works of organic unity, and *morality*, geared to the living of the proper life and to salutary interactions with others. While individual faculties could overlap in their objects of attention—for example, there could be a philosophy *of* art—each faculty had its own forms of being, its own values, and its own spheres of human pertinence. For example, insofar as art imitated life, it might appear to resemble morality or philosophy, but insofar as it also diverged from life through its formal properties of style and its imaginative distance, art could not really philosophize or moralize. One should not go to art for conceptual argument or for models of the good life. (Conversely, one should not go to morality to understand what art was about.) As Adler put it in one of the last footnotes of the book:

> What I have called "sociological criticism" makes two errors. First, it judges a fictional work according to its choice of theme and not according to the detailed treatment of the chosen subject-matter.... Second, in so far as it considers the subject-matter in detail it applies the standards of scientific rather than of poetic possibility.... [T]he sociological critic must recognize that a novel, for instance, can be good as fiction and bad as propaganda, or conversely. He must also be made to see that the didactic intention—whether logical or rhetorical—violates the medium of fine art, as a means of imitation, and not of proof or persuasion. (673–74)

For Adler, the greatest of the Great Books would be the works of philosophy, since there the practices of conceptualization and speculation most enabled human beings to rise up from the lower depths of animalistic appetite.[20] But insofar as art did something that philosophy did not do—namely, offer imaginative reworking of the world for nonphilosophic people who were not immediately in the realm of contemplation—art had its own essential place among human activities. There was no necessary incompatibility of art with greatness, and there was no reason to assume that the popularity of an art detracted from its ability to be great. As Adler enthused toward the end of his book, "I offer . . . the work of Walt Disney as lively art that also reaches greatness, a degree of perfection in its field which surpasses our best critical capacity to analyze and which succeeds at the same time in pleasing children and simple folk" (581). Like Scott Buchanan with his notion of translation between the myriad realms of human activity, both mental and manual, Adler recognized the diversity of human faculties, emotional and intellectual, but assumed they could find coexistence in a great conversation that cut across hierarchies of high and low.

It is not clear why the idea of the Institute of Cinematics went nowhere. But it is noteworthy that Adler, its fundamental source of inspiration, seemed to fall into a rhetoric of mass culture *critique* as he moved into the 1940s. He continued to engage with film through his efforts as speechwriter for Will Hays, but he increasingly preferred that his work on film stay behind the scenes and not be acknowledged.

Adler's next fat book after the enormous *Art and Prudence* brought him into a new encounter with mass culture but in a way that now pushed him increasingly to affirm the Great Books tradition *at the expense of popular arts like cinema*. In 1940, Adler published *How to Read a Book*, which became a best seller and made him into a popular culture icon in his own right.[21] With its title redolent of the self-help books of the day, *How to Read a Book* might appear to participate in that pragmatic instrumentalization that characterized the work of many of the middlebrow intellectuals. And certainly the book did offer a nuts-and-bolts approach to reading—readers could improve their skills by such tactics as parsing difficult words, using book titles as a clue to their content, taking notes and outlining arguments, and so on—that made it seem eminently practical. But if the expansive *Art and Prudence* had implied that, with enough time, one could find room for both Great Books *and* movies (and time enough even to engage in a long critique of the social science criticism of the movies), *How to Read a Book*, written under the shadow of imminent war, suggested that choices had to be made. Despite its general title, *How to Read a Book* was specifically about the reading of *Great* Books and about the need to single out and value their special virtues. The movies now were represented as a trivial pursuit: Adler offered lament about an age in which, instead of pushing ourselves to read the best books and participate in their great conversation, "we turn to gossip and scandal, or give up conversation entirely for bridge *or movies*" (vii; my emphasis). The highest culture had to be defended and made available as the primary cultural force in the fight for liberty: the cultural mediator, as Adler now defined the role, was "one who helps the less competent make more effective contacts with the best minds" (60). Where *Art and Prudence* had applauded cinema among the arts precisely because its popular nature allowed it democratically to reach across social divides to offer imagination to all constituencies at their own levels of cultural cultivation, Adler now hinted that society itself might *have* to be divided: "Even today, it may be true that some part of the population must be vocationally trained, while another part is liberally educated" (98). Plato, finally, seems indeed to have won the day.

By the late 1930s, the Great Books intellectuals appear to have given up on the movies as a site of education. Adler's change of heart in fact seems a local version of a larger shift in attitudes toward popular culture that was taking place among intellectuals toward the end of the decade. It was only a few short years, in fact, after Scott Buchanan's, Mortimer Adler's, and Mark Van Doren's 1930s ventures into film that Clement Greenburg declared war on mass culture in his notorious essay "Avant-Garde and Kitsch" (1939), and his opening salvo became only one in a series of fervent missions launched against popular culture.

The encounter of the 1930s Great Book intellectuals with the popular art of cinema serves as a fitting conclusion to the story I have presented in this book, since that favorable encounter represented one of most explicit acts of cinema appreciation on the part of high-culture intellectuals. This was a moment of rapprochement before the onslaught of that of mass culture critique that would come to predominate in the postwar period. Postwar discussion of contemporary mass culture evidenced what Andrew Ross has termed a "failure" of encounter between American intellectuals and the popular arts. Likewise, Jonathan Auerbach notes how the emergent postwar field of American studies—for which film might have seemed a perfect object for the field's "myths and symbols approach" to American everyday culture—virtually ignored the art of cinema, as if little of revelatory value could be found there; the professional journal of American studies, *American Quarterly*, published *nothing* on film in the 1950s (and only one essay up to 1973). Likewise, the New Critics of postwar America came to valorize hermetic works of high modernism against a mass culture they found facile and too democratically available: as Christopher Newfield explains, "Many observers have noted that the New Critics were avid canonizers of demanding writers like the metaphysical poets of the seventeenth century and the high modernists of the twentieth. . . . Truly literary language was not the common language that typified mass culture. The result was not only a certain arduous, even pleasureless tone in criticism, but also the creation of a professional firewall between the definable set of literary masters worthy of professional study and the kind of shallow entertainments favored by the folk." In such a context, as Greg Taylor argues, serious study of film was often forced to go underground and wait for the explosion of concerns in the 1960s that would once again bring academia to attend to the cinema as a form of cultural expression.[22]

With world war looming, figures like Mortimer Adler propagandized there were better things to do than waste time with movies (although he would write privately to Will Hays during the war that he was seeing three to four movies a week). Other intellectuals, like Clement Greenburg, had gone further to see mass culture as one of the very incipient threats that, along with fascism, called into doubt the future of Western society.

A little while later, however, at the beginning of another war, Hollywood cinema got its revenge perhaps, imagining that there were more important things to do than spend time with the books of the so-called great tradition. In 1951, the year before Adler's Encyclopaedia Britannica project reached fruition, a Korean War film, *I Want You*, directed by Mark Robson, offered what is probably one of the few discussions in classical Hollywood cinema on the merits—or lack thereof—of the Great Books of the Western World. The young heroine, Carrie (Peggy Dow), comes home on break from college and goes out for the evening with her occasional boyfriend, Jack (Farley Granger). Jack—an early version of those troubled youths who populate the American cinema of the 1950s—is a carefree loafer, interested in nothing but the pleasures of the moment such as his noisy hot rod. Carrie clearly likes Jack a lot, but she is bothered by his irresponsibility, especially since her time at college has given her a new sense of her own intellectual potential. The impetuous Jack is consumed with desire for Carrie, but she fends off his amorous declarations. "I've got plans for myself," she asserts. "Until I'm twenty-five, nothing serious."

Calculating with dismay that that means waiting five years for Carrie to decide if she will commit to him, Jack asks what she plans to do for those long years. Carrie's answer shows that she has given her future a lot of thought: "I'm going to finish college, travel . . . I'm going to grow up." Then she offers an example of what that means: "There's a whole list of books I'm going to read. Two hundred and eleven of them. . . . The *Iliad*, *The Critique of Pure Reason*, Aristotle. I'm going to be frivolous about men and serious about everything else until I'm ready."

However, the words I have quoted convey only one aspect of the scene. As Carrie is reciting her list of great works, she happens to look up as she mentions Kant and falters when she sees Jack gazing at her with puppy love.

Carrie finishes her speech, but it now sounds all the more like a recitation, as if she were mechanically defending the Great Books but knowing in her heart of hearts that there is something more out there.

Hollywood films, we know, are fond of setting up contradictions and then offering mythic resolution to them. A film from the moment both of the Korean War and of what Betty Friedan analyzed as "the feminine mystique," *I Want You* is no exception. Jack gets his draft notice and realizes a newfound maturity of purpose. There is more to life than hot rods and impetuous desires lacking in commitment and in responsible planning for the future. But Carrie, too, gains new purpose: she realizes that she does love Jack, that they need each other, and that he cannot go off to war without her marrying him. She abandons her college plans, and they wed. He leaves for the war with the full affirmation of his self-domesticating wife to inspire him.

Carrie's childish dreams of the Great Books are left behind. There are, the film suggests, more important things ahead for 1950s America. The volumes of Great Books that Mortimer Adler would soon hawk to the American public might sell like crazy, but most historians assume they became one more acquisition for suburbanites to put on their shelves in order to signal their social status. Perhaps Carrie would eventually become one of these purchasers who would find space for the volumes, unread, in her new domestic world. This certainly was a Hollywood sort of dream for the Great Books.

Notes

INTRODUCTION: TOWARD A DISCIPLINARY HISTORY
OF FILM STUDIES

1. Eugenie M. Fribourg, "What College Girls Think of the Movies: Barnard Regrets That Their Ideas Are So Far behind Their Technique," *Motion Picture Classic* 30, no. 2 (October 1929): 29.
2. Ellen Messer-Davidow, David R. Shumway, and David J. Sylvan, eds., *Knowledges: Historical and Critical Studies in Disciplinarity* (Charlottesville: University Press of Virginia, 1993).
3. David Bordwell, *Making Meaning: Inference and Rhetoric in the Interpretation of Cinema* (Cambridge, MA: Harvard University Press, 1989).
4. Jack C. Ellis, "Ruminations of an Ex-Cinematologist," *Cinema Journal* 24, no. 2 (Winter 1985): 50.
5. Bernard Rosenberg and David Manning White, eds., *Mass Culture: The Popular Arts in America* (Glencoe, IL: Free Press, 1957).
6. The exceptions include such figures as Parker Tyler, Manny Farber, and Robert Warshow, whom later film studies canonized as veritable avant-gardists who early on imputed to cinema an energy that often gave the medium edgy qualities not reducible to the bland conformities of middlebrow mass culture. For a strong assertion of these figures as 1950s rebels, see Greg Taylor, *Artists in the Audience: Cults, Camp, and American Film Criticism* (Princeton, NJ: Princeton University Press, 1999).
7. Joseph Gelmis, ed., *The Film Director as Superstar* (Garden City, NY: Doubleday, 1970).
8. Julie A. Reuben, *The Making of the Modern University: Intellectual Transformation and the Marginalization of Morality* (Chicago: University of Chicago Press, 1996).
9. For an excellent analysis of early initiatives to teach film in K–12, see Lea Jacobs, "Reformers and Spectators: The Film Education Movement in the Thirties," *Camera Obscura* 22 (January 1990): 29–49. As Jacobs notes, K–12 film ed-

ucation in the period tended to focus on either of two goals: to use films as vehicles to improve *moral* judgment *or* to treat films in themselves as artistic objects whose refined appreciation could help improve *aesthetic* discernment. Representative of the former position was the organization Teaching Film Custodians, which used films as a mode of visual education to make life lessons rich in immediate impact: in one typical activity, the Teaching Film Custodians reedited classical Hollywood films into short subjects that centered on a moral dilemma that students could then discuss. Representative of the latter position was the National Council of Teachers of English, which in the 1930s took an affirmative stance toward film's potential for cultural uplift and promoted appreciation of quality Hollywood narratives.

Another important pedagogy in the period came in the form of correspondence classes offered by private businesses such as the Palmer Photoplay Corporation. Most of the correspondence school classes focused on photoplay writing, although there were some production courses such as those offered by the New York Institute of Photography, which actually sent students a 16 mm camera loaded with film as part of its lesson plan. For a useful analysis of the photoplay correspondence classes, see Anne Morey, "Fashioning the Self to Fashion the Film: The Case of the Palmer Photoplay Corporation," in her *Hollywood Outsiders: The Adaptation of the Film Industry, 1913–1934* (Minneapolis: University of Minnesota Press, 2003), 70–113.

10. At this point, it is worth noting some mentions of additional ventures in film pedagogy in these decades of which there are few remaining traces. I encourage any readers who might have information about them to contact me (dana.polan@nyu.edu). To take these in order:

a. Yale University's *Obituary Record of Graduates Deceased during the Year Ending July 1, 1927*, notes that alumnus Dwight Macdonald Sr. (father of the famous New York intellectual) "in 1919 lectured at Yale on the history and development of the motion picture industry." There is no record of a course on the subject, however, and it is likely that Macdonald Sr., who worked as a lawyer for several motion picture companies, simply had given a lecture or two in a course on some broader subject or perhaps had spoken at the fraternal house he had been a member of and that he returned to from time to time. Dwight Macdonald Jr.'s biographer Michael Wreszin shared his thoughts on this with me, and I thank him for his assistance.

b. In a 1932 issue of *Educational Screen*, civil engineering professor R. V. Newcomb, identified as "Director, Motion Picture Activities," at the University of South Dakota, described a course he had initiated in motion picture production at the university. In his account, he had been taking amateur movies of events on campus and realized that such documentary efforts should be systematized. He set up an office to coordinate campus filmmaking, and this led to interest on the part of students in a production class. Newcomb tried to introduce such a course into the engineering curriculum, but his dean objected, and so Newcomb negotiated for the journalism department to offer it. The course, Cinematography, was very much a practical one, with sessions on such topics as

"Taking the Picture," "Titles," "Cutting, Editing, Splicing," "Processing," and "Trick Work," but it also devoted two sessions to "History of Motion Pictures" and "Evolution of Film." At first, students appear to have shot footage individually, moving from mere experiments in correct exposure to more complicated lessons in angle and composition. Soon, however, the owner of a local soda fountain offered to fund a film to promote his business, and the students formed a crew to make a modest fiction film, called *Date Night*, about an evening at the fountain. The class also seems to have engaged in some educational film work with production of a film entitled *The Testing of Construction Materials* for Newcomb's own department. While the course was clearly a hands-on effort, Newcomb ended his article with the suggestion that his instruction in techniques of production could have ameliorative impact on the viewing habits of student spectators. That is, his course was also, as he claimed, a training in aesthetic discernment and critical awareness: "Our students have taken a new interest in the motion pictures shown at the local theatre. Instead of just being interested in the story, they now notice and study camera angles, photography, lighting, tempo and methods of carrying out action. They are thus better equipped to enjoy the good dramatic motion pictures we have today." See R. V. Newcomb, "Cinematography at the University of South Dakota," *Educational Screen* 11, no. 3 (March 1932): 70–71, 90.

c. In its issue for March 1933, *Educational Screen* reported, "The College of the City of New York had instituted a course on 'The Art of the Motion Picture,' to be conducted by Irving A. Jacoby, and intended for the 'intelligent moviegoer, the student of comparative art, and members of the motion picture industry who seek the proper perspectives of films. Sixteen lectures will be given in the course, each lecture to concentrate on a different phase of the motion picture. The course is to be supplemented by showings of important pictures no longer exhibited.'" See *Educational Screen* 12, no. 3 (March 1933): 78. Jacoby's son Oren has shared with me a faded and somewhat illegible catalog entry that expands on that description and clarifies that the course was part of CCNY's adult education evening program. The course, it is said, will outline "a critical approach to the motion picture, its history, its present trends, and probable future, the Hollywood style, the influence of Hollywood culture on world culture, experimental practices, short subjects, and newsreels, animated cartoons, travel, education, and industrial films." It specifies that the films shown would include "epics of Griffith and DeMille, the comedies of Chaplin, the realist dramas of von Stroheim and von Sternberg, the phantasies of Clair and Lubitsch."

No other traces appear to remain of this course (e.g., CCNY archivists found nothing for me). This is regrettable, since Jacoby's course seems somewhat advanced in its canonic grasp of major trends in film history, its understanding of the diversity of genres, its recognition of the need for comparative study of Hollywood in relation to world cinema, its focus on auteur directors, and its deep concern for the study of film as part of general culture (the catalog entry describes the ways film impacts on knowledge in fields like economics, literature, sociology, and psychology).

Jacoby would go on to an important career in documentary and educational film production with such figures as John Grierson and Willard Van Dyke. His pedagogy would follow a trajectory typical of much film teaching from the 1930s to 1940s by moving from the more culturalist and generalist course of 1933 to practical instruction in filmmaking—especially, in his case, training in documentary film production as the needs for such increased with the coming of war.

d. In the mid-1930s, Lelia Trolinger, an assistant professor of visual instruction at the University of Colorado, offered an extension course, Education 136, Education through Motion Pictures. No trace appears to remain of this course other than a 1935 catalog description with reading list:

"A survey (1) of the experimental evidence of the value of motion pictures in classroom instruction with criteria for evaluating instructional films and (2) of the effects of the 'movies' upon youth, based upon the Payne Foundation studies, with considerable emphasis upon the work that can be accomplished by teachers in guiding pupils in motion picture appreciation."

Readings for the course included the volumes of the Payne Fund Studies on the influence of movies on children, as well as a number of books on K–12 teaching of film appreciation such as Edgar Dale's *How to Appreciate Motion Pictures,* William Lewin's *Photoplay Appreciation in American High Schools,* and Sarah Mullens's *How to Judge Motion Pictures.* Given the course's placement as an extension class within an education program, it is likely that it was intended as professional training for schoolteachers. It seems very much in keeping with a film-betterment trend in the 1930s that assumed that deleterious effects of motion pictures could be combated in large part at the point of reception, through the training of youthful spectators to be more discerning in their film viewing practices and to demand uplifting and well-made cinematic entertainment.

e. The magazine of the National Board of Review reported in its November 1934 issue on a one-month lecture series minicourse on photoplay appreciation at the Teachers College of Columbia University. The course was run by Alan Abbott, an English professor at Teachers College, and seems, like Trolinger's course at the University of Colorado, to have set out to offer K–12 schoolteachers some instruction in how to teach motion picture appreciation to schoolchildren. Thus, there were announced lectures on "Guidance in Motion Picture Appreciation," on "Standards of Adults and Children in Judging Films," on "Psychological Aspects of Motion Pictures, with Some Reference to the Payne Fund Studies," on "Stage and Screen: A Comparison of Dramatic Principles and Techniques," and on "The English Teacher and the Photoplay" (this last lecture was by William Lewin, author of the influential *Photoplay Appreciation in American High Schools*). See "Motion Picture Study," *National Board of Review Magazine* 9, no. 8 (November 1934): 14. The same article reports on an informal discussion group at Bennington College in Vermont on the art of the movies, sponsored by a professor of drama. Students evidently would see recent releases in the local movie houses and then come to the group to discuss the aesthetic contribution of technique and mise-en-scène. This venture appears, however, to have remained informal and not to have led to a bona fide course offering.

11. Quoted in Film Library Report, December 1937, available in Special Collections, MoMA Film Department.

12. Haidee Wasson, *Museum Movies: The Museum of Modern Art and the Birth of Art Cinema* (Berkeley and Los Angeles: University of California Press, 2005).

13. This comes from an undated memo in the MoMA archives from Griffith to Barry. Internal evidence would suggest the document was written between 1942 and 1945.

14. Iris Barry, "The Case for the Museum of Modern Art Film Library," unpublished document in MoMA archives, dated April 1948.

15. Ibid.

16. David Shumway, *Creating American Civilization: A Genealogy of American Literature as an Academic Discipline* (Minneapolis: University of Minnesota Press, 1994), 7.

17. David O. Levine, *The American College and the Culture of Aspiration, 1915–1940* (Ithaca, NY: Cornell University Press, 1986), 9.

18. Joan Shelley Rubin, *The Making of Middlebrow Culture* (Chapel Hill: University of North Carolina Press, 1992); Janice Radway, *A Feeling for Books: The Book-of-the-Month-Club, Literary Taste and Middle-Class Desire* (Chapel Hill: University of North Carolina Press, 1997).

19. John Hartley, *A Short History of Cultural Studies* (Thousand Oaks, CA: Sage, 2003).

20. Warren Susman, *Culture as History: The Transformation of American Society in the Twentieth Century* (New York: Pantheon, 1984); T. J. Jackson Lears, *No Place of Grace: Antimodernism and the Transformation of American Culture, 1880–1920* (New York: Pantheon, 1981).

21. Mortimer Adler, *Art and Prudence: A Study in Practical Philosophy* (New York: Longmans, Green, 1937), xii.

22. Richard deCordova, *Picture Personalities: The Emergence of the Star System in America* (Urbana: University of Illinois Press, 1990).

23. Edward Van Zile, *That Marvel, the Movie: A Glance at Its Reckless Past, Its Promising Present, and Its Significant Future* (New York: Putnam, 1923).

24. Laurence Veysey, *The Emergence of the American University* (Chicago: University of Chicago Press, 1965), 338.

25. John Higham, "The Matrix of Specialization," in *The Organization of Knowledge in Modern America, 1860–1920*, ed. Alexandra Oleson and John Voss (Baltimore: Johns Hopkins University Press, 1979), 15.

26. Raymond Williams, "My Cambridge," in *What I Came to Say* (London: Hutchinson Radius, 1989), 4.

CHAPTER 1: FIRST FORAYS IN FILM EDUCATION

1. The letter in question is dated November 10, 1945. The entire existing correspondence can be found in the "Hays, Will" folder of the Butler Papers in the University Collections of the Columbia University Library. Archival mate-

rials consulted for this chapter include that folder, as well as course catalogs, syllabi, memos, and letters in the Columbiana Archives of the university. There is also some material on the 1926–27 attempt by Columbia to set up a degree program in the Will Hays Papers (available on microfilm).

Film historian Peter Decherney has covered some of the same ground as this chapter in an excellent essay, "Inventing Film Study and Its Object at Columbia University, 1915–1938," *Film History* 12 (2000): 443–60; revised as "Overlapping Publics: Hollywood and Columbia University, 1915," in his *Hollywood and the Culture Elite: How the Movies Became American* (New York: Columbia University Press, 2005). My thanks to Peter for sharing the fruits of his research with me.

2. Laurence Veysey, *The Emergence of the American University* (Chicago: University of Chicago Press, 1965), 441.

3. Butler, quoted in John Angus Burrell, *A History of Adult Education at Columbia University* (New York: Columbia University Press, 1954), 81.

4. Egbert, quoted in ibid., 83.

5. One bit of evidence comes in the form of letters from home-study English secretary Ruth Needham to the National Board of Review, asking for an increased number of copies of the board's journal *Exceptional Photoplay*, which it provided to the class. The numbers went from 25 to 40 to 50 between 1925 and 1926. Needham's letters are in box 21 ("Columbia University") of the NBR files at the New York Public Library.

6. George Baxter Smith, *Purposes and Conditions Affecting the Nature and Extent of Participation of Adults in Courses in the Home Study Department of Columbia University, 1925–1932* (New York: Teachers College Press, Columbia University, 1935).

7. Arthur Leads, "Thinks and Things," *Writer's Monthly* 7, no. 1 (January 1916): 31.

8. Anonymous, "Home-Made Motion Pictures Predicted for Near Future: Films Will Be as Common as Phonograph Records Says Victor O. Freeburg, Head of Photoplay Department of Columbia," *New York Times*, April 22, 1917, sec. 8, p. 5.

9. See Peter Decherney, "Imagining the Archive: Film Collecting in America before MoMA" (Ph.D. diss., New York University, 2001). Decherney's published essay and book, cited in note 1, cover similar ground.

10. Anonymous, "Lasky Company Offers Scholarship to Columbia Students," *Moving Picture World*, October 30, 1915, 765. See also Anonymous, "Lasky Scholarship for College Scenario Course," *Motion Picture News* 12, no. 18 (November 6, 1915): 76.

11. Arthur Leads, "Thinks and Things," *Writer's Monthly* 8, nos. 5/6 (November/December 1916): 208.

12. Victor O. Freeburg, *Disguise Plots in Elizabethan Drama* (New York: Columbia University Press, 1915).

13. In an unpublished essay, "From Art in the American Lyceum to 'Photoplay Composition,'" film historian Kaveh Askari hypothesizes compellingly

that Freeburg may have derived his conception of composition from aesthetician Arthur Wesley Dow, who wrote a book on that topic in 1899, who came to head the arts department at Columbia's Teachers College, and who clearly imprinted his aesthetic philosophy on teachers of the arts in the university's extension program. In Askari's words,

> Freeburg modeled his analysis of cinema on the pictorial principles of static media in two ways: he extracted static compositions from moving scenes and he conceived of moving form as an extension of static form. For his static compositions he looked to mise-en-scène and the posing of actors. He reproduced stills from films and analyzed them as one would a painting. He looked for the effectiveness of line and balance in a still, sometimes abstracting his own diagrams that bear a striking resemblance to those in Dow's workbook. From this method he developed an elaborate theory of a "tableau effect" in the film spectator's perception.
>
> For moving forms, Freeburg developed the idea that film gave literal expression to those movements already suggested by the lines and shapes of static art. For example, the movement suggested in a sculpture of an athlete could be literally realized in a composed movement of an athlete for the camera....
>
> In building these concepts from Dow's basic paradigm, Freeburg developed a pedagogy of film art that allied cinema with the plastic arts rather than the performing arts. He did teach the importance of dramaturgy. Any practical course on screenwriting wouldn't get very far without covering the basic components of story, but he consistently maintained that dramaturgy must be integrated with effective composition.

My thanks to Kaveh for sharing his sharp research with me.

14. Freeburg, *Disguise Plots*, 30.

15. Victor O. Freeburg, *The Art of Photoplay Making* (New York: Macmillan, 1918), 29. Further references in text.

16. T. J. Jackson Lears, *No Place of Grace: Antimodernism and the Transformation of American Culture, 1880–1920* (New York: Pantheon, 1981).

17. In passing, it should be noted that Freeburg's notion of just what constituted contemplative and peaceful images was often harshly ideological. For example, at one point in *The Art of Photoplay Making*, he made the offensive assertion that in terms of visual appeals to the imagination, "[A] king of Babylon connotes more than a negro prize fighter" (106).

18. Victor O. Freeburg, *Pictorial Beauty on the Screen* (New York: Macmillan, 1923), 30.

19. Anonymous, "Home-Made Motion Pictures Predicted for Near Future."

20. Vassilos Koronakes wrote the paper, "Victor Freeburg, Frances Patterson and the Photoplay Studies at Columbia University—A Research Program," for John Belton's Rutgers seminar in film research.

21. Frances Taylor Patterson, *Cinema Craftsmanship: A Book for Photoplaywrights* (New York: Harcourt, Brace, 1920), vi. Further references in text.

22. Frances Taylor Patterson, *Scenario and Screen* (New York: Harcourt, Brace, 1928), 28–29.

23. Anonymous, "Screen: Here and There," *New York Times*, October 23, 1921, 73.

24. Anonymous, "Picture Plays and People," *New York Times*, July 2, 1922, 66.

25. Mary Kelly, "Columbia's Cinema Class," *New York Times*, December 7, 1930, 130.

26. Anonymous, *Variety*, August 31, 1938, 30.

27. Frances Taylor Patterson, "A New Art in an Old University," *Photoplay Magazine*, January 1920, 65, 124.

28. Anonymous, "From the Glare of Studio Lights to the Velvet Darkness of the Theatre," *New York Times*, October 4, 1925, X5.

29. These postcards are in my possession. I thank film historian Kathryn Fuller Seeley for offering them to me.

30. Richard Koszarski, *An Evening's Entertainment: The Age of the Silent Feature Picture, 1915–1928* (New York: Scribner, 1990), 335, referring to Frances Patterson, ed., *Motion Picture Continuities* (New York: Columbia University Press, 1929).

31. Hoberman describes the production of *Broken Hearts* in his *Bridge of Light: Yiddish Film between Two Worlds* (New York: Schocken Books, 1991), 107–10.

32. Anonymous, "Screen: Two Current Pictures," *New York Times*, December 25, 1921, 65.

33. Horace Coon, *Columbia: Colossus on the Hudson* (New York: Dutton, 1947), 147.

34. The clipping in the Lincoln Center Performing Arts Library unfortunately does not indicate which newspaper this December 24, 1930, article came from.

35. For one trace of Rogers's efforts in educational filmmaking, see Margaret I. MacDonald, "Interests Organizing to Further Cause of Educative Films in Public Schools," *Moving Picture World* 45, no. 3 (July 17, 1920): 316.

36. Anonymous, "Motion Picture Notes," *New York Times*, January 15, 1922, 72.

37. The letter can be found in the College Affairs Committee files in the Lester Cowan papers of the archives of Special Collections, Margaret Herrick Library, Academy of Motion Picture Arts and Sciences (AMPAS), Los Angeles.

38. Patterson seems to have also taught some versions of the more ambitious course with drama scholar Arthur Edwin Krows. Krows appears best known for a basic study of stagecraft in American drama (*Play Production in America*, 1916) but he also had experience of the cinema, both as a photoplay writer for several films of the 1910s and 1920s and as author of a 1930 book, *The Talkies*.

39. Burrell, *History of Adult Education at Columbia University*, 31.

40. For the list of advisers, see "Film Study at Columbia University," *School and Society*, July 19, 1937.

CHAPTER 2: A BRIEF INTERLUDE AS THE MOVIES MARCH ON

1. Peter M. Rutkoff and William B. Scott, *New School: A History of the New School for Social Research* (New York: Free Press, 1986), 25. Further references in text. The current chapter benefited from research in the archives of the library at the New School for Social Research.

2. Terry Ramsaye, *A Million and One Nights: A History of the Motion Picture through 1925* (New York: Simon and Schuster, 1926 [Touchstone Books reprint edition, 1986]), xiii.

3. Terry Ramsaye, "The Motion Picture," *Annals of the American Academy of Political and Social Science* (special issue on the "Motion Picture in Its Economic and Social Aspects") 128, no. 217 (November 1926): 1–19. Further references in text.

4. Robert C. Allen and Douglas Gomery, *Film History: Theory and Practice* (New York: McGraw-Hill, 1985), 51.

Ironically, because the existence of Ramsaye's New School course came to light only after the publication of *Film History*, the volume mistakenly asserts, "In 1914 or 1926 there were no college courses in film history to guarantee sales for a history of film" (59) to explain why Ramsaye (and Robert Grau before him) had to engage so heavily in publicity activity for their volumes. It now seems clear that Ramsaye's book did bear a direct link to a course in an institution of higher learning and that he may have seen his lectures precisely as a way to build sales for his history.

5. Ramsaye, *A Million and One Nights*, xiii. Further references in text.

6. Paul Rotha, *The Film Till Now: A Survey of the Cinema* (New York: Jonathan Cape, 1930), 22.

7. Under the title "Objection and Reproof," Ramsaye's letter to the editor ran in the January 30, 1927, edition of the *New York Times* (p. 3). Gerstein's review had appeared in the *New York Times Book Review*, November 28, 1926, 3.

8. From the same year as Ramsaye's *A Million and One Nights*, see, for instance, William Marston Seabury's *The Public and the Motion Picture Industry* (New York: Macmillan, 1926).

9. These fraught negotiations are to be found in the "Ramsaye" folder of the Horace Kallen papers at the American Jewish Archives, Hebrew Union College in Cincinnati. My thanks to the archivists at the AJA for providing me with copies of the letters.

CHAPTER 3: "YOUNGER ART, OLD COLLEGE, HAPPY UNION"

1. President A. Lawrence Lowell file in Harvard University Archives, folder 724, UAI 5.160 1925–28. Research for this chapter is based primarily on mate-

rials in four sites: the general University Archives of Harvard University; the archives of Harvard's Fogg Art Museum; the John F. Kennedy Presidential Library (papers of Joseph P. Kennedy), and, above all, the Historical Collection in the Baker Library of the Harvard School of Business. Most helpful at the latter were the correspondence files of Wallace Donham, dean of the School of Business in the period I am dealing with. For reasons of brevity, letters to and from Donham or his staff—which are organized alphabetically in the files—will not be given detailed reference.

2. See Terry Ramsaye, *A Million and One Nights: A History of the Motion Picture Through 1925* (New York: Simon and Schuster, 1926 [Touchstone Books reprint edition, 1986]), 806–7.

3. On Seabury and the Payne Fund Studies, see Garth S. Jowett, Ian C. Jarvie, and Kathryn H. Fuller, *Children and the Movies: Media Influence and the Payne Fund Controversy* (New York: Cambridge University Press, 1996). As the authors note, Seabury's attacks on the film industry were considered so inflammatory that the other organizers of the Payne Fund Studies gradually eased him out of the project, and he had no involvement with it after December 1928.

4. Joseph P. Kennedy, *The Story of the Films, as Told by Leaders of the Industry to the Students of the Graduate School of Business Administration, George F. Baker Foundation, Harvard University* (Chicago: A. W. Shaw, 1927). Further references in text.

5. For Kennedy's departure from the film business, see the short report in *Variety*, May 7, 1930, 3.

6. The controversy is described in Frederick Lewis Allen, *The Big Change: America Transforms Itself, 1900–1950* (New York: Harper, 1952), 241.

7. Thorstein Veblen, *The Higher Learning in America: A Memorandum on the Conduct of Universities by Business Men* (New York: B. W. Huebsch, 1918); Abraham Flexner, *Universities: American, English, German* (New York: Oxford University Press, 1930), 166–67.

8. Frank Cole Babbitt, "Plato and the Movies," *Harvard Graduates' Magazine* 35 (1926–27): 20–25. For Baudry, see his essay "The Apparatus: Metapsychological Approaches to the Impression of Reality in Cinema," in, among other places, *Narrative, Apparatus, Ideology*, ed. Philip Rosen (New York: Columbia University Press, 1986), 286–318.

9. Flexner, *Universities*, 134.

10. See Roger L. Geiger, *To Advance Knowledge: The Growth of American Research Universities, 1900–1940* (New York: Oxford University Press, 1986).

11. Jeffrey L. Cruikshank, *A Delicate Experiment: The Harvard Business School, 1908–1945* (Cambridge, MA: Harvard Business School Publishing, 1987), 18.

12. Wallace Donham, "Business Teaching in the Case System" in *The Case Method: A Related Series of Articles*, ed. Cecil Fraser (New York: McGraw-Hill, 1931), 11–25.

13. For background on the history of the HSB's use of the case method, see Melvin Copeland, "The Genesis of the Case Method in Business Instruction,"

in *The Case Method at the Harvard School of Business*, ed. Malcolm McNair, with Anita C. Hersum (New York: McGraw-Hill, 1954), 25–33.

14. Block-booking was the practice by which distribution companies required movie theaters to lease films in a block—rather than by individual title. This guaranteed rentals for the distributor but sometimes forced theaters to take on films they could not sell to their audiences. Reformers frequently disdained the practice of block-booking because they thought it gave exhibitors less control over film choice in relation to the moral needs of the spectators.

15. See, for instance, Janet Staiger's use of him in David Bordwell, Kristin Thompson, and Janet Staiger, *The Classical Hollywood Cinema: Film Style and Mode of Production to 1960* (New York: Columbia University Press, 1985), 320–22.

16. Howard T. Lewis, *Harvard Business Reports*, vol. 8, *Cases on the Motion Picture Industry with Commentary* (New York: McGraw-Hill, 1930).

17. Howard T. Lewis, *The Motion Picture Industry* (New York: Van Nostrand, 1933).

18. Howard T. Lewis, "Distributing Motion Pictures," *Harvard Business Review* 7 (1928/29): 267–79.

19. William Victor Strauss, "Foreign Distribution of American Motion Pictures," *Harvard Business Review* 8 (1929–30): 307–15; Edward R. Beach, "Double Features in Motion-Picture Exhibiting," *Harvard Business Review* 10 (1931–32): 505–15.

20. Film historian Ian Jarvie suggested this version of the events to me. I thank him for his reconstruction of what likely happened.

21. Lewis's correspondence with—and submission of proposals to—the Motion Picture Research Council can be found in the MPRC archives, series 4, boxes 57 and 58, which are housed at the Hoover Institute at Stanford University.

22. Jowett, Jarvie, and Fuller, *Children and the Movies*.

23. Howard T. Lewis in "First Symposium on Elements Out of Which a Program Looking towards National Film Policies in Motion Pictures Can Be Selected," unpublished transcripts, MPRC files, series 4, box 58, pp. 19–20.

24. Cruikshank, *A Delicate Experiment*, 170.

25. Andrew Ross, *No Collar: The Humane Workplace and Its Hidden Costs* (New York: Basic Books, 2003), 94–95. For Mayo's own summary of his work in this period, see his book *The Human Problems of an Industrial Civilization* (New York: Macmillan, 1933).

26. The report is available in the Mayo papers, GA 54, carton 2, "Donham, Wallace, 1925–1945," at the HSB Historical Collections in the Baker Library.

27. These are available in the Mayo papers as "MOVIES, REGARDING, 1934–35," GA 54, carton 3. These efforts appear to not have led to published essays.

28. On March 15, the *Harvard University Gazette* mentions that Hays would lecture that day at the Harvard Union and that the event would be "[o]pen only to Members of the Union and Guests." The event itself is reported

in a March 18 letter from the secretary of Union Board of Governors to Associate Dean David at the HSB. See box 19 in the Harvard Union papers at the University Archive (3859.5515). There were also news releases about it in such publications as the *Boston Transcript* (March 16).

29. John Kasson, *Houdini, Tarzan, and the Perfect Man: The White Male Body and the Challenge of Modernity in America* (New York: Hill and Wang, 2001). Kasson analyzes Arch Shaw's *System* in the context of a discussion of Edgar Rice Burroughs, who worked for a time at the journal.

30. Esther Yogev, "Corporate Hand in Academic Glove: The New Management Struggle for Academic Recognition—The Case of the Harvard Group in the 1920s," *American Studies International* 29, no. 1 (February 2001): 63.

31. Donham correspondence, box 46, "Paramount Pictures Corporation" folder.

32. See Samuel Eliot Morison, ed., *The Development of Harvard University since the Inauguration of President Eliot, 1869–1929* (Cambridge, MA: Harvard University Press, 1930).

33. Melvin T. Copeland, *And Mark an Era: The Story of the Harvard Business School* (Boston: Little, Brown, 1958), 83. It is perhaps worth noting that Copeland's history makes no mention of the film course either.

34. Film historian Peter Decherney also offers an account of the Fogg initiative for an annual film awards program in "Mandarins and Marxists: Harvard and the Rise of Film Experts," in his *Hollywood and the Cultural Elite: How the Movies Became American* (New York: Columbia University Press, 2005), 63–82.

35. Michael Augspurger, "*Fortune*'s Business Gentlemen: Cultural and Corporal Liberalism in the Early 1930s," in *Prospects: An Annual of American Cultural Studies*, vol. 26, ed. Jack Salzman (Cambridge: Cambridge University Press, 2001), 423–47. Augspurger has since expanded his analysis of *Fortune* into a book-length study: *An Economy of Abundant Beauty:* Fortune *Magazine and Depression America* (Ithaca, NY: Cornell University Press, 2004).

36. *Academy Bulletin*, no. 17 (December 22, 1928): 4.

37. Alfred B. Kuttner, review of *The Story of the Films, National Board of Review Magazine* 3, no. 1 (January 1928): 6.

CHAPTER 4: BETWEEN ACADEMIA AND THE ACADEMY OF MOTION PICTURE ARTS AND SCIENCES

1. Unidentified newspaper report, February 28, 1930, USC Moving Image Archives. Research for this chapter depended primarily on several key sources: the Lester Cowan Papers and the College Affairs Committee files at the Margaret Herrick Library; the Stanford University archives; the Boris Morkovin papers in the university archives of USC; and the materials collected on USC's film program and housed in its Moving Image Archive. Note: some of the press clippings collected at USC are missing references such as pages or exact dates. When it did not seem essential, I did not expend the effort to track these down.

2. Unidentified newspaper report, August 5, 1930, USC Moving Image Archives.

3. In some documents, the course name is given as Introduction to *the* Photoplay, although the shorter version is more common. I will adopt the Introduction to Photoplay usage except when referencing a text that pointedly uses the longer title.

4. Kevin Starr, *Material Dreams: Southern California through the 1920s* (New York: Oxford University Press, 1990), 151–52. Further references in text.

5. "A 4-Year College Course to Fit You for the Movies," *American Weekly*, 1928 (no further date in archive copy).

6. Milton Sills, "The Actor's Part," in Joseph P. Kennedy, *The Story of the Films, as Told by Leaders of the Industry to the Students of the Graduate School of Business Administration, George F. Baker Foundation, Harvard University* (Chicago: A. W. Shaw, 1927), 193–94.

7. References in this paragraph and the next to the content of this first College Affairs Committee meeting come from the useful document "Minutes of College Comm. Meeting, May 24," in the Lester Cowan Papers, Margaret Herrick Library, AMPAS.

8. C. B. Neblette, "University of Southern California to Sponsor Four-Year Course in Motion-Picture Technology," *Photo-Era Magazine*, February 1928, 110.

9. Unfortunately, no source information is available that would identify the newspaper in which this article ran.

10. David Bordwell, "The Mazda Tests of 1928," in David Bordwell, Kristin Thompson and Janet Staiger, *The Classical Hollywood Cinema: Film Style and Mode of Production to 1960* (New York: Columbia University Press, 1985), 294–97.

11. However, as Pierre Sands reports in his history of AMPAS, a short film of Edison offering his support of the Academy was shown at its annual meeting of members on November 5, 1930. One wonders if there is a connection between this film, shown six months after the USC course, and the original plan to have an Edison film produced for the course. See Pierre Sands, "A Historical Study of the Academy of Motion Picture Arts and Sciences (1927–1947)" (Ph.D. diss., University of Southern California, 1966), 78.

12. There was some sort of connection between Kate Gordon and Lester Cowan. In a November 21, 1927, letter to her, Cowan declared, "I want you to know, Dr. Gordon, that you have touched my life in a very significant way and that I shall always feel indebted to you for sympathy, understanding and inspiration." Cowan seems to have specifically tried to recruit Gordon to teach a version of Introduction to Photoplay at UCLA, but a survey of catalogs there reveals that no such film course made it onto the books.

13. Anonymous, "Course in Picture Appreciation," *Educational Screen* 8, no. 2 (February 1929): 42.

14. The first year's lectures, minus the opening day's remarks, have been collected in John C. Tibbetts, ed., *Introduction to the Photoplay* (Shawnee Mission, KS: National Film Society, 1977). Further references in text.

15. William Stull, A.S.C., "The Movies Reach College," *American Cinematographer* 7 (June 1929): 16–17.

16. Notice of MacDonald's summer course appears in the *Academy Bulletin*, no. 32 (June 7, 1930): 2. It is also mentioned as "a survey of the motion picture industry and discussion of current problems of motion and sound films" in H. Clay Harshbarger, *Some Highlights of the Department of Speech and Dramatic Arts*, internally published document, University of Iowa, 1976, p. 14.

17. See Walter Miles, "Muybridge Semi-centennial," *International Photographer* 1, no. 5 (June 1929): 18–19.

18. Paul Farnsworth, "Changing Our Artistic Tastes," *Childhood Education* 8 (1931): 234.

19. See *Academy Bulletin*, no. 34 (September 12, 1930): 6.

20. Sands, "Historical Study of the Academy of Motion Picture Arts and Sciences," 131–32.

21. Lester Cowan, ed., *Recording Sound for Motion Pictures* (New York: McGraw-Hill, 1931).

22. The comment comes from former USC film professor Mel Sloan in the transcript in the USC Moving Image Archive of a discussion among a number of retired professors from the film school. As an alternate version, another student, Bill Paulson, claimed the problem was that Morkovin did not restrict the number of people who could go on the class trips, and this led to too many persons showing up at the studios. The AMPAS papers of producer-screenwriter Howard Estabrook, who was on the AMPAS Board of Governors, contain a curious letter (folder 242) in which a student of Morkovin's defends the professor against an unspecified incident that happened during a visit to MGM: "The man who offended MGM was named Marble. . . . I am a bit vague as to just exactly what he did that what so unethical, but I do know that Dr. M. got the blame for it."

23. Victor Garwood, "I Remember Boris (1)," Memorial Text, USC Retired Faculty Association. Copy in possession of the author.

24. As his own son, Mark, who was left behind at age seven and brought over to live with his father only at age eighteen, just before he left for college, declared: "His American venture was an escape from a 'stultifying petit-bourgeois environment' with a possessive wife and squabbling children whom he did not know how to handle. And indeed America provided wide-open horizons for his tremendous energies." December 15, 1985, letter to Victor Garwood in preparation for a Boris Morkovin memorial. Copy in possession of the author.

25. Mark Morkovin put it this way, "For a while, during my stay 1935–1937, he was a little overimpressed by the celebrities whose cooperation he was seeking." Ibid.

26. Although it does not bear directly on the ways he used his sociological research in his pedagogy, it is worth noting one curious impact of Morkovin's sociology of film reception in his historical moment. His work came to the attention

of the Reverend William Short, the instigator of the Payne Fund Studies into the effects of the movies, and it is clear that Short took Morkovin to represent a serious voice and even potential rival on the topic. The files from Short's Motion Picture Research Council, now housed at Stanford University's Hoover Institute, contain a series of letters between Short and Morkovin that constitute a veritable pas de deux in which each cautiously tried to learn more about the other without giving away too much. When Short sent Morkovin a draft copy of his volume *A Generation of Motion Pictures,* a strange and highly unscholarly assemblage of random quotes from the movies, Morkovin did not at first respond, and Short went crazy with worry that the Los Angeles–based Morkovin might leak his materials to the film industry and thereby preempt Short's critique. (Short even sent President von KleinSmid a letter of complaint about Morkovin.) When Morkovin finally answered with a series of criticisms about the lack of scholarship behind Short's ad hominem attacks on the movies, Short responded coolly and distantly. When a colleague of Morkovin's wrote to Short to recommend that the Motion Picture Research Council consider funding Morkovin's research on the creative ideas at play in Hollywood, Short replied that the council was more interested in issues of reception than production and referred him to Howard T. Lewis at Harvard, who had been asked to do the one part of the Payne Fund Studies that might deal with industry issues. In many ways, the disagreement between Morkovin and Short—who both agreed that movies were a cultural form of great social impact—had to do with how they assumed effective reform or control of that impact could take place. Writing to Short on October 31, 1932, Morkovin, who had been getting increasingly involved in the teaching and sponsoring of student filmmaking, imagined that there could be an ameliorative effect at the point of production. As he said, "It is only logical that such an effort should be made to start a movement for the study *and extensive use of this medium* for constructive purposes. The study of dramatic, artistic, social, psychological and technical aspects of motion pictures should be introduced as a curriculum in leading schools of this country. Special attention should be paid as to how the sound camera could be used in presenting the greatest achievement of modern, natural and social science in a dramatic, fascinating way, as the motion picture is capable of doing.... Prerequisite to that should be the bringing up in universities and other schools of a generation of students mastering this medium of modern magic" (my emphasis). Short, in contrast, tended to think of cinema as an essentially corrupt art that could never really be improved or made beneficial for society, and he replied in a letter of December 1, 1932, that the movies offered little but lies and what he termed unworthy and abnormal representations to such a degree that forceful intervention *at the point of consumption* was necessary. In his words, "The social control of the motion picture, both for the child and the average adult, becomes a matter of life and death for organized society."

27. See Morkovin's summary in the *Bulletin of the National Cinema Workshop and Appreciation League,* no. 1 (December 1935): 3–4.

28. Boris Morkovin, "Regardless of Technical Advance Picture Leans Heaviest on Drama," *International Photographer* 7 (February 1933): 12.

29. Boris Morkovin, "The University Studies the Motion Picture," *National Board of Review Magazine* 13, no. 10 (October 1938): 4.

30. It is not clear how the association with Disney came about, although Disney was a frequent visitor to cinema classes at USC. On December 8, 1933, in a talk on "Psychological Aspects of the Animated Cartoon" at Caltech, Morkovin had emphasized Disney films and referred to Walt as a genius and a prophet. Perhaps this attempt to flatter Disney was one of the things that brought the professor to Disney's attention.

Disney had clearly been interested in finding ways to outsource the training of his animators to professional pedagogues and thereby render it solid and rigorous. It was in the very same period that he established connections with the Chouinard Art Institute, in Valencia, California, later to become the prestigious California Institute of the Arts with funding and decisive organizational input from Disney, and serving from the 1930s as a venue for instruction of Disney animators and for recruitment of talent into the studio.

31. Interview, *Daily Trojan*, June 25, 1931, 7.

32. *Motion Picture and the Family* 2, no. 3 (November 15, 1935): 2.

33. For one version of this tale, see Louise Spencer's account in "Mrs. Spencer Tracy's Own Story," *Ladies' Home Journal*, December 1972, 90, 116–20.

34. Boris Morkovin, "Psychotherapy and Techniques of Perceptual Re-education of the Acoustically Impaired," *Hearing Survey Quarterly*, no. 1 (1944): 1.

CHAPTER 5: POLITICS AS PEDAGOGY, PEDAGOGY AS POLITICS

1. Harry Alan Potamkin, "A Proposal for a School of the Motion Picture," in *The Compound Cinema: The Film Writings of Harry Alan Potamkin*, ed. Lewis Jacobs (New York: Teachers College Press, 1977), 587–92. Further references to *The Compound Cinema* in text.

2. Jay Leyda, "Advanced Training for Film Workers: Russia," *Hollywood Quarterly* 1, no. 3 (April 1946): 286.

3. Anonymous, "A Course in the Motion Picture Art," *National Board of Review Magazine* 7, no. 11 (November 1932): 15.

4. Anonymous, Harry Alan Potamkin obituary, *Nation*, August 16, 1933, 171.

5. The two-page draft, "Outline for a Text Book on the Movies," can be found in the "Potamkin" folder in box 42 of the National Board of Review papers, available at Special Collections, New York Public Library.

6. Russell Campbell, *Cinema Strikes Back: Radical Filmmaking in the United States, 1930–1942* (Ann Arbor: UMI Press, 1982), 55.

7. For the full list, see *Compound Cinema*, 585.

8. Peter Decherney also discusses the relation between Potamkin's philosophy of pedagogy and broader theory of culture in Brechtian terms in the chap-

ter "Everyone's a Critic: Harry Alan Potamkin's Marxist Film Library," in his *Hollywood and the Culture Elite: How the Movies Became American* (New York: Columbia University Press, 2005), 88–96.

9. Dudley Andrew, "Harry Alan Potamkin," *Film Comment* 10, no. 2 (March–April 1974): 56–57.

10. Peter Decherney offers important insights on Potamkin's "Library of the Motion Picture" in "Everyone's a Critic," 91–96.

11. Campbell, *Cinema Strikes Back*, 57.

12. William Troy, "An Academy of the Film," *Nation*, November 22, 1933, 605.

CHAPTER 6: APPRECIATIONS OF CINEMA

1. Course materials for Cinema Appreciation are to be found in the Sawyer Falk papers, box 4 ("Cinema"), University Archives, Syracuse University. Unless otherwise referenced, cited documents come from this collection. In many cases, Falk put dates on his lecture notes. In other cases, as we will see, since his course often revolved around discussions of films currently in the theaters, we can make good guesses by noting the release date of the film he was lecturing on. But in some cases, no date is given, and I will simply cite such material for its support of the overall argument. Some of this material comes from decades later than the 1930s. But, as I make clear, Falk's overall position on film did not change much over a three-decade period. Pronouncements from the entire span of his career in teaching Cinema Appreciation tend to fit in well with his overall aesthetic position, and I have therefore permitted myself to quote across the range of his film teaching.

2. Paul Rotha, *The Film Till Now: A Survey of the Cinema* (New York: Jonathan Cape, 1930). Falk even brought Rotha to his class in 1937 to lecture on documentary film. In at least one version of Cinema Appreciation in the second half of the 1930s, Falk assigned Gilbert Seldes's quirky textbook *An Hour with the Movies and the Talkies*, seeming in particular to find useful Seldes's argument that cinema was an art that transcended reality to create fantasy. By the 1940s, he had a much longer reading list, although quite an eclectic and even sketchy one, with texts of history (e.g., Bardèche and Brasillach's *History of Motion Pictures*, in its 1938 edition, translated by MoMA's Iris Barry) and industry analysis (e.g., Raymond Moley's *The Hays Office* and Mae Huettig's *Economic Control of the Motion Picture Industry*) overwhelming the more specifically aesthetic analyses—limited to Arnheim's *Film as Art* and Lindsay's *Art of the Moving Picture*—even though Falk himself said that his course would be neither historical nor industry-oriented.

3. David Bordwell, *On the History of Film Style* (Cambridge, MA: Harvard University Press, 1998), 20.

4. Subsequently, Richard Griffith did in fact offer a guarded but overall favorable review of the Deren films in *New Movies (The Magazine of the National Board of Review)* 21, no. 3 (March 1946): 22–23.

5. VèVè Clark, Millicent Hodson, and Catrina Neiman, *The Legend of Maya Deren*, vol. 1, pt. 1, *Signatures (1917–1942)* (New York: Anthology Film Archives/Film Culture, 1984), 184.

6. This article, from the May 18, 1934, edition of the campus newspaper, the *Syracuse Daily Orange*, is reproduced in *The Legend of Maya Deren*, 182.

7. In the Sawyer Falk papers, the clipping for this article from the *Syracuse Post-Standard* is undated, but it is clear that it appeared sometime in early 1935.

8. The editorial from the *Syracuse Daily Orange* is reproduced in *The Legend of Maya Deren*, 182.

9. Sawyer Falk, "Movie Enterprises at a University Theatre," *National Board of Review Magazine* 20, no. 1 (January–February 1945): 8.

10. Sawyer Falk, "Relating Community Activities with a University Interest in Motion Pictures," *New Movies (The Magazine of the National Board of Review)* 11, no. 4 (April 1936): 8.

11. Falk, "Movie Enterprises at a University Theatre," 8.

12. Ibid., 9.

13. For a useful examination of *La Cucaracha* as a nonrealist experiment in design, see Scott Higgins, "Demonstrating Three-Colour Technicolor: Early Three-Colour Aesthetics and Design," *Film History* 12, no. 4 (2000): 358–83.

CHAPTER 7: CINEMATIC DIVERSIONS IN SOCIOLOGY

1. Most of the research material for this chapter comes from the National Board of Review files archived at the New York Public Library, boxes 40 ("NYU") and 45 ("Frederic Thrasher, Correspondence"). There is also some material on Thrasher in the NYU archives, and the Academy of Motion Picture Arts and Sciences has some issues of the newsletter of the Metropolitan Motion Picture Council, the film-betterment publication that Thrasher worked on, in its Margaret Herrick Library, Beverly Hills.

2. See Fredric Thrasher, "The Movies and the Dime Novel," in *The Gang: A Study of 1,313 Gangs in Chicago* (Chicago: University of Chicago Press, 1927), 102–15.

3. Frederic Thrasher, ed., *Okay for Sound: How the Screen Found Its Voice* (New York: Duell, Sloan and Pearce, 1946). *Okay for Sound* was commissioned and funded by Warner Bros. to coincide with the heavily publicized twentieth anniversary of its first sound releases, such as *Don Juan*. The Warner company was very hands-on in the preparation of this volume (to the extent of militating for photos that emphasized Warner staff and stars), and it is not clear what precisely it meant to have had Thrasher as "editor." In a September 15, 1946, letter to Richard Griffith at the National Board of Review, Thrasher asserted that he had "edited" the volume but admitted that it was "not a scholarly production, but was intended to be a rather popular pictorial presentation." In fact, other than a one-page introduction signed by him, most of the textual material—including even photographic captions—appears to have been prepared in-house at Warner Bros. The extensive correspondence about the volume con-

tained in the files—now housed at AMPAS—of Warner publicist Marty Weiser includes many examples of input and advice about the volume, but none of these come from Thrasher, and there is no direct sign of his involvement. Instead, the advice comes from figures at Warner, including Jack Warner himself. For what it is worth, though, several points in Thrasher's admittedly brief introduction do complement the approach to film he would refine over the course of the years. Thus, he speaks of film as the one great art form born in modern times and mentions that it now has college courses devoted to it. He notes that the entertainment film reaches vast multitudes of the American population and that this in itself indicates popular cinema is "one of the greatest educational forces in modern times." Perhaps one should not make too much of Thrasher's contribution, such as it was, but the idea that the entertainment film is itself a form of pedagogy is certainly in keeping with the position he would develop progressively in the 1930s in which fiction films were as much to be considered modes of visual education as were documentary or instructional films.

4. Anne Morey, *Hollywood Outsiders: The Adaptation of the Film Industry, 1913–1934* (Minneapolis: University of Minnesota Press, 2003), 180–81.

5. Frederic M. Thrasher, "The Study of the Total Situation," *Journal of Educational Sociology* 1, no. 8 (April 1928): 479, 487.

6. Ibid., 487. Likewise, in "What Can Research Prove?" an essay published in the *National Board of Review Magazine*, Thrasher offered a sweeping faith in social science's potential predictive abilities: "If we had enough facts about a human being, it would be possible to predict exactly what he would do in a given situation. As it is, we are able to predict human behavior to a very large extent and this is becoming more and more possible as our researches into social behavior are developing." Thrasher, "What Can Research Prove?" *National Board of Review Magazine* 9, no. 4 (April 1934): 12.

7. Frederic M. Thrasher, "The Boy's Club Study," *Journal of Educational Sociology* 6, no. 1 (September 1932): 4.

8. Ibid., 5.

9. Mark Lynn Anderson, "Taking Liberties: The Payne Fund Studies and the Creation of the Media Expert," in *Inventing Film Studies*, ed. Haidee Wasson and Lee Grieveson, forthcoming.

10. Paul G. Cressey, "The Motion Picture as Informal Education," *Journal of Educational Sociology* 7, no. 8 (April 1934): 504–15.

11. Thrasher, "The Study of the Total Situation," 478; my emphasis.

12. Frederic M. Thrasher, "Motion Pictures and the Social Sciences," *National Board of Review Magazine* 11, no. 2 (February 1936): 6.

13. Frederic M. Thrasher, "Education versus Censorship," *Journal of Educational Sociology* 13, no. 5 (January 1940): 288–89. Further references in text.

14. Dr. Dan Dodson, "A Brief History of the Department of Educational Sociology and Anthropology from 1923–1966," unpublished typescript manuscript in the NYU University Archives.

15. Garth S. Jowett, Ian C. Jarvie, and Kathryn H. Fuller, *Children and the Movies: Media Influence and the Payne Fund Controversy* (New York: Cam-

bridge University Press, 1996), 130. Further references in text. Centering on Cressey's (and Thrasher's) unpublished research for their Payne Fund volume, this book offers rich background material on Thrasher's career, although it does not deal specifically with his classroom pedagogy.

16. Martin Bulmer, "The Early Institutional Establishment of Social Science Research: The Local Community Research Committee at the University of Chicago, 1923–1930," *Minerva* 18 (1980): 51–110.

17. Over the years, the course would come to benefit from affiliation with other organizations and institutions such as the Amateur Cinema League, the Museum of Natural History, the American Social Hygiene Association, the Hays Office, the Museum of Modern Art, the National Council of Teachers of English, and the New York Public Library.

18. Thrasher, "Education versus Censorship," 300.

19. Myron Lounsbury, *The Origins of American Film Criticism, 1909–1939* (New York: Arno Press, 1973), 159.

20. It is interesting to note that Gerstein herself wrote a piece for the *New York Times*, announcing one of the semesters of Thrasher's course (the semester, in fact, in which she lectured for him on René Clair). See Gerstein, "N.Y.U. Plans Program of Screen Lectures," *New York Times*, January 31, 1937, 44.

21. There is useful background information on such clubs and the larger context of film-betterment initiatives in the public schools of the 1930s in Eric Smoodin's chapter "Film Education and Quality Entertainment for Children and Adolescents," in his book *Regarding Frank Capra: Audience, Celebrity, and American Film Studies, 1930–1960* (Durham, NC: Duke University Press, 2004), 76–118.

22. William Lewin, *Photoplay Appreciation in American High Schools* (New York: D. Appleton-Century, 1934), 44–45.

23. See Robert L. Whitley, "The Case Study as a Method of Research," *Social Forces* 10, no. 4 (1932): 56–73.

24. Some of this first-person data show up in Cressey's unpublished Payne Fund material. See Paul Cressey, "The Community—A Social Setting for the Motion Picture" in Jowett, Jarvie, and Fuller, *Children and the Movies*, 137–216. The research of Cressey and Thrasher's Chicago sociology colleague Herbert Blumer on the impact of movies on college students' sexuality also relied heavily on interviews and first-person accounts. See Blumer, "The Motion Picture Autobiographies" and "Private Monographs on Movies and Sex," also in Jowett, Jarvie, and Fuller, *Children and the Movies*, 242–301.

25. Film historian Mark Lynn Anderson hints that Thrasher may even have been using his NYU course as a source of data collection for the project; that is, he may have hoped to employ the students who chose the "motion picture life history" option as a veritable control group whose accounts of the impact of movies on their lives would be compared or contrasted to data that came from the delinquents Cressey and Thrasher were also concerned with and had been interviewing for the Boys Club project and its Payne Fund spin-off. See Anderson, "Taking Liberties."

26. Anonymous, "The Motion Picture as Curriculum," *National Board of Review Magazine* 11, no. 7 (September–October 1937): 9.

27. Jowett, Jarvie, and Fuller, *Children and the Movies*, 86.

28. Frederic M. Thrasher, "The Sociological Approach to Motion Pictures in Relation to Education," *Education* 58, no. 8 (April 1938): 471; my emphases.

29. Thrasher, *The Gang*, 3. Further references in text.

30. Likewise, in an essay from 1931, when Thrasher quoted the account of moviegoing by a city youth, it was all about the spectacle in the auditorium—the crush of people, the rituals of picking up girls—and there was no reference to the show on the screen. In passing, Thrasher noted that adolescents got some of their ideas from movies, but these seemed to play only a small role in the larger sweep of vibrant narratives, the rich and active life stories, of the city dwellers. See Thrasher, "Social Attitudes of Superior Boys in an Interstitial Community" in *Social Attitudes*, ed. Kimball Young (New York: Holt, 1931), 236–64.

31. Thrasher, "The Sociological Approach to Motion Pictures in Relation to Education," 472.

32. Frederic M. Thrasher, "What Is a Good Movie?" *National Board of Review Magazine* 14, no. 9 (December 1939): 6, 10.

33. It may be that the idea that aesthetic achievement mattered as much as sociological correctness in an adult art was a notion that Thrasher had already elaborated in the years before 1939. For example, a summary of a lecture he gave in 1937 seems to indicate that there, too, he felt the primary qualities of good movies were basic technical proficiency and artistic accomplishment. The piece appears in the *Bulletin* of the Metropolitan Motion Picture Council, of which, we remember, Thrasher was technical director. It summarizes Thrasher as saying that "the moral issue of the film is no longer a vital one. A real field of interest for educational and community groups at the present time is the artistic adequacy and the sociological validity of film material." See *Metropolitan Motion Picture Bulletin* 1, no. 3 (November 1937): 12.

CHAPTER 8: MIDDLEBROW TRANSLATIONS OF HIGHBROW PHILOSOPHY

1. Hilton Kramer, "Studying the Arts and Humanities: What Can Be Done?" *New Criterion* 7, no. 6 (February 1989): 2. Further references in text.

2. Mortimer J. Adler, *Art and Prudence: A Study in Practical Philosophy* (New York: Longmans, Green, 1937), 302. Further reference in text.

3. Historical research for this chapter relies in part on the Mortimer Adler papers housed in the Special Collections of the Joseph Regenstein Library of the University of Chicago (his papers about cinema are in boxes 25, 69, and 70, primarily), as well as documents from the founding years of St. John's College in Maryland provided to me either by archivists at the college or by George Comenetz, professor of sciences at St. John's in the late 1930s.

4. Scott Buchanan, "Methods and Techniques in Adult Education," *University of Virginia Record Extension Series* 20, no. 4 (October 1935): 30–32.

5. Scott Buchanan, "In Search of a Liberal College: A Program for the Recovery of the Classics and the Liberal Arts," unpublished document. This plan for St. John's is found in the college archives. My thanks to the archivists for making a copy available to me.

6. Buchanan offers deeper commentary on economics and the mode of production in "Surplus Value," *Virginia Quarterly Review* 13, no. 1 (January 1937): 86–105. There, he applauds *Capital* as the great "poem" or "epic" of Man as Laborer, but he argues that the specific problem with the capitalist mode of production is not that the laborers' surplus is taken from them but that it is taken *to the benefit of owners who do no productive labor themselves*. Capitalism is not fundamentally flawed but is sometimes corrupted by slothful nonproducers. A clear inspiration for Buchanan was Thorstein Veblen's notion of wasteful, nonproductive conspicuous consumption on the part of the idle rich.

7. Buchanan even suggested that Mumford might be a perfect choice for director of the institute.

8. See Michel Foucault, *The Archaeology of Knowledge*, trans. Alan Sheridan-Smith (New York: Pantheon, 1972).

9. Mark Van Doren served as film critic for the *Nation* from mid-1935 to mid-1938, writing a biweekly column. Many of his film reviews were collected in his volume of criticism, *The Private Reader: Selected Articles and Reviews* (New York: Holt, 1942), where they were prefaced by one of his few general reflections on film art, a 1937 essay from *American Scholar* originally entitled "Let the Movies Be Natural" and retitled "The Limits of Entertainment" for inclusion in the larger volume of criticism. Except for this short reflection and one other brief essay—"The Movies as Entertainment," *National Board of Review Magazine* 13, no. 3 (March 1938): 4–5—Van Doren did not seek to elaborate a general aesthetics of film. Nonetheless, recurrent assertions about cinema run through Van Doren's film writings and easily complement Scott Buchanan's and Mortimer Adler's admiration for the popular art: Van Doren contends that film is most of all a narrative art geared to meaningful change over time (including—since, like Buchanan and Adler, Van Doren was an Aristotelian—the meaningfulness of moments of fateful recognition); consequently, that meaning should emerge from narrative logic rather than be imposed upon it, so that any message a film might convey had to be organic to its structure; consequently, that between forced messages (visible in propaganda and in pretentious attempts to "literaturize" film through adaptation of high-class novels and plays) and gripping narrative, the artist's and audience's preference should go to the latter; and that therefore each art had to discover its own formal virtues and highest potentials (film's were those of an engaging narrativity) and not set out to imitate other arts or discourses (again, as an Aristotelian, Van Doren divided discourse into the poetic and the historical, and he classified film as an example of the former so that its vocation should be not to try to communicate about the real world but to offer imaginative reconstruction of it). The following lines from a retrospective reflection (not included in *The Private Reader*) on his first two years of movie reviewing can stand as a summary of Van Doren's perspective

on cinema: "That I prefer poetry to history I have hitherto confessed.... [T]wo seasons of movie-going have convinced me of this: the camera, with brains and imagination behind it, is as much a master of the story-telling art as anything or anybody else. It will continue to attempt things which it cannot do as well as plays and novels do them, and possibly its duty to itself is still to make a great many mistakes from which the limits of its medium may be learned." See Van Doren, "Films," *Nation* 145 (August 7, 1937): 158.

10. James Sloan Allen, *The Romance of Commerce and Culture: Capitalism, Modernism, and the Chicago-Aspen Crusade for Cultural Reform*, rev. ed. (Boulder: University of Colorado Press, 2002).

11. Joan Shelley Rubin, *The Making of Middlebrow Culture* (Chapel Hill: University of North Carolina Press, 1992).

12. The classic account of Erskine is Gilbert Allardyce, "The Rise and Fall of the Western Civilization Course," *American Historical Review* 87, no. 3 (June 1982): 695–725. Also useful, especially since they emphasize the democratic impulse behind Great Books initiatives, are Katherine Chaddock Reynolds, "A Canon of Democratic Intent: Reinterpreting the Roots of the Great Books Movement," *History of Higher Education Annual* 22 (2002): 5–32, and Rubin's *Making of Middlebrow Culture*.

13. John Erskine, *My Life as a Teacher* (Philadelphia: Lippincott, 1948), 166. Further references in text.

14. The history of the People's Institute is well recounted in Robert Bruce Fisher, "The People's Institute of New York City, 1897–1934: Culture, Progressive Democracy, and the People" (Ph.D. diss., New York University, 1974). Further references in text.

15. There are several studies of the efforts of the People's Institute in the arena of film. The most detailed is William Uricchio and Roberta Pearson, *Reframing Culture: The Case of the Vitagraph Quality Films* (Princeton, NJ: Princeton University Press, 1993).

16. Harvey London, "Everett Dean Martin," *Dictionary of American Biography, Supplement Three: 1941–1945*, ed. Edward T. James (New York: Scribner, 1973), 511.

17. Scott Buchanan, *Possibility* (New York: Harcourt, Brace, 1927), 111. Further references in text.

18. Mark Van Doren, "The Limits of Entertainment," in *The Private Reader*, 297–98.

19. Mortimer Adler, "The Movies, the People and the Critics," *National Board of Review Magazine* 13, no. 4 (April 1938): 5–8. Further references in text.

20. Actually, the Thomist Adler held out faith in a realm *above* philosophy: that of Christian grace and revelation. At one point in *Art and Prudence*, Adler spoke of the dream of "the re-establishment of Christendom." But he also noted, "Those who do not share this faith and hope must move to a solution on a lower level" (653). To the extent that we are below the angels, we can engage in the rational labor of philosophy to raise us up toward the divine.

21. Mortimer Adler, *How to Read a Book: The Art of Getting a Liberal Education* (New York: Simon and Schuster, 1940). Further references in text.

22. Andrew Ross, *No Respect: Intellectuals and Popular Culture* (New York: Routledge, 1989); Jonathan Auerbach, "American Studies and Film, Blindness and Insight," *American Quarterly* 58, no. 1 (March 2006): 31–50; Christopher Newfield, *Ivy and Industry: Business and the Making of the American University, 1880–1980* (Durham, NC: Duke University Press, 2003), 146; Greg Taylor, *Artists in the Audience: Cults, Camp, and American Film Criticism* (Princeton, NJ: Princeton University Press, 1999).

Index

Film titles are followed by the name of the director and the date of production; titles of books are followed by the author's name.

Abbott, Alan, 380n10
Abbott, John, 88, 208, 279
Addams, Jane, 24
Academy of Motion Picture Arts and Sciences (AMPAS), 10, 80, 83, 86, 176–213
Academic disciplines, historiography of, 2–3, 20–21
Adler, Mortimer J., 12, 25, 27, 346–48, 349, 354–55, 362–74, 375
Allen, James Sloan, 355
Allen, Robert, 96–97
Alstock, Leon, 134–35
Anderson, Mark Lynn, 303, 305, 396n25
Andrew, Dudley, 251
Arnheim, Rudolph, 369
Art and Prudence (Mortimer J. Adler), 13, 27, 346, 354, 365–73
The Art of Photoplay Making (Victor Freeburg), 47–56
Ashley, William, 263–64
Askari, Kaveh, 382n13
Auerbach, Jonathan, 374
Augspurger, Michael, 161–64

Babbitt, Frank Cole, 121–22, 123
Ballard, Virginia, 171

Ballet mécanique (Fernand Léger, 1924), 287
Bardacke, Gregory, 270
Bare, Richard, 213, 227
Barnard College, 1
Barr, Stringfellow, 347, 355
Barrett, Wilton, 321
Barry, Iris, 17–18, 88, 193
Baudry, Jean-Louis, 121
Beaton, Welford, 179
Benjamin, Walter, 50
Bennington College, 380n10
The Birth of a Nation (D.W. Griffith, 1915), 100
Block-booking, 132–33, 387n14
Bloom, Allan, 355, 356
Blumer, Herbert, 311, 396n25
Borden, Neil, 133
Bordwell, David, 3, 188, 265–66
Broken Blossoms (D.W. Griffith, 1919), 66
Broken Hearts (Maurice Schwartz, 1926), 62
Bryn Mawr College, 16
Buchanan, Scott, 12, 14, 25, 346–74; at People's Institute, 359–65
Bulmer, Martin, 312
Burrell, James Angus, 82–83, 88–89

401

402 / Index

Butler, Nicholas Murray, 33–34, 36–37, 38, 79, 80–87, 88, 116

The Cabinet of Dr. Caligari (Robert Wiene, 1920), 64–65, 104
Cain and Mabel (Lloyd Bacon, 1936), 263
Campbell, Russell, 239–40, 261
Carnet de bal (Julien Duvivier, 1937), 297–98
Chapaev (Georgi Vasilyev, 1934), 288
Chase, George, 165
Chouinard Art Institute, 392n30
Cinema Appreciation (Syracuse University film course), 263–98
Clair, René, 249
Clark, Elizabeth, 76
Cleopatra (Cecil B. DeMille, 1934), 296
Cochrane, Robert, 87, 132, 147, 156
Cohen, Bernard S., 284
College of the City of New York (CCNY), 379n10
Columbia University, 8, 10, 17–18, 33–89, 90–92, 118, 122, 182–83, 314
Coon, Horace C., 75–76
Copeland, Melvin, 160
Cornell University, 16
Cowan, Lester, 178–212, 215
Craftsmanship, 26–27
Cressey, Paul, 299, 302, 303–5, 312, 329, 330, 334, 335–36
Cruikshank, Jeffrey L., 137

Dartmouth College, 16–17
Davies, Milton J., 39
Decherney, Peter, 43–44
Decordova, Richard, 27
DeMille, Cecil B., 142, 159
Deren, Maya, 268–69, 270, 287
Dewey, John, 108, 349, 367
Disney, Walt, 392n30
Disney studio, 224–25
Donham, Wallace P., 115, 125, 128–58, 160
Dow, Arthur Wesley, 383n13
Dumbo (Ben Sharpsteen, 1941), 289

Egbert, James, 38–39, 44, 76, 78, 79, 82, 87
Eisenstein, Sergei, 248
Eliot, Charles W., 126–27
Ellis, Jack, 4
Erskine, John, 13, 356–59, 362, 364

Fackenthal, Frank D., 34, 82
Fairbanks, Douglas, 177, 192
Falk, Sawyer, 11–12, 18–19, 24, 25, 236, 263–98, 308
Farber, Manny, 377n6
Farnsworth, Paul, 203–7
Fisher, Robert, 360, 361, 363
Flexner, Abraham, 120, 122–23, 352
Fogg Art Museum (Harvard), 119, 146–47, 161–73
Forbes, Edward R., 165–74
Foucault, Michel, 354
Fox, William, 82, 150
Francis, Alec B., 202
Frank, Waldo, 92, 95, 108–9
Freeburg, Victor, 8, 10, 19–20, 37, 40, 42–56, 57–58, 61, 63–64, 68, 77, 193
Fribourg, Eugenie M., 1
Fuller, Kathryn, 310–11, 320, 334
Fulton, Albert, 20
Fundamentals of Motion Picture Production (USC film course), 228–31

The Gang (Frederic Thrasher), 299, 305, 336–38
Gerstein, Evelyn, 107, 111, 318–19
Gessner, Robert, 342–43
Gilbert, Horace, 157
Gillespie, B.K., 228, 231
Glazer, Benjamin, 195
Gomery, Douglas, 96–97
Gordon, Kate, 191, 389n12
Gorham, Mack, 76
Greenburg, Clement, 374, 375
Grierson, John, 243
Griffith, D.W., 66–67, 100, 101, 107
Griffith, Richard, 17, 393n4

Hammons, Earle W., 149
Hartley, John, 25

Harvard Film Society, 173–74
Harvard Graduate School of Business Administration (HSB), 9, 25, 86, 113–74, 184
Hawley, H.C., 134
Hays, Will, 33, 36–37, 80–87, 110–11, 130–71, 183, 200, 210, 375
Hays Office, 25, 81–87, 88, 118, 125–26, 219, 231, 368
Hiatt, Amos, 134–35
Hickey, Eleanor, 227
Hoberman, Jim, 62
Hot Blood (Nicholas Ray, 1956), 281
How to Read a Book (Mortimer J. Adler), 373–74
Hubbard, Florence, 232
Hunt, H.R., 113
Hutchins, Robert Maynard, 347, 350

Indiana University, 16
In Old Kentucky (George Marshall, 1935), 282–83
Institute of Arts and Sciences (Columbia University), 39, 87–88
Intolerance (D.W. Griffith, 1916), 100, 101, 107
Introduction to Photoplay (USC film course), 176–233
Isaacs, Nathan, 132, 154–55
Ivens, Joris, 291
I Want You (Mark Robson, 1951), 375–76

Jackson, Daniel D., 82
Jacobs, Lewis, 236
Jacoby, Irving A., 379n10
Jarvie, Ian, 310–11, 320, 334
Jason, Joy, 219
Johnson, Alvin, 93, 110–11
Jowett, Garth, 310–11, 320, 334

Kael, Pauline, 20
Kallen, Horace, 110–11
Kasson, John, 152
Katz, Samuel, 156
Kaufman, Sidney, 262
Keaton, Buster, 176

Kennedy, Joseph P., 9, 114–71, 193
Kent, Sidney, 149
Knight, Arthur, 273
Knudsen, Vern, 212
Kohn, Ralph A., 156
Koronakes, Vassilios, 57
Kracauer, Siegfried, 291
Kramer, Hilton, 344–45
Krows, Arthur Edwin, 384n38
Kuhn, Thomas, 6–7
Kuttner, Alfred, 174

La Cucaracha (Lloyd Corrigan, 1934), 289
Laemmle, Carl, 36
Lands, Films and Critics (New School for Social Research film course), 237–58
Lasky, Jesse, 145, 162, 164–65
Lasky Company, 43–44
Leads, Arthur, 42, 45
Leahy, William, 132
Lears, T.J. Jackson, 27, 51, 163
Leavis, F.R., 106
Le Bon, Gustave, 54
Levee, M.C., 185–86, 188, 195–96
Levine, David O., 22
Lewin, William, 324
Lewis, Howard T., 129, 132, 133–37, 139, 143, 158, 172
Leyda, Jay, 236–37, 262
Lindsay, Vachel, 19–20, 27, 61, 68–69, 193
Loew, Marcus, 118, 160
Lot in Sodom (Melville Webber and James Sibley Watson, 1933), 268, 277, 287, 289
Lounsbury, Myron, 319
Lowell, A. Lawrence, 113–15, 116, 119–20, 124, 127, 147
Lynd, Robert and Helen, 23, 92

MacDonald, Dwight, Sr., 378n10
MacDonald, William R., 187–88, 193, 206, 228, 231
Malinowski, Bronislaw, 92
Marcuse, Herbert, 253

Maritain, Jacques, 271
Martin, Everett Dean, 360–62
Mass culture, 1950s critique of, 4, 374–75
Matthews, Brander, 57
Mayer, Louis B., 201
Mayo, Elton, 137–43
Mead, Margaret, 92
Méliès, Georges, 103
Mendelowitz, D.M., 16
The Merry Widow (Ernst Lubitsch, 1934), 283–84
Metropolis (Fritz Lang, 1927), 292
Metropolitan Motion Picture Council, 300
Middletown (Robert and Helen Lynd), 23, 92
Miles, Walter, 197–209, 215
Milliken, Carl, 83–84, 130–31, 170, 171
A Million and One Nights (Terry Ramsaye), 8–9, 90–108, 113, 115
Mills College, 191
Mission to Moscow (Michael Curtiz, 1943), 264
Mount Holyoke College, 16
Morey, Anne, 301
Morkovin, Boris, 10, 213–35, 238, 307, 340; abandonment of film pedagogy, 233–35
The Motion Picture: Its Artistic, Educational and Social Aspects (NYU film course), 307–43
The Motion Picture Industry (Howard T. Lewis), 134–36
Mumford, Lewis, 353–54
Münsterberg, Hugo, 5–6, 20, 27, 68–69, 193, 369
Museum of Modern Art Film Library, 15–19, 29, 88, 173–74, 208–9, 279–80, 342
Muybridge, Eadweard, Stanford University ceremony in honor of, 198–202

National Board of Review (NBR), 11, 62, 65, 291, 298, 299, 318–34, 360

National Council of Teachers of English, 378n8
Neblette, C.B., 182, 183
Newcomb, R.V., 378–79n10
Newfield, Christopher, 374
The New School for Social Research, 8–9, 11, 90–112, 122, 237–62
New York University, 12, 14, 16, 38, 73, 299–343
Nicoll, Allardyce, 369
Nye, Arthur, 212

Occidental College, 80, 86
Okay for Sound (Frederic Thrasher), 299, 394n3

Pagnol, Marcel, 288
Panofsky, Erwin, 20
Park, Robert, 311
Parker, R.B., 33
The Passion of Joan of Arc (Carl Dreyer, 1928), 276–77, 279
Patterson, Francis Taylor, 8, 10, 19–20, 26, 37–89, 123, 258
Patterson, Rowland, 56–67, 87, 89
Payne Fund Studies, 12, 116, 136–37, 310–13, 318, 319–20, 329, 330, 347, 368–70, 391n26
The People's Institute, 25, 359–65
Photoplay Composition (Columbia University film course), 8, 27, 33–77, 122–23, 314
Pomeroy, Roy, 180
Post, Chandler R., 162–63, 170
Potamkin, Harry Alan, 11, 111–12, 236–62
Potemkin (1925), 64–65, 322
Potter, Russell, 87–89
Princeton University, 16
The Private Life of Don Juan (Alexander Korda, 1934), 290
Progressivism, 24, 125, 360
Pudovkin, V.I., 369

Radway, Janice, 23
Ramsaye, Terry, 8–9, 11, 90–112, 115, 172, 237–39, 307

Ramsey, William E., 227
Reed, Robert Ralston, 44
Reuben, Julie, 13
Richards, I.A., 204
Robinson, James Harvey, 92
Rogers, Rowland, 78–80, 83
Room Service (William A. Seiter, 1938), 282
Ross, Andrew, 138, 374
Ross, Edward, 173–74
Rotha, Paul, 106, 265–67, 274, 393n2
Rubin, Joan Shelley, 23, 355
Rutkoff, Peter M., 91–93

Sachs, Paul J., 127, 165–73
Sands, Pierre, 211
Sarris, Andrew, 20
The Scarlet Pimpernel (Harold Young, 1934), 288
Scholastic Photoplay Clubs, 323–26
School of Moving Picture Technology (Columbia University), 80–87
Schulberg, B.P., 195
Schwartz, Maurice, 62
Scott, William B., 91–93
Seabury, William Marston, 116–17
Seldes, Gilbert, 288, 354, 369, 393n2
Seymour, James, 117, 129–30, 166–71
Shanghai Express (Joseph von Sternberg, 1932), 246
Shaw, Arch W., 127–28, 151–53
Short, William, 136–37, 318, 391n26
Shumway, David, 21
Sills, Milton, 139, 142, 178–78, 180, 188, 189, 191; death of, 211
Sir Arne's Treasure (Mauritz Stiller, 1919), 62–63, 64
Small, Ruth, 285
Smith, Charles Sprague, 359–60
Smith, George Baxter, 40–42
Social Aspects of Motion Pictures (USC film course), 220–28
Society of Cinematologists, 4, 343
Southall, James P.C., 82
Spottiswoode, Raymond, 369
Stanford University, 10, 16, 178, 197–209

Stanmyre, R.W., 272
Starr, Kevin, 177, 178
Stevens Institute of Technology, 16
St. John's College, 12, 14, 15, 344, 345–54
The Story of Louis Pasteur (William Dieterle, 1935), 306–7
Streibert, Theodore, 131–32, 139, 157, 167, 172
Susman, Warren, 27
Syracuse University, 11, 236, 263–98
Swain, R.E., 198, 199, 202
System (journal of business), 127, 145, 151–53

Teachers College of Columbia University, 380n10
Teaching Film Custodians, 378n9
Thiesen, Earl, 232
The 39 Steps (Alfred Hitchcock, 1935), 289–90
Thrasher, Frederic M., 12, 14, 15, 18, 23, 29, 251, 291, 293–94, 298–343
Thurlby, H.H., 134–35
Tracy, Louise, 234
Tracy, Spencer, 234
Transatlantic Tunnel (Maurice Elvey, 1935), 292
Trilling, Lionel, 362
Trolinger, Lelia, 380n10
Turnbull, Margaret, 44
Tyler, Parker, 377n6

University of Chicago, 16
University of Colorado, 380n10
University of Iowa, 197
University of Pittsburgh, 16
University of South Dakota, 378n10
University of Southern California, 10, 86, 175–235

Van Doren, Charles, 356
Van Doren, Mark, 13, 25, 308, 354–55, 374; cinematic principles of, 398n9
Van Zile, Edward S., 28
Vassar College, 17

Veblen, Thorstein, 33, 90, 93, 120, 122–23, 163
Veysey, Laurence, 30, 34
Von KleinSmid, Rufus B., 177–81, 191

Warner, Harry, 147–49, 150–51, 157, 321
Warshow, Robert, 377n6
Wasson, Haidee, 16
Waugh, Karl, 175–76, 181, 183, 185, 187, 191, 197, 202, 215
Way Down East (D.W. Griffith, 1920), 66
Webster, Eugene, 115
We Live Again (Rouben Mamoulian, 1934), 286–87
Whitley, Robert L., 329

Wilbur, Ray Lyman, 199, 208
Williams, Raymond, 30
Wilson, Carey, 85
Winterset (Alfred Santell, 1936), 264
Woods, Frank, 80, 83, 178, 183, 189, 190, 198, 200, 210
Woods, Lotta, 180
Workers Film and Photo League (WFPL), 239–40, 242, 245, 246, 261

Yale University, 155, 378n10
Yogev, Esther, 154
Yolland, Edgar H., 197
Yost, Dorothy, 213, 231

Zukor, Adolph, 34, 81–82

Text:	10/13 Aldus
Display:	Aldus
Compositor:	Binghamton Valley Composition, LLC
Printer and binder:	Maple-Vail Manufacturing Group

www.ingramcontent.com/pod-product-compliance
Lightning Source LLC
Chambersburg PA
CBHW020633230426
43665CB00008B/149